HAMPSHIRE
NUNNERIES

Romsey Abbey (*Paul Reeves Photography*).

HAMPSHIRE NUNNERIES

Diana K. Coldicott

Phillimore

1989

Published by
PHILLIMORE & CO. LTD.
Shopwyke Hall, Chichester, Sussex

ISBN 0 85033 673 2

Printed and bound in Great Britain by
Richard Clay Ltd.,
Bungay, Suffolk.

For Peter

Contents

List of Illustrations

Frontispiece: Romsey Abbey

List of Maps

Preface and Acknowledgments

Until their dissolution by Henry VIII there were four nunneries in Hampshire. The Benedictine abbeys at Winchester, Romsey and Wherwell had been founded in that order during the 10th century, while the small priory near the present Hartley Wintney – the first Cistercian nunnery in England – dates from the third quarter of the 12th century. A study of each house was included in Vol.II of the *Victoria County History (Hampshire)* which was published in 1903 but since then they have received varying amounts of attention from historians. Wherwell Abbey and Wintney Priory have attracted little notice; even the Wherwell cartulary remains unpublished. Work on the history of St. Mary's Abbey has been included in several local studies, most noticeably in the great volumes of *Winchester Studies* (1 and 2, of 1976-85). Since 1977 the L.T.V.A.S. Group have published several short studies on the local· history of Romsey, but the major books on the abbey are H.G.D. Liveing's *Records of Romsey Abbey* (1906) and the shorter *Pages from the History of Romsey and its Abbey* by Sir Richard Luce (1948). Between those two dates Eileen Power's magisterial *Medieval English Nunneries* was published in 1922 and remains the only major work on nunneries in England, in spite of the great growth in women's studies during recent years.

Although it is written as a local history, I hope that *Hampshire Nunneries* may be a small contribution to the subject of medieval nunneries in England generally. I have tried to trace the history of the four houses and a little of the life that was lived in them from the time of their foundations until their dissolution during 1536-9 when their corporate lives were suddenly brought to a close, their sites passed into other hands and most of their buildings were destroyed. Above ground, only the church of Romsey Abbey still stands as a glorious and living memorial to the nunneries that had once seemed so permanent a part of local life.

The sources I have used are set out in the notes and bibliography. From the end of the 13th century until the start of the 16th, the registers of the bishops of Winchester were the most valuable, while the papers of the Court of Augmentations provided most of the material for the period of the Dissolution. I first consulted them for a dissertation I wrote for Portsmouth Polytechnic on 'The Dissolution of the Hampshire Nunneries' which has formed the basis of my last two chapters.

I have received help from many people in the course of my work. Miss Rosemary Dunhill and her staff at the Hampshire Record Office have been unfailing in their assistance during my many visits there, and I have a file of letters in answer to my queries from the archivists of other counties where the nunneries had interests: from Wiltshire R.O., Berkshire R.O., Lincolnshire R.O., Somerset R.O. and Dorset R.O. In London I have been grateful for the facilities for readers at the British Library, the Public Record Office, the Institute of Historical Research and, not least, the London Library whose staff have posted me innumerable books. Abroad, I wish to thank I.F. Grigorieva of the Saltykov-Shchedrin State Public Library in Leningrad for providing me with a complete photocopy of the Wherwell Calendar which is in the Russian state collection. I also wish to record my gratitude to several specialists who have helped me understand different aspects of the sites of the nunneries. The Winchester Archaeological Office has kindly allowed me to use its plan showing the area of recent excavations on the site of St. Mary's Abbey, its photograph of one of the graves there and a drawing of the staff of office found inside it (illus. 35, 36). Mr. Mike

Morris was most helpful in arranging this and discussing the excavations with me. Similarly Mr. Kevin Stubbs, now of the Historic Buildings Bureau at Winchester, explained the excavation work carried out at Romsey Abbey during 1973-9 and allowed me to use two of the plans that were drawn at that time (illus. 11, 37). Two local historians who have kindly shared their knowledge with me are Mr. David Gorsky of Hartley Wintney and Ms. Phoebe Merrick of Romsey. For other specialist help I am indebted to Dr. John Harvey and Mr. Richard Warmington for information on architecture; to Miss S.M. Levey of the Victoria and Albert Museum on embroidery and dress; to Mrs. Marie Fitzpatrick Bennett on music; to Mr. T.A. Heslop on seals; to Dr. A.R. Rumble for his translation of the boundaries of Nunnaminster from the forthcoming *Winchester Studies*, vol.4; and to Miss Vera London for assistance with Appendix 1. Above all, I am grateful to Miss Katharine M. Longley, lately of the Borthwick Institute, who provided me with translations whenever my Latin was inadequate; where I have quoted translations from unpublished episcopal registers the work is hers. Once I had completed my first draft the late Dom S.F. Hockey kindly read the whole typescript, Dr. Barbara Yorke read the first two chapters on the Anglo-Saxon period, and Dr. Simon Keynes read the section of the first chapter on the foundation of Wherwell Abbey. I am very grateful for all their constructive comments.

Compiling a collection of illustrations has been a task in itself. My brother, Bryan K. Edgley, L.R.P.S., took a series of lovely photographs for me at Romsey Abbey, at Wherwell, Winchester and Hartley Wintney; 16 of them are included here (nos. 5, 7, 15, 17, 18a and b, 19, 20, 21, 38, 49, 54, 55, 57, 58, 59). He also photographed the seals of St. Mary's Abbey and Romsey Abbey that are among the muniments of Winchester College; the Warden and Fellows of the college have kindly allowed them to be published (nos. 27, 28). For other photographs I am indebted to Lt. Col. G.J.B. Edgecombe and the Army Air Corps (no. 53); Gordon Fraser Gallery (no. 12); Monumental Brass Society (no. 50); The National Trust (no. 6); Mr. Barry Stapleton (no. 52). I am also grateful to Mr. J.L. Jervoise of Herriard Park for allowing me to use the portrait of his ancestor, Abbess Avelina Cowdrey (no. 33) and to the following for permission to reproduce photographs from their collections: Abingdon Town Council, no. 51; Bodleian Library, nos. 16, 34; The British Library, nos. 1, 3, 4, 8, 9, 14, 22, 26, 30, 32, 40; The Syndics of Cambridge University Library, no. 13; Messrs. Christie's, no. 47; The Dean and Chapter of Durham Cathedral, nos. 10, 31; Hampshire Record Office, no. 29; Musées Nationaux, Paris, no. 44; National Portrait Gallery, nos. 42, 46; Public Record Office, nos. 27a, 28a; Saltykov-Shchedrin State Public Library, Leningrad, no. 25; The Master and Fellows of St. John's College, Cambridge, no. 23; The Master and Fellows of Trinity College, Cambridge, no. 24; The Vicar of Wherwell, Hampshire, nos. 17, 58; Winchester City Council, no. 48; In addition, no. 39 was taken from R.H. Clutterbuck's *Notes on the Parishes of Fyfield . . . and Wherwell*; and no. 41 from H.G.D. Liveing's *Records of Romsey Abbey*.

The maps were drawn by Mr. J.W.T. Johnson of the Cartography Unit at Portsmouth Polytechnic, and the family trees by Mr. K.W. Hearn of Andover Workshop Copying Bureau.

Finally I wish to thank Peter for all his patient support and his invaluable help with the index.

D.K.C.

Monxton
January 1989

Chapter One

Anglo-Saxon Foundations

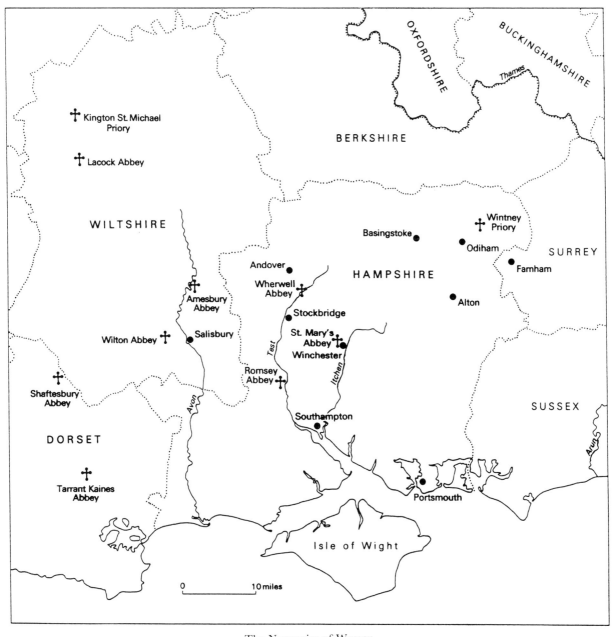

The Nunneries of Wessex.

Nunnaminster and Romsey Abbey before 960

The story of Hampshire's nunneries starts in the reign of Alfred the Great. When he succeeded his brother as king of the West Saxons in 871, he inherited a kingdom impoverished and devastated by successive Danish invasions. In Wessex, as in other parts of Britain, early monastic life and learning had been brought to a halt by the invaders but Alfred, amongst many other achievements, laid the foundations for its revival.

As a soldier, Alfred, through his victories over the Danes, secured as much peace for his people as it was possible to hope for in the ninth century. As a politician, he became lord over western Mercia as well as his own Wessex, so by the time of his death he was ruling a kingdom nearly twice as large as it had been at his accession. It was the nucleus of the future England. Peace enabled Alfred to draw up laws for his people and to encourage the spread of Christianity and learning. He himself translated Pope Gregory's 'Pastoral Care' into Anglo-Saxon for the benefit of the clergy, and he recruited scholars from far and wide to make other translations that could be copied and sent to the different bishops. This concern for the spiritual development of his people brings one nearest to the mainspring of his many-sided life: his faith in God.

As Alfred wanted to see monastic life revived in Wessex, he founded two monasteries. One at Athelney was for monks, who were all foreigners, and the other was at Shaftesbury for nuns. He endowed both with estates to provide them with an income, and appointed his daughter Ethelgifu as abbess of the nunnery in which there were 'many other noble nuns serving God in the monastic life in the same monastery'.[1] Both these foundations date from about 888. Shaftesbury Abbey was the more successful of the two and probably generated a certain amount of enthusiasm for monastic living among other well-born ladies in Wessex. Two years later another nunnery was started at Wilton.

It is not surprising that Alfred should have made plans to found one, and possibly two, other religious houses in Winchester as part of his general plan for the development and defence of the city. The recent extensive excavations in Winchester have produced a much clearer picture of the city in Anglo-Saxon times and of the changes made there by Alfred, probably during the 880s when there were still comparatively few people living in it. As an integral part of the defences, he constructed a street system covering three quarters of the city which is still the basis for the present roads. In the south east corner lay the Old Minster which was then a fairly small and probably overcrowded cathedral served by secular clerks.[2] Encouraged by Grimbald, a learned monk from St. Bertin at St. Omer, Alfred then planned the foundation of an adjacent New Minster which was used for royal burials as soon as it was completed.

It seems quite likely that Alfred may also have considered the possibility of founding a nunnery in Winchester and may have discussed it with his wife, Ealhswith. Some time before his death (for it is not mentioned in his will) Alfred granted her the land to the east of the Old Minster on which Nunnaminster was later built. It is not known when Ealhswith transferred this property to the new nunnery, but it may have been in her will which has not survived. However, there is a description of its boundaries in a book of Gospels that was once owned by Nunnaminster. The most recent translation of this passage reads:

> The boundary of the tenement which Ealhswith has at Winchester runs up from the ford on to the western [part of] the westernmost mill-yair, then east to the old willow and thence up along the eastern mill-yair, then north to the market street; then there east along the market street as far as king's city-hedge, on to the mill-yair, then there along the old mill-yair until it strikes the ivy covered ash, then there south over the double fords to the middle street, then there west again along the street and over the ford, so that it strikes again the westernmost mill-yair.[3]

The passage is interesting as a description of the earliest boundaries of the site of Nunnaminster, but in the absence of the original charter it is impossible to know Alfred's

1. The boundaries of Nunnaminster in the tenth century, taken from a book of Gospels that belonged to Nunnaminster. BL ms. Harley 2965, f.40v.

intentions when granting the land to Ealhswith.[4] Perhaps the most likely reason for his gift is that he wished, during his lifetime, to make provision for his wife in a place of safety which would remain her own in the event of his death. This is the more likely since there was a strong preference in the West Saxon royal house for keeping land in the male line, although there were a number of well-born ladies in Wessex who were landowners in their own right. The grant may also reflect Alfred's personal respect for Ealhswith whom he had married in 868, three years before he became king. She was the daughter of an ealdorman of Mercia and the granddaughter of a king of Mercia. They had five surviving children: two sons, including Edward the Elder who succeeded his father, and three daughters. Two of the daughters made politically important marriages while the third, Ethelgifu, became abbess of Shaftesbury and is mentioned in several early histories.[5]

The author of the *Liber de Hyda* wrote that Ealhswith was the builder of the monastery of nuns at Winchester, to which she had given gifts, and that she was buried with honour in the New Minster.[6] Her death, which occurred some time between 902 and 905, was also recorded by Florence of Worcester and he described her as

. . . the devout handmaid of Christ . . . and the foundress of a monastery for nuns at Winchester.[7]

Alfred had died in 899 and was initially buried in the Old Minster, but after the dedication

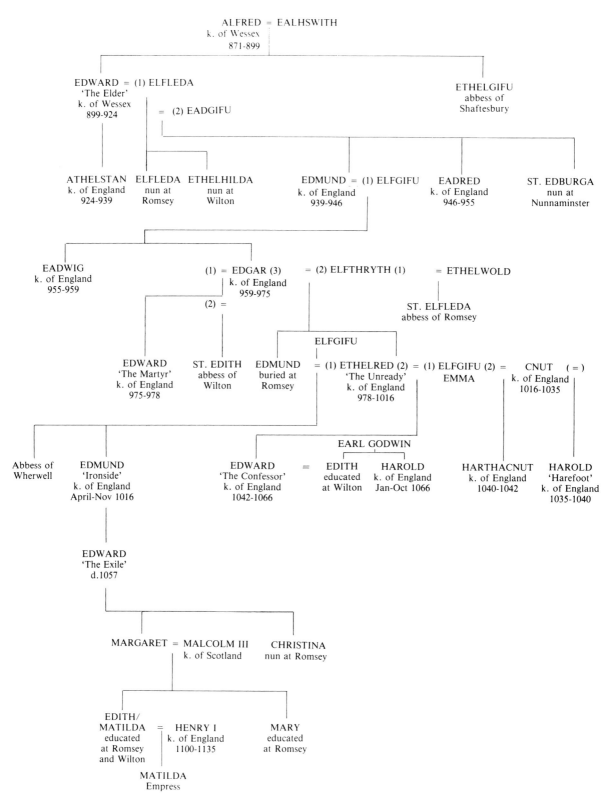

2. Descendants of Alfred the Great.

of the New Minster in 903 his remains were translated there and Ealhswith was buried beside him. After the New Minster was moved to become Hyde Abbey in 1110 their remains were buried together before the new high altar. (Leland wrote that two little lead tablets inscribed with their names were found in their tomb, which was itself finally destroyed during excavations for a new prison in 1787-8.[8])

Work on the buildings for the Nunnaminster was continued by Edward the Elder. Little is known about this first construction, but slight foundations were found during the excavations on the abbey site in 1981-3. One chronicler wrote that in 908 Archbishop Plegmund dedicated a very high tower in Winchester, whose foundations had been laid a little before that time in honour of Mary, mother of God,[9] and it is believed that that dedication may mark the completion of the nuns' first church. The only other recorded building from the first half of the tenth century was an oratory or chapel dedicated to St. Peter in or near the garden of the nunnery, which was probably identical with the later parish church of St. Peter in Colebrook Street.[10]

Although no date can be ascribed to the foundation of Nunnaminster, it was evidently recognised as a nunnery during the widowhood of Ealhswith, though that does not preclude the possibility that the community of ladies living with her may have been run on domestic rather than strictly monastic lines. The character of Ealhswith herself is likely to have set the tone of life there, but she is nowhere described as abbess. Probably the first person to become abbess during the decade following the death of Ealhswith was Etheldritha, a lady who was a member of the royal family.[11] She is first mentioned c.912 when she interpreted the vivid dreams of the young mother-to-be of the future Bishop Ethelwold. Her installation as abbess is mentioned in an early account of St. Edburga, who was entrusted to her care in early childhood.[12]

Edburga was the daughter of Edward the Elder by his last marriage. It is said that the king had become convinced of his little daughter's vocation to the religious life when, at the age of three, she had chosen to pick religious rather than secular objects from a selection put before her by her father. (One hesitates to say that many a little three year old would choose to pick up a small chalice and paten that could be handled and banged together rather than a prickly piece of jewellery!) Nevertheless the king decided to hand over the little princess to Abbess Etheldritha, and to mark his trust he made endowments to the nunnery and gave the community ornaments, a book of gospels and a chalice and paten for their church.[13] The king's faith in his daughter's incipient holiness proved justified. Edburga was to spend the rest of her short life at Nunnaminster, increasingly loved and revered by her contemporaries for her holy living. Although she died when she was only about 30 years old (c.951)[14] a cult had already started to develop around her during her lifetime, but it is not clear whether she ever became abbess of Nunnaminster.

When Edburga died she was buried humbly within Nunnaminster, but stories of miraculous healings at her tomb soon spread among the people and in time she became accepted as a saint. Osbert of Clare, who wrote a life of St. Edburga in the 12th century, recorded that the nuns themselves became convinced of her sanctity when they could not close a window that was overlooking her grave, and were only able to do so after they had reburied her by the high altar. Later he recounts, perhaps more reliably, that Bishop Ethelwold had her remains translated to a costly shrine with the assistance of Abbess Alfghena. It was later refurbished by Abbess Alfleda. Osbert recounted the splendour of the shrine at some length, with its gold, silver and topaz decorations.[15] It was included in a contemporary list of shrines, which no doubt brought Nunnaminster an increase in both visitors and prestige, but in spite of this the remains of St. Edburga were not allowed to rest in peace at Winchester. Accounts differ, but later in the century Bishop Ethelwold seems to have been among those who were responsible for sending some of her relics to the newly-founded Pershore Abbey, which was partly dedicated to her, so that in time her fame became as great in Worcestershire as in Wessex.[16] Today it is difficult to view the detaching and dispatching of parts of the body or skeleton of a saint with anything but repugnance, but the early church thought differently. The practice had been followed enthusiastically since the eighth century for men viewed such relics as contacts with the eternal.

To return to the beginning of the tenth century, Edward the Elder has an important place in the history of Hampshire's nunneries not only because of his many connections with Nunnaminster but also because he was the first founder of Romsey Abbey. It is an accident of history that Edward is so little known in comparison with his father. Whereas a quite surprising amount of contemporary material remains to illuminate something of the character and certainly the achievements of Alfred, very little has survived from his son's reign. But there is enough to be able to appreciate his main political and military achievements. Like his father, Edward doubled the area of Wessex rule in the course of his reign so that by the time of his death in 924 it extended over all England south of the Humber, even if he received only grudging obedience from many of his northern subjects. Edward's wars with the Danes and the resulting territorial expansion belong to the second decade of his reign (909-18). During the first years he remained in Wessex. Initially he had to subdue one of his cousins who had occupied the royal estates of Wimborne and Christ-church, but after the cousin had fled (leaving behind a nun whom he had abducted) his kingdom remained reasonably peaceful for several years, though the possibility of further Danish attacks can never have been far from the mind of any tenth-century ruler of Wessex.

At the start of his reign, Edward carried out his father's wishes and built the New Minster in Winchester on a site immediately to the north of the Old Minster, as well as completing the first Nunnaminster buildings after the death of his mother. It seems reasonable to assume that the foundation of Romsey Abbey also dates from these years of relative peace before 909. A date of c.907 is sometimes given and may well be right but it cannot be proved. The chronicles that can be cited are the *Liber de Hyda* which mentions that Edward's daughter Elfleda was at Romsey,[17] and Florence of Worcester who wrote that in 967

> Edgar the Pacific, King of England, placed nuns in the monastery at Romsey founded by his grandfather, Edward the Elder . . . [18]

Florence compiled his chronicle at the start of the 12th century, using the work of several early writers but he based it particularly on an earlier chronicle written by Marianus Scotus that has since been lost.

Archaeologists are now producing much new information about Romsey, both about the occupation of the area since Romano-British times and about the church buildings on the site of the present abbey.[19] Rammed chalk footings of an early Saxon church have been found and there is evidence of at least three charcoal burials, probably dating from the first half of the ninth century. (They were so called because the corpse was not itself burnt but was laid on a bed of charcoal. It has been presumed that the practice was reserved for people of status.)[20] This early church was subsequently demolished and a late Saxon church was built on the site of the earlier church and graveyard, presumably to meet the needs of the newly founded nunnery. In shape the new church was an equal armed cross, measuring 28 metres in length and breadth, with an apsidal east end. Parts of the original chancel end were discovered in 1900 and can still be seen below the crossing floor of the present church; the west end of the nave was also found at that time, but the transepts were not discovered until the recent digs – the north porticus in 1975 and the south porticus in 1979. The quality of the workmanship employed on this later church was high. The walls were of finely jointed ashlar blocks of stone from the quarries on the Isle of Wight and the roofing tiles were made from Purbeck stone. The mortar used between the stones and the plaster on the internal surfaces of the walls were both made by adding pulverised Roman brick to mortar, which produced a distinctive pinkish colour. (Similar mortar has been found at the Old Minster in Winchester.) The church was not without decoration, for parts of a stone frieze have been found, carved with a vine decoration. It has also been found that domestic buildings were erected to the south of the south porticus after the church was constructed but before the Normans started their rebuilding.[21]

Although one cannot know just why Edward the Elder decided to found another nunnery in Wessex or why he chose Romsey as its site, it is possible to suggest reasons. The geographical position of Romsey is interesting in relation to the other three towns where nunneries were already established. Winchester lay 10 miles away to the north east, while to the west there was roughly the same distance (about 15 miles) between Romsey and Wilton as there was between Wilton and Shaftesbury. Perhaps that was a coincidence, but all those three towns were included in the assessment for defence purposes that was known as the Burghal Hidage.[22] As it is evident from Edward's career that he was a thoughtful and patient planner, it seems likely that he would have noticed the relationship and perhaps looked forward to Romsey's development as a future *burh* with a defence potential. He would certainly have appreciated its plentiful water supply.

What other reasons are likely to have influenced Edward in his decision to found another nunnery? Probably, as with most of his enterprises, there were several. At the practical level he may have felt there was a need to make further provision for widows and unmarried ladies of the royal family. On the other hand, all that is known of Edward indicates that he had the same high ideal of Christian kingship as his father and an equal concern for the good of the church in his kingdom. (It was Edward who tackled the problem of the two impossibly large dioceses in Wessex. When the bishops of Winchester and Sherborne fortuitously died within a year of one another in 908-9, Edward divided the two into five so that the diocese of Winchester henceforward comprised the area of Hampshire and Surrey, while Wiltshire and Berkshire became a new diocese.[23]) Having seen the successful completion of New Minster, Edward may have wished to emulate Alfred by making another separate foundation for women. The success of the nunneries at Shaftesbury and Wilton had helped to stimulate an interest in the monastic life and ideal among many well-born ladies in Wessex. Indeed the interest seems to have been stronger amongst women than amongst men at the beginning of the tenth century, partly due to the influence of Ealhswith and other ladies of the royal family.[24]

Edward's first wife, Elfleda, was apparently as devout a lady as his mother and may be presumed to have encouraged her husband's plans for a new nunnery at Romsey. They may both have wished to mark its foundation by the consecration there of Elfleda, their eldest daughter, in the same way that a daughter of Alfred became the first abbess of Shaftesbury. Before her consecration Elfleda may have lived at Wilton Abbey with her sister.[25]

Besides their sons, Edward and Elfleda had six daughters. William of Malmesbury wrote about these princesses that

> Edward had brought up his daughters in such wise that in childhood they gave their whole attention to literature, and afterwards employed themselves in the labours of the distaff and the needle, that thus they might chastely pass their virgin age.[26]

Allowing for exaggeration and the turn of phrase of a 12th-century monk, it is still evident that the sisters were considered to have been carefully brought up. Diplomatic marriages were arranged for four of them but the first and third sisters, Elfleda and Ethelhilda, both became nuns. Whether this course was decided for them entirely by their father, or whether their own inclinations were considered at all remains unknown. However, in view of the later story about Edward and their youngest step-sister, St. Edburga, it is reasonable to assume that he may at least have taken their dispositions into account as an indication of the will of God.

Several early chronicles mention the three sisters who were each connected with a different nunnery: Elfleda with Romsey, Ethelhilda with Wilton and Edburga with Nunnaminster. One of them describes Elfleda as abbess of Romsey,[27] but there is no doubt that St. Edburga took pride of place amongst the sisters in the minds of the chroniclers. Her saintliness is referred to by one after the other whereas Elfleda is never called a saint. (The point is made because she has sometimes been confused with the later St. Elfleda of Romsey.)[28] References to the two elder sisters are usually brief but once again William of Malmesbury gives more details

> . . . vowing celibacy to God [they] renounced the pleasure of earthly nuptials; Elfleda in a religious and Ethelhilda in a lay habit; they both lie buried near their mother at Wilton.[29]

Evidently Ethelhilda did not take her full vows and remained unveiled; and according to the *Liber de Hyda* Elfleda was buried at Romsey rather than at Wilton.[30]

Edward the Elder and his eldest legitimate son both died in the summer of 924. His first-born son, Athelstan, was then elected as king and ruled most capably for the next 16 years. Helped by his personal knowledge of Mercia, where he had been brought up at the royal court, Athelstan aimed to weld the different territories that he had inherited into one nation. All were subject to the same laws and for the first time there was 'one coinage over all the king's dominion'.[31] Increasingly the church was becoming involved in the process of governing that dominion as a natural outcome of its virtual monopoly of literacy. Athelstan himself was a good churchman and a great collector of religious relics. William of Malmesbury said of him:

> . . . there can scarcely have been an old monastery in England which he did not embellish either with buildings or ornaments or books or estates. Thus he honoured recent foundations avowedly, old ones with tactful kindness as if incidentally.[32]

The nuns of Shaftesbury Abbey received a grant of land from Athelstan but there is no record of his having made similar grants to the nuns of either Romsey or Winchester. He did, however, make a personal gift to his step-sister Edburga of 17 *mansae* in Droxford,[33] but these did not become part of the endowment of Nunnaminster.

There were three kings during the 20 years between the death of Athelstan and the accession of Edgar (939-59). The first two, Edmund and Eadred, were both the sons of Edward the Elder's last marriage and therefore full brothers of St. Edburga. Their mother, Eadgifu, was not at court when Athelstan was king but she returned there during the reigns of her own two sons, when she was frequently among the witnesses to charters. She was a wealthy woman in her own right and an early friend and supporter of Dunstan and Ethelwold.[34]

King Edmund seems to have been surrounded by womenfolk with an intense interest in the good of the church generally, and of monasteries in particular. His first wife, Queen Elfgifu, was a benefactress of the nuns at Shaftesbury and was buried in their church when she died two years before her husband. She was later venerated as a saint. His second wife, Queen Ethelfled, evidently shared her husband's concern for Glastonbury Abbey where he had installed Dunstan as abbot and then endowed the house as a regular monastery. Many years later it was among the churches that received an estate under her will; so too did the church of the nuns at Barking in Essex.[35] However, none of these three royal ladies is known to have granted anything to either Nunnaminster or Romsey Abbey, although it is always possible that one of them may have encouraged Edmund to grant Nunnaminster a toll that was payable on all merchandise passing by water under the city bridge nearby, or by land through the Eastgate; or in 943 to give land at Clere in Hampshire ' . . . to the religious woman called Aelswith'.[36] (It is possible that this last was the property held later by Romsey Abbey at Sydmonton in the hundred of Kingsclere.)

Edward the Elder is said to have made large gifts to Nunnaminster, apparently after hearing Edburga singing a psalm at a royal banquet,[37] and it may be presumed that he gave endowments to Romsey Abbey although none are recorded. However, it is from the reign of Edmund's brother, King Eadred (946-55), that greater details are known about gifts to Nunnaminster. In 947 Eadred granted Eadwulf, a priest, 10 hides of land at Leckford in Hampshire with reversion to the nunnery of Winchester and the church where he was buried. Some time between then and the end of the reign Eadwulf the priest regranted this land. He gave five hides to Nunnaminster, which became known as Leckford Abbas, and the other five to New Minster (Leckford Abbots) 'where me lyketh my bodi for to rest aftyr my day'.[38] At the end of the reign all the three great foundations at Winchester received legacies under the king's will. The Old Minster and the New Minster were granted three estates each, while Nunnaminster received the estates of Shalbourne and Bradford in Wiltshire and Thatcham in Berkshire, as well as £30. The nunneries of Shaftesbury and Wilton were also left £30 each but no estates.[39]

The brief and undistinguished reign of Eadwig that followed is remembered for his quarrel with Dunstan, who was forced to leave the country, and for the loss of the greater part of his kingdom in 957 when the Mercians and Northumbrians renounced their allegiance to him and chose his younger brother Edgar as king. Unity was secured once again when Eadwig died in 959 and Edgar became king of all England.

The Tenth-century reformation

It is impossible to exaggerate the importance of the 16 years of Edgar's reign (959-75) to the history of monasticism in England. Several factors combined to make it such a fruitful period, not least the character of the young king himself who gave active and enthusiastic support for the reform and extension of monasteries in his kingdom. But the initiators of that reform were the three great church leaders, Dunstan, Ethelwold and Oswald, who were all monks. Each of them, to different degrees, had been influenced by the movement for monastic reform in Europe and had the vision and capability to extend it to England. Their task was made easier by the long period of peace during Edgar's reign.

Enthusiasm for the monastic ideal, once so strong in England in the pre-Viking days of St. Cuthbert and Bede, had been stirring in Europe for more than a century. There, the Rule of the sixth-century St. Benedict, which had been adapted by St. Benedict of Aniane (d.821) for use by his community, had been endorsed when the latter met his king at Aachen in 817. In the years since then the fame of several reformed communities such as Fleury and Ghent had grown and in time were to provide models for the later Benedictine houses in England.

Of the three English churchmen, Dunstan had possibly been the least affected by the reform movement until his exile in the 950s brought him into first hand contact with all the vigour of continental monasticism. Before then the old traditions of Glastonbury, where he had been educated, and the guidance of his kinsman Bishop Elfheah of Winchester had been the formative influences in the life of this saintly man. After King Edmund had installed him as Abbot of Glastonbury in about 940, he gathered a body of disciples there who lived in accordance with the Rule. Amongst those disciples was his friend Ethelwold, a native of Winchester, who had been ordained priest by Bishop Elfheah on the same day as himself.

Ethelwold later wanted to join one of the communities abroad to experience a more rigorous way of life, but his ability had already been recognised by the king's mother in particular and royal permission to leave the country was refused. Instead King Eadred gave him the derelict monastery of Abingdon to restore, as Dunstan had done at Glastonbury. During the next decade the community at Abingdon grew with the help of advice from the

3. King Edgar seated between St Ethelwold and St Dunstan, taken from the *Regularis Concordia*. BL ms. Cotton Tiberius A.iii, f.2v.

monasteries at Fleury and Corbie and with its life based on the Rule.[40] During some of this period Ethelwold was tutor to the future King Edgar. Oswald, the youngest of the three men, spent eight years as a monk in Fleury before returning to England in 958 and was therefore even more steeped in its way of life than Ethelwold.

When Edgar became King of Mercia and Northumberland in 957, he recalled Dunstan from exile to become both his adviser and a bishop. Two years later, when he became king of all England, he made Dunstan Archbishop of Canterbury and on his advice gave the dioceses of Worcester to Oswald and Winchester to Ethelwold in 961 and 963 respectively. The convictions and previous experience of these two monk bishops made it impossible for them to accept the situation they found in their new cathedrals, which were both staffed by secular, married priests. In February 964 Ethelwold had the clerks in the Old Minster expelled and replaced by some of his monks from Abingdon. At the following Easter a great synod was held, probably in Winchester itself, when the king agreed that he should take over ecclesiastical endowments held individually by clerks and grant them instead to newly formed monasteries.[41]

As a result of this policy the number of Benedictine foundations in the country grew steadily during the next few years. As Ethelwold's biographer, Aelfric, wrote:

> And thus it was brought to pass with the King's consent that monasteries were founded everywhere among the English people, partly by the counsel and action of Dunstan and partly by that of Ethelwold, some with monks and some with nuns, living according to the rule under abbots and abbesses . . . He was a father of the monks and nuns . . . [42]

This was nowhere more true than in Winchester itself. As in the Old Minster, monks soon replaced the former secular canons in the New Minster and Edgar granted them their famous Golden Charter in 966 when refounding the house as a Benedictine monastery. (Today this can be seen in the Exhibition Room of the British Library's Manuscript Department, where it normally lies next to that other great contemporary work of art from Winchester, the Benedictional of St. Ethelwold.)

The changes in the constitutions of the Old and New Minsters and the new endowments that the king granted them are well documented but no similar charters have survived for Nunnaminster alone, though there are two records of boundary changes that affected all three monasteries. On the evidence of one version of the Anglo-Saxon Chronicle which said that Ethelwold made two abbacies in Winchester, one of monks and one of nuns[43] it has been said that he refounded Nunnaminster early in 964, but perhaps reformed is a better word to use. There was after all no fundamental change to be made from seculars to religious as there had been in the other two Minsters. There were nuns at Nunnaminster before as well as after he became bishop and, even if their life had not been based on the Rule of St. Benedict until his time, he is unlikely to have been too harsh on a community that had nurtured St. Edburga until her death a few years earlier. As we have seen, it was Ethelwold who had her remains translated to a costly shrine in the nuns' church in the same way that he had St. Swithun translated into the Old Minster in 971. The year of St. Edburga's translation is not known but, like St. Swithun's, it took place in July. (Maybe the sun shone for her?) The two dates are recorded in Hyde Abbey's Calendar: St. Swithun on the 15th and St. Edburga three days later.[44]

Until Ethelwold's time the three Minsters seem to have been an integral part of the increasingly busy town of Winchester. Various buildings apparently huddled beside them and one imagines fairly continuous activity all around, particularly when the king was in residence in the palace alongside the Old Minster. But Ethelwold's concern was not that they should be part of the local community but rather the reverse. He wanted the monasteries set apart from the bustling urban life so that the monks and nuns could live in peace and solitude and concentrate on their spiritual duties. To this end, for it was surely Ethelwold's idea, some time between 963 and 970 the king granted land to the three monasteries which lay alongside them and which had been cleared of buildings.[45] It was foreseen that there might be some difficulties between the three houses if one of them owned property in the area allotted to one of the others, and should that happen then exchanges were to be made between the communities. Accordingly, a few years later, Nunnaminster surrendered a watercourse to the New Minster and received in exchange a mill which New Minster had owned in the town.[46] This may have been the mill inside the Eastgate that is mentioned in the survey of 1148.[47]

After the small buildings mentioned in the first charter had been cleared away, including the whole of the back street south of High Street from the later Little Minster Street eastwards, then the area occupied by the three monasteries was enclosed by ditches, walls and fences. For 30 years building work initiated by Ethelwold continued there; at times it was probably in progress at all three of the monasteries which must have put a strain on local resources. A thousand years later much of the western end of this original enclosure still remains free of city buildings near the cathedral. William of Malmesbury wrote that the original buildings of Nunnaminster (which he called *monasteriolium* – the little monastery) were almost destroyed by this time and were rebuilt by Ethelwold on the same site.[48] Some evidence of the rebuilding was found during the excavations of 1981-3. Beneath part of the nave of the Norman abbey church there were late tenth-century foundations which were probably from the west end of the second Saxon church. It had had much more substantially built walls than its predecessor built by Edward the Elder.[49]

A few years after Ethelwold became bishop, and probably at his instigation, another great Council of Winchester was held by the king in the presence of church leaders, abbots and abbesses who were gathered together in the Old Minster. The exact date is not known but it may have been early in the 970s. The *Regularis Concordia* which the king and the heads of the monastic houses agreed at this council marks the final settlement of the Benedictine revival in England. It was a code of monastic law, based on the Rule of St. Benedict, to which all the monks and nuns present vowed obedience. The 12 chapters of the agreement cover all aspects of life in the cloister – the pattern of daily life and worship, the variations of that pattern at the great festivals of the church, the giving of alms, the entertainment of strangers, the care of the sick and the burial of the dead.[50]

Henceforward the different monastic houses in England were to be united not only in their faith but also in the way they lived and observed the Rule. Unlike continental houses, English monasteries at this time were all brought under the patronage of the king and queen for whom prayers were said every day. Nunneries were brought under the particular care of the queen. In the words of the *Regularis Concordia*, the king,

> . . . saw to it wisely that his queen, Elfthryth, should be the protectress and fearless guardian of the communities of nuns, so that he himself helping the men and his consort helping the women there should be no cause for any breath of scandal.[51]

However, when a new abbess was to be chosen the consent and advice of the king himself was to be sought, as it was before the election of an abbot. This practice was observed by all Benedictine houses in England until the Dissolution.

One other section of the *Regularis Concordia* that applied only to nunneries was added by the archbishop:

> . . . that no monk, nor indeed any man whatever his rank, should dare to enter and frequent the places set apart for nuns, and that those who have spiritual authority over nuns should use their powers not as worldly tyrants but in the interests of good discipline. Wherefore . . . let the brethren take care so to arrange their going into the dwelling places of nuns that they in no way hinder their regular observance.[52]

Dunstan's sensible words would have been particularly relevant to Nunnaminster with its close proximity to the Old and New Minsters.

Unfortunately the only two manuscripts of the *Regularis Concordia* that have survived do not give the names of those who attended the Council, but as abbesses were there it is reasonable to suppose that the abbesses of Shaftesbury, Wilton and Nunnaminster at least were all present. There is a similar tantalising lack of names for the abbots and abbesses who evidently dined with the queen after Edgar's belated coronation at Bath in 973.[53]

The names of three possible abbesses of Nunnaminster have survived from the time of Ethelwold's episcopate but there is some confusion about two of them. Aelfric wrote that the bishop '. . . placed religious women in a nunnery, over whom he set Ethelthryth as mother superior'.[54] One is led to believe that she was the same lady who had interpreted the dreams of his mother more than half a century earlier but, even allowing for William of Malmesbury's description of her as an aged virgin, this is very hard to believe.[55] As Ethelthryth was a common name among West Saxon aristocratic women, it seems more likely that Aelfric was referring to another lady of the same name: either to an abbess otherwise unknown or to the queen herself being a mother to the nunnery within the meaning of the *Regularis Concordia*. Another abbess at the time of the translation of St. Edburga was called Alfghena.[56] And in the boundary adjustment charter already mentioned 'the abbess Eadgifu, the King's daughter' was named. This charter is likely to date from a later time than the translation of St. Edburga because the abbess was probably the 'abbess Eadgifu' who later witnessed a charter in Ethelred's reign. The phrase 'the King's daughter' has always puzzled scholars; Edgar was only 31 years old when he died, so he can never have had a daughter old enough to be an abbess in his own lifetime and it has been suggested that the phrase may have been interpolated at some later date by a scribe confusing Eadgifu of Nunnaminster with Edgar's daughter Edith of Wilton Abbey.[57]

It has been questioned whether an abbess of Romsey would have been present when the *Regularis Concordia* was agreed.[58] It all depends on when the Council was held: the later it took place, the more likely it is that Merewenna, the first abbess of the reformed nunnery, would also have been present.

The reform of Romsey Abbey by King Edgar under the influence of Bishop Ethelwold probably took place after the reformation of Nunnaminster, if only because it was further away from the seat of their power. Florence of Worcester dated the reformation to 967 when he wrote that Edgar placed nuns in the monastery at Romsey founded by his grandfather and appointed St. Merewenna to be their abbess, but the Worcester Annals give the following year 968.[59] It is more important that by the end of the 960s both houses had become true Benedictine nunneries.

Nothing beyond vague legend is known about Merewenna, one of the abbey's future saints, before Edgar placed her as abbess at Romsey, but it may be assumed that she was of noble birth and that her appointment was approved by Ethelwold as well as by the royal family. Some time, perhaps not long after the reform, the king and queen entrusted the abbess with the upbringing of the queen's stepdaughter Elfleda, the child of a nobleman called Ethelwold (d.962) who had been the queen's first husband.[60] Elfleda spent the rest of her long life at Romsey. She became abbess at the end of the century and in due course the patron saint of the convent church where both she and St. Merewenna were buried.[61] There is a delightful account of the two saintly abbesses in a 14th-century chronicle which at one time belonged to the nunnery. There is far more about St. Elfleda than about St. Merewenna in it, but the following passage concerns them both. One hopes there may be some truth in it.

> And right well did Abbess Merewenna behave as a most sweet mother to Elfleda, and Elfleda as a most loving daughter to Merewenna. The one taught the way of the Lord in truth as a most modest mother, and the other, by entire obedience as a dutiful daughter, retained zealously what she had been taught . . . The one on fasting days chastened her body by hunger, the other, whatever by abstinence from food she withheld from the body, she distributed to the poor in secret. The King and Queen, pleased with her saintliness, with the consent of the Blessed Merewenna, caused her to be consecrated by the Bishop of Winchester . . . And she lived henceforward under Abbess Merewenna for some time, abundant in virtues, generous in alms, constant in watches, in speech vigilant, in mind humble, of joyful countenance, and kindly mannered to the poor.[62]

The king and queen had another personal connection with the nunnery: their young son, the atheling Edmund, was buried there some time between 970 and 972.[63] He cannot have been more than seven years old for his parents were not married until 964, and he may have been much younger. Nothing is known about the cause of his death or the reason for his being buried there rather than in Winchester, so it is mere speculation to wonder whether he may have been staying there for some time or whether he was with one or both of his parents when they were visiting Elfleda or just breaking a journey at Romsey. Florence of Worcester wrote that he was 'honourably buried in the monastery at Romsey'[64] and his burial in the minster there is also mentioned at the end of an undated charter of Edgar in favour of Romsey.

In that charter the king confirmed the privileges of the nunnery including (surprisingly in view of the one of the agreements in the almost contemporary *Regularis Concordia*) the right of the nuns to choose their own abbess after the death of Merewenna and the right to hold their property freely. At the time of his son's death he granted the nuns a wood whose bounds were recorded at the end of the charter together with those of their other local property. In return for the woodland the nunnery gave the king valuable gifts of a 'finely wrought dish, armlets splendidly chased and a scabbard adorned with gold, to the value of 900 mancuses'.[65] (A mancus was a money of account valued at 30 pence.) There is a copy of this charter in the Edington Cartulary but modern authorities are divided in their views about its authenticity. It has been pointed out that it is very similar to a group of equally

4. A leaf from the 14th-century Chronicle with Lives of the English Saints which was once owned by Romsey Abbey. It shows part of the life of St Edburga of Winchester and the start of the lives of St Elfreda and St Merewenna of Romsey.
BL ms. Lansdowne 436, f.43v.

suspicious charters relating to the abbeys of Abingdon, Pershore and Worcester, though others have accepted it as genuine in spite of its having only survived in a medieval copy without the names of any witnesses.[66] But whether the whole charter is genuine or not, its description of the abbey's estate in Romsey is probably accurate. Twice this century it has been considered in great detail and related to the land as it is today.[67]

There is no doubt about the authenticity of another earlier charter of King Edgar which is also recorded in the Edington Cartulary. It is dated 968 and in it the king granted land at Edington (Edyndun) in Wiltshire to Romsey Abbey, free of all but the three common dues: the provision of bridges, fortifications and military service.[68] In the previous century Edington had been the scene of Alfred's victory over Guthrum in 878, and later he had given it to his wife Ealhswith in his will.

However, gifts to the religious houses were not only made by the king. Others were also touched by the enthusiasm of Ethelwold's reform movement and were able to make material contributions to the reformed and new monasteries and the monastic cathedrals which were developing in the wake of the *Regularis Concordia*. The ealdorman Ethelmaer was one of these. When he died in 982 he left generous gifts of land and money to the New and Old Minsters and the next beneficiary he named was Nunnaminster that was left two pounds of pence (i.e. 480 silver pence). The same bequest was made to the abbeys at Romsey, Wilton and Shaftesbury, in that order, as well as nine other abbeys and churches.[69] In the previous decade Elfgifu, a lady who was probably a member of the royal family, left a paten to Nunnaminster and her estate at Whaddon in Buckinghamshire to 'Christ and St. Mary at Romsey'. She left another estate to Bishop Ethelwold.[70]

The bishop himself may have made a gift of a different sort. At the request of Edgar and Elfthryth, and in return for an estate in Suffolk, he translated the Rule of St. Benedict from Latin into Old English for the sake of those who could not understand Latin. It is possible that the original translation was intended for a nunnery because it contains so many feminine pronouns and it has been suggested that it may have been made for the nuns at Winchester, but that is not certain.[71] However, it is reasonable to suppose that the two nunneries within his diocese would each have had a copy. One surviving text of the translation is followed by further contemporary writings, probably by Ethelwold himself, which include instructions to abbesses to be

> ... deeply loyal and to serve the precepts of the holy rule with all their hearts, and we enjoin the commands of God Almighty that none of them shall presume senselessly to give God's estates either to their kinsmen or to secular great persons, neither for money nor for flattery.[72]

The bishop was evidently not without reservations about the ability of women to manage the business affairs of a large monastic house.

No documentary evidence survives about other gifts to either Nunnaminster or Romsey Abbey at this time. It is not known whether the small Saxon rood which dates from this period, and is now used as a reredos in St. Anne's chapel in Romsey Abbey, was given to the nuns during the tenth century or at some later date. One must just be grateful that both it and the larger rood outside (which is believed to date from c.1025) have survived for so long.

The Foundation of Wherwell Abbey

King Edgar died suddenly and unexpectedly in July 975 when he was only thirty one. He left two young sons: Edward, the son of his first wife, and Ethelred, the surviving son of his marriage to Queen Elfthryth. Neither was old enough to rule alone. Edward had never been formally recognised as the heir and, in spite of his youth, had managed to offend many people of importance by the violence of his language and behaviour. Perhaps for this reason

5. The small Saxon rood, now used as a reredos in St Anne's chapel, Romsey Abbey.

6. The ruins of the Norman Corfe Castle, Dorset.

there were many nobles who sided with the queen and tried to secure the election of Ethelred as king. But Edward had the support of Archbishop Dunstan and his influence in the choice of the elder brother as king was probably decisive.[73] (Although by this time it was becoming customary to choose the eldest son of a king to succeed his father, an election was still necessary.)

The character of the young king and the discontent not only of those who would have preferred his half-brother, but also of many who resented either the monastic reforms or the endowments of land made during the previous reign, gave rise to growing dissension in the country. The situation was made worse by a severe famine in 976.[74] The two brothers themselves remained on friendly terms so it was perfectly natural that Edward should make his way to Corfe Castle to stay with his stepmother and Ethelred on the evening of 18 March 978 after a hard day's hunting nearby, but the outcome was anything but natural. That evening the young king was murdered by thegns at the gap of Corfe and his body was thrown into a bog where it remained for nearly a year. On 13 February 979 it was retrieved and taken to Wareham and five days later the remains were buried at Shaftesbury Abbey, where the king was later venerated as a saint and martyr. The repercussions from that night were felt into the next century and the story of it continued to be part of English folklore throughout the Middle Ages.[75]

Who was responsible for the murder? The chroniclers who wrote after the Conquest, and knowing the many troubles of Ethelred's reign, laid all the blame for it upon Queen Elfthryth whose character became increasingly blackened as one version was built upon another. Their accounts have been copied unquestioningly until the present century, but in recent years scholars have looked at the surviving evidence with more critical eyes and have at last exonerated the queen.[76] No contemporary writers ever maintained that she was responsible for the murder in any way. She is referred to affectionately in the will of her grandson Athelstan whom she had brought up[77] and she continued to witness charters until the end of the century.

The earliest circumstantial account of the murder implies that Edward was murdered by thegns who thought the gentler Ethelred would be more amenable as their lord. They can have had little thought for the effect on Ethelred himself. Although he was far too young to have been implicated in any way he became king with a terrible handicap. The queen was in just as difficult a position. The murder had been carried out on her estate and by men who were supporters of herself and her son. It is no wonder that she may have felt a personal sense of responsibility as well as anguish. Indeed the better the queen's character the more likely it is that she would have felt the need to make some recompense to God. And for her, how natural that this should take the form of founding a nunnery. As we have seen, she had been personally involved in the monastic reforms of her husband's reign, and in the *Regularis Concordia* she had been made the guardian of English nuns and encouraged by Edgar to take thought for their welfare.[78] There is no reason to doubt that her interest in monasticism was genuine and that she took her responsibilities towards nuns seriously. In this she would have continued to receive encouragement and support from Archbishop Dunstan and Bishop Ethelwold during the first decade of her widowhood, and to have had their blessing for her foundation of a nunnery at Amesbury soon after the death of her stepson. It is thought that there may have been an earlier monastery at Amesbury. However, the choice of site for the new nunnery there in c.979 may also have seemed appropriate because King Edward had held one of his only two church councils there during the year before his death.[79]

Traditionally Queen Elfthryth is also given credit for the foundation of Wherwell Abbey a few years later in c.986. (Wherwell is about 15 miles east of Amesbury and 10 miles to the north west of Winchester – similar distances to Romsey's in relation to Wilton and

Winchester.) Certainly the queen made generous endowments to Wherwell and she probably lived there during her last years, but there is conflicting evidence in the Wherwell Cartulary about the name of the actual founder. Charter 58 names Elfthryth but no.353 states that it was founded in 962 by Alfred son of Osgar, Ealdorman of Devonshire.[80] The latter record is a copy of a 14th-century petition to the king from the then abbess and convent concerning their rights over Harewood forest. In it they maintained that Alfred, the owner of the land, had founded their abbey to the honour of God and the True Cross in 962, that he was buried in their church and that he had granted them Harewood.[81]

The clerk who drew up that petition in 1344 must surely have based it upon some earlier writing for the facts put forward seem to make sense. Since Queen Elfthryth was the daughter of Ealdorman Ordgar, and it is quite possible that the name of Alfred's father given in charter 353 was a corruption of 'Ordgar', then Alfred was either the queen's brother or half brother.[82] And 962 is a significant date for it was the year of the death of Elfthryth's first husband, Ethelwold (the father of St. Elfleda at Romsey). The story told by William of Malmesbury that King Edgar murdered Ethelwold in Harewood forest so that he could marry Elfthryth has been discredited, but could Alfred perhaps have felt some responsibility for his brother-in-law's death there?[83]

If the date of 962 is about right, it becomes possible to give some credence to the story of Edgar's pursuit of a young nun from Wilton called Wulfhilda. Her aunt, Wenfleda of Wherwell, is purported to have asked the girl to visit her on some pretext in order to help the king's suit. Thanks to Wulfhilda's determination, virtue was triumphant, and in due course she became abbess of Barking Abbey. If there is any truth in this story it throws little credit on either Wenfleda or Edgar, who subsequently switched his attentions more successfully to another Wilton nun who became the mother of his daughter, the future St. Edith of Wilton Abbey. These youthful escapades are meant to have occurred in the early 960s, before the king's marriage to Elfthryth.[84] They certainly present another side to Edgar's character.

To return to the Wherwell Cartulary, charter 58 records Queen Elfthryth's death and describes her founding the monastery of Wherwell and enriching and endowing it with manors and gifts. It then launches into the usual medieval story of the queen's sins and the murder of her stepson Edward, before recording her foundation of the church of the Holy Cross and her living in penitence at Wherwell for the rest of her life. This founding of the church, as opposed to the monastery, is confirmed by another short charter which again records her obit as well as her foundation of the church in honour of the Holy Cross.[85] Perhaps the impetus behind its building was to provide a burial place for her brother. Whether there was some earlier wooden church in Wherwell which may have been the mother church for the area is not known, but it is a possibility that has recently been suggested.[86] At any rate it is reasonable to assume that Elfthryth's new church was built in stone and that from this time the nunnery became a Benedictine house, as Romsey Abbey had after Edgar's refoundation there.

There could well be some truth in the traditional date of 986 as the time of the queen's main involvement with Wherwell. Since she did not witness any of the surviving royal diplomas that were issued between 985 and 990, it has been assumed that she was not at court during the five or six years following the death of Bishop Ethelwold in 984. Free from his guidance the young King Ethelred was then, understandably, going through a phase that has been called his 'period of youthful indiscretions' by his modern biographer.[87] None of the queen's original diplomas to Wherwell have survived so one cannot be sure when her gifts were made, but the properties themselves are named in a later charter of confirmation from her son.

After the Conquest Queen Elfthryth's endowments to Amesbury and Wherwell were regarded as expiation for her purported sins, while in our own more secular day it has been suggested that they are evidence of her concern to strengthen her influence in her son's kingdom.[88] Perhaps there may be an element of truth in this but, given the queen's own time and circumstances, it is surely not unreasonable to assume that the motives for her generosity were mainly religious, and if that is so, it is sad that they have been misunderstood for so many centuries. Equally sad is the abbey's neglect of her memory. Although it was known that Elfthryth had died on 17 November, that day is conspicuously blank in the nunnery's surviving calendars so her obit was not commemorated. As founders were usually remembered so conscientiously by monastic houses, one wonders whether the nuns of Wherwell were really rather ashamed of their connection with her. (There is some doubt about the actual year of the queen's death. Charter 58 is mistaken in giving 1002; probably it occurred in 999 or during 1000-1001.)[89]

Soon after the queen's death Ethelred granted various privileges to the nuns at Wherwell and confirmed their title to 70 *mansae* in various places in the vicinity of the abbey. He granted them a further 60 *cassati* in Aethelingedene in Sussex which had formerly belonged to his mother, with the intention that the income from them should provide the nuns with food and clothing.[90] He also gave them the right to elect a successor to their abbess after her death, though with the advice of their bishop. Later a memorandum was added that 29 messuages in Winchester, and the income from them, belonged to the nunnery, and in 1008 the king granted the community a further 10 *mansae* at Bullington, near Wherwell.[91]

At about the same time Ethelred granted a similar confirmation of title to the nuns at Amesbury, also giving them the right to choose their own next abbess. This has since been lost. When it was produced in court in the 15th century the clerk transcribed the name of the abbess in 1002 as 'Heahpled', and as the name of the abbess at Wherwell was Heanfled it has been suggested that the same abbess may have ruled over both houses at that time.[92] If that was so then granting each community the right of election would have been a simple way of dividing the two communities, since each could probably be relied on to choose one of their own number. Certainly their future courses were different. Wherwell Abbey was to remain a Benedictine house until the Dissolution, but the reputation of Amesbury declined in the 12th century until it was refounded by Henry II as a priory in the Order of Fontevrault.

Chapter Two

Before and After the Conquest

Before the Conquest: 979-1066

For Wessex, and indeed the whole country, the years of Ethelred's long and interrupted reign were difficult. The Danish invasions that had been held at bay ever since Alfred's time irrupted again and eventually led to the king's exile. The first serious landings were in 980 when Southampton was sacked and many of its citizens killed or taken captive. Other coastal raids followed but these may have seemed isolated incidents in 984 when Bishop Elfheah succeeded Ethelwold. In fact they were the first of increasingly large invasions which brought so much terror and destruction that eventually the king and his advisers raised large sums in order to buy off the invaders. There was a respite for a couple of years after the great ceremony of Olaf Tryggvason's confirmation at Andover in 994, when the king himself had stood sponsor to the greatest of his country's invaders. (Maybe the abbess of Wherwell was among those present. Even if she was not, news of the event would surely have travelled quickly to the abbey.)

Later in the decade the raiders returned, systematically plundering the Wessex coast and terrorising the inhabitants. The king's government remained shakily intact but, perhaps in desperation, Ethelred stupidly ordered the murder of all Danes in England on St. Brice's day, 13 November 1002. In revenge King Sweyn of Denmark returned the following year and harried Wessex as far as Wilton and Shaftesbury. The Anglo-Saxon Chronicle does not mention the fate of the nuns there. The invaders returned again and again, generally during the milder weather, but in 1006 their army raided through Hampshire and Berkshire in winter and defeated the Wiltshire militia near Avebury before sweeping down with their booty past the walls of Winchester on their way to the coast. The relief within those walls must have been immense. In 1011 they landed in Kent where they murdered Archbishop Elfheah, the former bishop of Winchester, after he had refused to pay a ransom. Two years later, when Ethelred fled to Normandy, Sweyn of Denmark became king of England but he died the following year. Ethelred and his son, Edmund Ironside, then returned but by the end of 1016 they too were both dead and Sweyn's younger son, Cnut, became the undisputed ruler of England.[1]

Throughout those years there can have been little peace of mind for anyone in Wessex, whether in or out of a monastery. Instead of springtime bringing thoughts of new life, it must have rekindled the fear and dread of yet another savage invasion. For anyone of property there was the additional worry of taxes that would have to be paid to buy off the raiders. Osbert of Clare recorded that the nuns of Nunnaminster had to despoil the shrine of St. Edburga in order to redeem people captured by the Vikings; this incident may have followed the Viking raid on their estate at All Cannings in 1010. Five years earlier there had been another enemy: in 1005 there was a great famine throughout the country 'such that no man ever remembered one so cruel'.[2] Although this is the only famine mentioned in the Anglo-Saxon Chronicle at this time, it is likely that there were other years of great want especially in the south.

Sometime during this unhappy period, probably in the 990s, the abbess of Romsey is said to have heard a voice from heaven when she was praying, warning her of the coming of the Danes. She and her nuns immediately gathered up the abbey's most precious possessions and fled for protection to Winchester, where their sisters at Nunnaminster took them in.

This incident is believed to be the subject of an early wall painting in the retrochoir of the present abbey, which shows a woman stooping down to pack a trunk. Later, the Danes, who were led by Sweyn, arrived by the river and burned the deserted church and buildings.[3] Presumably the nuns returned to Romsey as soon as it was practical to do so after the danger was past. However welcoming the Nunnaminster nuns may have been in the hour of need, the evacuees are likely to have put a considerable strain on their sisters' resources which could not have been sustained for long.

Once Cnut became king the growing stability of his reign gave the country 20 years of welcome peace. Right from the start Cnut set himself to be a good son of the church, in spite of his upbringing in Denmark where Christianity and heathenism still jostled uncomfortably together. He was prepared to learn from its teaching as well as to fulfil the role expected of him as its protector, and in this capacity he and his wife, Queen Emma (the widow of Ethelred), repaired the monastic houses that had suffered during the years of invasions and became benefactors to many of them.[4] The king's gifts to the cathedral are recorded in the Winchester Annals but the writer did not name the monasteries that were repaired around 1023. However, it seems reasonable to assume that Romsey Abbey would have benefited from the king's desire to make amends for past wrongs since he himself was said to have been with his father when the Danes laid waste to that area.[5]

The most interesting record concerning the nunneries at this time is in the *Liber Vitae* of New Minster. This manuscript, which includes a contemporary drawing of Cnut and his wife placing a cross on the altar of the Minster, contains various lists of benefactors and churchmen, and amongst the illustrious women for whom the monks were to pray are the names of the Romsey abbesses Merewenna and Ethelfled. More unexpected is a later list of 54 nuns of Romsey, headed by their abbess Wulfwynn. This list was apparently written without later additions so that it provides a unique census of the Romsey sisters around 1030.[6] Its inclusion in the *Liber Vitae* indicates that the abbey had confraternity links with New Minster, as indeed it had with the Old Minster. In its turn the Old Minster was also linked to Wherwell Abbey but not to the neighbouring Nunnaminster.[7]

Queen Emma shared her husband's enthusiasm for the church and became an avid collector of relics, but her efforts were generally regarded with some mistrust. Maybe she lacked the true faith of some earlier royal ladies for she seems to have been a rather vain and autocratic person, quite unlike the meek and mild statue representing her on the present cathedral reredos. Nevertheless, she made generous gifts to several monasteries, including the Old and New Minsters at Winchester. The only grants that she is known to have made to a nunnery were in favour of Wilton Abbey; nothing is known of any gift to Nunnaminster although she would presumably have known it well, since she lived in Winchester for much of the time after her marriage to Cnut.[8]

The only recorded connection between Queen Emma and the Hampshire nunneries is with Wherwell, and even that is uncertain. To understand the circumstances one must recount the well known story about Emma being the only English queen to have been married to two kings and mother of two others. By Ethelred she had two sons, including the future Edward the Confessor, but when she married Cnut she left the boys in her native Normandy and virtually abandoned them as she identified herself entirely with Cnut and his fellow Scandinavians. After the death of Cnut in 1035, all her ambitions were fixed on their son, Harthacnut. He eventually became king but then died suddenly only seven years after his father. (Early in his reign Emma's biography was written, a work heavily biased in favour of the queen and her second family. The only contemporary copy of *Encomium Emmae Reginae* includes a portrait of the queen receiving the book from the author.[9])

After the death of Harthacnut, Emma's neglected first born son Edward became king, but it is hardly surprising that he apparently felt little affection for his mother who had

7. The large Saxon rood, *c*.1025, by the abbess's doorway, Romsey Abbey.

8. King Cnut and Queen Emma (Elfgifu) present a cross to New Minster, Winchester, taken from *Liber Vitae*.
BL ms. Stowe 944, f.6.

done nothing to forward his interests. It was perhaps to assuage some deep seated grudge against Emma that the new king rode into Winchester one day with three of his earls, accused his mother of treason and deprived her of all her property including her jewellery. One chronicler maintained that the king gave orders for Emma to be supplied with necessaries and for her to remain quietly, apparently in Winchester, but in the Winchester Annals it was written that she retired to the abbey of Wherwell in that year. If that was so, the aftermath of the traumatic encounter with her son seems the most likely time, especially as it was later said that she travelled from Wherwell to Winchester to face further accusations.[10] Whatever the truth, Edward later repented of his high-handed action and restored his mother to her own property in Winchester where she died in 1052. She was buried in the Old Minster near Cnut and Harthacnut, and when the present cathedral was built their remains were moved into it. Two hundred years later Emma's tomb was covered with a costly quilt on the orders of Henry III.[11]

Less than a decade later the king meted out rather similar treatment to his wife, Queen Edith, whom he had married in 1045. She had been an excellent choice, being young, attractive, well educated by the nuns of Wilton Abbey and the daughter of Earl Godwin, the most powerful man in the kingdom. However, Edward increasingly resented his father-in-law's power and in 1051 he determined to break it. Godwin and his sons fled abroad, refusing to face charges against them, and his daughter was repudiated by the king and sent to a nunnery. As in his quarrel with his mother, Edward soon cooled down and all was forgiven the following year when the queen was restored to her position at court and the earl and his son Harold enjoyed royal favour once again.[12]

9. An illustration taken from *Encomium Emmae Reginae* (written *c*.1040), showing Queen Emma receiving a copy of the work from the author, watched by her sons Harthacnut and Edward (afterwards 'the Confessor'). BL Add. ms. 33241, f.1v.

There is a conflict between the two earliest accounts about the nunnery to which the queen was sent during her banishment. The *Waverley Annals* and the two versions of the Anglo-Saxon Chronicle that mention Edith's banishment all say that she was sent to Wherwell Abbey. One version of the Chronicle says

She was brought to Wherwell and they entrusted her to the abbess.

The other version states that

> . . . the King put away the lady who was consecrated his Queen and deprived her of all she owned, land and gold and silver and everything, and entrusted her to his sister at Wherwell.[13]

This was followed by other chroniclers who added that she was sent there with only a single handmaid.[14] But in the *Vita Edwardi Regis*, which was written in honour of the king after his death, there is a different account. The archbishop is made the scapegoat for the situation to which the king reluctantly assented:

> And so, with royal honours and an imperial retinue, but with grief at heart, she was brought to the walls of Wilton convent, where for almost a year in prayers and tears she awaited the day of salvation.[15]

It is impossible to know which account to believe. It may be that there is truth in both versions. The queen could have been sent to Wherwell where the king's sister was evidently abbess and then sometime later, perhaps at her own request, escorted the 20 odd miles further west to the scene of her childhood at Wilton where she would have been a welcome and honoured guest.

These possible connections with the two queens are all that is known of Wherwell Abbey during the half century before the Conquest. For Romsey Abbey there is just the list of nuns, while no information at all seems to have survived about Nunnaminster. This gap in information is not peculiar to Hampshire's nunneries; it is true of nearly all monastic houses throughout the country. Many records relating to the English church during the years immediately preceding the Conquest were deliberately destroyed by the Normans in their efforts to obliterate the recent past, and those that survived – like the Anglo-Saxon Chronicles – were concerned with national affairs rather than the inner life of the monasteries where they were written and copied.[16]

In the absence of any evidence to the contrary one assumes that life in the three nunneries continued along the lines taught them by Bishop Ethelwold, even if there may have been some falling away in vigour and dedication, as there was in many of the monastic houses. But as news reached the nuns in 1065 that Queen Edith was replacing the old wooden church of their sisters at Wilton with a new stone one,[17] it would not have occurred to any of them that the old order was about to give way to a new one and that in future the connections between the nunneries and the royal family would be rather more distant.

After the Conquest: 1066-1100

The events of 1066 need no long recital here. The death of Edward the Confessor at the beginning of the year, the brief, battle-strewn reign of Harold (Queen Edith's brother) and the triumph of William of Normandy's invading army at Hastings in October are known to everyone. All that concerns us here is the effect of the Conquest on the Hampshire nunneries.

Romsey was not in the way of the invading army and Wherwell possibly escaped its attention as well, since it lay between the two routes probably taken by the spearheads of William's forces as they marched through north-west Hampshire on their way to Wallingford and London after the surrender of Winchester.[18] That surrender had been made in November by Queen Edith herself without any battle being fought, but though the inhabitants were spared immediate bloodshed and destruction, the effect of the invasion was soon felt. Many English laymen were dispossessed of their property within the city, but amongst the religious houses only New Minster lost a part of its site that William wanted for his new palace. The right of the monasteries to keep their other holdings in the city was recognised, and this benefited not only the three minsters but also the abbeys of Romsey and Wherwell who both owned property there.[19]

Although the nunneries and other religious foundations in the old Wessex seem to have escaped fairly lightly during the invasion, it is not difficult to imagine what a time of fear it must have been for every woman living anywhere near the soldiers' route. Some young women were evidently sent into nunneries by their families for protection which sometimes led to misunderstandings later on about their status, particularly if they had worn a veil for increased protection. Had they thereby become nuns or were they free to leave the house and to marry when the danger had passed? In the following decade Archbishop Lanfranc wrote to one of his bishops that

'As to those who as you tell me fled to a monastery not for love of the religious life but for fear of the French, if they can prove that this was so by the unambiguous witness of nuns better than they, let them be granted unrestricted leave to depart. This is the king's policy and our own'.[20]

The king's general policy for the church in his new realm became gradually apparent. At first he moved cautiously and even Archbishop Stigand, in spite of being excommunicated by five popes, continued to hold both Canterbury and Winchester until the spring of 1070 when he was finally deprived. He was replaced at Winchester by one of the King's chaplains, Walkelin, who soon started work on the present cathedral. Abbot Lanfranc of Caen, a monk trained at Bec and one of the foremost intellectuals in Europe, reluctantly agreed to become archbishop and, in spite of his lack of enthusiasm, his appointment as the metropolitan was a success for both church and state. In the course of the next two decades William and Lanfranc succeeded in their aim of normanising the church in England and the authority of the archbishop became recognised throughout the country for the first time.

Naturally the English monasteries were one of Lanfranc's first concerns. There were many similarities between them and the houses he knew so well in Normandy. The broad framework of their ideals and their lives within the Rule were the same, and both were an integral part of the church and state with the ruler (the duke in Normandy and the king in England) occupying a position of influence over them that was unknown elsewhere in Europe. They differed in that the relationship in England between monarch and monastery, although close and interdependent, had been fairly loose and undefined, whereas in Normandy the monastic houses were in strict subordination to the duke as their feudal lord; and in the spiritual realm the English houses lacked that sense of enthusiasm that was so much a feature of monastic life in the newer monasteries of Normandy in Lanfranc's day. That same spirit had been present in English houses a century before but since then many of the great monasteries had become wealthy and more complacent which had led to a decline in their spiritual and intellectual life. They were soon to receive a jolt as Norman abbots and bishops were advanced when vacancies occurred, a new liturgy was introduced to replace their own variety of Gregorian plainsong and a new church calendar appeared with many of the revered Old English saints' names removed.[21]

It is not known how far or how fast Lanfranc's reforms were applied to the English nunneries. It has been suggested that most of them continued to be ruled by Anglo-Saxon abbesses well into the late 11th century[22] but the evidence from the Hampshire nunneries is mixed. At Winchester, where Nunnaminster came to be known as the Abbey of St. Mary, Abbess Beatrice (a Norman name) died in 1084; her successor was referred to as Alice in the Winchester Annals but Anselm addressed her by the Saxon form of the name, Athelits.[23] At Romsey it is not certain whether Christina, who belonged to the Old English royal family, was ever abbess, but there was certainly an Abbess Athelitz around the turn of the century.[24] An unnamed sister of Edward the Confessor was abbess of Wherwell in 1051 but it is not known whether she survived her brother; however, the first of the next three known abbesses before 1113 had a Saxon name, Aelstrita, but her two successors were Norman.[25]

When Lanfranc became archbishop there were 10 nunneries in England, all in the south and six of them in Wessex. In the aftermath of the Conquest their importance declined for a number of reasons; one was the decline in the status of women generally in Norman

England, while another was the loosening of their ties to the reigning family, particularly the queen regnant. Queen Edith continued to be associated with Wilton Abbey where she probably spent much of her widowhood, although she was in Winchester when she died in 1075. However, she was a figure from the past. Queen Matilda, the wife of William the Conqueror, seems unconnected with any of the Wessex nunneries. Her own interest lay with the nuns' houses in Normandy, especially with the Abbey of La Trinité at Caen which she had built and where she was later buried. (Among the bequests in her will, she left that abbey her tunic 'worked at Winchester by Alderet's wife'.[26])

William the Conqueror evidently confirmed the ancient rights of Romsey Abbey sometime during his reign but the first mention of the house in the chronicles is in 1086 when Christina, granddaughter of Edmund Ironside and the sister of Queen Margaret of Scotland, 'sought refuge in the convent at Romsey and took the veil'.[27] William of Malmesbury described Christina as growing old at Romsey in the habit of a nun and three other chroniclers recorded her being there; their testimony has been accepted by most modern authorities although Eadmer implied that she was at Wilton.[28]

Orderic Vitalis, the monk who wrote his ecclesiastical history within 50 years of these events, was among those who wrote that Christina was at Romsey, and his history continued with an account of her two nieces. They were the children of Queen Margaret who 'sent her two daughters, Edith and Mary, to her sister Christina, who was a nun in Romsey Abbey, to be brought up and taught sound doctrine. There they were cared for by the nuns for a long time, and educated both in letters and in good morals'.[29] Later, Edith was sent

10. The seal of Matilda, Queen of England 1100-18.

to the nuns at Wilton, possibly after her father had discovered her wearing a veil at Romsey. That circumstance led many people to suppose that she had taken the vows of a nun, including Archbishop Anselm who wrote indignantly to the bishop of Salisbury in 1094 about a marriage that had been proposed for her by her father.[30] (By that time she was known as Matilda.) That marriage did not take place, but six years later the newly crowned Henry I determined to marry the lady himself, for purely political reasons. However, since her status was open to question, he needed permission from the archbishop. Matilda herself went to see Anselm and told him of the circumstances that had led to her wearing a veil:

> But that I did wear the veil [she said] I do not deny. For when I was quite a young girl and went in fear of the rod of my Aunt Christina, whom you know quite well, she to preseve me from the lust of the Normans which was rampant and at that time ready to assault any woman's honour, used to put a little black hood on my head and, when I threw it off, she would often make me smart with a good slapping and most horrible scolding, as well as treating me as being in disgrace. That hood I did indeed wear in her presence, chafing at it and fearful; but as soon as I was able to escape out of her

sight, I tore it off and threw it on the ground and trampled on it and in that way, although foolishly, I used to vent my rage and the hatred of it which boiled up in me. In that way, and only in that way, I was veiled, as my conscience bears witness. And if anyone says that I was dedicated, of that too the truth may be gathered from the fact, which is known to many persons still living, that my father, when by chance he saw me veiled snatched the veil off and tearing it in pieces invoked the hatred of God upon the person who had put it on me . . .[31]

Later in the year a church council decided in the king's favour so Anselm gave his reluctant consent to the marriage and performed the ceremony himself; afterwards the new Queen Matilda corresponded with the archbishop as her mother had done with Lanfranc.[32]

The Domesday Survey

Information about the nunneries' wealth and possessions before the Conquest rests on the chance survival of early charters, but from 1086 that knowledge comes from the remarkable survey of the country that was compiled into the Domesday Book. The survey was ordered by William the Conqueror at Christmas 1085 because, as the Anglo-Saxon chronicler said, the king wanted to know 'about this country – how it was occupied or with what sort of people'.[33] Among those people were the abbesses of Romsey, Wherwell and St. Mary's Winchester. Like all tenants-in-chief who held their land directly from the king, their manors and lands are detailed in the survey, though it is impossible to know exactly how many acres they held since the measurements of hides and ploughlands varied from one place to another.

The clerks collecting evidence in the shire moots were basically concerned to record the fundamentals of the agrarian economy: the arable and pasture, the woods, waters and waste, with their values at the time of Edward the Confessor's death and their current valuation. The manor was the unit used for the inquest, in spite of its varied nature, but the hide was the old basic unit for the purposes of taxation and the apportionment of common burdens such as military service and the upkeep of bridges.[34] (Originally a hide theoretically represented the amount of land that could be ploughed in one year to support a family using one ploughteam of eight oxen.)

The manors that the abbess of Wherwell held beyond the village were entirely in the abbey's possession and were all within a six-mile radius of Wherwell. The land granted to them by King Ethelred at Dean in Sussex had evidently been lost by 1066. The holdings of St. Mary's, Winchester and Romsey were a more scattered and assorted collection, reflecting their acquisition at different times and from various donors. The most valuable properties of both houses were in Wiltshire where great estates were common. There, St. Mary's held Urchfont and All Cannings while Edington and Steeple Ashton belonged to Romsey Abbey.[35] All four manors were within six miles of Potterne, south of Devizes.

The three nunneries all had property in Winchester; this included the abbess of Wherwell's own house which was held free of taxes. The tenements there of Romsey and Wherwell were noted with their other Hampshire property but the entry for St. Mary's only gives its holdings outside Winchester.[36] The city itself was not included in Domesday Book, but the two surveys of landholding in it that were made in c.1110 and in 1148 are believed to give a reliable guide to the nunneries' estates there in the pre-Conquest period.

The buildings regularly recorded were churches and mills. The churches in Romsey and Wherwell were both noted but on the nunneries' manors further afield only Froyle had a church apparently. Mills were far more plentiful and were owned on most of the manors held by the nuns. Leckford was an exception, but there the abbot of St. Peter's (New Minster) was the mill owner. At Totton, near Southampton, the abbess of Romsey's *salina* was recorded so the nuns evidently owned one of the valuable salterns there.[37] Two small points are of interest amongst the returns for the abbess of Winchester: the income from

Ovington, Hampshire, was used for the support of the nuns and was therefore not assessed; and in Berkshire the manor of Coleshill had been granted to the abbey by Walter de Lacy 'with his daughter'.[38]

The valuations of the different properties and how they were determined remain a puzzle for any user of Domesday Book. Many of the figures given were artificial, as valuations so often are. Although they cannot be converted into present-day values, they can be used to compare the wealth of the three nunneries; in simple terms, Romsey Abbey was the best endowed, St. Mary's Abbey came next and Wherwell had the smallest income. The surprising feature of the values is that the 1086 figures are mostly the same or slightly more than they had been 20 years earlier. Today inflation seems normal, but in the first 20 years of Norman rule in England values generally declined rather than increased. It tends to confirm that the property of the nunneries seems to have escaped the attentions of the Conqueror's army.

The findings of the Domesday inquest were soon found to be useful in any dispute over titles to property, so copies of the relevant entries were transcribed into the cartularies of monastic houses. In the Wherwell cartulary charter 354 seems to be such a copy but it gives the number of hides that the abbess held in 1066, not 1086.[39] The cartularies for Romsey Abbey and St. Mary's Abbey have not survived, but at the start of the Edington cartulary there are copies of the Wiltshire entries relating to Romsey Abbey's holdings at Edington and Ashton, and to St. Mary's Abbey's manor of Coleshill.[40]

Chapter Three

Peace and War in the Twelfth Century

Anselm and the reign of Henry I

The earliest surviving letters to abbesses in Hampshire were written by Anselm, probably during the prolonged vacancy in the diocese of Winchester that followed the death of Bishop Walkelin in 1098. William Rufus had refused to fill the vacancy so that he could keep the revenues of the diocese himself, but after his sudden death Henry I appointed the chancellor, William Giffard, to be bishop and recalled Anselm from exile. However, the archbishop refused to consecrate Giffard and two other bishops elect who had accepted investiture from the king. The dispute lasted until 1107.[1]

When the abbess of St. Mary's Abbey, Winchester heard that William Giffard was to be banished from the country on account of his loyalty to the church, she evidently wrote to Anselm in some distress. In his reply the archbishop reminded her of the honour of suffering for God and, in words that could still be used about any priest suffering persecution, he finished his letter,

> Therefore may his friends rejoice and exult, because he could not be vanquished by any violence or fear, nor be parted from the truth by any desire for gain. Let this be your consolation for his banishment, and let your daily prayer be to this end, that God may strengthen and console him. I salute and bless your daughters and mine, so far as in me lies.[2]

Anselm's two letters concerning Romsey could hardly be more different. They were apparently written at the same time, one to the Archdeacon of Winchester and the other to Abbess Athelitz, who had already asked for his advice. She was troubled about a deceased noble, probably Earl Waltheof, who had been executed for conspiracy by William the Conqueror and then buried in the abbey. Some people, including his son, were trying to encourage the growth of a cult around his tomb by suggesting that he should be venerated as a saint. Anselm was without sympathy. The archdeacon was ordered to go and see the lady abbess and her nuns to forbid them or anyone else from taking such a view, and also to send the young man away from the town.[3] When Anselm wrote to the abbess and nuns he was just as firm, even if he chose to soften his words at first:

> Did I not love you dearly, I would greatly rebuke you, because, after you yourselves had sent your messenger to me and had sought our advice as to what you should do about that dead man whom some persons wish to be considered as a saint, you have not stood by our advice, but, moreover, you remain disobedient to our instruction. Wherefore I direct you by mandate that, if you wish to avoid suspension from the divine office, from henceforth you cease from paying any honour to that dead man, such as is due to a saint, and neither make oblation to him nor, if it has been made, take it towards your work. And as for his son, who has taken up his abode at his tomb and loiters there, send him away from the town, and leave him no further means of remaining therein. Farewell.[4]

The archbishop was clearly appalled at this attempt to secure canonisation by popular demand in the old Anglo-Saxon manner.

Anselm died in 1109 but Henry's reign continued for another quarter of a century. His firm rule over a long period provided a welcome time of consolidation for the country and the church after all the disturbances caused by the Conquest. In the monasteries a sense of stability and continuity developed which was probably shared by the older nunneries. It was partly fostered by the work of several monastic historians such as William of Malmesbury, who were writing at this time; but more importantly, it was a time of real spiritual fervour in the English houses for men. Within their walls life continued to be centred on the liturgy, with little time for private prayer.[5]

The amount of spiritual fervour in the nunneries is impossible to gauge. They remained the preserve of noble families and performed a real service in providing refuges for widows, although the influence of those ladies on the communities may have been mixed. Many of them were perhaps just as interested in keeping in touch with this world as in making spiritual preparation for the world to come.

The nunneries continued to be used as places of informal education for the daughters of the nobility, though they were not schools. Young and old alike would have been busy with embroidery, for the benefit of lay patrons as well as the church, but the application of at least some of the nuns and their pupils to more academic pursuits is harder to discover. French was the language of the nobility and it seems to have been the natural medium for nuns both then and later, but there were some ladies learned in Latin at this time. Queen Matilda's education had equipped her to write in both Latin and French,[6] and in 1113 one of the nuns at St. Mary's Abbey contributed memorial verses in Latin to the Mortuary Roll of the late abbess of Caen when it was sent round to many of the English houses. The nuns of Amesbury and Shaftesbury also contributed a short Latin verse each, but when it reached Wherwell the nuns there just added the names of some former members of their own community.[7] Romsey Abbey was not on the itinerary of monasteries visited in 1113, but nine years later when the Mortuary Roll of a French abbot was being circulated the messenger visited the nuns there after he had been to Winchester and before going on to Salisbury and Shaftesbury. None of the nunneries produced any verses for that Roll.[8]

The stability of Henry's reign (1100-35) made it a good period for new building work. Within Hampshire, Hyde Abbey was built for the monks of New Minster who had been far too close to the new cathedral. Henry and Matilda were both present when it was consecrated. A few years later the king founded the Priory of St. Denys near Southampton for Augustinian canons who were to have confraternity links with Romsey Abbey.[9] At St. Mary's Abbey the domestic buildings were remodelled in the late 11th or early 12th century; modern excavations have shown that a vaulted undercroft (perhaps for the frater) was added during this period.[10] The changes to the abbey church were more sweeping. The Saxon church was dismantled and work started on a much larger building, emulating the new cathedral. It was dedicated to the nunnery's own St. Edburga in 1108, so that it became properly known as the Abbey of St. Mary and St. Edburga.[11] This was its title in the Mortuary Roll of 1113. Nothing is known about Wherwell Abbey at this period, apart from the possibility that the king may have stayed there in 1105 on his way to Romsey.[12]

At Romsey itself it had been decided to rebuild the abbey church on a much grander scale. There had been some preliminary work at the end of the 11th century, but the main work on the new chancel and transepts was carried out during and just after the last half of Henry's reign, c.1120-40, with another stint in the 1150s. During this period the Saxon church remained in use, its stout walls and roof providing some insulation from the noise of the builders beyond it. Once the walls of the new transepts had reached a good height a temporary screen was built from one side to the other, thus partitioning off the new chancel.[13] Even so, concentration must often have been difficult for the worshipping nuns.

In the absence of a cartulary for the abbey, it is very difficult to look beyond the stones themselves to the people and finances responsible for the building operations. It is just not known whether any substantial gifts were made to the community during Christina's time there at the end of the 11th century, or whether Anselm was referring to the new constructions when he mentioned oblations being taken 'towards your work' in his letter to Abbess Athelitz.[14] Large sums must have been needed to pay for the building that started around 1120, but who gave them? Henry de Blois might have done so, but Liveing suggested that

ROMSEY ABBEY
MAJOR PHASES OF CONSTRUCTION

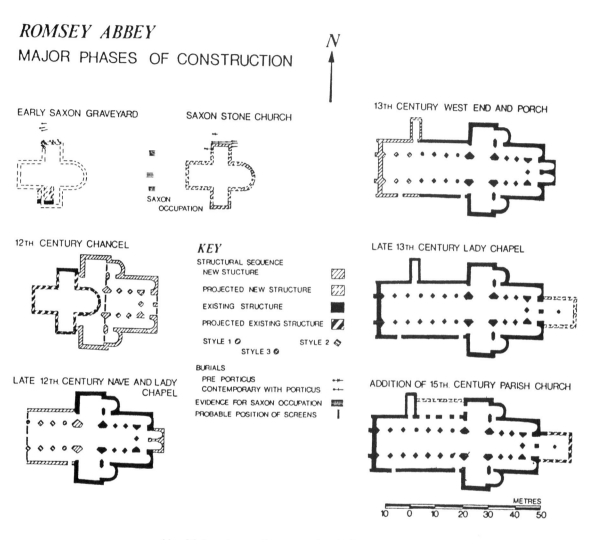

11.   Major phases of construction in Romsey Abbey.

the king could have been responsible, seeing the work as a memorial to Queen Matilda who had died in 1118,[15] although she appears to have had little contact with the abbey after her marriage. Her later years were spent at Westminster but she may have been with the king in February 1105 when he stayed at Romsey on his way to France. He sealed several charters on that occasion, including one 'with the advice and assent of Matilda my wife' in favour of Abingdon Abbey.[16] (That monastery really was one of the queen's interests on account of her friendship with its abbot Fabricius, who was physician to her and her husband.) Henry stayed in Romsey again the following year and also in 1110, but apparently he was not there after Matilda's death.[17] His known benefactions to the abbey included tax exemptions and the grant of seven charters, including one that gave the nuns the right to hold a yearly fair lasting four days and a market in the town every Sunday.[18]

Civil War and the Nunneries

The marriage of Henry and Matilda produced only two children: William, who was drowned in the wreck of the White Ship in 1120, and Matilda who had been married at an early age to the Emperor Henry V and was subsequently the wife of Geoffrey Plantagenet, Count of Anjou. The king remarried soon after the death of his son but his hope of another male heir was not realised (which must have been frustrating for a man with at least 20 acknowledged bastards). Later he induced the English barons to swear an oath accepting Matilda as his heir, though there was enthusiasm neither for the novel idea of a woman sovereign nor for Matilda herself. She was haughty, tactless and grasping and her second marriage was particularly unwelcome to the Norman barons.[19]

When Henry died in Normandy in 1135, his nephew Stephen de Blois quickly crossed to England where he was well known and liked. After being elected king by the citizens of London, he hurried down to Winchester to secure the treasury and take the castle, thanks to the influence of his brother Henry de Blois, Bishop of Winchester. If Matilda and her supporters had only been prepared to accept Stephen's kingship as a *fait accompli* the country, including the city of Winchester and two of Hampshire's nunneries, would have been spared a great deal of suffering and destruction. But she was a fighter like her father, and by 1141 the fighting was taking place in Hampshire.

That February Matilda's forces under her half-brother Robert of Gloucester (the eldest bastard son of Henry I) had beaten Stephen's army at the battle of Lincoln. The king was imprisoned at Bristol and Matilda made her way towards Winchester. Henry de Blois, who had become papal legate, was by then supporting her cause because of quarrels between Stephen and the church. Nevertheless Matilda had to agree to leave all ecclesiastical matters in the hands of the bishop before she was allowed to enter the city. Once there she was acclaimed by the citizens and received in state in the cathedral on 3 March 1141.[20] A month later she was formally elected *Domina Anglorum* at a legatine council in Winchester that had been called by the bishop and was attended by Archbishop Theobald and many other bishops and abbots. William of Malmesbury was also present.[21]

However, sovereigns were no longer crowned in Winchester but at Westminster. The citizens of London had been persuaded that they should accept Matilda, albeit reluctantly, but within a short time of her arrival there in June, her arrogant and unforgiving behaviour caused a riot. She was lucky to escape with her life. At first she fled to Oxford, still supported by Robert of Gloucester but no longer by Henry de Blois whom she had managed to antagonise. Within a short time she gathered her scattered followers together and rode to Winchester again at the head of them, reaching it towards the end of July. She took up residence and started to besiege the city and the bishop, who was now actively siding with Stephen. On Saturday 4 August, during the fighting between Matilda's forces under Robert of Gloucester and those of the bishop, firebrands thrown from the bishop's keep set fire to St. Mary's Abbey and destroyed it. Other buildings suffered the same fate, including Hyde Abbey and many parish churches.[22] Afterwards Stephen's forces, which were led by his wife (another Matilda), concentrated on cutting off supplies from their opponents. The besiegers were themselves then besieged.

As the situation became increasingly difficult for Matilda's forces in Winchester, they hastily established a garrison in Wherwell, no doubt to the consternation of the abbess and her nuns. There in September they were attacked and defeated in a battle on the outskirts of the village by William of Ypres and his followers who were supporting Stephen. Many were killed. Others took shelter in the abbey church which was then fired and burned to the ground by William's soldiers, after they had pillaged vestments, books and ornaments from it. The fire also spread to the domestic buildings.[23] As one contemporary wrote:

It was indeed a dreadful and wretched sight, how impiously and savagely bodies of armed men were ranging about in a church, a house of religion and prayer, especially as in one place mutual slaughter was going on, in another prisoners were being dragged off with thongs, here the conflagration was fearfully ravaging the roofs of the church and houses, there cries and shrieks rang piercingly out from the virgins dedicated to God who had left their cloisters with reluctance under the stress of the fire.[24]

When the news reached Winchester, Matilda and her remaining forces immediately left the city but their orderly retreat was soon turned to a rout after both they and the city were once again attacked by the king's troops. Matilda was lucky to escape. Robert of Gloucester was captured in Stockbridge and then exchanged for Stephen himself the following November.[25]

Intermittent fighting between Stephen and Matilda dragged on for several more years. Wilton Abbey was burned in the course of a battle in 1143 but none of the Hampshire nunneries was caught in the front line again. Romsey Abbey alone had apparently been left unscarred by the war, and perhaps it became a refuge for some of the sisters from Winchester and Wherwell while their houses were being restored and rebuilt.

In his history of Romsey, Sir Richard Luce suggested that three of the main figures in the civil war may have made contributions to the 12th-century work on the abbey church: King Stephen himself, Henry de Blois and Robert of Gloucester.[26]

Mary de Blois, the daughter of Stephen, was abbess at Romsey for a short time and a carving on one of the capitals in the south transept supposedly represents them both. Yet it is far from certain that Mary was a nun at Romsey during the lifetime of her father, so there are doubts whether Stephen was ever particularly generous to the abbey on her account, though he did grant it three charters in the course of his reign.[27] His daughter had been educated by the nuns at Stratford-atte-Bow, Middlesex but her own attendants there had been nuns brought over from St. Sulpice at Rennes. It is hardly surprising in the circumstances that friction and misunderstandings between the two sets of nuns developed. As a result the young princess departed with the French nuns to found a new nunnery at Lillechurch in Kent, with herself as its first prioress. Sometime between 1150 and 1152 it was formally agreed in the presence of the queen and Archbishop Theobald that they should receive the profits from the manor there which had originally been granted for Mary's support at Stratford.[28]

Sometime later Mary left the new priory for Romsey. We do not know why or when, but if it was during her father's lifetime then it would have been near the end of it, for he died in 1154. However, it was Mary's subsequent career that caused a scandal in her lifetime. She was abbess of Romsey by 1160 but then, in spite of her vows, she married Matthew, count of Boulogne, the son of the count of Flanders.[29] Undoubtedly her cousin, Henry II, was largely responsible for promoting the marriage but it is difficult to exonerate Mary entirely. There was so much disapproval of the match in high places that she could surely have avoided it had she been determined to do so. (Eventually, after the birth of two daughters, the couple parted and Mary passed her remaining years in a French convent at Montreuil.)[30]

Princess Mary's uncle, Henry de Blois, may well have made some gifts to Romsey in his capacity of diocesan from 1129 to 1171 but nothing has been recorded, unlike so much of his patronage at Glastonbury, Winchester and Cluny. But if he did so it is likely that this would have been during his later 'mellow years of generous patronage'.[31]

Finally it is an interesting possibility that Robert, Earl of Gloucester might not only have been a benefactor of the abbey but also the ROBERTUS commemorated on one of the capitals in the south aisle of the abbey chancel. There is no known connection between Robert of Gloucester and Romsey, but that faithful ally and half brother of the Empress

12. Norman capital in St Anne's chapel, Romsey Abbey. To the left of the photograph, *ROBERTUS ME FECIT* is carved on the chevron scroll; on the right, the words on the other scroll are less clear but are usually read as *ROBERT TU TE CONSULE XDS.*

Matilda was a patron and scholar as well as a soldier and statesman. His wife was the heiress of Robert fitz Haymon, who had been one of the earliest supporters of Henry I, and two of her sisters were abbesses: one at Shaftesbury and the other at Wilton.[32]

The foundation of Wintney Priory

In spite of the weak government and adverse conditions that prevailed during and after the civil war, Stephen's reign was a surprisingly fruitful time for English monasticism. In France new orders had been developing, above all the Cistercian order under the inspired leadership of Bernard of Clairvaux. New houses were founded there during the 1120s and 1130s as he and his followers became an inspiration to many. It was just a matter of time before his ideas spread across the Channel.

How did Bernard's Cistercian order differ from the Benedictine order to which all the Wessex monasteries and nunneries belonged at that time? Briefly, Cistercian monks sought to worship God more perfectly and follow the precepts of the gospel of Christ more faithfully by living their communal lives away from the temptations and distractions of the world. As a result their houses were always founded on poor land – forest, moor or marsh – at a distance from towns and villages; and there, with the help of a large force of uneducated lay brothers, they proceeded to make a living from the soil. They also differed in their organisation. Whereas each Benedictine house was autonomous before the Lateran Council of 1215, the Cistercians were part of a hierarchy independent of both the state and the local bishop. Each new house was the daughter house of an earlier foundation whose abbot was responsible for visiting all the daughter houses of his monastery regularly. These relationships can be shown in family tree form.[33] The corporate nature of the organisation was further strengthened by a General Chapter which was held annually and attended by all the male heads of Cistercian houses.

In England the Cistercians made their greatest impact in the north, but their first house was at Waverley, near Farnham, in the diocese of Winchester. This was founded in 1128 by Bishop Giffard and the monks of L'Aumone, and was so successful that by 1150 it had five daughter houses.[34] Almost certainly it was also the parent house of Wintney Priory.

Initially the Cistercians were strongly opposed to the idea of having any nunneries in their order at all. Their attitude was that women in general represented one of the temptations of the flesh and should therefore be avoided. And there were indeed practical difficulties. For instance a certain amount of contact, however limited, would be inevitable between a parent monastery and a daughter houses for nuns, and that in itself would be incompatible with strict Cistercian discipline. Then, since no woman could be a priest, it followed that one would have to be provided to say mass, yet if he were a monk that might endanger his eternal salvation. Furthermore, since no abbess or prioress could be expected to travel to the General Chapter, the house would tend to lose touch with the wider family. And how could ladies be required to work in the fields?

But enthusiasm for the new order was so great that it was inevitable that houses for women following the Cistercian way of life would come into being. The house generally described as the first Cistercian nunnery was founded at Tart, near Dijon, about 1132,[35] and Wintney Priory was the first in England. Similar English houses soon followed so that by the end of the 12th century there were 27 in the country, the majority of them in Yorkshire and Lincolnshire. At that time the priory at Wintney was the only such foundation in the south of England, though in the following century Tarrant Abbey in Dorset became a Cistercian nunnery.[36] All the early houses were in a somewhat anomalous position. Although the nuns and their patrons considered that they were Cistercians, their houses were not actually incorporated into the Cistercian order at that time. The General Chapter virtually ignored the question of nunneries until 1213 but it then finally recognised their *de facto* existence and issued a decree regulating their position. From that time onwards they can properly be described as Cistercian houses.[37]

Against this background of external enthusiasm for the order but official internal disapproval of women within it, Wintney Priory came into being. Little is known about its foundation but that little does include the name of the founder, Geoffrey fitz Peter, his original grants and a rough idea of when they were made.[38] His name first occurs in Hampshire in the Winton Domesday of 1148.[39] Five years later he witnessed a charter of Duke Henry shortly before he became Henry II, and then in the following decade he was named twice in the Pipe Roll returns for Hampshire.[40] In the second entry he rendered an account for the vill of Sparsholt whose history was to be linked with Wintney Priory until the Dissolution.[41] Geoffrey fitz Peter granted three charters to the church and nuns of Wintney which, with other later charters, were inspected by the prior of St. Swithun's, Winchester, at the end of the 13th century and then enrolled.[42] They were granted for the good of the souls of Geoffrey himself, his wife Cecily and their ancestors in the normal manner. However, it was less usual that he first named the souls of Henry II and his successors, but there was some connection between the royal family and Geoffrey's mother, Alina, who had been granted 'Hurtlege' by Henry I at the time of her marriage.[43] (Such gifts in frank marriage were normally only made by the father or close relative of a bride.)

In the first charter the nuns were granted the church of Hartley and all the town except one virgate, together with the tithes from Geoffrey's demesne of Coldrey, in return for their saying regular masses for their founder and his wife in perpetuity; among the witnesses were the abbot and prior of Waverley Abbey, and Alexander the priest of Hartley. The second charter granted them the chapel of St. Nicholas in Geoffrey's court at Coldrey, while the third gave them the rent from his mill at Newbridge in Winchester with its land in Colebrook Street.[44] (The nuns first made payments to the Exchequer on this Winchester property in 1181-2.[45]) Geoffrey was thus fulfilling the accepted role of a founder and patron of a Cistercian house by supplying the land and starting the endowment of the house; he would also have been expected to provide for the initial building fund.

The obit of Geoffrey fitz Peter is one of the original entries in the priory's calendar.[46] He evidently died in April, but there is no clue about which April. Neither is it known when he granted his first charter to the nuns; as with most 12th-century documents, it is only possible to have a general idea of that date by a process of subtraction. Thus from the charter itself we know that Henry II was already king so it cannot pre-date 1154; however, one of the witnesses was Abbot Henry of Waverley who at that time was abbot of Tintern Abbey, but he was at Waverley by 1161.[47] Then, letters of protection were granted to the church and nuns of Wintney by Henry de Blois[48] who died in 1171, so one is left with a foundation date some time after 1154 but not later than 1171.

In spite of the Cistercian order's official attitude to nunneries at that time, Geoffrey fitz Peter evidently discussed the proposed foundation with the abbot of Waverley nearby, and involved him in it. As we have seen, both he and Richard the prior there witnessed the first charter, and in it Waverley was credited with being the parent house of Wintney.[49] However, Waverley Abbey never seems to have publicly acknowledged its connection with Wintney Priory which is not mentioned in its annals.

On Wintney's side, a bond between the two houses is implied in a Norman-French prayer in their calendar which starts:

> Aus ke lisez cest escrit'
> Dez que frere Symon dit.
> Jhu' crist que unc ne menti
> Gard le Cuvent de Winteni
> et le cuvent de Waverle'.[50]

The calendar also includes the obit of Adam, abbot of Waverley from 1216-19;[51] his inclusion may perhaps be connected to the fact that he was in office at the time of the General Chapter of 1213.

Geoffrey fitz Peter and his wife Cecily were apparently childless since no heir was mentioned in his foundation grants to the priory and the name does not occur again in the records of the house, but the family of his sister, Juliana, continued to be benefactors of the nunnery. At the time of Juliana's marriage to Stephen de Bendeng of Winchfield, Geoffrey fitz Peter gave his sister one third of the vill of Hartley (presumably the virgate he had withheld from the nuns in his original grant). That property later passed to their son Maurice, but after the death of his son, another Stephen, it was quitclaimed to the nuns by his widow in 1258.[52] Both Stephens and Maurice Bendeng are named in the Wintney calendar along with six other members of the family.

In the 13th century other local families became benefactors of the little priory, especially the interconnected Herriard, Sifrewast and Colrith families. The obits of seven Herriards are included in the calendar, including Richard de Herriard who was described as the founder of the nunnery's stone church in his April obit; another Richard de Herriard is entered in the calendar for October, but it is not known which one was the father.[53] The sister and heiress of the younger Richard was Matilda who married Richard de Sifrewast.

They are both among the seven members of their family who appear in the calendar, Matilda herself being named as Matilda Sifrewast *domina* de Herriard.[54] Some of the grants which she and her family made to the priory church still survive among the Herriard Papers, one of them with Matilda's large seal attached.[55] Another family of early benefactors were the Colriths; two ladies' names are in the *Martyrologium* of the house and seven other obits were recorded in the calendar, including Dionisia *domina* de Colrith whose heart was buried before the high altar in the nuns' church.[56] The family apparently maintained their connection with the priory as one of their descendants was Christine, the wife of Richard Holt; they were both benefactors of the house in the 15th century. On the same folio to which their obits have been added there is an original entry for the obit of Matilda de Quincy who provided the dormitory for the nunnery.[57]

The motives for the generosity of these families who supported Wintney Priory were undoubtedly varied. Duty, thankfulness and sympathy probably played a part, and the earliest benefactors would have been influenced by the climate of enthusiasm for the Cistercians. Later patrons may have felt a family interest in the little nunnery where they were always welcome visitors, even if the prayers of those nuns were not considered to be quite so effective as those of monks – for above all medieval benefactors looked for spiritual rewards for their generosity, for themselves and for their ancestors and successors, particularly in the world to come.

Chapter Four

People Within the Cloister

When looking at the nunneries in their early days the historian has to try to build up a picture from a very limited amount of knowledge, but from the 13th century the surviving state records, episcopal registers and a few other scattered sources provide an increasing amount of information about all monastic houses. As a result it becomes impossible to continue with a more or less chronological account of the nunneries' history, which must instead be considered from different angles.

The individual nun
In spite of our greater knowledge about the nunneries after the start of regular record keeping, there is a real limit to the amount that is known about any individual nun. Historical knowledge is always partial and the further back one tries to go the harder it becomes to find those personal details that bring a character to life. Among English medieval nuns only Christina of Markyate has left a personal chronicle, and she had no connection with Hampshire.[1] But the names of many more of the nuns become known as the centuries progress.

The state records provide several names, particularly during the 13th and 14th centuries when it was the custom for two nuns to be sent in person to inform the king whenever the abbess of one of the Benedictine houses died. These ladies were then given the royal *congé*, the licence permitting the convent to elect a successor, and this was recorded on the patent rolls with the names of the two messengers. This custom may well have been older than the start of the rolls but it is only known from 1230. In that year Eustachia de Fauconburg and Hillaria de Percy reported the death of the abbess of Romsey,[2] and seven years later Hillaria was again chosen to inform the king when the next abbess, Matilda de Barbflé, died.[3] Abbess Isabella of St. Mary's, Winchester died in 1236 and the news was taken to court by Joan de Sancto Albano and Natalia,[4] but it was more than 20 years before two Wherwell nuns, Denise le Vele and Letitia de London, had to travel to Windsor following the death of their aged abbess, Euphemia.[5]

This personal reporting by two chosen nuns gradually died out by the middle of the following century. Matilda Haudelon and Hawisia de Mattisdon reported the decease of Abbess Elena de Percy of Wherwell at the end of 1297 but her successor, who ruled for over 30 years, was replaced before her death.[6] It was not until 1340 that an abbess next died in office there and by then the custom may have been forgotten, or else it may no longer have been thought necessary or appropriate for nuns to ride about the country. In 1333, when Abbess Sybil Carbonel of Romsey had died, a man was chosen to take the news up to Tweedmouth where the young Edward III was fighting the Scots.[7] The nuns of St. Mary's, Winchester continued to observe the traditional reporting for longer than the other two houses. Christina la Gayte and a companion took the news of their abbess's death to the king in 1337 and again in the plague year of 1349, but after that the custom lapsed there too.[8]

The state records provide the names of a few ladies who were nominated to a place in one of the Benedictine houses by the king. This undefined right of nomination was only claimed by the sovereign occasionally. Between 1263 and 1385 there were five royal nominations to both Wherwell Abbey and St. Mary's Abbey Winchester, and three to

Romsey Abbey. There is a homely ring to the background of the first nun who was nominated. She was Alice de la Chaumbre who was a kinswoman of the former nurse of the future Edward I, and when she was veiled at Wherwell Abbey in 1263 Henry III ordered a tun of wine to be sent to the nunnery.[9] The only group of nominations occurred at the start of the reign of the boy king Richard II. After his coronation in 1377 he, or rather his advisers, claimed that it was his right to nominate a lady to each of the three nunneries. Accordingly Margaret Camoys was admitted to Romsey Abbey and Agnes Denham to St. Mary's Abbey at the request of the Countess of Norfolk.[10] At Wherwell Abbey there was some confusion for Alice de Parys and Mary Bacoun were both nominated, but it was Mary who became a member of the community because five years later the king made the abbey an annual gift of venison during her lifetime.[11]

The registers of the bishops of Winchester are the best source for the names of individual nuns. By the end of the 13th century the elections of new abbesses were being recorded, and from the mid-15th century it became the custom to list the names of all the nuns voting at an election. Some of these names may already have appeared in the register if the nun had been nominated by the bishop. This right was exercised by most bishops before the 15th century and, unlike the sovereign, they nominated to Wintney Priory as well as the abbeys; each record normally included the names of the young lady and her father, and sometimes the reason for the favour being granted. Occasionally a nun was named in the episcopal injunctions that were sent to a house after a bishop or his deputy had held a visitation there, but invariably that was in connection with bad rather than good behaviour. Lists of novices appear in episcopal letters if the task of professing them was being delegated. Thus, when writing to the bishop of Salisbury in 1362, Bishop Edington named four ladies who were to be professed at Romsey Abbey[12] and in 1400 his successor, Bishop Wykeham, commissioned the bishop of Annadown to receive 13 novices into St. Mary's Abbey, Winchester and on the following Sunday to receive another 13 at Romsey.[13]

Sometimes an individual nun can be encountered in other contemporary registers. Archbishop Chichele claimed that he had the right of nomination after his enthronement and sent Joan Otterbourne to Wherwell Abbey and two other young ladies to Wilton and Shaftesbury.[14] An earlier archbishop, Simon de Meopham, had similarly written to the bishop of Winchester and nominated Dionisia de la Rye to Romsey Abbey, but she was not accepted there so the bishop himself nominated her to St. Mary's Abbey a few weeks later.[15] (A small sketch of a nun was made in the margin of his register against the entry.) A few individual nuns were also mentioned in the papal records when they were granted the right to choose a confessor to give them plenary remission at the hour of their death. Abbess Matilda Spyne of Winchester was granted such an indulgence at the request of Queen Isabella (the widow of Edward II) and two years later another long list of indults included Joan Poleyn, a nun at Wintney Priory. After the Black Death similar grants were made to three Romsey nuns.[16]

Generally the early records of the nunneries themselves are less helpful in producing the names of the sisters than might be expected. Few of the early obits give family names. However, by the end of the 13th century well-to-do families had generally adopted surnames so it becomes possible to know a little more about the background of some of the novices entering the nunneries. It hardly comes as a surprise to find that all the Benedictine nuns were well-connected, although no royal widows or princesses joined any of the Hampshire houses in later medieval times. (Just across the Wiltshire border Queen Eleanor, widow of Henry III, became a nun at Amesbury and through her influence so did her granddaughter Mary, daughter of Edward I.[17]) Agnes Longspée, who later became abbess of Shaftesbury, was at Wherwell Abbey[18] and another famous name there was Abbess Elena de Percy. Both she and the prioress of Amesbury were correspondents of Queen Eleanor of Castile.[19]

Sometimes a nun belonged to the family of a bishop. Jonate de Stretford was surely related to Bishop Stratford who nominated her to Romsey Abbey shortly before he was translated to Canterbury, and a Johanna Stretford was a nun at Wherwell according to her psalter. Later, Bishop Orleton described Johanna de Bourghull as his cousin when he asked the abbess of Wherwell to receive her.[20] It also seems likely that Abbess Matilda de Pecham of Winchester was related to the archbishop. However, as one goes through the names of known nuns it is clear that the majority of ladies came from locally prominent families. In earlier years some of them may have had wider connections, such as Joan the daughter of Adam Despenser who was at Wherwell,[21] but more usually they are good Hampshire names like Wintershull, Inkepenne, Tichborne and Coudray. They were country gentry with land, and either more or less influence as the centuries progressed. For them the local nunnery was a natural refuge in which their unmarried daughters and sometimes their widows could be placed with a suitable dowry, since no other occupation was really open to them in the way that trade, domestic or field work were to unmarried women lower down the social scale. The dowry alone made it impossible for any but ladies to become nuns in the Benedictine houses. However, as a prosperous middle class began to emerge their womenkind also became acceptable, particularly at the urban nunneries in Winchester and Romsey. Elizabeth, the widow of John Forster of Romsey, who was professed in 1400, was surely one of them.[22]

In some circumstances girls were sent to a nunnery as mere children. The church did not disapprove of the practice provided there was an understanding that they would probably make a career there. No doubt most of them did so in accordance with the wishes of their families, and knowing little of any other way of life. The few who felt unsuited to it could always leave before their profession, provided they had sufficient moral courage and somewhere else to go. Sometimes the motives of those who sent them at an early age were open to question, for nunneries could be used as dumping grounds for orphan heiresses whose inheritances were coveted, for girls with some physical or even mental defect and for the offspring of illicit unions.[23]

The usual age for the profession of young novices was 16 years old. Archbishop Pecham wrote to the abbess of Wherwell in 1284 that no virgins were to be admitted to the habit and veil of a nun before the completion of the year when they were fifteen.[24] A few years later Bishop Woodlock directed that when the community at Wintney Priory were assembled to consider important business, all ladies who were 16 years of age or more and had lived in the house for two years were to take part in the discussions.[25] The episcopal registers only start to mention the ages of individual novices during the last years of the nunneries. Maria Martyn was 16 when she was professed at St. Mary's, Winchester in 1524, and on the same day five girls aged 15 took their first vows. They were all fully professed by 1527 when they were among the nuns voting for a new abbess; and that list included two other girls aged 12 and 17 who were present but did not vote. In the following decade when nine novices took their vows at Romsey seven of them were aged between 14 and twenty.[26]

For the sake of the community, anyone entering one of the nunneries was naturally expected to be well behaved and of good reputation, and the bishops do seem to have made enquiries on that score before nominating a particular girl. Bishop Wykeham, for instance, who nominated three novices during his episcopate (two to St.Mary's, Winchester and one to Wherwell Abbey) always mentioned that he was informed to their *bone* or *bone et honeste* condition when he wrote commending them to the abbess of the house.[27]

Among the surviving books from St. Mary's Abbey there is a slim folio with the order of service for the consecration of nuns, which was given to the abbey by Bishop Fox early in the 16th century. It was written especially for the nuns there (the dedication is in the same hand as the rest) and is full of instructions in English about the service as well as the Latin

13. Two leaves from the *Ordo consecrationis sanctimonialium* given to St Mary's Abbey by Bishop Fox (Bishop of Winchester 1501-28). The explanations concerning the order of service are in English. Cambridge UL ms. MM.3.13, ff.3r., 6v.

liturgy. The following extract (with the English modernised) is an example of its mixture of helpful comment interspersed with the responses.

> And when the collect is said, and the bishop set before the middle of the high altar, then such a person as the bishop shall appoint, standing at the east door of the quire, and looking toward the place where the virgins that then shall profess do array themselves, shall sing unto them:
>
> *Prudentes virgines aptate vestras lampades, ecce sponsus venit, exite obviam ei.*
>
> And [after] that song, forthwith the said virgins conducted by an honourable priest in a cope, every one of them clothed all in white, and bearing upon her right arm the habit that the religion and profession requireth, with the veil, ring and scroll of her profession attached upon the said habit, and in her left hand bearing a taper without light, must come from the place where they were arrayed, towards the west door of the quire: softly in manner of procession, so that the elders go before the youngers, inclining their faces towards the ground, singing all together this response:
>
> *Audivi vocem de coelo dicentem: Venite omnes virgines sapientissimae. Oleum recondite in vasis vestris dum sponsus advenerit.*[28]

Far more formal is an English pontifical written a century earlier which included the order

14. A bishop consecrating a nun whose black habit lies on
the ground; taken from a 15th-century *Pontificale ad usum
Ecclesiae Romanae et Anglicanae*. BL ms. Lansdowne 451, f.63v.

for the installation of abbots and abbesses, followed by the order for the consecration of nuns. In the historiated initial at the start of the latter section a bishop can be seen with a novice in white, her black habit lying beside her.[29]

The size of the communities

Numerically all four nunneries present a similar picture: there were too many nuns before the plague years in the middle of the 14th century and afterwards there were too few. The unique list of 54 nuns at Romsey just before the Conquest has already been mentioned. One can only speculate about the numbers there and in the other convents during the next 200 years but it is fairly certain that a shortage of sisters was not a problem, though a shortage of income to support them was another matter. The financial state of the nunneries was to exercise the minds of most bishops of Winchester in the first half of the 14th century, but before that period of cautionary injunctions a more positive note sounds from Wherwell. There it was counted amongst the achievements of the beloved abbess Euphemia (c.1219-57) that in her day the number of 'the Lord's handmaids' had increased from forty to eighty.[30]

It is not surprising that the subject of too many nuns and too little income should first have been raised at Wintney. Like most nunneries founded after the Conquest, the priory was underendowed and was always much poorer than the three Benedictine houses. Bishop Pontissara stayed there early in his episcopate[31] and at a visitation held before 1286 he forbade the prioress to admit any more nuns into the community because of its poverty.[32] Later the bishop was similarly worried about the situation at Wherwell where those extra nuns were possibly costing more than had been expected. He sent the abbess an inhibition forbidding her to accept any further nun or sister until an enquiry had been held into their resources.[33]

Bishop Pontissara was succeeded by Bishop Woodlock, the former prior of St. Swithun's, who held a visitation at St. Mary's Abbey, Winchester in 1309. Afterwards his injunctions included a clause criticising the careless admission of too many nuns and forbidding the convent to accept any more until their numbers had been reduced.[34] Two years later a similar instruction was dispatched to Romsey Abbey: because their church was so overburdened no more nuns were to be received until their community had been reduced to its original number.[35] It is unfortunate that the bishop did not give an actual figure for the original number, but at the start of the 16th century the abbess stated that it was forty.[36]

Wherwell Abbey seems to have escaped official criticism from Bishop Woodlock when he visited it in March 1311, immediately before travelling down to Mottisfont and Romsey.[37]

No injunctions were entered in his register, and there were none for Wintney Priory in 1308 after it was visited on his behalf by the archdeacon of Winchester.[38] Maybe the advice given was only verbal. However, when the bishop sent his officials to Wintney again in 1315 to hold a formal visitation in the chapter house, their report led to a list of nine injunctions being sent to the prioress. One of them pointed out that because of bad advice in the past, the house had accepted and veiled too many nuns and as a result the income was insufficient to support the number of people living there. The nuns were told not to add to their numbers until the community had been reduced to 26 dames in addition to the prioress, since that number could reasonably be maintained out of the income of the house.[39]

The whole question of the size of the four communities was raised again by Bishop Stratford during his difficult decade as the diocesan before becoming archbishop of Canterbury. During the interval between his belated enthronement (which had been opposed by Edward II) and before he had to go into hiding in the aftermath of the king's murder in 1327, he wrote to each nunnery on the subject. Unfortunately he had already contributed to the problem himself by exercising his right of nomination. Two days after his enthronement in November 1324 he had written to the abbess of Wherwell nominating Maud Spircock,[40] whose family were prominent in the wool trade in and around Andover nearby. In May 1325 the bishop nominated Katherine, the daughter of Robert de Colyngbourne, to St.Mary's Abbey, Winchester,[41] but the religious life there had become slack. The following year he wrote again to the abbess criticising the number of ladies who had been living there too long without being professed, and ordering that they should be ready to take their vows by the feast of the Ascension.[42] Later that summer he held a formal visitation at the abbey and evidently realised that the house was 'overburdened both with nuns and with debts' and ordered that no more novices were to be received beyond the established number (unspecified) without his permission.[43]

Having appreciated the problem, Bishop Stratford sent orders about the need for balancing means and numbers to all the other nunneries in the course of 1327. Abbess Isobel of Wherwell was the first to hear from him. In a letter sent from Southwark in February he wrote that he knew she was being urged to accept more damsels beyond the established number, but he forbade her to do so until he had visited Wherwell.[44] The next letter in his register is rather more sharp. It was written to the Prior of Winchester on the same subject:

> We have already, for lawful reason, twice forbidden the abbess and convent of Wherwell to accept any damsel to be a nun; nevertheless these ladies, not long since as we understand, have accepted certain damsels. Wherefore we have once more forbidden them to accept any more, or to let those accepted receive the veil, until we have made a full enquiry in visitation as to whether their means would suffice nowadays to support more than the established number. We are absolutely determined not to be moved from this resolve, so kindly hold us excused.[45]

It sounds as though the prior had been asked to use his influence to get some would-be novice accepted at Wherwell.

In October the bishop wrote to the abbess and convent of Romsey with the familiar criticism that they had more nuns than their established number and ordering them not to accept any more before his next visit.[46] Six weeks later it was Wintney Priory's turn to receive a similar letter.[47] There is an actual figure for the number of nuns at Romsey in 1333; there were then 91 named nuns taking part in the election for Abbess Joan Icthe,[48] including Katherine Warham whom the bishop had himself nominated only eight months after his letter of reprimand. Soon afterwards they were joined by his last nominee, Jonate de Stretford.[49]

Bishop Edington was the last bishop to be worried about the nunneries being too full. Soon after his consecration he sent identical letters to the three abbeys forbidding them once again to receive more ladies than was allowed in their ancient constitutions,[50] though only after he had himself exercised his right to nominate to each of them after becoming bishop.[51] Wintney Priory was spared a letter, but the nuns there still had to receive one of his nominees in spite of their poverty.[52] In 1346 the abbess and convent of St. Mary's, Winchester complained to the pope about their excessive numbers,[53] perhaps on the advice of one of their prebendary priests or of the poor clerk responsible for their accounts. Fortunately they did not know how fearfully the problem was about to be solved – not by pontiff but by nature.

The plague known as the Black Death ravaged England for about a year from the winter of 1348-9. It had a devastating effect on the whole country and few monastic houses, in Hampshire or elsewhere, ever really recovered from it. By the time William of Wykeham became bishop in 1366 there was no question of any of the communities in his diocese being overfull. Instead, he was writing to the abbesses in 1387 directing them to increase the number of nuns in their houses which were then very much diminished below their statutory number.[54] They were never able to do so. During the 15th century the lists of nuns at the times of elections show that the three abbeys normally had between 20 and 30 professed nuns, while at Wintney the numbers declined from 14 in 1415 to only six in 1497. When an archiepiscopal visitation was held at two of the nunneries in 1492 there were 21 nuns at Romsey Abbey but only 15 at St. Mary's, Winchester.[55]

Nuns in authority

In any society the character of the person at the head of it is important to the members and this is particularly true of an enclosed community. The influence of a good abbess who used her authority wisely was reflected in a well-run convent, serving God and held in high regard. Conversely a weak or an immoral head could rapidly lower the whole tone of a nunnery – and it is unlikely that such news took long to travel abroad.

All the abbesses of the three Benedictine houses are known from the middle of the 13th century until the Dissolution. (They are listed in Appendix 1.) Each had become head of her community after a process of election which was well defined by the 14th century. Presumably it was always followed, but some elections were recorded in the episcopal registers in far more detail than others. The process started in the wake of the death or resignation of the previous head by the grant of a *congé d'élire*. The abbeys received theirs from the king; he was also entitled to their income during the interregnum, although he sometimes waived the right. Permission for elections at Wintney Priory came from the 'founder and patron'.[56] He was not usually named but when the sub-prioress wrote to the bishop after the resignation of the aged prioress in 1497 she mentioned Richard Holt as a founder and then named other members of his family as patrons who had granted the licence for an election.[57]

The bishop himself was occasionally present at an election but more usually it was directed by a lesser dignitary such as the archdeacon of Winchester. Diocesan officials always seem to have played an active part in elections. At the end of the 13th century when Bishop Pontissara wrote a letter of condolence to the nuns of St. Mary's, Winchester after the death of their abbess he said that he had commissioned his vicars to arrange an election and advise them as to their choice.[58] In 1297 he wrote similarly to Wherwell when Abbess Elena de Percy died[59] and a few years later Bishop Woodlock sent the archdeacon and a monk from Hyde Abbey to aid and advise the nuns at Wintney about the choice of a new prioress when Alice de Dummer resigned. He tactfully mentioned that he was sending them in case of the nuns' possible ignorance of the law and without meaning to prejudice the rights of the convent in any way.[60] He was rather more involved in the election process held at St. Mary's, Winchester in 1313; after technical objections were raised to the original election of Matilda de Pecham the bishop had to declare it void, but then himself appointed the same lady as abbess four days later and wrote immediately to the king requesting that the nunnery's possessions should be restored to her.[61]

In practice most of the elections were probably rather tame affairs. No doubt plenty of gossip went on privately amongst the nuns about possible candidates, but usually the lady with the best family connections was the one most likely to be chosen. The bishops' registers provide few examples of genuinely contested elections taking place. The earliest one recorded was at Romsey in 1333 when the former cellaress, Joan Icthe, was chosen by most of the 91 nuns and the prebendary priests, who were also entitled to vote.[62]

In the following century the nuns' individual votes were recorded at two contested elections, one at Wherwell and the other at St. Mary's, Winchester. At Wherwell three abbesses died in quick succession in 1451-2. The first two elections that resulted were only briefly recorded but there is a full account of the third which was decided by ballot. The prioress, Johanna Mersshe, was one of the two candidates but she only received six votes from the nuns, while the new abbess, Juliana Overey, was chosen by 18 of them.[63] At Winchester there were four candidates in 1488 and once again the prioress was unsuccessful; she only received one vote and that was from the new abbess, Johanna Legh, (tactful lady) who herself was voted for by 11 nuns, while Agnes St. Jone and Agnes Austell had six votes between them.[64] At both these elections three nuns were appointed as tellers and did not vote.

An unprecedented election took place at Romsey in 1478 during the unhappy time of Abbess Elizabeth Brooke. She had been abbess for six years when the scandalous fact emerged that she had been guilty of adultery and perjury (perhaps she had denied the charge at first). Bishop Waynflete accepted her resignation himself at Romsey, but when a ballot was held there two months later as part of the election process only one other nun besides herself voted for a different abbess.[65] Evidently she was a lady who inspired loyalty. Even the pope agreed that she could continue as abbess[66] but it was still unfortunate that she did so since her authority had been irrevocably undermined, and the archbishop's visitation in 1492 showed that the nunnery suffered as the result of her conduct during her second term of office.[67]

The two more usual types of election for an abbess were either by acclamation if there was only one candidate, or by the choice of someone such as the bishop who had been delegated by the chapter to act on their behalf. This type of election by compromission was held at Wintney in 1329 when Bishop Stratford chose and was present at the election of Prioress Alice de Westcote[68] and there are many other instances of such elections held for the abbeys. There never seems to have been a ballot at Wintney Priory and by the 16th century they were no longer held at the other houses. When Bishop Fox was diocesan there were four elections at the Benedictine nunneries; three were decided by acclamation and at the fourth he appointed St. Mary's last abbess, Elizabeth Shelley, in his capacity as compromissary.[69] Time confirmed the wisdom of his choice, but at Wherwell the ever-absent Cardinal Wolsey was responsible for the unfortunate choice of Abbess Anne Colte who was to bring discredit on the nunnery during its last decade.

All elections held by ballot, and most that were not, were conducted in the chapter house of the nunnery. Some others took place in the bishop's chapel in Southwark with a procurator (proxy) appearing on behalf of the convent.[70] Two Wherwell elections were held in the parish church at Farnham when the bishop was resident in his castle there[71] and there is one instance of a new abbess from Romsey, Lucy Everard, being proclaimed in the Lady Chapel of Winchester Cathedral.[72]

In earlier days, particularly if the bishop was personally present, many of the formalities attendant upon an election took place at the same time. Thus after Bishop Orleton had travelled to Wintney from Farnham in November 1336, he presided in the chapter house to accept the formal resignation of Prioress Alice and then the entire community *per inspirationem sancti spiritus* elected Covina de Mareys. Afterwards they all started to sing the Te Deum as they conducted the new prioress to the High Altar of their church, where the bishop blessed her and then led her to the prioress's accustomed stall in the choir. After he had installed her there he directed all the nuns to make their obedience to her as their new head, in accordance with the rules of their order. Three of the bishop's officials were present that day as well as a lawyer, Roger Franceys, who probably wrote the record of the occasion.[73]

In time the election process became more complex and took longer as an increasing number of officials became involved. From the time of Abbess Matilda Holme's election at St. Mary's, Winchester in 1410[74] the records usually occupy many folios in the bishops' registers. Citations, licences, certificates, schedules, articles, acceptances, confirmations and mandates to install are among the items regularly recorded before the bishop's benediction and, for the abbeys, the sovereign's restitution of their spiritualities and temporalities. By 1527, 18 sides of Bishop Fox's register were needed to write up the election of Abbess Elizabeth Shelley, whereas the Wintney election of 1336 occupies less than one side in Bishop Orleton's register. By the end of the 15th century many of these records include the oaths that were taken in English by the elected lady. The first recorded use of an English oath was on the occasion of Abbess Elizabeth Brooke's second installation in 1478.[75] (Perhaps the bishop was determined that she should understand what she was re-undertaking.) The oaths taken were usually to obey the bishop and to administer the property of the house wisely but in 1494, when Henry VII had been on the throne for less than a decade, Abbess Matilda Rowse of Wherwell took an English oath of loyalty to the king.[76] The service of installation was the same as for an abbot, and was included in contemporary pontificals.[77]

Once an abbess or a prioress of Wintney was in office she was normally there for life, though resignation or deprivation was always possible. The most usual reason for resignation was illness or old age, and in those cases the retired abbess seems to have remained at the nunnery with her own attendants but to have kept a little apart from the rest of the community. Normally the retiring head was not present at the election for her successor. Thus Juliana Overey did not attend the election that followed her resignation as abbess of Wherwell in 1494 after more than 40 years in office, though her interests were represented by Thomas Overey who was present and an annual pension was arranged for her;[78] but when the prioress of Wintney was forced to resign in disgrace in 1415 she appointed the sacristan as her proxy for the ensuing election claiming, diplomatically perhaps, that she was too ill to leave her room.[79]

After an abbess was elected she moved into her own apartments. At Winchester the abbess's lodging was a separate building lying between the convent church and the frater, with its own kitchen and other domestic offices.[80] The lodging of the abbess at Wherwell stood with other buildings in the quadrangle there, and the abbess of Romsey also had her own house with an adjacent chapel.[81] It seem unlikely that the prioress of Wintney ever had a house separated from the rest of the nunnery, though no doubt there were one or more particular rooms that she traditionally occupied. The heads of Cistercian houses were not expected to eat or sleep apart from the rest of the community, and no prioress's lodging is mentioned in any of Wintney's Dissolution papers.

The main reason for there being separate houses at the abbeys was to enable an abbess to entertain guests without interrupting the internal life of the nunnery too much. Offering hospitality to important travellers was the duty of a superior as well as a probable pleasure, but this domestic separation could easily have unfortunate consequences. It could sometimes result in an abbess becoming too independent and remote so that her rule became autocratic rather than motherly. She was always a person of importance in the life of her town or village, and in Romsey and Wherwell she probably had more power and influence than anyone else, especially during the earlier centuries. As well as fulfilling her duties within the abbey, she was expected to be a good neighbour, to provide for her tenants in time of trouble and to dispense justice when necessary. It was not a position that encouraged the development of humility, particularly in a lady who was proud of her family connections.

Families could indeed be a cause of trouble if they expected favours, and partly for this reason abbesses were often admonished by the bishop not to make sales or grant corrodies, pensions or other benefits without the consent of the chapter. Favouritism was another danger mentioned by several bishops, but it must have been hard to avoid. An abbess, like anyone else, needed companionship and when Archbishop Pecham visited Romsey at the end of the 13th century he suggested that she should have at least one other nun in attendance upon her, partly for company and partly as a witness to the purity of her life, and that these companions should be changed each year.[82] It was a sensible arrangement, but dependent for its success upon the characters of all concerned. At its best, a year spent in closer contact with an admirable superior would be beneficial to any nun, but if that superior lacked wisdom and discretion then an elite and self-perpetuating little clique could easily emerge in the abbess's lodging, leading to jealousy among the other ladies. One of the complaints at Romsey against Abbess Elizabeth Brooke was that she kept three nuns in her own house[83] and a few years later an injunction forbade the nuns there to visit the abbess's chamber after dinner and supper, and especially after compline.[84] As the reprimand followed warnings to Abbess Joyce Rowse about over-eating and drinking, especially at night, there is perhaps a suggestion of midnight feasts rather than companionable conversation.

In earlier days at least it was usual for one of the companion nuns to be chosen as the abbess's chaplain for a year. Bishop Wykeham wrote to the abbesses of Romsey and Wherwell that he looked upon that year as one when

> ... the nuns themselves who shall have been with you in the aforesaid office shall (by means of laudable instruction) be the better enabled to excel in religion, while you will be able immediately to invoke their testimony to your innocence if (which God forbid) any crime or scandal should be imputed to you by the malice of any person.[85]

One such lady chaplain was mentioned by Chaucer in the prologue to *The Canterbury Tales*, at the end of his description of the Prioress:

> Another Nun, the chaplain at her cell,
> Was riding with her, and three Priests as well.

At the three abbeys the deputy was the prioress, while at Wintney she was the sub-prioress. The duties attached to that office were probably rather vague and undefined when the head of the house was present and in good health, but during her absence the deputy filled a most necessary role. This was particularly so during the period following the death of an abbess, when the prioress took charge automatically and was responsible for informing the king and the bishop to ask for an election. These interregnums provided an opportunity for other members of the house to see how a prioress performed in a position of authority, but judging from the rather small number who became abbesses they do not often seem to have been impressed.

In the 13th century two abbesses at both Romsey and St. Mary's, Winchester had formerly been prioresses, and in the following century so had abbesses Christina la Wayte of St. Mary's and Matilda de Littleton of Wherwell.[86] Matilda had nearly a year in full authority at Wherwell while she was still prioress, after she had been placed in charge there by the prior of Winchester Cathedral on the authority of the bishop. The old abbess had been ruling for 34 years and was evidently 'impotent' – possibly senile.[87] During the last hundred years three more prioresses and one sub-prioress became abbesses of Wherwell, but Abbess Joan Brygges at Romsey and Abbess Matilda Holme in Winchester seem to have been the only two at the other abbeys. At Wintney there are no recorded instances of a sub-prioress becoming prioress, but that is not to say that it never happened. As there were no royal confirmations of elections there, which would have given the previous office held by the newly elect, it is impossible to know who the early sub-prioresses were.[88]

By the 16th century a 'terprioress' was being appointed at Wherwell and St. Mary's, Winchester[89] but earlier the most important obedientiary seems to have been the sacrist who was in charge of the church and responsible for providing everything needed in it. At Wherwell the office of sacrist had its own separate sources of income.[90] In 1497, when there were only five nuns present at Wintney for the election of a new prioress, only two nuns filled offices: the sub-prioress and the sacrist.[91] But at the abbeys nuns were appointed to many other offices. At Wherwell in 1518 the refectrix (in charge of the refectory) is listed before the precentrix who arranged the services, probably because she had been professed longer.[92] Similarly at Romsey in 1502 the nuns, other than the prioress and sub-prioress, seem to be named in order of length of service rather than seniority of office. No doubt it made for less trouble all round. The list at that election gives more office holders than any other; besides the sacrist there was an almoness, a cellaress, a kitchener, an infirmaress, two refectorians and the mistress of the school, as well as four chantresses and sub-sacrists; in fact only five of the fully professed nuns did not fill some office.[93]

Lay sisters and servants

Although the dowry system precluded women from a poor background from becoming professed nuns, in the early days they were able to become members of the community as lay sisters. They took simple vows and in church they recited short prayers by heart instead of the Divine Office. They were recruited from amongst the poor and were only too happy to have their keep and a roof over their heads in return for helping with the domestic chores in the kitchen, at the wash tub and elsewhere. At Wherwell Abbey Felicia and Alicia, whose obits were observed in January, were two early lay sisters.[94]

At Wintney Priory there were two types of women who were not fully professed: the ordinary lay sisters and *conversae*. The word *conversa* cannot really be translated, but it can be understood in relation to the *conversi* in the male Cistercian houses who had been an essential part of each community from the start. They were generally illiterate and were responsible for most of the manual and outside work so that other help did not have to be employed. (The ruins of some of the great Cistercian abbeys are still a monument to their labours.) In the Wintney calendar eight sisters were described as *conversa* in their obits and twelve, who would have taken lesser vows, as just *soror nostra*. All these obits were original entries and therefore date from the earlier years of the priory, but one lay sister was recorded later: Johanna Rose, *bone memorie soror nostra*.[95]

The calendars of Wherwell and Wintney show that lay brothers were members of both communities in the early days; four were recorded at Wherwell and eight at Wintney, including a member of the de Port family.[96] Presumably their main task was to run the demesne farms. One of Bishop Woodlock's injunctions to Wintney Priory ordered the prioress to assemble all the community if possible whenever any lay brothers or sisters were taking their perpetual vows, as it was one of the great occasions in the life of the house.[97] That was in 1316. After society had been changed by the Black Death the system of lay helpers living under vows gradually lapsed. There are no later references to them at Wintney, but at Wherwell the term *conversae* was used once in a certificate sent to Cardinal Beaufort.[98]

The officials that were increasingly employed by the nunneries – chief stewards, receivers and collectors – were hardly servants in the normal sense of the word. Beneath them were those who really did serve on a full time basis. Higher servants such as stewards were meant to be chosen by the whole community according to Archbishop Pecham, but evidently the steward at Wherwell Abbey did not meet with his approval for he was dismissed two days after the archbishop's visit.[99] No doubt there were many stewards and bailiffs who served the nunneries well but few are known. Their names sometimes appear on account rolls but otherwise it is the stewards who were criticised, such as Terbocke and Bryce at Romsey, that are known by name.[100]

There is little in the episcopal registers that is charitable about the domestic servants in the nunneries. Usually they are only mentioned whenever the bishop wanted one or more of them removed because there were too many employed, or because they were insolent, quarrelsome, badly behaved or pregnant. Bishop Woodlock wanted any servant removed from Wintney Priory who was a source of strife, or replied to the nuns impertinently, or was living an immoral life.[101] Later in the century Bishop Wykeham devoted a section of the injunctions that he sent to the abbeys to the ill-doings of women servants and chiefly to their chattering and gossip; he reasoned that such behaviour would bring discredit on the community itself.[102] It would not have occurred to him, of course, to mention that the women were fulfilling a most necessary role.

Chapter Five

The Nunneries and the Church

The wider church

In the chapel of St. Laurence in Romsey Abbey the reredos now used is part of an early 16th-century panel painting which was painted during the last years of the nunnery.[1] In the bottom left-hand corner the abbess of the day (either Anne Westbroke or Elizabeth Ryprose) is shown holding her crosier. Such crosiers represented the authority of an abbess over her flock – an authority given and held within the body of the church in which the abbess was herself responsible to the bishop, the archbishop and ultimately to the pope.

The popes themselves may have been remote figures but their influence was certainly felt in the nunneries during the centuries following the Conquest. Before that time the supremacy of the pope had been acknowledged as a matter of theory, but in practice the papal yoke had sat very lightly on Anglo-Saxon shoulders. The Benedictine nunneries had been founded without any reference to Rome but the Conquest had coincided with the start of a rapid growth in papal power. By the 12th century both the old and the new monastic houses in England were looking to the pope as their supreme authority and support in matters temporal as well as spiritual. They soon discovered the benefits to be derived from having their possessions and customs recited and confirmed by him, though this protection did not come free of charge.[2]

Pope Gregory IX sent his confirmation of all Romsey Abbey's possessions to the abbess in 1236.[3] The possessions were not listed in that document, but in the Wherwell Cartulary a group of seven detailed privileges and confirmations that were granted to the abbey there in the 13th century are recorded, three of them concerning the tithes of Wallop.[4] Tithes were the subject of several disputes. The pope was not usually involved in them, but there is a letter from Pope Innocent III appointing three local judges to hear one such case in 1200; they included the abbot of Waverley and the prior of Hyde Abbey.[5] The cartulary also records a papal bull issued by Pope Nicholas IV in 1291 which granted an indulgence to anyone visiting the abbey church at the principal feasts of the Virgin Mary and the Holy Cross; Archbishop Edmund Rich had granted a similar indulgence for 40 days in 1236.[6]

Such papal privileges, letters and mandates were undoubtedly recorded in the missing cartularies for the other nunneries, but in spite of their absence some details of the popes' involvement in their affairs can be traced from the papal registers. For instance, Clement VI was petitioned by the abbess and convent of St. Mary's Abbey to allow their appropriation of two churches in the 14th century, and Wintney Priory was granted a generous indulgence for penitents visiting their church and giving alms for its repair and conservation in 1397.[7] Papal mandates were also issued in connection with new developments at St. Mary's Abbey, Winchester and at Romsey. In 1317 Roger de Inkepenne, a citizen of Winchester, was granted a licence to found and endow a chapel in the nuns' cemetery in the city which was to be served by two priests, and a century later the papacy was again involved when the chapel had fallen into disrepair.[8] At Romsey the mandate issued by Calixtus III in 1457 was for the benefit of the parishioners rather more than the nuns: it allowed the appointment of an extra priest to say mass within the abbey, for more or larger bells to be installed there as the existing ones could not be heard throughout the parish; for the provision of a clock to tell the hours and for the people to go in procession through the fields and common places with their vicar and chaplain at Embertide, as happened elsewhere in the area.[9]

15. The abbess of Romsey depicted on the reredos now in the chapel of St Laurence, Romsey Abbey (*c.*1525). On her scroll are the words *Surrecsit dominus de sepulcro.*

The largest number of papal documents recorded for both England as a whole and for the Hampshire nunneries were the so-called 'papal provisions'. Using these mandates successive popes, or their legates in England, usurped the rights of ecclesiastical patrons such as the nunneries by appointing priests to vacant benefices and prebendal stalls within the abbeys. These will be discussed later. This enlargement of papal power had started in a modest way at the beginning of the 13th century but it later grew into a large and well-defined legal system, in spite of many English protests. Eventually Parliament enacted the Statute of Provisors (1351) which ordered that local elections and presentations were to be free from papal pressure. This and subsequent legislation loosened the popes' hold on church appointments and there is only one example of a papal provision being made to one of the nunneries' churches afterwards.[10]

At the start of the 13th century Pope Innocent III worked hard for the improvement of monastic life throughout Europe. The Fourth Lateran Council in 1215 initiated various reforms which were furthered by Pope Gregory IX and his successors during the next 50 years. At a local level all the surviving papal charters and confirmations to Wherwell and

Romsey abbeys date from this period. In the middle of the century councils were held in England to implement some of the reforms, including the Council of Oxford that was held under Archbishop Langton in 1222. This gave the bishops increased control over the monastic houses in their dioceses, and particularly over the nunneries. Their responsibility for appointing confessors for nuns, for regulating their numbers according to the revenue of the house, for authorising the admission of secular women and the sale of corrodies in nunneries all date from this council. Some time later the abbot of Athelney and the precentor of Glastonbury sent notice to the abbess of Wherwell of their intention to visit the abbey on the second Saturday in Lent:

> They exhort the sisters to correct and reform all things before their arrival, that they may, as they wish, find them worthy of commendation rather than of rebuke.[11]

(But as the letter was sent from Dummer only three days earlier there was little time to act on that pious exhortation.)

The system of episcopal visitation of monastic houses grew out of the reforms. For the most part the papacy did not take much notice of these visitations, but in 1232 Pope Gregory IX ordered the English bishops to visit all the non-exempt monasteries in their dioceses, either in person or by deputy. (Many of the newer orders of monks were exempt from visitations but not the nunneries such as Wintney Priory.[12]) Formal visitations by a bishop, as distinct from simple visits, followed a standard procedure. The initiative came from the bishop or archbishop himself, who sent the head of the house a notice of the day when he expected to be there. A month's notice seems to have been quite common but it could be less. Sometimes the date had to be changed, as in 1311 when Bishop Woodlock wrote to the abbess of Wherwell on 25 January announcing that he would be visiting the abbey on 25 February; however, something – maybe the weather – intervened and he wrote again on 2 March to say that he would be with them on the 11th.[13] There could be a change of plans if some more urgent business arose: in December 1308 the bishop postponed his visit to Wintney Priory and then wrote again two days later to say that he was too much occupied to hold the visitation in person and was therefore sending two commissioners instead.[14]

A bustle of spring cleaning, earnest discussions with the steward about animals that could be slaughtered and preparations for baking surely followed, especially at a little house like Wintney Priory that may not have had many visitors. And if anything was seriously amiss then consciences were likely to be pricking at the thought of his grace's probing questions, for visitations were essentially for finding out all aspects of life within the house.

After the arrival of the bishop and his retinue, the visitation would start with his being formally received in the nuns' church and then led to the high altar to celebrate mass. Later he would move to the chapter house and preach a sermon to the whole community. When Bishop Orleton held his first visitation of the Winchester archdeaconry in November 1334 he preached in French at St. Mary's Abbey on the 9th and at Romsey on the 28th, when he chose the parable of the wise and foolish virgins for his text[15] – an appropriate but hardly an original choice one imagines. In the course of the 15th century the choice of language would have changed; certainly Bishop Fox would have addressed the nuns in English at the start of the 16th. Outsiders were welcome to go and hear the sermon but they had to leave the chapter house before the bishop started his enquiries.

Each nun would be examined by the bishop in the presence of his clerks and her depositions taken down. These *detecta* were then read out publicly at the end of the visitation, along with any discoveries (*comperta*) made by the bishop and his assessors in the course of their enquiries.[16] None of the depositions made by the nuns have survived in the Winchester registers, but the register of Archbishop Morton contains the *detecta* from the visitation to the abbeys of St. Mary's, Winchester and Romsey in 1492.[17] The expense of these visitations was normally met by the nunnery. In the country generally, four marks was the usual procuration fee.[18]

At the end of the visitation the bishop or his representative would again address the community. He would make any criticism that he thought necessary and presumably give words of encouragement as well, for the visit was intended to be pastoral as well as judicial. These remarks were not recorded, but if it was apparent that all was not well then injunctions about future conduct were drawn up afterwards and sent to the abbess. Their purpose was to order any reforms that the bishop thought were needed, but as there is a certain repetitiveness about many of the clauses from one bishop to another there does seem to have been a consistent need for reminders. Usually about a dozen points were made. They dealt with the practice of religion, the life of the nuns within the community and the need to cut down contacts with the outside world (a forlorn hope this) as well as business affairs such as the need for an annual audit and the safe-keeping of the convent's seal. At the end there was usually a direction that the injunctions should be read out in chapter four times a year.

The first known episcopal visitations in the diocese of Winchester were made by Bishop Nicholas of Ely. In 1271 he held visitations in Winchester at the Cathedral, at Hyde Abbey and at St. Mary's Abbey; and the whole process was repeated three years later by Archbishop Kilwardby.[19] Bishop Nicholas had earlier visited the nuns of Wherwell Abbey; their cartulary records that he had been their visitor for 11 years before his death and that he had not accepted any maintenance money for his visitation.[20] It seems likely that the bishop may also have visited the nuns at Wintney. He was one of their benefactors,[21] as he was to their fellow Cistercians at Waverley Abbey which was to be his burial place, though his heart was interred in the Cathedral.

After the death of Bishop Nicholas in 1280 more than two years elapsed before disputes about his successor were finally ended by the pope's consecration of John de Pontissara in Rome. Early in 1284 Archbishop Pecham held a visitation of the diocese to deal with any remaining difficulties, and the abbeys of Wherwell and Romsey were among the monastic houses that he chose to visit. The injunctions that he sent them later give some of the earliest known details about life within them.[22] Five years earlier he had written to the abbess of Wherwell nominating a lady to the abbey, and in 1281 he had found it necessary to issue an ordinance against nuns leaving their convents and being exposed to the moral dangers of society[23] (but as it was recorded in the Worcester episcopal register it is not likely that the conduct of the nuns in Hampshire was the cause of his immediate concern).

Visitations to the nunneries by or on behalf of all but two of the 14th-century bishops of Winchester are recorded. One of the exceptions was Bishop de Asserio who was in office for less than four years. The other was Bishop Edington whose visitations were held by an official; however, it is known that he stayed in Hartley Wintney towards the end of his life and the nuns at the priory later recorded his obit and his visit in their calendar.[24] No visitation injunctions for any of the nunneries were entered in the register of Bishop Wykeham, though his reprimand to the abbess of St. Mary's about the lack of discipline is in it.[25] He visited all the religious houses in his diocese in 1373, 1380 and 1387 and when he sent injunctions to Romsey Abbey in 1387 he mentioned that they were being sent after his third visitation there, but nothing is known about the earlier ones. He sent similar injunctions to Wherwell that year; in fact the two sets were so alike that the scribe only kept a full copy of the Romsey one, adding a note at the end of the few points that were different for Wherwell. According to a note at the end, a copy of the injunctions was also sent to St. Mary's Abbey.[26] Half a century later Bishop Beaufort's visitation to Wherwell is only known because of an entry in the Wherwell Cartulary.[27]

During the fifty years before the Dissolution two visitations were held on the authority of

Canterbury. The visitation made by Robert Shirborne to St. Mary's Abbey, Winchester, and Romsey Abbey in 1492 has already been mentioned. Nine years later, when there were interregnums at both Canterbury and Winchester, the prior of Christ Church, Canterbury, grasped his brief opportunity of power and commissioned Dr. Thomas Hede to hold a visitation of all the non-exempt religious houses in the diocese of Winchester. At the nunneries all was well in Winchester and Wherwell, and even at Wintney the new prioress had managed to reduce the outstanding debts, but at Romsey there were still many difficulties and complaints during Abbess Brooke's final year in office.[28]

Many of the bishops of Winchester were benefactors of the nunneries in their diocese. In the Wintney Calendar Bishops Godfrey de Lucy, Peter des Roches, John of Exeter, Nicholas of Ely and John de Pontissara were all described as such.[29] Bishop Pontissara (d.1304) is the last to be recorded there, but his contemporary Philip de Barton, archdeacon of Surrey, is also included in it as a benefactor.[30] Several of the later bishops left legacies to the nuns in their wills. Bishop Edington (d.1366) was apparently the first; among many bequests to monastic houses and individuals he left the abbess of Romsey a ring set with a ruby and £20 to pray for his soul, while another £20 was to be distributed among the sisters. St. Mary's, Winchester and Wherwell Abbey were only left 20 marks each.[31] William of Wykeham left legacies to the abbesses of Romsey (5 marks) and St. Mary's (4 marks) and one mark each to the other nuns of those houses, except his cousin Felicia Aas, who was

16. Title page from *The Rule of Seynt Benet* (1517), translated into English by Bishop Fox for the benefit of the four nunneries in his diocese.
Bodleian Library. Arch. A. d.15.

soon to become abbess of Romsey, and she was to have £5. He also cancelled a debt of £40 which he had lent the Romsey nuns to help with the cost of repairs.[32] Bishop Waynflete remembered all the monasteries in the city of Winchester: his legacy to the abbess of St. Mary's was 13s. 4d., and 2s. to each professed nun but only 16d. to the non-professed.[33] Bishop Langton bequeathed St. Mary's a silver standing cup and cover.[34]

Bishop Fox did not leave any legacies to the nuns when he died but during his lifetime he made them a more enduring gift. Soon after resigning as Keeper of the Privy Seal in order to devote himself to his spiritual duties, he translated the Benedictine Rule for the nunneries in his diocese and sent each of the four houses a manuscript copy before having an edition printed in London in 1517. Two of these printed copies have survived. In the introduction the bishop himself describes why he made the translation into English:

We . . . revolving in our mind that certain devout and religious women, being within our Diocese and under our pastoral charge and cure, have not only professed them[selves] to the observance of the Rule of the holy confessor Saint Benet but also be bound to read, learn and understand the same when they be Novices and before they be professed. And also after their profession they should not only in themself keep, observe, execute and practice the said rule, but also teach other their sisters the same; in so much that for the same intent they daily read and cause to be read some part of the said Rule by one of the said sisters amongs[t] themselves, as well in their Chapter house after the reading of the Martyrology as some time in their Frater in time of reflections and collations: all the which reading is always done in the latin tongue whereof they have no knowledge nor understanding, but be utterly ignorant of the same . . . We, the said Bishop, knowing . . . that we may not without like peril of our soul suffer the said religious women, of whose souls we have the cure, to continue in their said blindness and ignorance of the said Rule, to the knowledge and observance whereof they be professed, and especially . . . that the young Novices may first know and understand the said Rule before they profess them[selves] to it. So that none of them shall . . . afterward probably say that she wyste not what she professed, as we know by experience that some of them have said in time past. For these causes, and especially at the instant request of our right dear and well beloved daughters in our lord Jesus, the abbesses of the monasteries of Romsey, Wherwell, St. Mary's within the city of Winchester, and the prioress of Wintney . . . we have translated the said rule into our mother's tongue, common, plain, round english, easy and ready to be understand by the said devout religious women.[35]

The local church and clergy

At the local level a number of priests were attached to each of the nunneries, though the nature of the attachment varied greatly. In the three Benedictine abbeys the prebendal priests enjoyed the highest status and income, but from the 14th century it was the vicars of the local parish and the unbeneficed priests who served in their own churches whom the nuns would have known.

The original position of prebendaries is well summarised in charter 54 of the Wherwell Cartulary. At first they had been expected to reside in their own houses near the nunnery for at least part of the year. They each had a small area of land (the prebendary of Wherwell had four acres) and were entitled to receive food from the convent kitchen. The main endowment was a parish church of which the prebendary was rector; as such he received the great tithes and was responsible for chancel repairs. He was not normally responsible for the people of the parish since the cure of souls lay with the perpetual vicar whom the rector presented to the living. In most cases that church was some distance from the nunnery but at Romsey and Wherwell the prebendal parish church was immediately adjacent to the nun's church. Each prebendary had a stall in the choir of the abbey church and was a full member of the chapter with the right to speak and vote at the time of elections. He was expected to help the nuns with their legal and financial affairs, including the auditing of their bailiffs' and other accounts, and to be present at the annual audit. If he was absent he was liable to provide a chaplain to minister in his place, who would then receive the daily portions of bread, ale and a dish from the kitchen.[36] (However, a bad prebendal priest was worse than useless: the dissolute William Shirlock was such a menace to the nuns at Romsey Abbey that Archbishop Pecham had to forbid him entering the nuns' cloister or the abbey church.[37])

Unfortunately by the end of the 13th century it was becoming common for the offices to become sinecures as non-resident prebendaries ignored their duties. The system was also undermined by the abbesses being forced to present nominees of the pope, or his delegate, to prebendal stalls instead of nominating priests of their own choice. In one of the Wherwell charters it was recorded that

> The arrangements for the prebendaries no longer tend to good but to harm because the ladies are obliged at the urgent request of the masters to present such men to be prebendaries as never reside there.[38]

The abbess of Wherwell sent a petition to the pope complaining about one such priest, Nicholas Talemache, who had been non-resident and neglectful of his prebend over a period of 20 years. Evidently her plea was not ignored for Nicholas later resigned and exchanged the prebend for another benefice.[39]

The nuns were similarly unable to present priests of their own choice to the parishes whose advowson they held. Two uncompromising letters written on behalf of the papal

17. A view of the former Wherwell parish church before it was pulled down in 1858. It shows the north aisle, with bell turret over the west gable; the cusped outer arch above the three-light large west window is characteristically 13th-century. There was probably a narrow south aisle lit by the two-light west window of lancets divided by a slender shaft. This watercolour painting of 1830 is now in Wherwell parish church (*see also* plate 58).

legate in July 1268 forbade the abbess of Wherwell to present anyone to any benefice as the legate, Cardinal Ottobono, intended their next vacancy for his chaplain Master Ardicio Tridino. However, after throwing out threats of excommunication if the order were disobeyed, the writer did have the grace to add that he did not believe the nuns would think of attempting to do so.[40] This naming of Master Ardicio highlights another problem that arose with many papal nominees at the time, for they were often Italians who never set foot in England. But at least one bishop of Winchester was ready to question the powers that Rome had assumed, and in the 1290s there was a protracted dispute between Bishop Pontissara and the papacy about the presentation to Wherwell Abbey's prebend of Middleton. The pope won eventually, but only after the bishop had been called to Rome.[41]

    The provisions that different popes made to benefices and prebendal stalls, with the correspondence concerning them, account for the majority of records concerning the nunneries in the papal registers. Apart from one in 1402, all the provisions to prebends were made during the 30 years before the Statute of Provisors (1351) when Pope John XXII and Pope

Clement VI were making full use of their powers. However, it is interesting to see that by that time both the king and the bishop of Winchester had learned to play the system and would petition the pope on behalf of any priest whom they wished to see rewarded with a particular prebend. Thus during the last 12 years of his pontificate Pope John provided a dozen priests with nominal canonries in the nunnery churches (five at both Romsey and Wherwell, and two at Winchester) but only three of those canonries came with actual vacancies to prebendal stalls – and the three priests provided to them were all Englishmen; in 1328 Edward III had petitioned the pope for a prebend for John de Crockford in Romsey Abbey and for William de Synkale, one of his clerks, in Wherwell Abbey, while three years later Robert de Stratford was provided with a stall at Romsey on the petition of his kinsman the bishop.[42]

Later, Robert de Stratford was to be the cause of contention. He was a prebendal priest of Wherwell as well as Romsey and both these stalls automatically fell vacant when he became bishop of Chichester in 1337. Six years later, and knowing that they were then 'unlawfully held by others', Pope Clement VI provided one of his Italian papal writers with both the prebends.[43] In the meantime the king had granted the tithes of the Romsey prebend of Edington to Gilbert de Bruera, the dean of St. Paul's, who later became the prebendary and apparently remained so in spite of opposition.[44] There was similar confusion at Wherwell Abbey where Peter de Inkepenne, who already occupied one prebendal stall there, thought he had also been provided with the bishop's former prebend of Middleton. Papal pressure forced him to resign it, although he was allowed to keep the income that he had already received. Within a short time he was occupying it once again, thanks to a royal patent and the timely death of the papal writer.[45] (There were further disputes about the right of presentation to this prebend a few years later.)

The whole affair is a good example of the type of papal interference that was increasingly resented in England and was shortly to be brought to an end by Parliament, although it did not follow that the nunneries were then able to exercise their own judgment about presentations. The king continued to find that the gift of a prebend made a welcome reward for any cleric whom he wished to advance, and he used his powers regardless of whether the nunnery was actually in his hands during a vacancy or not.

Four prebendal priests had stalls in the abbeys of Wherwell and St. Mary's, Winchester and there were three in Romsey Abbey. Each prebend took its name from the parish church attached to it. Three of the four Wherwell Abbey prebends were endowed with churches in parishes that had belonged to the nuns at the time of Domesday: Wherwell itself, Goodworth and Middleton which are all adjacent. A papal bull in 1257 gave the nuns the right to give or withhold permission for any new chapel within that total area, so the chapels of Bullington and Tufton which belonged to the prebend of Wherwell may date from that time. A more distant chapel at Compton, Berkshire was attached to the prebend of Goodworth and was included in the nuns' appropriation of the prebend in 1444.[46] The fourth prebend was attached to the parish church of Bathwick in Somerset; there the manor of 'Wicke and Woolley' had come into the possession of the abbey following the death in 1093 of Bishop Geoffrey of Coutance who had held it at the time of Domesday. This prebend, like Wherwell and Middleton, continued in being until the Dissolution. Apparently these Wherwell prebends had come into being at the end of the 13th century. A charter in the cartulary of the house says that it was believed that these 'portions' were ordained by John Pecham, formerly archbishop of Canterbury, at his metropolitan visitation, without other authority or confirmation.[47]

The four prebends in St. Mary's Abbey were all endowed with parish churches that served estates that had belonged to the abbey before the Conquest. Two were in Wiltshire, at All Cannings and Urchfont, and the other two were local, at Itchen Abbas and Leckford.

The four recorded priests who held this last prebend in the 14th century were all English and were presented by the king.[48] In Wiltshire the churches of All Cannings and Urchfont both date from the early 13th century, and by the end of that century the greater part of their revenues had been appropriated to the two prebends. At All Cannings the prebendary owned 12 acres of arable and some pasture by 1260 but most of his income was from tithes; out of that he was liable to pay a pension to the abbess.[49] At Urchfont the prebendary was receiving two thirds of the tithes from the abbey's demesne lands; he also owned a house and garden there.[50]

At Romsey Abbey the three prebendal stalls were all occupied in the 13th century. The first prebend was known as the portion in the parish church of St. Laurence of Romsey, but the endowment also included the church of Timsbury nearby and the chapel of Imber, Wiltshire. It was the only prebend in Romsey Abbey which continued until the Dissolution. The second prebend was endowed with the church of Edington and the chapel of Bradley. Like the Wiltshire estates of St. Mary's Abbey, Edington had been held by the nuns of Romsey before the Conquest and at least by 1241 the church there was a prebend of the abbey. In 1351 this prebend came to an end when Bishop Edington founded his chantry there. At first the warden of it became a canon in the abbey but when the chantry was converted into a religious house of Bonhommes in 1358 the religious (but not manorial) connections between Edington and Romsey Abbey ceased.[51] The demise of the third prebend, the co-portionary prebend of St. Laurence in the abbey church, also occurred in 1351 when it was appropriated to the nuns by Bishop Edington. Officially this was because of their poverty after the Black Death, but no doubt it was also a reward for their co-operation over Edington; from that time the income out of Sydmonton became their own apart from an annual pension for the bishop and his successors of 6s. 8d.[52] Earlier there are records of the four priests who held the prebend in the first half of the 14th century and of the dispute over the presentation of one of them. This occurred in the 1320s when the abbess and convent had the temerity to try and present a priest to the vacant prebend themselves, instead of accepting the pope's nominee who also had the backing of Edward II. They lost of course, but only after the case had gone to the papal court.[53]

Vicars were first instituted to the parishes in which the abbeys were situated between 1318 and 1321. (Legally the establishment of vicarages had to follow a successful appropriation.)[54] At Romsey Bishop de Asserio established a perpetual vicarage in 1321 and instituted Henry de Chulmarke as the first vicar. He had been presented by the two prebendaries of Romsey, and was to receive allowances of food and drink from the abbey each day (double the quantity given to a nun!) as well as the small tithes and other emoluments.[55] At Wherwell the prebendary there was the patron of the parish church and remained so, in spite of the abbess's petition to the pope asking that the convent might appropriate it so that 'there would be an end to the frequent disputes between the ladies and the prebendary'.[56] The first vicar of Wherwell was Bartholomew Bovet who was instituted in April 1318, six days after the abbess and convent of St. Mary's Abbey had presented William de Laurence to the church of St. Peter in Colebrook Street, Winchester.[57] (But St. Peter's was never prebendal to the abbey.)

The parish church of 'Hurtele Monialum', which is now known as St. Mary's Old Church, was about a mile away from Wintney Priory. No prebendaries were ever attached to it. The advowson was in the hands of the prioress and convent, and since it had been decided in 1295 that the king had no rights over the house as a patron he never nominated to the benefice on their behalf.[58] Richard de Heghe was instituted to the vicarage in 1302.[59]

Inevitably relations between the local vicar and the nunneries would have varied over the centuries according to the personalities of those in office. They may have been easier at Hartley Wintney where the one mile walk between the parish church and the priory would

18a. The site of the medieval parish church of St Laurence, Romsey.

18b. The adjacent chapel of St Laurence in Romsey Abbey today.

19. St Mary's Old Church, Hartley Wintney. Until the 19th century, the church comprised a chancel and nave of the 13th century with 14th- and 15th-century details. The transepts were added in 1834 and the tower in 1842.

20. Chancel window in St Mary's Old Church, Hartley Wintney, showing some of the medieval fleur-de-lys pattern now uncovered. Other wall paintings uncovered between 1977-80 include three saints: St Christopher, a large St George spearing a dragon and a female saint, probably St Catherine.

have provided time to soften the sting behind any rebukes that were about to be made by either vicar or prioress. One imagines that Henry Sewghel, who was vicar early in the 16th century, was a friend to the priory for he left legacies to the prioress and to all nuns there.[60]

At Romsey and Wherwell there was no such safety margin. At Romsey the parish church was adjacent to the north side of the abbey church and tempers ran high enough on one occasion for a nun, Margaret Poyns, to attack the vicar physically. No reasons were recorded, only that she was later absolved from the excommunication that followed.[61] A few years later John Foliot seems to have been a trouble-seeking vicar of Romsey. In 1372 he objected to the part played by the sacrist in the traditional blessing of palms on Palm Sunday, and the following year he was in dispute with the abbess over repairs to the parish church.[62] By the end of the century this was anyway too small for the town so Bishop Wykeham granted a faculty to enlarge it in 1403, and at the same time wrote a letter to the abbess asking her to encourage and assist the vicar (now John Umfray) in the undertaking.[63]

At Wherwell the parish church was a separate building that lay just to the north of the abbey church. When the abbess of Wherwell petitioned the pope in the 14th century she wrote that it would be very convenient to be allowed to appropriate the parish church because it was

> ... as it were, adjacent to their church and even situated inside the precinct of the conventual church and within the boundaries of the monastery, so that part of the conventual church, or a chapel of the same, is very close to it, as is commonly the case in conventual churches having parish churches so close . . .[64]

Originally the parish church only had the status of a chapel and some aspects of its inferiority remained. On certain feast days no services or bell ringing were allowed in it, and on Palm Sunday and at Candlemas the services and processions were held in the abbey church where the vicar had to preach and the 'accustomed oblations' were made. He also had to baptise all the village babies in the convent church as there was no font in the parish church. As was written in the cartulary:

> In the church of the nuns' convent, in the nave or body of the same, is one stone font for use as a baptistry, anciently ordained for the baptism of the children of the whole vill and parish of Wherwell, in which all the children of the whole parish have always from the first foundation of the same been baptised there by the vicar of the said parish, nor is there any other font in the parish church of the said vill.[65]

However, at the beginning of the 15th century certain parishioners thought that this should be changed. They obtained a suitable stone vessel which they carried secretly to the entrance of the parish church, but they had reckoned without the vigilance of the abbess's chaplain, William Serle. On instructions from Abbess Alice he removed the vessel from the entrance and put it into the nuns' church where the holy chest for the parishioners had stood before the construction and ordination of the parish church. Feelings ran high. Six parishioners brought a writ of trespass against William Serle and other servants of the abbess, but friends intervened so that four arbitrators were appointed to settle the matter instead. They met at Andover in May 1415 and decided that the abbess should retain the vessel which would henceforth be used in the convent kitchen, but the parishioners – who were never again to presume to place anything resembling a font in their church – should be reimbursed with its value of 26s. 8d. That was immediately paid by Margery Graas.[66] (The vicar was not mentioned.) At Winchester in the 1340s the nuns of St. Mary's Abbey had been involved in a similar disagreement with their neighbours in Colebrook Street who had attempted to install a font in St. Peter's church.[67]

At the other end of life all the abbeys provided cemeteries within their precincts. At Romsey and Wherwell the burial grounds for local people were attached to the parish churches and in their wills parishioners would name the churchyard of St. Laurence in

Romsey or the cemetery of the church of the Holy Trinity in Wherwell as their burial place. At Wherwell some sort of desecration took place in the graveyard around 1380 as the bishop then issued a commission to compel the parishioners to pay the vicar a fee for reconciling it.[68] At Winchester the Holy Trinity Chapel stood within the cemetery of St. Mary's Abbey; this was the chantry that was founded and endowed by the Inkepenne family in 1318. Two centuries later it was visited by Leland who wrote:

> There is a fair chapel on the north side of St. Mary Abbey church in an area thereby; to the which men enter by a certain steps; under it is a vault for a carnerie. One Inkepenne . . . was founder of it. There be three tombs of marble of priests, *custodes* of this chapel.[69]

In the early 14th century many chantries were founded by men of means who wished to perpetuate their names in this world and secure the salvation of their souls in the next. They were endowed for the benefit of the donor and his family in at least two of the abbey churches at this time. In 1328 Robert de Wambergh, archdeacon of Wells, founded the chapel of St. Peter as a perpetual chantry in the church of St. Mary's Abbey by agreement with the abbess; it was located on the south side of the choir, toward the east.[70] Three years later the Braishfield chantry, the chapel of St. Nicholas, was endowed in Romsey Abbey and provided a burial place for members of that family, including the father of Emma de Braishfield whose corpse was moved there from the cemetery.[71] The site of that chantry is not known but the chapel of St. George which was founded as a chantry in 1476 remains in the north choir aisle of the abbey church with some of its interesting tiles still in position.[72] At Wherwell there is no record of a chantry chapel being dedicated but several endowments were made between 1323 and 1331 by the prebendary of Goodworth, Henry le Gayte (als. Wayte), to provide a chaplain to celebrate divine service daily in the abbey church for the souls of Roger le Forest and his family.[73]

Some of the many chaplains who served the churches of the nunneries are known by name, especially those who were appointed to the chantries. Others are known because their misdeeds reached the episcopal registers, though sometimes the sins were minor. Thus Bishop Sandale dispatched a horrified letter to the abbess of Winchester after he spotted one of her chaplains, John de Ashley, walking in the city in a parti-coloured gown![74]

Other priests in regular contact with the nuns were their confessors who were normally appointed by the bishop after the Council of Oxford. In the 13th century it was customary for a monk from St. Swithun's Priory to be chosen for the nuns of St. Mary's Abbey; when Bishop Pontissara appointed John de Sibbesdon, the infirmarian, to be their sole confessor he ordered that he must go to the abbey when sent for and not the nuns to the priory as had happened in the past.[75] Later, secular priests were sometimes appointed, including the rector of St. Peter's, Colebrook Street.[76] Similarly two of the confessors to the Wintney nuns were both rectors of Elvetham nearby.[77] At Wherwell Abbey one of the confessors in the 14th century was Walter Chapellayn, a Minorite friar from Winchester, but his licence was later withdrawn by Bishop Wykeham who urged the nuns there to accept one of the monks from St. Swithun's.[78] He also appointed this same monk, Ralph Basyng, as one of three confessors to the Romsey nuns in 1396; one of the others was John Umfray who was vicar of Romsey when the parish church was enlarged. Earlier the abbess of Romsey had been empowered to choose one or two chaplains herself to be confessors to herself and her nuns, but in his injunctions of 1387 the bishop ordered that confessions were normally only to be made to a confessor appointed by himself.[79] A century later Bishop Langton licensed a Carmelite friar to hear confessions at Romsey, but for some reason the sub-prioress, Anabelle Dyngley, was granted a licence to choose her own confessor.[80]

Chapter Six
Life Within the Cloister

One of the constantly reiterated themes of episcopal injunctions to the nunneries was that nuns should stay within their cloisters. The manner of their life there and the pattern of their days cannot really be appreciated so many years later, but some attempt will be made in the next three chapters to gather together the little that is known about them.

The Divine Office

At least since the time of Bishop Ethelwold's reforms in the tenth century the nuns in the three Benedictine abbeys would have had their day ordered in much the same way as their male counterparts. The canonical hours, collectively called the Divine Office, were matins, lauds, prime, terce, sext, none, vespers and compline. Their observation set the pattern of the monastic day but the actual times when they were observed are only approximately known, and anyway varied considerably not only on Sundays and feast days but also with the time of year. Mass was celebrated twice daily before none and in time other offices were included in the day, particularly the chapter office each morning.

21. The north side of the cloister of Romsey Abbey lay alongside this south aisle wall. The large Saxon rood can be seen on the wall of the south transept.

The routine of life was different in winter from summer and Lent made a third variation. The winter horarium started on 13 September and continued until Ash Wednesday; during that time the nuns' day would have started with matins at about 2 a.m., followed immediately by lauds then prime after the first light of day. At Wherwell in the 14th century there was trouble when prime, which was held in the choir of the church, often clashed with the first mass in the Lady Chapel nearby. It is not difficult to appreciate that

... on account of the confusion of voices and sound, which arises from the position of the music on both sides, a great discord is caused in the ears of the hearers and various other inconveniences are brought about ... [1]

Bishop Wykeham proposed that prime should not begin until mass was finished, though this had to be sufficiently early so as not to disrupt the times of later services.

The chapter office was held during the morning in the chapter house; it combined business with devotions and included readings from the Rule of St. Benedict. Terce and sext were both held in the morning, and over the years the hour for none moved forward and is thought to have been sung at about midday in later medieval times. There was then a considerable space for other activities before vespers in the late afternoon and compline at about 7 p.m. in winter. Afterwards the nuns were expected to go to bed. During the summer horarium compline and bedtime were about an hour later and the night office was earlier, so it became customary to have another period of sleep before prime.

It is impossible to know how well the Divine Office was observed down the centuries. Probably every bishop at every visitation stressed the importance of faithful attendance when he was addressing the communities, but the need for some flexibility seems to have been recognised. Obedientiaries sometimes had to attend to their other duties, and so did the heads of the houses. When Archbishop Pecham wrote to Abbess Elena de Percy of Wherwell in 1284 he referred to the possibility of her not having time to attend compline, apparently because of her obligations as a hostess. He ordered that on those occasions she must be informed when it was over by the nun presiding over .the choir, who would be accompanied by two other sisters of good standing; all drinking had then to cease and her guests were to leave so that she could say compline herself so as to be prepared for the night vigils – provided she was not ill.[2]

Only a few episcopal injunctions about the Divine Office have been recorded. Amongst them Bishop Pontissara ordered the nuns at Romsey to rise earlier than they had been used to do, in order to sing matins and the other hours at their proper times so that High Mass could always be celebrated before none.[3] The Wherwell nuns may have been more conscientious as he did not mention this in the injunctions he sent them the following week, and since his successor, Bishop Woodlock, never sent injunctions to Wherwell at all after his two visitations, there was presumably nothing serious to criticise. However, Bishop Woodlock did send injunctions to the other three nunneries urging greater observation of their spiritual duties. In 1309 he wrote that the nuns at Winchester were not to engage themselves in private work or conversation during the hours of divine service, or to be absent from it without leave – and the abbess was urged not to grant such leave without good cause.[4] Two years later the Romsey nuns were once again having to be reminded about the need to rise earlier for matins, and for an earlier start to the daily celebration of mass in the infirmary which should no longer be attended by lay people who were living within the precincts.[5] And, unable to visit Wintney Priory himself in 1316, he started his decree to the house by reminding the nuns that the religious state had been established principally for the performance of the service of God, and directing them to perform that service 'with the solemnity that becomes it and better than it has been performed heretofore'.[6] Like their sisters at Romsey they were told to rise earlier for matins; they were to be in the choir in good time for the service of God and everyone except the obedientiaries was to remain there until the service was finished; fasting was prescribed for those nuns who absented themselves without leave.

The injunctions that Bishop Stratford sent to St. Mary's Abbey in 1326 started in a similar way. He observed that the requirements of the Rule relating to the Divine Office had been very badly kept and that all nuns were to attend both by day and night, unless given permission to be absent, or else be punished according to the Rule; and should their non-attendance persist they were to fast on bread and water each Friday and receive further punishment at the discretion of the abbess.[7] (This was more severe than the Wintney nuns' fasting mentioned by Bishop Woodlock: he had at least allowed bread and ale.)

At the end of the 14th century Bishop William of Wykeham started his injunctions to the abbeys by ordering that the canonical hours and masses were to be said and sung daily and that nuns were not to be absent without permission, but this seems to have been written more as a matter of form rather than to redress any specific backsliding.[8] A century later, however, there certainly was a great deal wrong at Romsey. Among the *detecta* at the time of the visitation held for Archbishop Morton in 1492, several of the nuns said either that divine service was not observed there or that 'religion was not kept', while one mentioned people chatting in the middle of the choir.[9] This was during the notorious period of the rule of Abbess Elizabeth Brooke when discipline in the house was at its lowest. In its absence it must have been all too easy in the cold of a winter's night to stay in bed rather than attend matins in a freezing church.

Nine years later, when the religious houses in the diocese were being visited in 1501, there seems to have been an improvement. Although Abbess Brooke did not die until the following year, the prioress of Romsey testified that both the night and day offices were observed there. Abbess Matilda Rouse of Wherwell said that there was regular attendance at the night and day hours, while at Winchester it was the sub-prioress who stated that all the convent rose at night for matins except the sick and aged.[10] As their most likely weak point, all the nunneries seem to have been asked specifically about the night services.

Books, music and seals

By the late 13th century books were as essential a part of English Benedictine life as music. Those few that survive from the nunneries are a tangible link with the nuns who once owned them. It is impossible to know how many volumes were in the libraries of the three abbeys since no catalogue of contents has survived from the library of any English nunnery, though Bishop Wykeham did order an inventory of books to be made at Wherwell Abbey which implies that there was a reasonable number there.[11] Two continental catalogues of nunnery libraries are known, including one compiled in the 15th century of the books belonging to the Dominican nuns of Nuremburg who owned 350 volumes; but the very fact that a catalogue was compiled may indicate that the nuns there had an unusually large collection.[12]

All the surviving books which are known to have belonged to one of the Hampshire nunneries, or to individual nuns within them, are listed in Appendix 4. Six psalters still remain but there are only single examples of other types of book. This is probably not a coincidence for psalters were of central importance as prayer books and were one of the earliest books of the Bible to be illuminated. Like most copies, these six were each bound with a calendar of saints' days, festivals and the obits of benefactors and former members of the community, particularly the heads of the house. It will be seen from the so called Romsey Psalter that the evidence of these obits can be crucial when ascribing the original ownership of a book.

There is no record of any English nunnery having its own great copy of the Bible, either the vulgate or in translation, though nuns are known to have studied such translations and in Europe were their most numerous orthodox users; neither is any surviving Gospel Book connected with the Hampshire nunneries. The oldest book listed in the appendix is the Anglo-Saxon Book of Nunnaminster (BL MS. Harley 2965), a prayer book which had probably belonged to Ealhswith, wife of King Alfred, and later to the nuns at Winchester. They also owned an 11th-century prayer book (BL MS. Galba A.xiv) and a 12th-century copy of some of the writings of the early Church Fathers, including Smaragdus and St. Augustine (Bodleian 451). All the houses would have had their own martyrologies with lives of the saints, and two of these are in the British Library collection: Wintney Priory's 13th-century Martyrology which is bound with a calendar and an early version of the Rule of St. Benedict (BL Cotton Claud D.iii), and a slightly later volume that used to belong to Romsey Abbey which contains a Chronicle of the Saxon kings as well as the lives of English saints (BL Lansdowne 436).

The Nuremburg catalogue includes notes on how each book came into the convent's collection; some were given by nuns when they were admitted or else copied by them in the scriptorium, while others were given by benefactors. In the absence of such a helpful list either the Hampshire books themselves have to supply the information or it remains unknown. None of them is likely to have been copied by the nuns. In England there is no reason to suppose that nuns themselves copied any of the books in their libraries, and indeed it is highly improbable that they did so.[13] It is true that there were good scribes at Romsey at both the beginning and end of the 15th century but they are more likely to have been clerks than nuns.[14] However, ignoring post-Dissolution ownership descriptions, five of the six surviving Hampshire psalters can be connected with individual nuns and two of them give the name of the donor.

The oldest of the six psalters is a large and beautiful copy (St. John's Coll. C.18) that was written in the scriptorium at St. Alban's Abbey in the 1160-70s. Although there are no miniatures in it there are 20 major initials, nearly all historiated. It was originally intended for a Flemish monastery but apparently it was never sent there. It is likely that the first owner of the psalter was Matilda de Bailleul who had become abbess of Wherwell by 1180.[15] Her niece, the revered Abbess Euphemia who succeeded her may also have owned it personally for the obits of several members of her family are in the calendar, including her mother Margaret de Walliers. It is possible that Abbess Euphemia may have given it with other books and valuables to the abbey church,[16] or perhaps it may first have passed to the other Matilda de Bailleul who was prioress in the last half of the century. Her obit is in its calendar and so is Abbess Mabel de Ticheburne's (d.1281) but the obits for Abbess Euphemia and her two successors are missing.

A 13th-century psalter (Trinity Coll. B.11.4) is inscribed with the name of a Winchester nun, Joan de Roches, who was presumably related to Bishop Peter des Roches. The contemporary note is written in French at the end of Psalm 26, and when translated reads:

> Memorandum that Dame Ida de Ralegh has lent to Dom Walter Hone, Abbot of Neweham, this psalter for the term of his life. And if the said Dame Ida outlives the said abbot, let the said Dame Ida have it back. And if the abbot aforesaid outlives the said Dame Ida, let the abbot charge his monks to entrust the said psalter to Dame Joan de Roches, nun of the abbey of Our Lady of Winchester.[17]

One cannot be sure that Dame Joan received the psalter, but the calendar does include St. Mary's own St. Edburga in July as well as St. Swithun. The whole psalter is splendidly written and illuminated and includes a picture of an abbess and a nun kneeling before an altar in one of the historiated initials (fol.103v).

A small early 14th-century psalter with canticles and litany that is now in the British Library (Add. MS.27866) once belonged to Johanna Stretford who was a nun at Wherwell. She wrote that the book belonged to her in one of the few available spaces, which happened to be nearer the end than the beginning of the volume. Another psalter of similar size and date (Fitzwilliam Mus. McClean 45) which was at Wherwell contains the obits of Abbess Matilda de Littleton and three members of the de Columbers family; these were all later additions to the calendar. Perhaps the abbess gave this psalter to her abbey as well as the ornate silver gilt chalice which is described in the Wherwell Cartulary.[18]

Two psalters now known as the Wilton Psalter (Royal Coll. Physicians MS.409) and the Romsey Psalter are connected with Romsey. Prayers at the end of the litany indicate that the 13th-century Wilton Psalter was originally written for an abbess of Wilton Abbey, possibly in the scriptorium of Salisbury cathedral. As the calendar does not include the octave of the nativity of the Virgin, it was written before 1252. Few additions were made to

A put chorinchium: beati dionisii epi. qui claruit tempi
bz marcii antonini. et lucii aureliani. Turonis: sci pe
tri epi admirande sctatis uiri. V idus aprilis. luna.

A B C D E F G H I K L M N O P Q R S T
xviiii xvi xiiii x iii i iiii xxiiii xiiii vi xv xxvii viii xx vi xvi xxvi iii i xiiii xxv vii

N atale beati pchori. qui fuit unus de septem primis di
aconibz. Hic aput antiochiam martirio coronatus e.
In syrmio: passio sctarum septem uirginu. IIII. id aprilis.

A B C D E F G H I K L M N O P Q R S T
xii i i iii xiii iiii xxiii xxvi vi xvi xxvii vii xx xxi ii iii xviii vi xv xxvi vii

E zechielis pphe: qui a iudice populi israel aput babiloni
am interfectus. in sepulcro sem. atqz arfaxad est sepultus
Rome beatorum mrm plurimoy quos scs alexander papa
baptizauit. hos omnes aurelianus princeps in pfundum
maris mergi fecit. Alexandrie: sci apollonii presbiteri et
aliorum septem. quinqz IIII idus aprilis. luna.

A B C D E F G H I K L M N O P Q R S T
xxii iii iiii xxiii iiii v xxvi vii vi xxvii xx x xxi iii ii xi xxvii xxiii vi xvi xxvi xxviii viii

R ome natale beati leonis pape: cuius temporibz extitit
sca sinodus calcidonensis. Aput cretam in urbe gorti
na: sci philippi epi. In dalmatia ciuitate salona: sci do
mnionis epi cummilitibz octo. Hicomedie: sci euistorgii pbri
In britannia: sci gudlaci confessoris et anachorite. PRIDIE ID APL E

A B C D E F G H I K L M N O P Q R S T
xxii iii iiii iiii xxiii xxiii vi vi xxvi xxvi viii iiii xxi i xi xxii iii iiii xx vi xvi xxvii ix

R ome uia aurelia: natale beati iulii pape. sub consta
tio impatore decem mensibz tribulationes et exilia
ppessus post cuius mortem cum magna gfa ad sua
sedem reuersus quieuit in pace. Eodem die: sci zenonis

23. An historiated initial 'Q' from a 12th-century Psalter that belonged to Wherwell Abbey. It shows Ahimelech the priest handing Goliath's sword to David, having already given him the sacred bread that is on the table. They are watched by Doeg the Edomite, a servant of Saul (1 Samuel 21). Cambridge, St John's Coll. ms. C.18, f.70v.

24. A leaf from an early 13th-century Psalter that may have belonged to Joan de Roches, a nun at St Mary's Abbey, Winchester. The historiated initial shows (above) Christ as judge with two angels and (below) an abbess with crosier and a nun with scroll kneeling before an altar. Cambridge, Trinity Coll. ms. B.11.4., f.103v.

its calendar in the succeeding centuries and no obits of nuns were entered into it. It is not known how long the psalter remained at Wilton, but by the early 16th century it belonged to Ralph Lepton who was a chaplain to Bishop Fox. A well written inscription in English records that in 1523 he gave it to his great niece, Elizabeth Langrege, who became a nun at Romsey. Presumably the inscription was added some time after the psalter had been given because it contains details of other donations that Master Lepton made at the time of Elizabeth's veiling. Rendered into modern English it reads:

> The xth day of October in the year of our Lord God one Thousand five hundred and XXIII, the XVth year of King Henry the VIIIth and the XXIIIth year of the Translation of my lord Richard Fox Bishop of Winchester, master Raufe Lepton parson of Alresford and of Kings Worthy, servant and chaplain to my said lord Richard, gave this book to Elizabeth Langrege whose Grandfather John Warner, gentleman, was uncle to my lady dame Anne Westbrook, abbess of Romsey; to the said Elizabeth 'mynchynne' of Romsey the said master Raufe was great uncle unto. Above that the said master Raufe gave first at the veiling of the said Elizabeth in money five pounds delivered to John Raye, bailiff of Romsey. Above that the said master Raufe gave to the said Elizabeth one goblet of silver, all gilt covered, with three lions on the foot. And two spoons, the one crystal garnished with silver gilt with an image on the end; the other all white.[19]

As Elizabeth Langrege was 17 years old when she was professed in 1534, she could only have been six years old in 1523. (Perhaps the gift may have been made if and when she first attended school at Romsey Abbey where her mother's cousin was abbess at the time.)

The so-called Romsey Psalter, which was written in the 15th century, was owned by St. Mary's Abbey before the Dissolution. There is no actual inscription to that effect but the obits of nearly all the abbesses of St. Mary's between 1100 and 1419 are recorded in the calendar, showing that it was in regular use there. In spite of that it was thought at the beginning of this century that it had once belonged to the nuns of Romsey, so when it came up for sale in 1900 the money was raised locally to buy it for the abbey church where it can still be seen.[20] It may be confusing that it is now known as the Romsey Psalter but it is only thanks to the generosity of the townspeople of Romsey that there is still one book in Hampshire which originally belonged to one of its nunneries.

As well as complete books, two separate calendars survive. The earlier one (BL MS.Cotton Nero A.ii, fols.3-13) is believed to have once been part of the 11th-century prayer book of St. Mary's Abbey (BL MS.Galba A.xiv). The other (Leningrad Q.v.I.62) is a calendar that was originally written at St. Alban's Abbey but was at Wherwell Abbey by the end of the 12th century. Various additions were made to it over the next century, both local obits and the dates of national events such as the coronations of Richard I, John and Henry III. Like the abbey's psalter that was written at St. Alban's, this calendar is particularly associated with the early 13th-century abbesses Matilda de Bailleul and Euphemia. Their obits (and Richard I's) were entered in large letters on coloured bands, and near the end of the manuscript there are two Latin poems lamenting the death of Abbess Matilda, and also a letter of consolation on it.[21]

None of the four nunneries' own copies of Bishop Fox's translation of the Rule of St. Benedict is known. However, the manuscript copy of the Order of Consecration of Nuns which he gave to St.Mary's Abbey has survived (Cambridge U.L. MS. Mm.3.13); on a blank leaf at the beginning there is a note that he gave the book to the monastery of nuns in the city of Winchester and was a benefactor of the house. It is both an order of service in Latin 'pertaining to the solemn profession, benediction and consecration of holy virgins'[22] and also a commentary on that service in English with detailed instructions for all involved. The two are interspersed. (Illustrations on p. 41.)

It was the normal practice for monastic books to be kept in the place where they were needed. Thus the nunneries' service books such as psalters, missals and gospel books would have stayed in church, the book being currently read aloud at meal times would have remained in the refectory and books for private study would have been kept in their general library, wherever that was. There is no record of any actual book room or scriptorium in any of the nunneries, but it seems possible that at St. Mary's Abbey such books may have been kept in the treasury house with its 'charters, evidences, writings and muniments' which were kept in 'divers coffers and almeres' at the time of the Dissolution.[23] Similarly it seems reasonable to imagine that any books which could collectively be called the libraries of the other nunneries were more likely to have been kept with their muniments than anywhere else.

Generally the precentor of a monastic house was the person responsible for its books, although in time a librarian was often appointed. At the start of the 16th century St. Mary's Abbey had a sufficient number of books for one of the nuns, Elia Pitte, to be librarian[24] but the term was not apparently used at any of the other nunneries, or indeed at Winchester at the time of the Dissolution. At Wherwell the sacristan was responsible for the care of the books kept in church for the divine office. When Bishop Wykeham noticed that they were 'broken, badly bound, full of mistakes and completely unfit for use' he ordered the abbess and sacristan

> ... without delay to have these books which need repair duly re-made and repaired, causing an inventory to be made of all these books, one copy of which we desire to remain in the possession of the abbess and another in that of the convent.[25]

To what extent did the nuns study and understand those books which they did have? It is impossible to know of course but it seems likely that all the choir nuns were literate. The nuns of Godstow were said to be well learned in English books in the 15th century[26] and there is no reason to suppose that the same was not true of the nuns in Hampshire. Their ability to write may have been more limited but some ladies were able to do so, or otherwise Bishop Stratford would not have found it necessary to forbid the nuns at Winchester to write letters 'on parchment or on tablets' without permission from the abbess or prioress.[27]

Their knowledge of Latin was another matter. Although there were some exceptions, it seems that the majority of English nuns knew none during the late Middle Ages. Bishop Fox was quite clear when he translated the Rule into English for them that

> ... in the Latin tongue ... they have no knowledge nor understanding, but be utterly ignorant of the same.[28]

Two hundred years earlier Bishop Woodlock had also realised the nuns' limitations so when he sent injunctions to the nunneries at Winchester and Romsey he had them translated into French. At the time it would have been the natural tongue of well born ladies, even if it was the French of Chaucer's prioress:

> And well she sang a service, with a fine
> Intoning through her nose, as was most seemly,
> And she spoke daintily in French, extremely,
> After the school of Stratford-atte-Bowe;
> French in the Paris style she did not know.

It has already been mentioned that Bishop Orleton spoke in French when he preached at Romsey and St. Mary's Abbey in 1334, but by the start of the 15th century English had become the mother tongue for all sections of society. By 1478 the newly elected abbesses were using it when taking their oaths, instead of the French they had used in Bishop Wykeham's time.[29]

As nuns were expected to be able to sing, they needed some knowledge of music. In the mortuary roll of 1122 two Winchester nuns who had been *cantrice* were recorded, but a similar term is not used again until 1502 when there were four *cantaristae* at Romsey Abbey.[30]

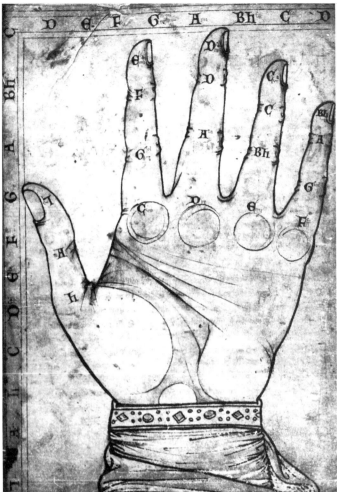

25. A 12th-century Guidonian Hand, with the letter names of the pitches, which was used to teach singing at Wherwell Abbey. It is included in the Calendar of the abbey which is now in Russia. Leningrad, Saltykov-Shchedrin ms. Lat. Q.v.I.62, f.23.

26. Two Marian antiphons from the 14th-century Wherwell Cartulary: *Sancta Maria non est tibi similis*, followed by *Sancta Maria virgo intercede*. BL ms. Egerton 2104a., f.2.

Normally it was the duty of the precentrix to lead the singing. As the standard of English music, particularly church music, was high at the end of the Middle Ages, one assumes that only nuns with real musical ability were appointed to the office.

In the nunneries' own books there is musical scoring for the Te Deum in the small psalter owned by Johanna Stretford of Wherwell, and the antiphons have musical notes in The Order of Consecration of Nuns that belonged to St. Mary's Abbey. However, the most interesting musical item is at the end of the Wherwell calendar now in Leningrad. Three pages show how the nuns were taught singing by the use of the Guidonian Hand; on one page a hand was drawn which included the letter names of the pitches, while on the other two there is information within circle diagrams about the syllables and the music for practice exercises.[31] This technique, known as solmisation, was the medieval equivalent of the tonic sol-fa system. It was a very common method of teaching singing in the Middle Ages and was sufficient to give novices the rudiments of musical knowledge that they needed for plainsong and polyphony.

Sometimes the episcopal registers mention which anthems were sung when the bishop was present in one of the nunnery churches. *Veni Creator spiritus* was often sung at the start of a service, while the *Te Deum laudamus* would follow the installation of a new abbess. The Wherwell Cartulary includes the music for two other polyphonic pieces.[32] They are settings, each in three parts, of two Marian antiphons: the first, which was used for processions, is a setting of the text *Sancta Maria non est tibi similis* and this is immediately followed by the second *Sancta Maria virgo intercede*. They are complete except for an inch or so on the left side of the page that may have been stripped away when the cartulary was bound.

At the Dissolution no instructions were given to the commissioners about the books and literary manuscripts in the monastic houses, so their fate was left to chance. Those later owners who are known are mentioned in Appendix 4, but the Wherwell Cartulary is the only item whose continuous ownership from 1539 is fairly certain, for it seems to have remained with the deeds of Wherwell manor until the 19th century. (A note at the start records that it was produced in court in 1762 during an action involving a member of the Iremonger family.)

Cartularies are of course in a different category from other books since each is individual to the monastery whose title deeds and charters have been copied into it. The Wherwell Cartulary (BL MS. Egerton 2104a) is the only one that survives from the Hampshire nunneries, although some early material and charters relating to Romsey Abbey and St. Mary's Abbey are included in the Edington Cartulary (BL MS. Lansdowne 442). The Wherwell manuscript contains copies of grants and a narrative history of the abbey down to 1261, as well as royal, papal and episcopal charters. Apart from some miscellaneous items there are 463 numbered entries and these are followed by another 32 charters concerning the income of the sacrist. As the cartulary dates from the late 14th century it seems likely that it may have been compiled in the wake of the criticisms made by Bishop Wykeham about discrepancies in the various records of the house, both books and rolls, concerning money due to the community. He ordered that one book or customal should be made which would then be the basis for assessing all future allocations for food, pittances and other doles – but two copies were to be made.[33]

All the original grants recorded in the Wherwell Cartulary, and many other later deeds, would have had the abbey's seal attached to them but not a single specimen is known to have survived. However, seals are extant from the other three nunneries. There are seals from the abbeys of Romsey and Winchester at both the P.R.O. and among the muniments of Winchester College. At the P.R.O. a 12th-century seal of Romsey Abbey shows an abbess (generally assumed to represent St. Elfleda) who holds a crosier in one hand and a book in the other. Abbess Mary of Winchester is also depicted with a crosier and a book on her

27. Seals of Romsey Abbey: (*left*) 12th-century seal showing St Elfleda (PRO. E326/11100) and (*right*) 15th-century impression from a matrix of *c*.1160 showing the annunciation (Winchester Coll. no. 16378.).

personal late 13th-century seal; in a surprisingly complex design she is shown standing between two figures under a canopy with the coronation of the Virgin above.[34]

At Winchester College there are four seals, or fragments of seals from St. Mary's Abbey and two from Romsey Abbey. (Among the muniments there is also a small 14th-century seal of a Romsey merchant, William Valentyn, on an agreement between him and Abbess Joan Icthe.) One of the Romsey seals is particularly interesting: it is preserved on a deed of 1458 but from a matrix of *c*.1160 and it shows the annunciation in a very rare form with the archangel airborne, while the Virgin, instead of the archangel, holds the scroll with 'Ave Maria' upon it. Two of the impressions from St. Mary's Abbey are from the same matrix which dates from the 1170s or 1180s although the deeds that are sealed are both mid-14th century. The one illustrated (no.1271) is less sharp but more complete than the other (no.1266) which lacks the Virgin's head. A later and larger seal (no.808a), which was probably from a mid-15th century matrix, survives on a deed of 1537; the shield that can be seen at the bottom right is England quartering France modern.[35]

The surviving seals from Wintney Priory are all at the Hampshire Record Office. Three documents among the Herriard Papers bear its seal; the earliest is on a deed of Prioress Lucy (c.1256-c.1263) which has a fragment of a seal attached that was from a different matrix from the others. The two later seals are almost complete and show the patron saint

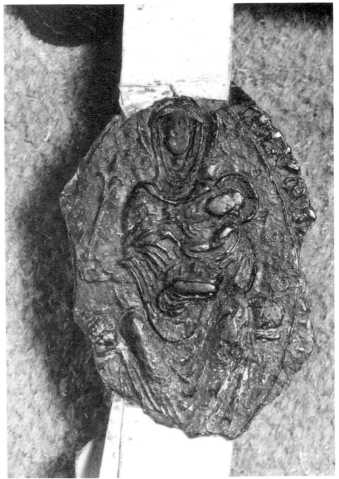

28a. (*above left*) Personal seal of Abbess Mary, abbess of Winchester *c*.1285-8, showing the coronation of the Virgin at the top (PRO. E42/481).

28b. (*above right*) St Mary's Abbey seal: a 14th-century impression from a matrix of *c*.1170, showing the Virgin and Child (Winchester Coll. no. 1271).

28c. (*left*) St Mary's Abbey seal: a 16th-century impression from a matrix of mid-15th-century date (Winchester Coll. no. 808a.).

of the priory, St. Mary Magdalen, standing under a canopy with a jar of ointment, which was her emblem. Both impressions were made from the same matrix within a week of one another in May 1337 but the one illustrated is much sharper than the other. A fourth fragment of a seal from the priory is attached to a deed of 1415 among the Kingsmill Papers.[36]

Food and Drink

Normally three mealtimes punctuated the monastic day. The first, whether or not it was actually called breakfast, was a light snack of bread and ale that was taken after prime. The nuns then had to wait for the main meal of the day until after none; during the winter horarium this would have been about two o'clock but it was probably rather earlier during the summer, so that they could have a siesta afterwards. (This was one of the results of the monastic day having evolved in a Mediterranean climate.) Another light meal was then taken between vespers and compline, but after that no eating or drinking was officially allowed, even in the abbess's chamber. Archbishop Pecham had to remind the abbesses of Romsey and Wherwell about that prohibition,[37] but later abbesses were equally guilty of ignoring it.

29. Seal of Wintney Priory c.1330, showing St Mary Magdalen with a pot of ointment (HRO. Herriard Collection. C83).

The basic foods eaten in England before the 16th century were bread (of varying degrees of coarseness), bacon, fowls, fish, eggs, cheese and milk. The diet of the better off also included different meats and game. The common vegetables were onions, leeks, parsnips and cabbage, while the seasonal fruits were apples, plums, and cherries. Fruit was sometimes eaten raw, but uncooked vegetables were mistrusted which was unfortunate since valuable vitamin C was lost. Potage was the universal dish and that came in various forms according to the availability of ingredients: basically any soupy, stewy concoction was called potage. A pot of it can be seen simmering away in one of the illustrations in the little psalter that belonged to Johanna Stretford of Wherwell. It was often served on thick brown bread trenchers which absorbed the gravy. White bread probably graced the table of the abbesses at times, but like white porray (made from white meat, ground rice and bacon or eel) it was only for the better off.

Besides an orchard, each nunnery would have had its own herb garden to grow the wide variety of herbs needed for medicines and used in cooking – often to disguise rather than enhance the flavours. Spices were equally popular for the same reason, and honey was the universal sweetener. Pepper and salt had to be bought in, but Romsey Abbey had its own salt pan at Totton in Eling, while the nuns at Winchester received one pound of pepper each year in rent from one of their tenants.[38] Drink, in the absence of tea, coffee or even safe drinking water, was restricted to wine, ale and cider.

The cellaress of each nunnery was responsible for organising the catering arrangements and supervising the servants actually doing the work, probably with some assistance from

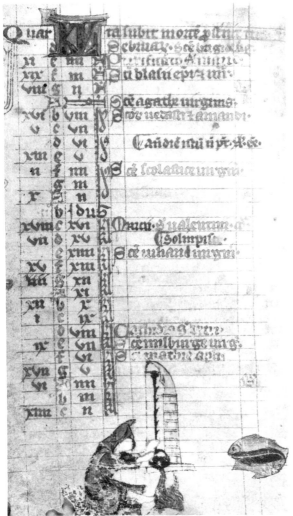

30. Tending the pot: the leaf for February from the 14th-century Psalter and Calendar which belonged to a nun at Wherwell Abbey. A hooded figure warms his feet and adjusts the black pot which hangs from a cotterell above the fire; two blue fish lie ready for cooking. BL Add. ms. 27866, f.6v.

the steward of the house. A few of the names of the later cellaresses in the Hampshire abbeys are known, but for a description of the work that the office involved one must turn to an account that was written by the cellaress of Barking Abbey for the benefit of her successors.[39] Like any good manager this lady started her 'charthe' with the sources of income available to her, notably from the abbey's manors which provided goods in kind from their demesne farms as well as rents. She mentioned the different 'rewards' that she paid to the servants responsible to her at Christmas, and then continued with many details about the food that she provided for the community. There are gaps in her account for some everyday items and there is little about fish or vegetables beyond the lenten dried peas and beans, but she had much to say about meat, grain, butter and eggs, provisions for Lent and 'pittances' which were small dishes of delicacies served in addition to the normal fare. Using this account of the unnamed cellaress as a guide, it is possible to add a few details about the actual catering in the nunneries in Hampshire.

By the time the cellaress was writing, meat was normally being eaten three times a week at Barking on Sunday, Tuesday and Thursday, except in Advent and Lent. It was usually beef. An exact amount, called a 'mess', was allocated to each nun and it was the responsibility of the cellaress to make sure that the fortnightly slaughtering of oxen would produce enough. If it did not, she had to buy extra in the market. This would not have been a problem in Romsey, and even less in Winchester which was an important centre for the marketing of livestock for slaughter. Mutton was not esteemed in the Middle Ages and little was eaten at Barking, but in that respect the diet in the Hampshire nunneries may have been different. The abbeys of Winchester and Romsey each owned manors in Wiltshire with large flocks of sheep, and some of the compotus rolls for St. Mary's manor of Froyle in north east Hampshire show that many sheep were sent down to Winchester for food, as well as calves for veal and pigs for the larder.[40] After the recent excavations at St. Mary's Abbey the animal bones that had been discovered were analysed and it was found that lamb, pork, beef and rabbit had all been eaten there, as well as venison from fallow and roe deer.[41]

The cellaress of Barking did not mention venison, but several royal gifts of it were made to the Hampshire abbesses, particularly by Henry III. His first gift was in 1237 when he ordered five bucks from the New Forest to be sent to Romsey for the feast following the installation of Abbess Isabella Neville, and two fallow deer were similarly sent to Wherwell when Abbess Constance was installed in 1259.[42] As two of his other gifts of venison were made in the year following the installation of a new abbess they may have been intended as a compliment to mark the occasion, even if they were received too late for the accompanying festivities. Thus in May 1266 three does from Chute forest were sent to Abbess Euphemia of Winchester eight months after her election, and one doe was sent from Clarendon forest in Wiltshire to Abbess Alice Walerand in 1269 after she had become abbess of Romsey.[43] (This was the only time that one of the abbesses was sent venison from beyond the county boundary but Clarendon, south east of Salisbury, was not so very far from Romsey.) There are no records of the king sending other deer to the nuns at Winchester or Romsey, but he made further gifts to the abbess of Wherwell. He broke his journey there in December 1256 when he was on his way to Winchester and afterwards ordered two fallow deer to be sent to Abbess Euphemia, while in 1267 he sent three does to a later abbess.[44] However, the most valuable gift came in the following century when Richard II ordered that two fat bucks and two winter does were to be sent to the abbess each year during the lifetime of Mary Bacon, who was a nun at Wherwell.[45] (At the time the royal secretary was John Bacon.)

Earlier nuns would (or should) have been shocked by the amount of meat eaten in the nunneries by the later Middle Ages. The Rule of St. Benedict forbade the religious to eat flesh-meat, and in the 13th century the authorities did their best to impose a meat-free diet on communities. But it was a losing battle. Poultry and pigeons were not included in the prohibition but the major loophole was the need to give extra nourishment to the sick. They were always allowed 'special food' as flesh-meat was called, provided the house could afford it, as Bishop Woodlock wrote to both St. Mary's, Winchester and Wintney Priory.[46]

The only fish that the cellaress of Barking mentions in her account were the supplies purchased for Advent and Lent. At Advent she laid in over 1,000 red herrings (which were smoked) and for Lent there were extensive supplies of both red and white (pickled) herrings – enough for four fish each day for every lady – as well as other salt fish, including salmon. The diet was made more palatable by the addition of almonds, figs and raisins, rice and mustard. Each nun received 2 lbs. of almonds and ½lb. of rice to last for the whole of Lent and 1 lb. of dried fruit each week, but the logistics of this system of rationing are not mentioned. The quantities of fish being brought directly from Southampton by the cellaress of St. Mary's Abbey can be traced for the year 1443-4 in the Southampton Brokage Book. This shows that she had ordered fresh hake for the week before Christmas, and two smaller loads of it were sent on 1 August.[47] The other seven cartloads of supplies were purchased either during Lent or in preparation for it. One load with red and white herrings, salt fish and onions was for the hospice of the abbey but four days later on 10 February, which was a fortnight before Shrove Tuesday, three cartloads left for the nunnery itself. Two were full of salt and there was more salt in the third, along with 3,000 red herrings and 2,000 white ones in barrels. Another cart with wine, onions and hake left for the abbey on the Sunday before Ash Wednesday, and more hake was sent on 23 March; that was followed by a cartload of oysters two days later for the feast of the Annunciation.[48]

Fish was also sent from Southampton to Romsey but the Brokage Book does not actually record that any of it was for the abbey there, so perhaps the cellaress bought her supplies from local fishmongers; but in 1527 there is one record of it being sent 'for my lady'.[49] At Wherwell the nuns were entitled to receive three herrings each on every Friday between Michaelmas and Christmas, but by the time of Bishop Wykeham's visitation they were being given three pence instead which they evidently regarded as a poor substitute. The bishop ordered the abbess to allocate them the actual herrings once again.[50] Sixty years later the Brokage Book recorded two loads of herrings leaving Southampton for Wherwell on 12 September 1444,[51] and in 1478 the abbess sent her own cart and servants to collect hake, herrings and fruit for her storeroom.[52]

The cellaress at St. Mary's Abbey would have had no trouble buying fish in the city. Winchester was a regional centre for marketing it so there were plenty of fishmongers, particularly in the 14th century; at one time there was one trading in the High Street just opposite the abbey.[53] When the fish bones from the abbey site were analysed it was found that they were from 20 different species; in addition to the common varieties there were some rare species such as sturgeon and porpoise that were only eaten by people of status.[54] (A porpoise was treated as a fish rather than a mammal in the Middle Ages in order to conform with fasting rules.)

Freshwater fish were usually kept in a stewpond so that they were easily caught and a good flavour, for rivers were sometimes polluted. There was one at St. Mary's Abbey,[55] and at Wintney the site of the stew can still be seen. Presumably the prioress also had riparian rights in the River Hart that flowed past the priory. The tributaries of the river Test would have been ideal for stews at Wherwell and Romsey, and both abbesses had fishing rights in the river, though poachers could be a problem. In 1435 two of them appeared before the manor court at Romsey charged with stopping the watercourse 'next Stretmede' with a dam and taking the abbess's fish there with pots and other instruments.[56]

The abbess of Romsey received fish each year from at least two of her tenants. Since the end of the 12th century she had been receiving honey and eels from the tenant of Testwood in Eling, and later he agreed to send her a salmon or its value as well, in substitution for the services of 13 men for one day a year. At the end of the 14th century 6½lbs. of honey, 300 eels (instead of the original 12 dishes of them) and a salmon were still being paid.[57] More fish came from the tenant of the abbey's property at Welles in Romsey whose rent included 2,000 herrings and 300 eels each year for his house, land, two water mills and fishery.[58] (At Barking eels baked with wheat and rice were a pittance served on Maundy Thursday.)

The cellaress wrote little about poultry, except for the geese that were eaten twice a year on the feast of the Assumption and on their Foundress's day, when each lady had half a goose (surely not eaten at one sitting?). Possibly the cellaress took it for granted that capons, chickens and pigeons would always be available from the demesne farm, as they undoubtedly were at Wherwell, Romsey and Wintney. The nuns at Winchester had no demesne farm and no dovecot was recorded there, but poultry could easily be purchased in the city and they received chickens and eggs from their manors, including Froyle.[59] Bones from 26 species of birds were found on the abbey site, including such exotic table delicacies as cranes and whooper swans.[60]

At Barking the cellaress normally had to provide 32 eggs each week for the priory and an extra eight when there were vigils, but only 16 in Advent and none during Lent when they were forbidden. She also had to provide each nun with her own 'ey silver' (eggs being 'eyren') so that they could purchase further supplies themselves; the amounts varied at different times of the year but was between 1¼d. and 1¾d. a week, with an extra ½d. at each vigil of the year when no meat was eaten. On Shrove Tuesday there was an allowance of 2d. each as a pittance for their pancakes which were called 'cripcis' and 'crumkakers'. It is not known whether the same system of egg money was operating in Hampshire by the 15th century but it seems likely that it may have been. Certainly the nuns at Wherwell were being given 2d. a week for their provisions after the church at Goodworth Clatford was appropriated to their house in 1453.[61]

Butter measured in 'cobets' was referred to by the cellaress, but she did not mention cheese although it was an important part of the staple diet of the time. At Wherwell the portion of the prebend included a cheese from the convent dairy on Trinity Sunday – and a pig at Martinmas.[62] Neither did the cellaress devote much space to bread and ale in spite of their importance, but they were not neglected in the injunctions of the 14th-century bishops. Bishop Woodlock wrote to three of the nunneries on the subject, starting with St. Mary's Abbey in 1309:

> Whereas necessities must be provided for the servants of God, we ordain and direct that suitable loaves of due weight, and like those traditionally made, also ale and potage, all well cooked, together with all other foodstuffs which they have been accustomed to receive as victuals shall be supplied to the nuns . . . [63]

He must have heard complaints at Romsey too, for he ordered that the convent bread there should be brought back to its former quality and quantity,[64] and similarly when he wrote to the prioress and nuns at Wintney Priory he mentioned the importance of their bread not being reduced in quality or their ale weakened, and that their customary pittances should be supplied.[65] A few years later Bishop Stratford wrote to the abbess of Winchester on the subject:

> . . . the daily portions that the nuns ought to receive for the kitchen must henceforth be given them faithfully at the end of each month, and suitable vegetables in season and good ale, not too weak, must be provided for them.[66]

He went on to stipulate that she was responsible for providing the cellaress with the necessary funds from the income of the house.

Bishop Wykeham charged the abbess and their officers to see

> . . . that you cause the nuns of the convent to be served with bread and drink and other food suitable and proper as respect for Religion demands and in accordance with the ancient laudable custom of your house and its means.[67]

He returned to the subject when sending additional injunctions to Wherwell Abbey where the catering seems to have been going through a bad phase, perhaps because of the incompetence of the cellaress or the laxity of the abbess. Meals were evidently being prepared in the chambers of the nuns instead of communally in the convent kitchen. The bishop insisted that the practice should stop, that brass vessels and other kitchen utensils should be purchased for the convent kitchen whenever they were needed and repaired at the common expense, and that the abbess should restore the distribution of certain pittances in both money and goods which the nuns had formerly received (including those Friday herrings).[68] As to the expense, repairs to the kitchen pots and the replacement of broken pottery cost Romsey Abbey £2 13s. 8d. in 1412-3, while the kitchen expenses as a whole (but not including the abbess's household) were £82 10s. 2d.; together the two sums were about one fifth of the abbey's total income that year.[69]

At Winchester and Wherwell there were separate baking and brewing houses which were allowed to remain after the Dissolution. although the convent kitchens were not. Romsey Abbey probably had similar facilities although only the kitchen in the outer court was recorded.[70] At Wintney Priory, where catering would have been on a much more modest scale, there was a brewing house but baking was apparently done in the kitchen; both places were 'in great decay' by the 16th century.[71] It is reasonable to assume that the quality of the bread and ale produced in the nunneries varied greatly over the years and that any deficiencies quickly became the subject of murmuring among the ladies. In many monastic houses by the 15th century there were complaints at visitations about the quality of the bread provided, especially if it was not made from wheat, and about ale that was thin and weak or even murky.[72] At the visitation of Romsey Abbey in 1492 three of the nuns complained about the quality of the beer, which may have been at least one of the reasons for the prioress's complaint that they frequented the taverns in the town without permission.[73] The convent's bread was apparently not mentioned on that occasion but nine years later there were complaints about the reduced amount of bread and cheese provided for the nuns, due to the much disliked steward.[74]

At Barking Abbey wine was served on special occasions such as Maundy Thursday when the abbess was served with a bottled wine and the rest of the community shared two gallons of an ordinary red wine; two days later on Easter Eve they had another gallon as well as three gallons of ale. In Hampshire the nunneries were well placed to receive supplies of French wine from Southampton for feast days and to serve their visitors. The cart leaving there in February 1444 with onions, hake and a pipe of wine (126 gallons) for St. Mary's Abbey would have been one of many with similar loads over the centuries.[75] In 1478 the abbess of Wherwell sent her servants down with her own cart to collect two pipes of wine for the abbey and another pipe for a neighbour. (The cart was evidently a strong one, for two months later they made the trip again to collect new millstones which would also have been imported from France.[76]) By 1527 the abbesses of Wherwell and Romsey were both using independent carters to collect their wine and other goods from Southampton; John Gardener and John Marchant (or Marshall) were the carters for Wherwell, and John Evesse was employed by the abbess of Romsey.[77]

In the 13th century Henry III made gifts of wine to the nuns of Romsey and Wherwell in the same way that he sent them venison. On two occasions the tun of wine (252 gallons) that he gave was to celebrate the veiling of a particular nun; at Romsey she was the niece of the anchorite of Westminster, and at Wherwell she was the former nurse of Prince Edward who had been admitted to the nunnery at the king's request.[78] His other gifts were made to the abbesses, presumably in return for hospitality; in 1272 he had a tun of wine sent to Abbess Alice Walerand of Romsey, and there had been four earlier gifts for the abbess of Wherwell.[79] The king kept his own small cellar at Wherwell Abbey and regularly sent orders to the bailiffs of Southampton to despatch a couple of tuns of wine there, particularly during the 1240s and 1250s,[80] and on two occasions the wine he was giving the abbess was from that cellar. Apparently he never sent any wine to the abbess of Winchester since he would have stayed at the castle when he was in the city and was therefore not under any obligation to her. It is not surprising that he did not send any to little Wintney Priory, but in the spring of 1265 when Eleanor de Montfort was in residence at Odiham Castle she made five small gifts of wine to the prioress of Wintney after entertaining her at the castle.[81]

It is a matter for conjecture whether the nuns ever drank their own wine. It was produced at some English monasteries, so maybe the summers were sometimes hot enough to ripen the grapes that grew on the vine over the inner gate at Wintney Priory, or in the vineyards that Abbess Euphemia planted at Wherwell.[82]

Originally the monastic ideal of the Rule had been that all meals should be cooked in a common kitchen and eaten in the refectory, but gradually this simplicity was modified. Inevitably the sick needed their food served in or near the infirmary, including their permitted portions of meat. In the 13th century this led to some nuns taking advantage of meat being available there, so at Romsey those who were in good health were ordered only to eat in the refectory or in the abbess's chamber.[83] In 1316 one of Bishop Woodlock's injunctions to Wintney Priory had directed

> . . . that you eat more often in common and in greater number in your refectory that you have done heretofore, that is to say, one assembly for all at least once a day; and that the dames who are directed or enjoined by the prioress or the keeper of order to eat in the refectory are to go there without objecting . . . [84]

In accordance with the Rule meat was never served in the refectory proper but from the

14th century onwards, as it came to be eaten by everyone in practice, the refectory was sometimes divided into two storeys, the upper part being the frater and the lower part the *misericord* where meat was served.[85] It is not clear whether this happened in any of the Hampshire abbeys, but at the end of that century Bishop Wykeham repeated the prohibition about meat eating in the refectory, and he also ordered that at least two thirds of the nuns were to eat there together every day.[86] One imagines them in a room similar to the present parish church of Beaulieu which used to be the refectory of the abbey there. At Wintney Priory the refectory would have been on a far more modest scale. When Alice Preston, who had been in charge of it, died in 1420 someone made an inventory of the goods relating to her office and copied it into the calendar of the house. It is a modest list:

> ii worn tapestry hangings from the wall at the back of the high table
> ii choice seat cushions
> xv table napkins
> iiii tablecloths of Paris work
> ii linen tablecloths
> x hand towels
> a worn basin with the lavatory
> i pewter salt cellar
> ii laten candlesticks and i of pewter[87]

At the beginning of the 16th century the nuns at Winchester were still having their meals served to them in the frater, except for one very elderly nun, but at Romsey they no longer did so. It is one more example of the laxity of life there. In 1492 one of the nuns complained that none of them served in the refectory on the days when they should, though at least that showed that it was still in use then. Nine years later the abbess herself told the visitor that the nuns did not take their meals in the frater but in certain rooms that she had assigned to them.[88] This breakdown into separate households had happened in some other English nunneries and was the practice that Bishop Wykeham wanted eradicated at Wherwell for all nuns except the abbess herself.

The custom of the head of the larger monastic houses having a separate chamber became widely accepted during the 12th century. By the end of the 14th century, as society became more civilised, there was an increasing wish for comfort and privacy so that in most large monasteries that one chamber extended first into a suite of rooms, and later into a separate establishment with a large hall, parlour, chapel and bedchamber as well as domestic offices.[89] Each of the three Hampshire abbesses had her own 'lodging' as it was called. They were run independently with their own staff and accounts for which the cellaress of the house was not responsible. The abbess dined there with her own household and guests, except at the great festivals when she joined the rest of the community. Food was normally prepared in her own kitchen, and there were no prohibitions about flesh-meat which she or any other nun who was invited to her table could eat other than in Advent or Lent – though Bishop Langton gave Abbess Johanna Legh permission to eat meat in Advent.[90] When Archbishop Pecham had visited Romsey and Wherwell in 1284 he had not criticised the arrangement for normal times but in view of an impending famine he ordered the abbess of Romsey, who had been accused of extravagance, to dine in the refectory so that everyone could see that the food available was being shared fairly.[91] Abbess Elena de Percy of Wherwell was reminded rather sharply that an abbess

> . . . acts cruelly and sacrilegiously whenever, at a time when the convent is suffering want and lacks necessities in bread, drink or pittance to which the house is accustomed, she quite shamelessly has sumptuous meals prepared for her in her own chamber.[92]

The archbishop stipulated that she should eat with her community and not even allow her guests to have a table set for them in her chamber; instead they were to have their meals in the outer hall of the convent.

At least the archbishop assumed that meals of some sort would be served in the refectories, even when food was in short supply, but some time later Archbishop Reynolds was concerned to hear that the nuns at Wintney had actually been leaving their priory because of the lack of food. He attributed this to negligence and poor administration in the house. He may have been partly correct but, in fairness to those in charge at the time, his correspondence on the subject was in 1316 when the whole country was in the grip of a three-year famine.[93]

Chapter Seven

Diversions from Routine

In his Rule, St. Benedict acknowledged the need for variety in the lives of the religious and wrote of the balance needed between time spent in prayer, in manual work and in reading. By the Middle Ages this balance had been lost in the nunneries. There was little manual work for the nuns because domestic chores, both inside and out, were generally done by servants, as they would have been in the households from which the ladies were drawn, though perhaps some of the younger sisters at Wherwell and Wintney may have helped a little at haymaking or harvest time if there was a shortage of cottagers to help the regular farm servants. (If so one hopes that none of them invited as much gossip as the sub-prioress of Gracedieu Priory who went haymaking on her own with the chaplain of the house.[1]) Some of the nuns would have read a little, but it has already been mentioned that there is no evidence of nuns copying manuscripts. Work with their hands was therefore confined to the distaff skills of spinning and needlework. Other diversions in their lives, however simple and innocent, tended to be criticised by the bishops who sometimes seemed to lack an understanding of the human need for variety.

Needlework and Clothes

Nuns in Anglo-Saxon times had been famous for their needlework. It is likely that the surviving stole, maniple and girdle that were embroidered for Bishop Frithestan of Winchester early in the tenth century were made by Hampshire nuns, probably at Winchester. They were later given by Athelstan to the shrine of St. Cuthbert at Durham.[2] The fingers of the nuns must have worked many other fine vestments and church hangings in later centuries but there is little evidence that one can cite to prove it. Needlework is not signed like a document, and normally it cannot be expected to last for several centuries anyway.

During the 13th century the skill of English embroiderers became renowned, and by the end of the century *opus anglicanum* was being prized and presented throughout Europe. During this period the household roll of Eleanor de Montfort shows that she paid the nuns of Wintney Priory 10s. in 1265 for making a cope for her chaplain, Brother J. Angeli, for Easter,[3] but this is the only known instance of local nuns being paid for their needlework. A little earlier vestments were among the many gifts that Abbess Euphemia gave to her community at Wherwell but one cannot be certain that they were made by the nuns there.[4] In the following century John de Inkepenne made bequests of cloth to St. Mary's Abbey, obviously intending that they should be made up for liturgical use: there were pieces of red and gold cloth for use in the Holy Trinity Chapel and another piece of green and gold cloth that was left to the sacrist of the abbey.[5]

In time, many of the larger pieces of embroidery were produced in commercial workshops. Two such pieces are associated with Romsey Abbey: a powdered panel of which only a fragment survives, and a pall that can still be seen displayed in the church today. It has been made from at least one but probably two identical green velvet copes that were embroidered in England in the late 15th century. It is easy to see their original curves and to pick out the 'stars of six points, wavy, worked in gold' and the embroidered borders of 'tawny coloured velvet, exquisitely stellated and adorned' which were described by Charles Spence in 1862. Another antiquarian had also seen the pall by 1860 and both writers mention that it was kept in the vestry then, so presumably it was sometimes still used at

31. The maniple and stole of St Cuthbert, early 10th century. The embroidered figures show (*left*) Peter the Deacon and (*right*) the Prophet Jonas.

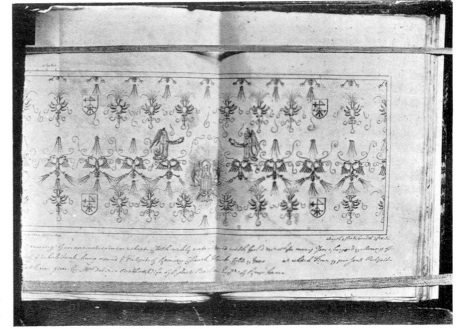

32. Powdered panel that belonged to Romsey Abbey, early 16th century, as drawn by Dr. Latham in 1805. BL Add. ms. 26, 777, ff.132-3.

funerals. By Liveing's time it was on display in its present position.[6] However, this fascinating relic was not mentioned by Dr. Latham at all and this fact alone makes it almost certain that it was not given to the abbey until after he had ceased to add to his notes (he died in 1837, aged 96).

The early 16th-century powdered panel which Dr. Latham drew in 1805 was probably an altar cloth or dossal originally, but the doctor described it and its use as

> . . . an ancient crimson velvet cloth richly embroidered with gold and which for many years, beyond ye Memory of any of ye inhabitants, hung round ye pulpit of Romsey church . . . Length 9ft. 10in. breadth 3ft. 8in.[7]

His drawing shows four identical shields in the embroidery and one of them is actually pasted into the fourth volume of his notebooks where the faint sparkle of metal threads can still be seen under a magnifying glass. As identical shields were incorporated into a carved decoration above the fireplace of an old house in Romsey, they were presumably the merchant marks of the man who owned the house and who gave the powdered panel to the abbey.[8] Neither his identity nor that of the embroideress is known but, because of the similarity of the work to surviving panels elsewhere, it is thought more likely that it was made in a London workshop than by the nuns.

Embroidery at its best is both a skill and an art. It is unlikely perhaps that even a majority of nuns ever had that skill, and of those that did how many were able to continue with it as their eyesight began to decline in middle age? But sewing can be on a more simple level. The writer of the medieval *Ancren Riwle* provides a glimpse of both the type of sewing that a woman religious should do and should avoid doing:

> I am always the more gratified, the coarser the works are that ye do. Make no purses, to gain friends therewith, nor bloodbends of silk; but shape and sew and mend church vestments, and poor people's clothes.[9]

Spinning was easier for both the fingers and the eyes, and that was a skill that most women in the Middle Ages possessed. Aubrey quotes an old man in Dorset who remembered seeing the nuns of Kington St. Michael '. . . come forth into the nymph-hay with their rocks and wheels to spin',[10] and no doubt some of the Hampshire nuns did the same.

It is not known whether any of the spun wool was used by the nuns for knitting, or whether any of them had a hand in making their own clothes, but the subject of their dress is of interest. Originally it had been the duty of the chambress of a nunnery to buy any material needed for clothes, and she was then responsible for having it made up and the garments distributed to the nuns. This rather impersonal approach soon broke down and by the 13th century it was becoming customary (however inconsistent with the Rule) for monks and nuns to be paid an annual allowance, called a *peculium*, to buy their own clothes and personal necessaries. Since the money came from the common fund, the system was not criticised by the bishops; indeed at some convents the head of the house would be reprimanded if the *peculium* was not being paid.[11] It seems likely, however, that novices joining a community would normally bring suitable cloth or clothing with them; certainly a young novice joining Barking Abbey in 1244 was given five marks from the Exchequer to buy cloth for going there.[12] By that time the nuns at Wherwell were receiving a *peculium* and the amount allowed to each lady was increased by 12d. each year by Abbess Euphemia,[13] but unfortunately the basic amount is not known. At Romsey the accounts of 1412 do not record the amount of individual payments but the total amount paid for clothing expenses was £23 7s. 8d.[14] so each lady probably received the best part of £1.

It is not clear whether or not the *peculium* system was used at Wintney Priory. Under an early charter made by one of the benefactors of the house, Maud de Heriard, the community received 20s. a year in rents for the purchase of good clothing.[15] In 1216 Bishop Woodlock mentioned the 'good custom' relating to clothing amongst those practices that should be maintained, but without saying what it was.[16] A century later one of the many criticisms of Prioress Alice Fyshide was that for several years she had not provided the nuns there (other than her two favourites) with necessary clothing,[17] so perhaps the precarious finances of the priory were not sufficient for personal allowances even in theory.

In the three Benedictine abbeys the nuns wore the correct black habits of their order, like the abbess shown in the 16th-century panel picture in Romsey Abbey. It is not known whether the Wintney nuns wore white habits like the Cistercian monks, though they were certainly worn in some nunneries; the priory is not mentioned in an early record which listed seven houses of white nuns, *moniales albae*, including Amesbury Abbey, though that was not a Cistercian house.[18] The writer of *Ancren Riwle* made a few sensible suggestions about clothes: they were to be plain, warm and well made and as many as were needed both for the day and night; underclothes were to be made of coarse canvas rather than linen and shoes were to be thick and warm, though they could be discarded in summer when 'hose without vamps' could be worn. And in case any lady had considered it, no iron, haircloth or hedgehog skins were to be worn, though later the writer seems to contradict himself when he wrote 'A woman may well enough wear drawers of haircloth very well tied, with strapples reaching down to her feet, laced tightly'.[19]

In the 13th century Archbishop Pecham had been critical of the flowing, pleated habits of fine cloth that were being worn by the nuns at Godstow Abbey in Oxfordshire,[20] but there is no record of him mentioning the subject when he visited the abbeys at Romsey and Wherwell. However, in the next century two bishops of Winchester were brave enough to criticise the clothing of the nuns in their diocese. The first was Bishop Woodlock, but he was careful to start off his seventh injunction to St. Mary's Abbey, Winchester by saying that he was merely following the instructions of the archbishop (Robert Winchelsey) in decreeing:

> . . . that in future no nun shall use silken veils of purple or any other colour than black, purses or girdles of silk, laced shoes, or coloured hangings round her bed . . . If any nun who has been rebuked for any of the aforesaid matters does not mend her ways . . . let her purple veil, laced shoes, silken girdles or purses, or coloured curtain be taken away from her by the abbess . . . and let her be provided with another veil and other shoes, girdle, purses and curtain appropriate to the Order.[21]

At the end of the century Bishop Wykeham wrote to the three abbesses:

> . . . we forbid you . . . to wear in public veils or robes of silk, pins of gold or silver, or silken belts ornamented with gold or silver; and only a consecrated nun may wear a ring and must be content with one ring only.[22]

Poor ladies! In an age when people loved colour and ornament it must have been hard to have their small vanities criticised. But their silk veils and girdles probably reappeared before long. A Winchester nun was bequeathed a girdle with its buckle, pendant and six studs of silver, and it is unlikely that she never wore it.[23] Two other nuns inherited warm wraps: Anneys Boneville of Wherwell Abbey was left her brother's best coat with fur, and one of the priests at Romsey bequeathed Agnes Harvey his red mantle and a tapestry coverlet.[24]

Although most of the nuns can be expected to have kept an observant eye on the clothes being worn by their visitors, fashion can only have made occasional slight inroads into their own dress. But some women have the knack of wearing anything with style. As Chaucer described his prioress:

> Her veil was gathered in a seemly way . . .
> Her cloak, I noticed, had a graceful charm.[25]

When Bishop Fox's chancellor visited Romsey in 1523 he evidently found the nuns wearing

33. Abbess Avelina Cowdrey, abbess of Wherwell 1518-29. The church (*top left*) is that of Wherwell Abbey, showing the spire of commanding height that was built by Abbess Euphemia in the mid-13th century.

their veils in rather too seemly a manner and directed that in future their foreheads must be covered to the middle with their veils.[26] Perhaps some of them had been wearing fashionable supports for their veils, like Abbess Avelina Cowdrey of Wherwell whose portrait was painted around that time.

Pets and Processions

If their choice of clothes offered little light relief to the nuns, their pets certainly did so. Their presence in most nunneries was criticised from time to time by different bishops, whose strictures helped to control the numbers, but they were too important to many of the nuns to be banished altogether. The author of *Ancren Riwle* had written gently that 'Ye shall not possess any beast, my dear sisters, except only a cat'[27] (puss being too useful a member of a community to be barred). But that official teaching was regularly ignored by many of the sisters who lavished their frustrated maternal love on a variety of small pets. Again, one turns for the best picture to Chaucer's description of Madam Eglantyne:

> As for her sympathies and tender feelings,
> She was so charitably solicitous
> She used to weep if she but saw a mouse
> Caught in a trap, if it were dead or bleeding.
> And she had little dogs she would be feeding
> With roasted flesh, or milk, or fine white bread.
> Sorely she wept if one of them were dead
> Or someone took a stick and made it smart.[28]

At Romsey in the 13th century Abbess Walerand evidently kept pet monkeys as well as a number of dogs in her own chamber. She was forbidden to continue keeping the monkeys by Archbishop Pecham but he seems to have allowed her to retain one well behaved little dog.[29] A century later Bishop Wykeham was understandably critical when he found that several nuns at Romsey Abbey were bringing birds, rabbits, dogs and other pets into church with them, and thus distracting the attention of both themselves and others during the services. He forbade the practice, though he does not seem to have actually forbidden them being kept. Later he returned to the subject of dogs, particularly hunting dogs which were roaming round the buildings, fouling both church and cloister and costing money to feed which should have been spent on alms for the poor. They were forbidden absolutely.[30] Hunting dogs belonging to the abbesses of Winchester and Romsey had been recorded earlier[31] but there is nothing to indicate that the nuns themselves went out with them, though some medieval ladies did enjoy both hawking and hunting. Sport in the nunneries is more likely to have been confined to simple ball games, as in a contemporary illustration that shows nuns joining in an early form of rounders or cricket.[32]

Although there are no references to pets in the other Hampshire nunneries it would be incorrect to imagine life there without them. At St. Mary's Abbey among the bones which were found during the recent excavations, there were those of a skylark which may have been kept as a cage bird. Then, innumerable little dogs must have scampered through the cloisters and gardens at times, whether they belonged to the nuns or their visitors, and many a cat stalked around before seeking the warmth of the nearest fire. In the barnyards where the hens scratched there would have been the delight each spring of newly hatched chicks, while on the streams going through their grounds individual ducks would have been known by sight and the annual appearance of their broods of ducklings excitedly welcomed.

Formal entertainments within the nunneries were probably rare, but the nuns would often have heard strolling minstrels. In 1441 the boy choristers from St. Swithun's Priory and St. Elizabeth's College dressed up as girls and sang and acted before the abbess and nuns of Winchester in their public refectory on Holy Innocents' Day, three days after

fiert lacianor que lefcu li fair fendre
e plus hardi des lor z fi eftoit le mendre
n les ert othelene el champ le fift eftendre
i la mort abatu lame li eftuet rendre
A fes vaches garder ne porra mes entendre

34. Nuns at play, *c.*1340: a marginal illumination from the *Romance of Alexander.*
Bodleian ms. 264, f.22.

Christmas.[33] Early in the 14th century the young nuns there were accustomed to celebrate
all three days after Christmas in a light-hearted way. Bishop Stratford referred to their
celebrations as feasts and solemnities, but evidently he did not consider them solemn
enough:

> The feasts and solemnities hitherto kept among the young nuns on the days of St. Stephen, St.
> John and Holy Innocents are to cease, being more productive of vainglory and excess than those on
> other days; the verses and trifles uttered after the blessings at each reading on the said feasts and on
> any others are henceforth forbidden.[34]

Attendance at religious ceremonies outside the nunnery precincts can hardly be called a
diversion, but sometimes the funeral of a benefactor would have made a break in the normal
routine. Then there were processions which were such a feature of medieval life. In October
1321 for instance, during Edward II's troubled reign, Bishop Rigaud de Asserio ordered the
prior and monks of St. Swithun's to assemble in the cathedral with the abbot and monks of
Hyde Abbey and the abbess and nuns of St. Mary's Abbey and then process through the
city with all the other religious and clergy of Winchester, publicly praying for peace in the
kingdom and encouraging others to do likewise.[35]

There were undoubtedly many other occasions when the Winchester nuns joined in such
processions, though since Cardinal Ottobon's Constitutions of 1268 the practice of nuns
processing beyond their own boundaries had been officially frowned upon. As Bishop
Wykeham cited that prohibition in his injunctions of 1387[36] perhaps the nuns did not
publicly join in the prayers and processions for peace that he himself ordered several times
in the diocese during the Hundred Years' War.

Within the nunnery precincts processions were a feature of any important service, such as the installation of a new abbess, the veiling of new nuns and the great festival services. At Romsey on Palm Sunday it was customary for the abbess and nuns to process together with the vicar and chaplains after the sacrist (one of the nuns) had blessed the palms before the High Altar, but in 1372 there was a dispute between the abbess and clergy. Apparently the vicar and chaplains had objected to the part played by the sacrist. The sight of a woman pronouncing a blessing, even on greenery, was perhaps too much for them. Unfortunately only the temporary inhibition that was laid on the clergy while the matter was investigated was recorded, and not the final outcome of the action brought against them by the abbess.[37]

Visitors and Visiting

Probably the greatest diversion for the nuns, as for most ladies down the ages, was receiving visitors and paying visits. The bishops tried to cut down the number of visitors to the nunneries and the amount of disturbance that many of them undoubtedly caused, but it was a losing battle. The idea that nunneries, like all monasteries, had a positive duty to provide hospitality was too ingrained in the medieval mind. Founders and benefactors of a house, such as Wintney Abbey's Colrith family, had a natural claim on the hospitality of a house, and there were times when both bishops and monarchs were as glad as any other travellers of the shelter provided by the nunneries.

When Winchester was still an important royal centre the king often made use of the abbey guest houses at Wherwell and Romsey. King John stayed at Romsey in 1200 when he was travelling from Portsmouth to Winchester, and he was there twice early in 1210. His only visit to Wherwell was in June 1205, after leaving the nuns at Wilton Abbey and before going on to Ludgershall.[38] Henry III stayed many times at both houses during his long reign, and some of the gifts of wine and venison that he subsequently made to their abbesses have already been discussed. He also repaid their hospitality with gifts of timber for building work that they had in hand. Edward I visited three Hampshire monasteries in the last week of January 1275; he was at Beaulieu on Sunday 27th, then at Romsey for the Monday and Tuesday before travelling on to Wherwell for one day. He continued his journey to Windsor Castle via Overton, Caversham and Reading.[39] Few later monarchs stayed at the nunneries. Edward III was at Wherwell in 1331, and one assumes that when Henry IV was in Romsey in 1409 he stayed at the abbey, but it is less likely that Henry VIII planned to do so in 1535 when he intended travelling to Salisbury via Romsey.[40]

Bishops and their representatives stayed in the guest houses of the nuns at Romsey, Wherwell and Wintney both when holding visitations and in the course of other journeys, and occasionally they sought their hospitality on behalf of other people. In 1244, when Henry III was disputing the election of William de Ralegh to the bishopric of Winchester, he sent a mandate to the abbess of St. Mary's Abbey asking her to treat two of his supporters, Joan de Bidon and Margery de Tornay, with honour.[41] And in the next century, during the Hundred Years' War, Bishop Wykeham wrote to the abbesses of both Romsey and Wherwell asking them to offer their hospitality to Dame Elizabeth de Berkele while her husband was absent on service.[42] (Presumably her husband was with her kinsman, the Earl of Pembroke, who was then making an unsuccessful bid to relieve La Rochelle.) Earlier in the war the Wherwell nuns nearly had a different type of visitor thrust upon their lands: many of the king's great horses were about to be stabled at Wherwell, but at the last minute it was learned that the French had plans to invade so orders were given for the horses to be taken out of Hampshire and far from the sea.[43] There was no mention of the nuns being moved!

All monasteries provided guest houses for their visitors and met the cost of their upkeep. The expenses involved would have been a regular feature of all the nunneries' annual accounts. In the Romsey Abbey account roll for 1412-3 'spices for the guest house' were included with liveries for the abbess's household and together came to £18 14s. 4d., while the cost of wine for guests visiting the abbess was £6 13s. 4d.[44] Food provided in the guest house that year was not costed, but the expense is unlikely to have been negligible. The donations of short term visitors and the more regular contributions of longer staying boarders presumably helped to offset the cost of providing hospitality, but it could be a financial burden. Unless one detects special pleading, the nuns at Winchester were evidently finding it so in 1468 when they complained to the king that they were so overburdened with the expenses of building repairs and the payment of tenths that they were unable to fulfill the obligations of their Order as to hospitality.[45] (Their plea did not fall on deaf ears.)

However, the presence of visitors living in their guest house, dining with the abbess and walking in their grounds surely provided the nuns with many a pleasant topic of conversation, but the church itself was concerned about their disruptive influence. From the end of the 13th century various regulations about visitors were evolved, though their very repetition in successive injunctions suggests that they were frequently ignored. One of the aims was to prevent male visitors from sleeping in the nunneries, so one finds Archbishop Pecham forbidding any man to enter the precincts of the cloister at Wherwell after sunset.[46] Later the nuns there apparently thought that this did not apply to friars, although their reputation was dubious by then, so Bishop Wykeham sent them a mandate on the subject in 1368:

> Lately it has come to our ears by popular report of trusty men, that contrary to the honesty of religion you admit various religious men, especially of the mendicant orders, lightly and promi-scuously to pass the night in your habitations, from which grows much matter for laxity and scandal, since the cohabitation of religious clerks and nuns is altogether forbidden by the constitution of the holy fathers.[47]

The bishops also aimed to keep visitors of either sex out of some parts of the nunneries at all times. In this they were following Ottobon's Constitutions and the papal Bull *Periculoso* that put the dorter, frater, infirmary, chapter house and cloister out of bounds to all but nuns, though a confessor, doctor or near relative would be allowed in a nun's chamber in the event of illness. When he was writing to Romsey Abbey on this subject Archbishop Pecham ordered four nuns to be appointed as scrutineers '. . . who shall expel from the cloister as suspect all persons . . . wishing to stare at the nuns or to chatter with them.[48] But one wonders just how long that arrangement lasted. Similar injunctions that aimed to keep secular visitors out of the cloisters were given by Bishop Pontissara to Wherwell, by Bishop Stratford to St. Mary's, Winchester and by Bishop Wykeham to Romsey Abbey.'[49]

Then there were the regulations about nuns talking to their visitors. Officially permission had to be obtained from the head of the house before a nun could have a conversation with any visitor, particularly a man. Such meetings were meant to be held in a public place, such as the parlour or the abbess's hall or (at Romsey) the side of the church next to the cloister, and in the presence of one or two other nuns.[50] But these rules can only have applied to conversations with short term visitors and not to long term guests such as the female boarders and corrodians.

All nunneries took in lady boarders and corrodians from time to time. The corrodians paid a lump sum and were then entitled to the hospitality of the convent for life, while the boarders paid for services rendered in the normal way. The bishops seem to have had an ambivalent attitude to boarders. Archbishop Pecham and Bishop Edington wrote that they could stay at a nunnery with episcopal permission,[51] but some bishops attempted to get rid of secular visitors altogether. They did not succeed because the nunneries welcomed the extra income and their guests were glad of their safe and relatively inexpensive hospitality. The only record of permission being given for a boarder at one of the nunneries was in 1367 when Bishop Wykeham granted the prioress of Wintney a licence to receive Beatrice Paynell as a paying guest for several months; she was the sister of Sir John Foxley of Bramshill nearby.[52]

Permanent guests, such as widows ending their days, were probably little trouble. The difficulties usually arose over ladies who just needed a temporary refuge, for they could be gossipy nuisances. One such lady may have outstayed her welcome at Wintney in 1308, and three years later Bishop Woodlock tried to get rid of secular ladies, both married and single, from Romsey Abbey because they were disturbing the tranquillity there and causing scandals.[53] At St. Mary's Abbey, Winchester, Bishop Stratford found the convent 'more than usually burdened with unprofitable and harmful persons' when he visited it in 1326 and ordered them to be sent away and never re-admitted.[54] But it is only too likely that Abbess Matilda discovered several exceptions to this ruling. In 1364 the heads of all four nunneries received a copy of the same letter from Bishop Edington ordering them to remove all boarders lodging in their houses.[55]

An example of the type of scandal that Bishop Woodlock may have had in mind occurred at Romsey in 1375. One of the boarders staying at the abbey then was Joan, widow of Peter de Brugge. One night she was 'ravished and abducted' by a party of a dozen or so men who broke into the buildings and removed her, together with all her jewellery, clothes and furs. To make matters worse, her chaplain was also involved in the plot, but as he and all the perpetrators were pardoned in the course of the next seven years one wonders if the lady herself had been been not unwilling?[56] But one can imagine how the whole incident and the subsequent enquiries would indeed have disturbed the tranquillity of the house.

Children, both girls and young boys, were received as boarders at most nunneries from time to time. They are seldom mentioned in records but there are references to children at each of the Hampshire houses. At Romsey Bishop Woodlock said that boys and girls were not to share the same dormitory as the nuns or be led into the choir for the celebration of mass, and at Wintney he forbade secular children eating in the refectory with the nuns.[57] Presumably he thus drew a distinction between children sent there for a short stay and girls who were intended for a religious life. At Wherwell Abbey Archbishop Pecham had earlier ordered that no boys were to be educated with the nuns.[58]

It is impossible to know the extent to which children were sent to the nuns for simple education as well as safe keeping. In 1501 one of the Romsey nuns, Alice Whytingstale, was described as 'mistress of the school' but this seems to be the only mention of a school there.[59] At that time there do not seem to have been any schoolchildren at Wherwell, where the abbey was in a village rather than a town, but the school at St. Mary's Abbey, Winchester is well documented. At the visitation of 1501 one nun, Agnes Cox, was called the Senior Teacher and she presumably taught the children since another nun was referred to as the Mistress of Novices.[60] More is known about the school in the 1530s. In 1536 the 26 girls there were recorded, all of them from well-to-do families, and at the head of the list was Bridget Plantagenet who was the youngest daughter of Lord Lisle. She had been placed at St. Mary's Abbey, and her step-brother at Hyde Abbey, during part of the period when her father was at Calais. Three of the letters that Abbess Elizabeth Shelley wrote to Lady Lisle have survived; they are mainly concerned with clothes for her pupil that were either needed, had arrived or, in the case of an ermine 'cappe', had failed to arrive. In one an account of money both due and received is set out in a chatty fashion that does not disguise the fact that the abbess knew exactly how much was owed to the abbey, while in the last she writes of a visit that Bridget had made to friends from which she had apparently not returned.[61]

As well as receiving visitors of all descriptions, the nuns themselves also went visiting. It was accepted that they could pay short visits to their family home from time to time, accompanied by a servant, but though their family connections were maintained they were not supposed to stand as godmother to any new arrivals.[62] Archbishop Pecham wrote a general letter to the nunneries in his province stipulating that nuns were not to linger for more than two days, even at the house of their parents or kinsfolk, but when writing to the abbess of Romsey he extended this to three days, adding that the sisters were only to go out in staid company.[63]

None of the Hampshire nuns is known to have joined in pilgrimages, those favourite medieval outings, and few are likely to have done so. Episcopal permission would have been needed for such a jaunt, but in 1195 the Council of York had forbidden nuns to go on pilgrimage 'in order that the opportunity of wandering about may be taken from them'.[64] The bishops remained discouraging, and in view of the primitive sleeping conditions along the way and the bawdiness of some of the likely company their attitude is not surprising. Chaucer does not tell us how Madam Eglantyne managed to obtain permission from her diocesan. Perhaps she asked afterwards.

There was always the possibility of short visits to nearby towns. The nuns from Wintney Priory would all have known Odiham, and would have passed through it on their way to visit Eleanor de Montfort at Odiham Castle in 1265,[65] while in the other direction Farnham was only about eight miles away. Andover was the nearest market town for the Wherwell nuns (perhaps the material for their cartulary came from the parchment makers there) and the abbesses of Romsey and Wherwell must often have journeyed to Winchester where they each had their own house. However, town visits for the nuns of Wherwell and Wintney involved planning and travel, but their sisters at Romsey and Winchester only needed to walk through their gateways to be into town or city with all their bustle, life and temptations. Both Bishops Pontissara and Woodlock found it necessary to forbid the nuns of Romsey to eat, drink or spend the night in the town,[66] but it was so easy of access that the problem inevitably remained. At the visitation of the abbey in 1492 Abbess Elizabeth Brooke admitted to the archbishop's vicar-general that her nuns were suspected of going into town by the church door, and feebly asked him to forbid them frequenting taverns or going outside the nunnery without her licence. The authority of her office was certainly at a low ebb. And the prioress stated firmly that the nuns did indeed frequent taverns and went into the town continually without leave.[67]

In his injunctions of 1326 Bishop Stratford tried to give some guidelines about outside visiting to the nuns of St. Mary's, Winchester. They were only to go into the city or up St. Catherine's Mount if they had permission from the abbess and were accompanied by a mature, respectable and discreet nun; and they were not to dally there with any suspect person, whether priest or layman. Neither were they to go to St. Swithun's Priory or the other houses of male religious, except in solemn processions, or dine there unless they were accompanying the abbess or prioress, or visit their workshops unless on business and in the company of another nun.[68] And for visits further afield,

> When it happens that nuns sojourn outside the dormitory or refectory, let it be only with a decent escort (except in case of sickness) and if they need the services of a secular woman, let them be content with one servant of good life and honest behaviour.[69]

It is clear from later entries in Bishop Stratford's register that these quite reasonable orders fell on some deaf ears within the abbey, including those of the abbess. The scandal that resulted will be mentioned in the next chapter. But over the years there were not many scandals. More happily one can reasonably imagine many a young nun riding down leafy lanes on a summer's day, with full permission and properly accompanied, for a few days' holiday in her childhood home. There she would be greeted by those she loved, feasted in the hall and told all the latest family news before going out to see the garden, the orchard and any new building. And a few days later she would settle back into the ordered life of the cloister, her mind full of new pictures of those for whom she prayed.

Chapter Eight

In Sickness and in Health

Longevity, sickness and plague

It is an impossible task to try to throw much light on the health of women who lived five or more centuries ago. However, one of the few indicators of reasonable health is longevity, but even that is difficult to assess in the days before parish registers were kept. In one respect nuns were more likely than married women to reach old age since they were not exposed to the dangers of pregnancy.

Before the 16th century the age of a nun was rarely mentioned, so one can only look for actual evidence of reasonably long lives among the abbesses. The length of their terms of office can be calculated from the records of their elections and deaths, and to get some idea of their ages a minimum figure of 25 years must be added, though most ladies were probably older than that when they were elected. From the figures available, four abbesses remained in office for over 40 years so they were certainly old ladies when they died. Two were from Romsey Abbey: Matilda Lovell who was abbess for 45 years and Isabella Cammoys who ruled for only one year less. At Wherwell Matilda de Bailleul was abbess for 40 years according to the cartulary and her niece Euphemia for at least 38 years, while Juliana Overey was in office for 42 years before she resigned. No abbess quite managed 40 years at Winchester, but Agnes Buriton and Johanna Legh came very close with 39 years' service each. Other abbesses who were in office for more than 30 years can be seen in the lists in Appendix 1. Although such long periods of rule could bring their own problems to the communities, these ladies did indeed live to a good age. No doubt there were other elderly sisters at all the nunneries but their names can only be picked out when they appear in widely spaced voting lists: thus Agnes Harvey of Romsey was a novice in 1478 and chantress 45 years later.[1]

Health, or rather the treatment of illness, was taken seriously in medieval England, in spite of much ignorance on the subject. Doctors were resident in most large towns such as Winchester by the 12th century; in fact they were probably more eminent there at that time than they were later in the Middle Ages.[2] Doctors were allowed into convents to see any sick nun,[3] though the ministrations of a good infirmarian were probably just as effective. Like many secular ladies, a nun holding the office of infirmarian would be expected to be knowledgable about the concoction of herbal remedies, about the dressing and bandaging of wounds and even the setting of dislocated and broken bones. She was also meant to be skilled in the practice of blood letting, that medieval cure for all ills, so that there was no need for barbers to enter the nunneries.[4] (The nuns at Romsey were meant to receive a pittance of 6d. each whenever they had blood let.[5])

Bishop Woodlock seems to have shown more concern about sick nuns than any other prelate. Writing to St. Mary's, Winchester he said that all sisters who were infirm should be visited daily by the abbess, prioress or other nun given that task, and that they should be provided with necessary food and medicines so far as they could be afforded by the community.[6] He repeated the direction about special food for the sick to the nuns of Romsey and Wintney, meaning that meat was to be provided if the house could afford it.[7] In the same injunction to Romsey Abbey he ordered that the chaplains were to be restrained from visiting the infirmary frequently, and suggested that a gate leading into the garden should be made in an inconspicuous position so that it could be used by nuns who were unwell.

One cannot help wondering whether the original idea for such a gate may have occurred to some convalescent nun who later remembered to mention it when being interviewed at the visitation.

Little is known of the infirmaries themselves except at Wherwell. There Abbess Euphemia, amongst her many other building works in the mid-13th century, had a new, large infirmary constructed away from the main buildings, with a watercourse beneath it to carry off the refuse.[8] She also assigned five marks a year to its custodian that were payable out of the tithes the house received from Inkpen in Berkshire and from Fullerton nearby.[9] Perhaps the new infirmary may have been near the abbey's mill, for it is named immediately before the mill and millhouse in the list of buildings that were to be left standing when the house was dissolved in 1539. At Winchester the infirmary of St. Mary's was then deemed to be superfluous and was due to be demolished.[10] After Abbess Euphemia's work there is no record of other improvements being made in the infirmaries of the three abbeys, but it is interesting to read Dom Knowles's comments on later changes in many monasteries:

> It might be argued that the monks were in the van as regards domestic improvements, as they had long been as water engineers and plumbers. The move towards comfort developed during this period chiefly in the infirmary, which was very commonly rebuilt with rows of private rooms for the sick and aged . . .[11]

Nuns with contagious diseases did not have to remain within their convents. That official ruling in the Bull *Periculoso* was the only exception to the rules about enclosure. One cannot point to any example from the Hampshire houses, but in another diocese a nun with leprosy was to be sent away to a hospital.[12] But from 1348 the fear was not so much of leprosy but of the plague, which contemporaries called 'the great pestilence'. It is known more commonly now as the Black Death.

The disease first reached the south coast of England in the summer of 1348. On 24 October Bishop Edington sent out mandates alerting all his clergy: 'We are struck with the greatest fear lest, which God forbid, the fell disease ravage any part of our city and diocese'.[13] He charged them to see that their congregations attended the sacrament of penance and took part in penitential processions, walking with bare feet through the market places of towns and round the cemeteries of village churches. On Sundays, Wednesdays and Fridays the religious were to join in saying the seven penitential and fifteen gradual psalms in their choirs, and on Fridays the monks of St. Swithun's were also to chant the long litany while walking in procession through the market place of Winchester, together with the clergy and people.[14] The nuns of St. Mary's were surely among them, while at Romsey, Wherwell and Wintney the simpler processions were probably led by the nuns and their chaplains with the local vicar. Their hearts may have been apprehensive as they walked but none can have envisaged the horror of the coming year.

In November 1348 the bishop authorised the superiors of all the nunneries in his diocese to appoint two or three suitable priests to hear the confessions of the nuns, in case their own chaplains all died suddenly.[15] By the following month the plague had reached Winchester and the first priest died of it on 1 January 1349. By the end of that month the death toll was so high in the city that it became difficult to cope with the burials. The death rate among the beneficed clergy rose steadily each month. The peak of new institutions to vacant benefices was reached in May; after that it subsided but by the end of the year 48.8% of the beneficed clergy had died – more than in any other diocese in the country.[16]

All the monastic houses in the country suffered badly and the Hampshire nunneries were no exception. Accurate figures are only known for the heads of houses, but of those four who were in office in January 1349 only Abbess Amicia Ladde of Wherwell survived the year. Abbess Joan Icthe of Romsey died in April; her coffin lid still survives in the abbey.[17] The following month the surviving nuns at Winchester were mourning the death of their abbess, Matilda de Spyne, and a few weeks later the prioress of Wintney died.

It is to the credit of Bishop Edington and his clerks that the administration of the diocese did not break down, though in the emergency many priests were ordained more rapidly than usual and at an earlier age. When the abbesses died the correct procedure for the appointment of a successor was followed without delay and duly recorded. At both abbeys the election was made by the proclamation of the nuns, i.e. by common consent without voting. The king sent his assent to the election of the new abbess of Romsey on 7 May, nine days after he had issued the *congé d'élire*; it was confirmed by the Prior of Winchester on behalf of the bishop a week later and the bishop himself sent his benediction from Esher on the 21st.[18] (During the vacancy the prebend of the Portion of St. Laurence had also died so the abbey's right of appointment had been exercised by the king; two successive vicars of Romsey were also to die later that summer.[19]) In June the election process for Abbess Margaret de Molyns of St. Mary's, Winchester was equally efficient. It is only surprising in the circumstances to find that two of the nuns, Christina la Gayte and Margaret Inkepenne, had personally taken the news of the late abbess's death to the king, who issued the *congé* from Woodstock.[20]

Signs of strain and emergency measures are apparent in the episcopal records following the death of Prioress Covina de Mareys of Wintney in July. The scribe accidentally called her Covina Gervaise, and instead of the archdeacon or other officials attending the election and installation of her successor, the bishop wrote to the rector of Burghclere, John de Beautre, asking him to examine the election of Emma de Wynterburn as the new prioress and to install her if he confirmed it. The rector wasted no time and replied two days later from Winchfield that he had installed her.[21]

Although those three are the only nuns known to have died in 1349 many others would have been victims of the plague, no doubt including some of the 90 sisters who voted at Romsey in the election of 1333.[22] Only the imagination can supply anything of the fear and panic that everyone within the nunneries, as in the world outside, must have felt that terrible year. Faith may have been the only support for the living as they saw one member of the community after another develop the fever and dreaded swellings of the bubonic type of plague, or succumb to the even more infectious pneumonic form of the disease, and as they heard their cries and smelt the sickening and pervasive odours given off by the bodies of the victims.

By the end of 1349 the worst was over and the survivors were struggling back to normal life. However, the plague returned again in 1361-2 and it was then that Abbess Amicia Ladde of Wherwell died. As she had been in office for over 20 years her death in September 1361 may have been from natural causes, but it was followed in November by the death of her successor, Constance de Wyntreshulle, and the previous month the abbess of Winchester had also died. In the following century plague appeared in England at intervals but never on such a devastating scale as in 1349. There were several outbreaks in the years 1447 to 1454[23] and it was in that period that Wherwell Abbey lost three abbesses in 13 months, between November 1451 and December 1452.

In normal times nuns were buried in the cemetery of their convent and all the funeral expenses were borne by the community, as well as the provision of pittances for the sisters on the day of the funeral.[24] Probably many of the abbesses were buried within their churches, like Matilda Rowse who was interred in the nave at Wherwell Abbey in 1518.[25] Benefactors could also be buried in the monastic churches. Twenty six medieval burials were found in the nave and aisles of the church of St. Mary's Abbey, Winchester during the excavations of 1981-3 (and others were found elsewhere on the site). Two of the 26 burials were children while the others were of men and women in almost equal numbers. The average height of

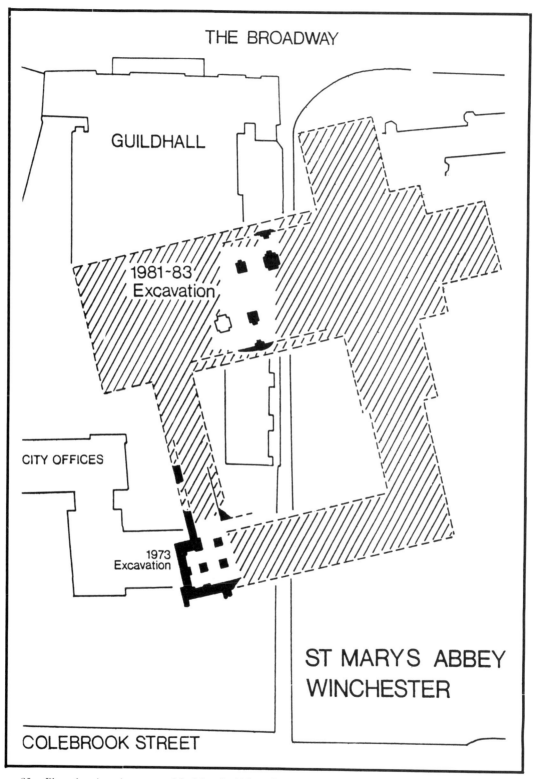

THE BROADWAY

GUILDHALL

1981-83 Excavation

CITY OFFICES

1973 Excavation

ST MARYS ABBEY WINCHESTER

COLEBROOK STREET

35. Plan showing the areas of St Mary's Abbey, Winchester, that were excavated in 1973 and 1981-3. Scale 1:715.

the men was 5ft. 8ins. and of the women 5ft. 3ins. Many of them showed signs of various joint diseases. The provisions for their interment varied; some had only shrouds, others had wooden coffins, but the more important had been buried in stone. Those coffins had either been constructed from worked chalk blocks with carved headpieces or from single blocks of stone. Five were excavated, including one in the south aisle of the church which held the remains of a lady who had been at least 45 years old at the time of her death and 5ft. 2ins. tall. Her coffin was carved from a single block of Purbeck limestone and by her side lay the remains of her staff of office which was made from ivory and carved bone with an iron shank set in wood. Her grave (no. F.35) pre-dated and probably formed the focus of a chapel in the church which was partly enclosed by cross walls by the 14th century; subsequently the chapel was enclosed on the north side by another tomb.[26]

Morality and Lapses from Grace

In the wake of the Gregorian reforms of the 11th and 12th centuries that tried to impose clerical celibacy, there was a greatly increased devotion in the church to the Virgin Mary, and the concept of virginity as an ideal state took a firm hold on the medieval mind. Nuns, as virgins consecrated to Christ, were thus regarded by the church as separate and superior to other women. It was this excessive regard for the importance of virginity that lay behind all the episcopal strictures on the need for enclosure and the elimination of visitors and visiting.

Bishop Woodlock regarded dorters as a possible danger area, seeming to have little idea of natural female modesty. At Winchester some of the nuns had been obtaining a measure of privacy for themselves in the dorter by draping coloured hangings from the tester over their beds. Their different colours would have appealed to most medieval eyes but the bishop refused to allow them, although he did permit the sisters to have some curtains of common cloth, provided that they were only partly drawn so that anyone who passed by could see them getting into bed.[27] Two years later he decided that even common cloth curtains were inadvisable and ordered that all curtains were to be permanently removed from the nuns' beds at Romsey. He also forbade any children sleeping in the nuns' dorter there.[28] Later this prohibition was extended by Bishop Wykeham to include any secular woman, and he also ordered that each nun was to have a separate bed.[29] Bishop Woodlock was probably being optimistic if he really thought he could insist on silence being kept in all the dorters, but he mentioned it in his injunctions to both the abbeys, while at Wintney Priory he gave as his reason for ordering silence in the cloister, refectory and dormitory that 'excessive speech does not accord with virginal simplicity'.[30]

Virginal simplicity was an ideal that the church longed to see realised in its nuns. Successive bishops urged them to follow the paths of righteousness and did their best to protect them from the temptations of the outside world, but many of the nuns had no real vocation for the religious life. It probably did not occur to the bishops and their officials, who were constantly moving from one place to another, that some of the young nuns probably suffered at times from both boredom and sexual repression. And even those who felt a vocation may sometimes have experienced the lassitude and despair of *accidia* for similar reasons. It did not help that many of the younger sisters who did not have the responsibility of one of the offices were probably underemployed.

Generally it is remarkable that the great majority of nuns adapted themselves to the life of the cloister and kept their vows of chastity. There were rare scandals at each of the four Hampshire nunneries which were dealt with officially and so reached the episcopal registers, and there would have been others hushed up, but they seem to have been fewer than in many dioceses, particularly in the north.[31] Most scandals in the registers involved apostasy, which usually meant that a nun had left her convent to live with a lover. Excommunication

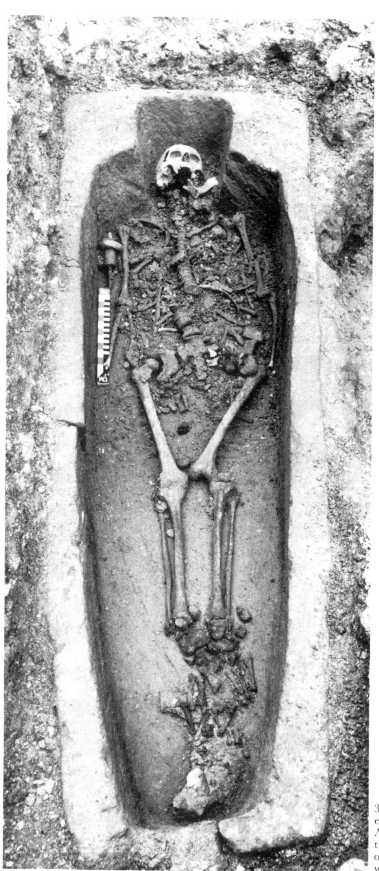

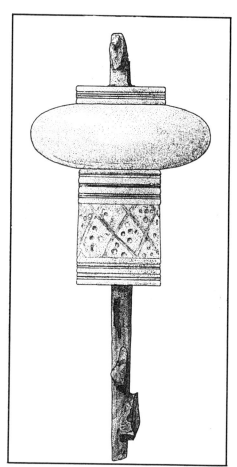

36. (*above left*) Coffin and female skeleton excavated in the south aisle of St Mary's Abbey. A staff of office lies to the side of the lady's remains. (*above right*) The staff of office, made from ivory and carved bone with an iron shank (actual height: 17 cms.).

would follow because all the monastic vows had been breached and the life of religion brought into dishonour, whereas a nun found guilty of unchastity but remaining in her nunnery would only be given a penance. But excommunication could be absolved, and the tendency everywhere was for erring nuns to return to their convents sooner or later, finding the censure of church, state and public opinion too great to bear.

To turn to specific instances, at Wherwell Abbey there was only one recorded scandal in the two and a half centuries covered by the registers, apart from an accusation involving the abbess in a possibly trumped-up charge on the eve of the Dissolution. The offending nun was Katherine Fauconer whom one may reasonably suppose to have been a member of the Fauconer family of Hurstbourne Priors, and if so she was the second member of the family to have been in trouble in a short time.[32] Katherine ran away from the abbey but her abductors were not known in June 1393 when the bishop excommunicated them.[33] It is unlikely that the name of her lover remained unknown for long, but it was never recorded. Presumably the pair remained together for some time, but in the end the pressures were too much for them and seven years later Katherine sought absolution from Bishop Wykeham who then wrote to the abbess asking her to receive the penitent back into the nunnery.[34]

At the other country house, Wintney Priory, it has already been mentioned that the nuns had horrified the archbishop of Canterbury early in the 14th century by leaving their house during a time of famine in order to look for food.[35] But it was early in the 15th century that the reputation of the house really declined. Alice Fyshide had been prioress there since the mid-1380s and at least by 1404 she had evidently become unworthy of her office. In April that year Bishop Wykeham commissioned his official, M. John Elmere, and another priest to hold a visitation at the priory on his behalf.[36] Possibly on account of the bishop's death that September, the record of their findings reached the papal ears and a year later Pope Innocent VII issued a mandate to the archdeacon of Taunton and to a canon of Wells to hold another visitation at the priory. The mandate listed the findings of the first enquiry which, among other points, maintained that the prioress supported Thomas Ferring, a secular priest

> . . . as companion at board and in bed, who has long slept and still sleeps, contrary to the institutes of the order, within the monastery, beneath the dormitory, in a certain chamber in which formerly no secular had ever been wont to sleep, and in which the said priest and Alice meet together at will by day and night to satisfy their lust . . . [37]

It was also said that she was supporting and giving food and clothes to two immodest nuns of the house: one was her sister, who had abandoned her vows, left the priory and had children, and the other was a nun also living an immoral life although she was not an apostate. But was the visitation ever made? Perhaps not. At any rate Alice Fyshide remained prioress for another 10 years, but in February 1415 a second, rather muddled, papal mandate on the same subject was sent to the dean of Chester with similar charges, including one which said that the prioress had had children. If he found her guilty he was to remove her from office.[38] Evidently he did, and less than a month later Alice Fyshide resigned. She remained at the priory, at least for a time, because it was noted that at the election for her successor she was 'too ill to leave her room' to go to the chapter house with the other 13 nuns, but she appointed the sacristan of the house as her proxy. In fact Johanna Benbury was chosen as the new prioress by acclamation, but had it come to a contested election the proxy vote would presumably not have been accepted, for at the start of the proceedings:

> Dame Leticia Brakenham, sub-prioress, at the desire of all the nuns, gave written warning that if any excommunicate took part in the election her vote would be invalid.[39]

As Cardinal Beaufort's second register is missing, little is known about the priory over the next three decades until 1453 when the election of Prioress Alice Somerset was confirmed.[40] A year later one of her nuns with the charming name of Petronilla Pygeon was in trouble, and this time her seducer was known and was ordered to do penance. The mandate sent to the vicar of Odiham reads:

> Whereas the bishop has imposed a penance upon William Pratte of Basing, for having violated Petronilla Pegion, a nun of Wintney Priory, by having carnal knowledge of her, the vicar is to call and to bring the said William to perform the said penance, viz. on 31 August next (a Saturday) dressed only in shirt and breeches, and carrying a taper, he is to go round the market-place of Odiham, and kneeling at two different places there is to receive discipline by the rod from the vicar (wearing surplice and stole). The following Sunday, in a similar condition, he is to go before the processional cross round Odiham church at procession time, then to prostrate himself in the middle of the nave until the Offertory of the High Mass, and then to place his taper in the hands of the celebrant. The vicar to certify the bishop of his actions before returning this mandate. Given at Waltham, 23 August 1454.[41]

Petronilla's penance was not recorded.

Normally a nun who had been involved in such a public scandal would have been debarred from future office. It is therefore surprising, and some reflection on the moral state of the priory, that only six years later Petronilla Pygeon was chosen as prioress and installed by the archdeacon of Winchester, following the death of Alice Somerset. But the choice was limited indeed. Only four nuns were actually living at the priory at the time, though there were two others who had run away – Katherine Founteyn and Matilda Trussell.[42] Katherine Founteyn later returned and in 1498 she was sub-prioress when Petronilla Pygeon resigned from office after nearly 40 years as prioress.[43] To have had both a prioress and sub-prioress with flawed reputations cannot have been good for either morale or the local reputation of the house.

At Winchester the respect and affection felt by the citizens for the nuns of St. Mary's Abbey lasted until the Dissolution. At most periods the good reputation of the house was well deserved but there were two unfortunate periods in the 14th century when there were weak abbesses, and earlier there had been the isolated case of Matilda de Bauoun. She had apparently returned to the abbey after committing the usual sin and in April 1310 the bishop directed the sub-prior of St. Swithun's and one of the diocesan officials to receive her purgation.[44]

The two abbesses who were weak, particularly during their last years, were Matilda de Pecham (1313-37) and Alice de la Mare (1365-85). Matilda de Pecham had become abbess after a disputed election,[45] but there is no reason to doubt her reputation during her early years. (Roger de Inkepenne is unlikely to have founded his chantry within the abbey grounds if it had been otherwise.) But by 1326 life at the abbey had become slack and Bishop Stratford found much to criticise in his injunctions. Five years later, in June 1331, the abbess was issued with a summons and evidence was taken about her conduct at another visitation.[46] The following month this was followed up by the bishop who ordered the vicar-general to examine and investigate everything that had been found at the visitation against 'Dame Matilda who calls herself abbess' and to make a final pronouncement on the findings 'even if it leads to her removal and deposition'.[47] But the abbess was not removed, though it would have been better for the reputation of the house if she had been. In May 1333, when she and one of her nuns were again summoned to appear before the bishop or his deputy in the abbey's chapter house, the nature of the charges became apparent. The new vicar-general then wrote that:

> He has received complaints that certain nuns, having put aside their religious habits and returned to secular clothes, have associated with various religious persons and others, and against the judgment of conscience, after a way of life dedicated to God, by unchaste and sacrilegious union have produced daughters. These things are said to have happened several times through the abbess's notorious

negligence and fault; by her dissimulation these and similar actions have long remained, and still remain, uncorrected.[48]

The findings were not recorded, and in November Bishop Stratford left the diocese to become Archbishop of Canterbury.

A year later the new Bishop Orleton held a personal visitation of St. Mary's Abbey, preaching his sermon to the nuns in French.[49] Perhaps that and his visitations immediately beforehand to the Cathedral Priory and Hyde Abbey were courtesy visits rather than occasions for searching enquiries, for more than a year passed before the bishop became concerned about the moral and economic state of the abbey and ordered a commission to enquire into its affairs. The four members included his official, M. John de Usk, and the future bishop, William de Edington who was then Master of St. Cross.[50] Since their findings evidently gave cause for concern, in July 1336 the bishop commissioned John de Usk to correct the faults found at the abbey, which stemmed from the negligence of the abbess, the prioress and others in authority. Some of the nuns had been visiting unsuitable places and, as an inevitable corollary, scandal had been caused by the admission of undesirable people into the abbey.[51] Abbess Matilda did not resign, for she was still the superior in 1337 when there was another visitation,[52] but there may have been some private sighs of relief at the news of her death that November.[53]

Thirty years later, when the size of the community had been much reduced, a nun called Isabella Gervays was abducted from the abbey by 'a great number of evildoers' who also took abbey property to the value of £40 with them.[54] Although unnamed they were excommunicated by Bishop Wykeham in January 1370.[55] In June that year the bishop was writing to Abbess Alice de la Mare in a very different tone, asking her to re-admit Isabella, who was pregnant, and to keep her in safety until the birth of her child.[56] After that her story is lost. Presumably that was just an isolated case but a general slackness and lack of discipline crept into the house at the end of Abbess Alice's life. She was censured by the bishop in November 1384 for not correcting her nuns, and they were ordered to obey the abbey's obedientiaries under pain of excommunication.[57]

That was the last recorded criticism of any of the nuns at St. Mary's Abbey. No injunctions apparently followed after the visitation of the house in 1396 by the archdeacon of Wiltshire and John Elmere, the official,[58] and the reputation of the house during the 15th and early 16th century was good.

It will already have become clear, however, in the references to Abbess Elizabeth Brooke that the same could not be said about the reputation of Romsey Abbey during its last years. Before her time there seems to have been no more trouble at Romsey than at the other nunneries, but after her death in 1502 the abbey never really recovered its good name.

In the 14th century there had been three recorded scandals involving nuns from Romsey, but none apparently concerned nuns being abducted. The first may or may have not involved the murder of Alice de Wyntershull in May 1315, four months after she had been elected abbess. News of her death was taken to Edward II by two of the nuns, Alice de Roffa and Margaret de Middleton, who were given the congé d'élire on 11 May.[59] On the 28th the king issued a commission of oyer and terminer 'touching the persons who killed Alice de Wintreshulle, late abbess of Romsey, at Romsey . . .',[60] and a few weeks later, when one of the commissioners was replaced, the patent referred to the commission 'touching the persons who, plotting the death of Alice de Wyntreshulle, late abbess of Romsey, caused her to be intoxicated'.[61] Nothing else is recorded about the commission, but in Bishop Woodlock's register there is an undated letter which he wrote to the archdeacon of Winchester ordering the excommunication of anyone found guilty of spreading the slander that the abbess had been poisoned.[62]

The second case concerned a nun called Margaret Poyns who had been excommunicated after attacking the vicar of the parish church. The record of the commission to absolve her in November 1347 does not give any reason for her 'laying violent hands' on him, so one can only wonder just how innocent was Nicholas the vicar over the incident.[63] Two decades later the name of the erring nun was either Marion or Margery de Rye. She seems to have been one of life's rebels. She is first encountered after she had deliberately removed her veil and gone to sit in the nave of the church with lay women instead of sitting in the choir; both there and in other places she gossiped and chatted, not joining in the worship of the church or saying the Hours. In February 1369 the abbess was told by the bishop to admonish her and get her to resume her veil and abide by the Rule. The following month he licensed the rector of Michelmersh to hear her confession and absolve her from her sins before the feast of St. George. But Margery was not easily tamed. She persisted in her disobedience so that in September the bishop wrote again to Abbess Isabella Cammoys authorising her to use any discipline to compel her to conform to the Rule, provided it did not endanger her life.[64] Poor girl. She was obviously quite unsuited to the monastic life, but from the point of view of the abbess she must have been a most unsettling influence in the community.

No other scandals at Romsey were recorded until the time of Abbess Elizabeth Brooke. Her affairs have already been mentioned, and Liveing describes in detail how she had confessed to adultery with John Placy, how she had tendered her resignation to Bishop Waynflete in 1478, only to be re-elected, and how subsequently she had succumbed to the charms and come under the influence of first one steward and then another.[65] A papal decree of 1482, which followed petitions from both the abbess and the bishop, gives some further details about this unfortunate lady and her affairs. Both morals and money were involved. Elizabeth Brooke admitted 'that she had allowed herself to be carnally known and feared that she was pregnant' but said that in future she would live piously and chastely. (But pride she did not regard as a sin. She was careful to let His Holiness know that she had good family connections: '. . . of a noble race of barons'). Pope Sixtus IV allowed her to choose her own confessor to absolve her from her sins 'once only', and inhibited the bishop from making further enquiries about her past conduct or that of her chaplains and household; he also allowed her the right to grant corrodies. Bishop Waynflete's subsequent petition evidently mentioned that Elizabeth Brooke had always led an immoral life and for that reason he had deprived her of her office. He gave new light on her re-election when maintaining that '. . . at the prayers of many of the nobles of those parts she got herself elected anew . . .' and that his confirmation had been given on the condition that she would mend her ways and not grant further corrodies except in cases of need or for the benefit of the community. But, financially at least, the abbess had not mended her ways. With her chaplains and others she had resumed her old style of life, giving money to the undeserving (other matters not mentioned) so the bishop received papal permission to make enquiries about any of the abbess's crimes that had been committed subsequent to her original absolution.[66] But in spite of those enquiries and of the archiepiscopal visitation in 1492, Elizabeth Brooke remained abbess until her death in 1502. Unfortunately the community then chose another weak abbess, Joyce Rowse. If only a dedicated sister with natural powers of leadership had been elected she might have transformed the nunnery, but such a one was either not there or not recognised.

Another nun who had not been an influence for good was Emma Powes. Before joining the community at Romsey she had been removed from at least two other nunneries, including Lymbrook Priory in Herefordshire where she had been prioress before being accused of immorality and deprived in 1488.[67] She was probably the sister whom Joan Paten had wished to see sent back to her original house in 1492.[68] In 1501 Emma was accused of having immoral relations with the vicar of the parish church but she was still at the abbey, where she was sub-sacrist, the following year.[69]

Possibly there was similar trouble in 1507 when a subsequent vicar of Romsey parish church was publicly admonished not to enter the precincts of the house, except the chapel of the Holy Rood, or to have any communication with the abbess and nuns.[70] Two days earlier the bishop's vicar-general had similarly warned a certain Master Folton that in future he was not to visit or communicate with any nun of Romsey, under pain of excommunication.[71]

The last ladies to have their misdeeds recorded before the Dissolution all appeared before the vicar-general in the chapter house at Romsey on 16 January 1527. Alice Gorsyn was seen first and reprimanded for uttering slanders about her fellow nuns. (As she had still been a novice in 1523, her fault was probably due to youthful sharpness rather than crabbed old age.[72]) Then Clemence Malyng was removed from her office of sub-prioress and sacrist, ostensibly for being negligent and careless but really because she had often met a priest, Richard Johans, in church in the evening after leaving out a key for him and had taken him something to drink in the sacristy, though nothing else improper had ever occurred. The third miscreant was Margaret Dowman, who had also been a novice in 1523; she had committed adultery with Thomas Hordes and was ordered to be imprisoned for a year, wearing no linen on her outer garments, nor the ring of her profession which she had violated and in any procession she was to carry her candle point downwards.[73]

These various scandals at the four nunneries are not a selection. They are the only cases recorded that involved individual nuns. It has already been mentioned that there were undoubtedly other incidents that were hushed up and kept from the episcopal glare and the episcopal register, but even so they are really very few considering how many nuns there were in Hampshire during the two and a half centuries before the Dissolution. With some exceptions at different times the four houses do generally seem to have been worthy of good conduct marks.

Chapter Nine

The Economy of the Nunneries: Income

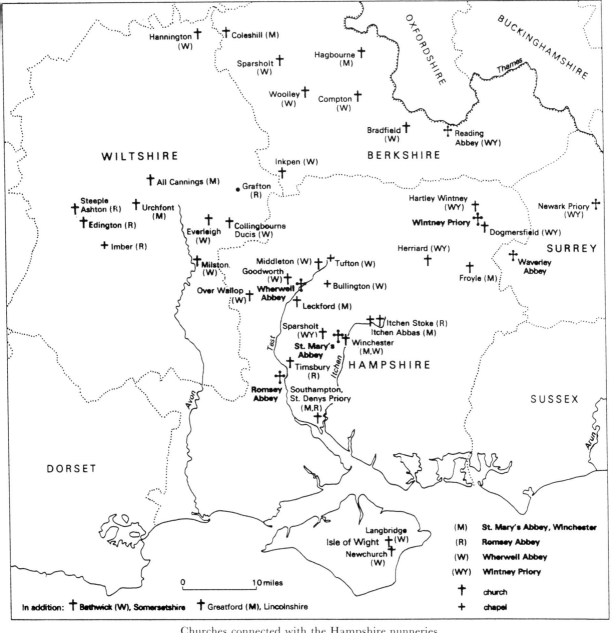

Churches connected with the Hampshire nunneries.

Like all monastic houses the nunneries derived their income from two sources: their spiritualities and their temporalities. Spiritual income came from grants made to each nunnery in its capacity as a religious house, while temporal income was derived from its rents, the profits of its manors, and contributions made by guests and the parents of children being boarded there. The ownership of these spiritualities and temporalities was vested in the head of the house, so after each election the new abbess (or prioress of Wintney) had to be formally admitted into their possession. During an interregnum the income of the abbeys was meant to revert to the king through his escheator, although that process could be set aside; if it was, the nuns had to pay a fine for the privilege.[1]

Their churches and other sources of spiritual income *(see Appendix 2)*

The main source from which the nunneries derived their spiritual income was the benefices that had been appropriated to them. After appropriation they normally received the great tithes from that parish in their capacity as corporate rector, while the vicar whom they presented looked after the spiritual welfare of the parishioners in return for a fixed income and the lesser tithes. It was quite usual, particularly in the 14th century, for monastic houses in financial difficulties to seek the necessary episcopal and papal permission to appropriate a benefice of which they were already patrons. In the case of the nunneries the advowson might either have been owned by the abbess and convent since pre-Conquest days, or by a prebendary in one of the abbeys, or appropriation could follow on soon after the gift of an advowson as it did at Herriard. The process could be completed within a reasonable time, as it apparently was when Itchen Stoke was appropriated in 1317, but sometimes it could drag on for years if the matter was disputed. The appropriation of Froyle by St. Mary's Abbey took nearly a quarter of a century.

Altogether the four nunneries had nine rectories appropriated to them between the late 12th and the mid-15th centuries, five of them between 1317 and 1354.[2] Wintney Priory and Romsey Abbey had three each, although one of Romsey's was just a portion of the parish church within the abbey church. St. Mary's Abbey, Winchester had two for certain (Froyle and Urchfont) but they obviously hoped that Greatford, Lincolnshire was to become their third; papal permission for its appropriation was obtained in 1352 but it was apparently not carried out. Wherwell Abbey had only Goodworth (Clatford) which they appropriated in 1444; but a century earlier the nuns had prepared a case for their appropriation of the rectory of Wherwell parish,[3] but they were never successful so it remained in the hands of a prebendary.

The great tithes that the nunneries received from these parishes were by their very nature in kind, but the steward of the house could then sell any crops that were surplus to requirements. There is a brief mention of this in a deposition that was made by Elizabeth Martyn, the last prioress of Wintney in 1572. The priory had then been dissolved for 36 years, but she was asked various questions about its former properties including the parsonage of Sparsholt, Hampshire, and its tithes. Her replies start:

> To the first article Elizabeth Martin of the age of 60 years, being late Prioress of Wintney in the county of Southt. deposeth and sayeth that she knoweth the parsonage of Sparsholt very well, and that it did belong unto the said Priory of Wintney.
>
> To the second article she deposeth and sayeth that all the corn and grain growing within the parish of Sparsholt did always belong unto the said parsonage and the tithe thereof was yearlie sold by the Baylie of the said house, one Abbot, to their most advantage as it did arise.[4]

The appropriated benefices were the most valuable of the nunneries' spiritualities but all the houses derived some income from various other sources. Each received small pensions and annual payments whether from their own prebends, from other monastic houses, from a portion of the tithes of some parish not otherwise connected to them, or from the rector of a parish in the wake of some ancient dispute. The cartulary of Wherwell Abbey gives the origins of some of these payments, such as the pensions of 30s. and 10s. p.a. that were still being paid to the abbess at the Dissolution out of the rectories of Over Wallop and Barton Stacey respectively, following disputes about tithes in the 13th century. Because their cartularies have not survived this type of information has been lost for the abbeys at Winchester and Romsey unless it is recorded elsewhere, like the small pensions paid to St. Mary's Abbey at one time by the Priory of St. Denys near Southampton. A little more is known about the pensions that the prioress of Wintney was still receiving in the 16th century. The origin of the 2s. p.a. that was paid to her by Romsey Abbey out of its manor of Itchen Stoke is not known, but a pension from the rector of Dogmersfield can be traced back to the 12th century, and two others from Reading Abbey and Newark Priory to the early 13th. The names of the abbot of Reading and the Prior of Newark who first granted those pensions were entered into the Wintney Calendar, and two other obits there are for priors of Southwick Priory whose canons provided the nuns with two quarters of salt each year.

Other spiritual income came from alms given by visitors to the monastic churches and from offerings made at shrines within them, such as the shrine of St. Edburga in the church of St. Mary's Abbey. Mortuaries, which were paid whenever someone was buried in one of their churches, were also an occasional source of revenue or valuable gift. A few of the people buried are known from their wills. In 1361 John de Inkepenne continued his family's association with St. Mary's Abbey, but he asked to be buried beside his brother Robert in the convent church instead of in the Holy Trinity Chapel; he bequeathed 6d. to every nun there on the day of his funeral and 20s. to the abbess.[5] At the start of the 16th century a former mayor of the city, John Stratford, was buried in the Lady Chapel of the abbey between his two wives.[6] (One wonders about his relationship, if any, to Edburga Stratford who was a nun there at the time of the Dissolution.) Another will shows that Thomas Faukes asked to be buried in the church of Romsey Abbey before the altar of the Holy Cross, leaving the nuns there a plain silver bowl; and at Wherwell a priest left the abbey his chalice 'in recompense and satisfaction for my mortuary'.[7]

All the nunneries benefited from other legacies as well. The Wherwell Cartulary records a mid-13th century bequest of 20 silver marks which Philip de Falconberg, archdeacon of Huntingdon, left to the abbess and convent of Wherwell so that his obit could be kept.[8] Some other legacies were more disinterested, and by the 14th century they were being left to individual nuns as well as to the community. Bishop Edington did both when he left £20 to be distributed among the sisters at Romsey and another £20 and a ring for Abbess Isabella Cammoys (perhaps in gratitude for the nunnery's co-operation over Edington). One of the nuns there who would have benefited from his legacy was Thomasina Blount who was later left an individual legacy of 40 marks by her sister, Lady Alice West; the will also included 100s. for the community.[9]

Several wills which survive from the beginning of the 16th century were made by neighbours of the nunneries such as John Cornyshe, another former mayor of Winchester, who left a valuable rosary to the Lady Chapel of St. Mary's Abbey.[10] However, most legacies were received from clerics rather than laymen. Two Wherwell priests, William Howell and John Burgess, who probably served as chaplains to the nuns, obviously had the well-being of the abbey in the forefront of their minds. They both asked to be buried within the monastery church (Howell in the nave and Burgess before the image of the Holy Cross) and left money for their obits, for repairs to the nunnery and for distribution amongst the community. William Howell left Abbess Matilda Rowse 20s. for being an overseer of his will, while John Burgess made Abbess Alice Cowdrey and her brother John his executors, leaving them 40s. each and the residue.[11] At Hartley Wintney the vicar of the parish church, Henry Sewghel, had only a modest amount to distribute but he left Prioress

Anne 6s. 8d., smaller legacies to three other named nuns and 12d. each to every other nun at Wintney Priory.[12] However, this type of legacy is missing at Romsey at that period, presumably because of the poor reputation of the abbey then. Even a native of the town, Ralph Hall, did not mention the nuns, although he left bequests to five other monastic communities in Hampshire.[13] The only benefactor seems to have been Gilbert Stanton, who was probably a chaplain, but although he left small legacies to the different altars in the abbey church and two small bequests to one of the nuns, Christine Dackham, he did not mention the community as a whole.[14]

The dowries that came with novices or were paid at their veiling are more difficult to discover. Many of the small properties that later produced rents for the nunneries (and were thus temporal income) probably came as dowries originally, such as the lands given to Romsey Abbey early in the 12th century by William Escuet 'with his daughters' and by Ernulf Deschuit 'when he placed his daughter in the abbey'.[15] Bishops were later concerned about the possibility of simony. When Bishop Stratford sent his injunctions to St. Mary's Abbey in 1326 he drew the distinction between money paid by agreement at the veiling of a nun and offerings made freely:

> No money or other peculiar advantage henceforth to be received for the veiling of nuns according to any pact or agreement; but when by gift or by some privilege free offerings are made to the house by the friends of nuns received without a pact, these may be freely and gratefully accepted.[16]

Sixty years later Bishop William of Wykeham came across the same problem at Romsey Abbey and criticised the 'considerable sums' of money that had been paid at the reception of some nuns 'by prior agreement and an entrance pact, not without the stain of the sin of simony'.[17] But the line drawn between gifts by or without an agreement must have been a fairly fine one in practice. The last record of a gift made at the veiling of a nun comes in the Wilton Psalter. It has already been mentioned that this book was given to a nun at Romsey by her great-uncle, Ralph Lepton; the inscription in it records that he also gave her a silver goblet and two spoons and that at the time of her veiling he gave the abbey £5 which he delivered to the bailiff there.[18]

The spiritual income that the nunneries received was always less than their temporal income. Assessing just how much it was in any one year is impossible, but in Appendix 2 there is a list of the different churches from which the nuns derived most of their spiritual income, together with contemporary valuations. The first such valuation of church property, the *Taxatio* of Pope Nicholas IV, was made around 1291 but the interpretation of its figures is open to question, and this criticism must also apply to the valuation of the archdeaconry of Winchester in the 14th century which was based on the *Taxatio*. More accurate valuations can be found in some of the Dissolution accounts and in the *Valor Ecclesiasticus* of 1535, although the returns that were made for Hampshire are not as detailed as they are for some other counties.

Their manors and other property (*see Appendix 3*)

The most important source of income for each of the nunneries was the profits that they received from their estates. Most of the money was derived from rents paid by their tenants in town and country and from their possession of extensive agricultural land on their manors. Their mills and woodlands also brought in income, and the abbesses' courts were another regular source of profit. It is impossible to do justice to the subject in a few pages. Whole books have been written about medieval estates, and there are sufficient records for another to be devoted to those of the Hampshire nunneries.

The manors owned by the four nunneries have been listed in Appendix 3, together with other properties that are known. Thanks to the survival of its cartulary the list of Wherwell's

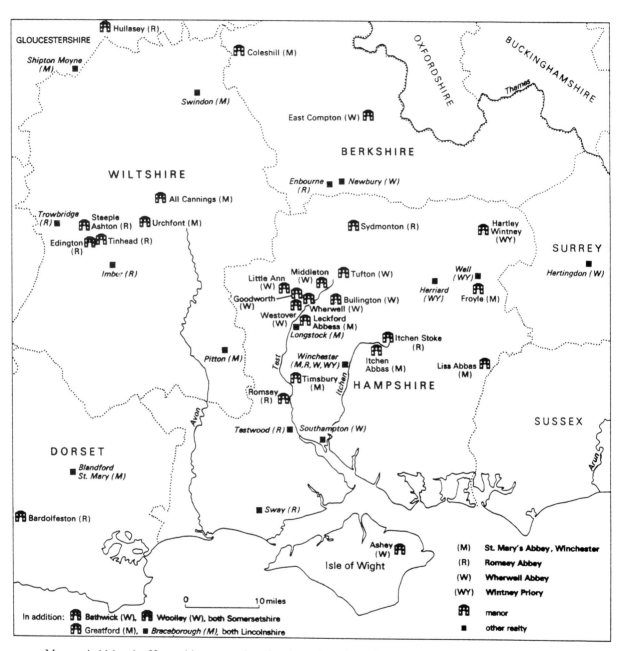

Manors held by the Hampshire nunneries, showing other places from which they received at least £1 p.a.

individual properties is probably virtually complete, but it is likely that in those for the other two abbeys there are omissions of property that had been lost before the 16th century. Most of the manors owned by the abbeys had been in their possession by the time of the Conquest and were still owned by them at the Dissolution. One exception was the manor of Coleshill, Wiltshire which St. Mary's, Winchester held in 1086 but later surrendered for the benefit of Bishop William of Edington's new foundation.

The best recorded non-manorial properties were in Winchester. There the three abbesses each held one of the seven great fiefs by the 11th century and even poor Wintney Priory was granted property in Colebrook Street at its foundation which it always kept. The extent and value of Wherwell Abbey's estate was very much diminished by the time of the Dissolution but at least some remained, whereas Romsey Abbey had lost all theirs. The abbesses of Winchester were better placed to keep an eye on their properties and, thanks to its good reputation with the citizens, the abbey received four further grants of property in the city between 1298 and 1415.[19] Even so, the real value of their holdings at the Dissolution was possibly a quarter of what it had been in 1148.[20]

Manorial lands that were adjacent to a rural monastery were normally held in demesne so that the home farm, which provided much of the community's food, was under the direct control of the head of each house. One of the Dissolution papers shows that Wintney Priory employed 13 outdoor servants who were referred to as 'hindes'.[21] However, most of the records that survive relate to manors at some distance from the nunneries. In the century or so after Domesday Book was written the more distant manors were probably let out, but by the start of the 13th century it had become normal in England for large estates to be taken into direct management, so as to increase the income received from them. It was a time when new lands were being acquired both from gifts and from the clearance of land, and there were growing markets for the crops and livestock reared on them. By the end of the century these manors were probably at the peak of their efficiency, and thanks to the accounts that were drawn up to show the financial position between the local official and landlords such as the abbesses, a remarkable amount is known about them.[22]

A hierarchy of different servants was needed to run the system. At the lowest level on a 13th-century manor a reeve would be responsible for collecting rents, organising the cultivation of crops and remitting any profits to the abbess. He was usually one of the unfree tenants who would be rewarded by being excused from paying rent and giving other services. A paid bailiff, who was usually a free man, supervised the work of the reeve. At first each manor had its own bailiff, but later it became common for one man to oversee two or more manors in the same district; this would have been simple to organise in Wiltshire where Romsey Abbey's two manors of Steeple Ashton and Edington were adjacent, and Urchfont and All Cannings which belonged to St. Mary's Abbey were only four miles apart. The bailiff was not responsible for any extensive woodland; areas such as Harewood forest were in the hands of a woodward.[23] Based at each abbey were the financial officials, the receiver and the auditor, who were responsible for running the estate and holding any courts on behalf of the abbess.[24]

The names of several of the nunneries' reeves and bailiffs are known from surviving records, especially the compotus rolls which set out their accounts in the greatest detail in the 13th and 14th centuries when the manors were being farmed directly. There is a splendid collection of these account rolls from the Hampshire manor of Froyle, which belonged to St. Mary's Abbey, Winchester. The first series of its rolls, for the 30 years from c.1233, probably includes the earliest surviving account rolls for an individual manor in England.[25] After 1263 there is a break for a century, but from 1363 the rolls continue intermittently until the eve of the Dissolution.[26] The first known reeve was just John. He had collected rents of assize of £19 16s. 0d. in 1236; he was the only man presenting the account then, which suggests that there was no bailiff at the time.[27] But in 1252 the account was made by 'W'[28] (later William) who was probably bailiff although he and his successors were described as *serviens*.[29]

As an example of one of the compotus rolls, a few of the items in the Froyle roll for the year from Michaelmas 1260 will be considered.[30] Though chosen almost at random because it is well written and set out, it has at least two interesting features. On the personal level it shows that Abbess Agnes visited Froyle in the course of the year, and on the estate side it provides a good example of the abbess and her steward taking overall decisions concerning their manors. They had evidently decided to increase the size of the sheep flock at Froyle and in order to do this more than 400 extra sheep had been driven there from three of the abbey's other manors.

The account was presented by Robert, *serviens*, and John de Kupper the reeve. It is set out in the usual manner with the cash position first. The arrears from the previous account were 28s. 7¼d. but £23 3s. 8½d. had been collected in rents of assize; among the acquitances the reeve was excused 5s. in return for his services, the hayward 2s. 6d. and the shepherd who had custody of the sheep also 2s. 6d. After the defaulters were noted, including Emma de Kupper who owed 5s. rent for a virgate of land, the cash in hand with arrears came to £20 16s. 7¾d. The profits of the manor started with 9s. 1d. for pannage of pigs and came to £10 7s. 0d. altogether, excluding the sale of corn; pledges and perquisites brought in another £8 6s. 0d., so the total value with arrears was £40 19s. 2¾d. These credits were followed by debits. There were the expenses of the ploughman and the carter and many other necessary outgoings; expenses of 30s. 2¼d. had been incurred according to two tallies when the abbess visited the manor (this presumably included the value of the five sheep slaughtered then) and 8d. was costed for her travelling there. Finally the account listed the quantities of crops grown, including barley and oats, and this was followed by a long list of all the stock. It started with the same two carthorses (*equi' carect'*) as last year, but there had been changes with the draught horses (*affri*). Twenty-six had been accounted for the previous year, but since then one had been received as a heriot and three had arrived from the abbey's manor at Urchfont, Wiltshire; however, three had died, three had been sold and one had been sent to Winchester so only 23 remained by Michaelmas. Oxen (*boves*) had also gone down in numbers but only because seven had been sent to Urchfont, leaving 21 at Froyle. The same bull was still there, but the herd of cows had increased from eight to 12; two had been sent from the manor of Liss, one had been bequeathed and two others had been calves the previous year, but one had been slaughtered at Martinmas.

The dramatic change in the size of the flock has already been mentioned. At Michaelmas 1260 there had been 212 sheep (*multon'*) but 12 months later the number was 577. This had been achieved by bringing in 222 from Itchen (Abbas), about 24 miles away, 184 from Urchfont and 38 from (All) Cannings, both these involving a walk of nearly 50 miles for shepherd and sheep along the drove roads, possibly via Weyhill. The two flocks from Wiltshire were not sent together. From the possible total of 656 sheep, 79 had been lost; these included 28 slaughtered at Martinmas, six natural deaths, 22 sent to Winchester (to the abbey) and the five mentioned to feast the abbess on her visit. Finally each pig and piglet and all forms of poultry were listed before the eggs, bacon and mutton.

The expansion and increased profits of demesne farming did not last. Often they had come to an end by the beginning of the 14th century, and the position was made much worse by the shortage of labour after the Black Death. It was this situation of falling incomes from their manors that led to the desire amongst the abbesses for appropriated rectories. Many large landlords started to lease out their manors 'at farm' so that they received a fixed rent from the lessee (the farmer) who himself retained any profits from the manor, other than those retained by the landlord. (Woods were often reserved. The abbess of

Wherwell for instance excluded the woods, warrens and hunting rights when she leased the manor of Westover early in the 16th century.[31])

In Wessex monastic landlords such as the abbesses of Winchester and Romsey did not usually make the change from farming their manors directly to leasing them out until the early 15th century. In Wiltshire the abbess of Winchester started to lease out her demesne at Urchfont some time between 1434 and 1441 and at All Cannings by 1449. Both these manors had been producing food supplies for the abbey on a large scale and they continued to do so under the new system, the farmer paying in kind for the arable lands he had leased. However, the nuns still retained their own flocks of sheep there for a few more years; there were over a thousand at Urchfont and 600 at All Cannings until the 1470s.[32] By 1535 money rent was being paid to the abbess by both manors, the farmers and the reeves making separate accounts of the money due to Winchester.[33]

At Froyle the changeover to leasing took place some time between 1425, when the account was rendered by a bailiff for the last time, and 1430 when it was made by Richard Holt as 'farmer'. He already held the manor of Coldrey within the parish of Froyle by his marriage with Christine Colrithe (and they were both benefactors of Wintney Priory). On the evidence of the surviving compotus rolls, the leases seem to have been for terms of seven years; Richard Holt held for 14 years and his successor, William Whithere, for seven years.[34]

Although rents and the profits from farming activities were the most important sources of revenue that the nunneries received from their estates, there were others such as the profits from the ferry which sailed from the Isle of Wight over to Portsmouth. This was run by the abbess of Wherwell's manor of Ashey. (There was also a windmill on the manor, at least from 1274, in contrast to the watermills on its other properties.[35]) Another source of income for all the houses came from their various manorial courts. The jurisdiction that the abbesses had on their manors over their local tenants was based on their feudal relationship: the tenants, both free and villein, owed suit to the abbess as their lord and were thus as obliged to attend her court as she was obliged to hold one. (In the same way each abbess, as a tenant-in-chief, owed suit to the king.[36]) Naturally the functions of these courts did not remain static over the centuries. The original suit of court owed to an abbess at her court every three weeks declined in importance, though it was still being quoted in 1367,[37] but the jurisdiction of the court baron and the court leet continued on the manors. The steward of each abbey normally held court on the different manors twice a year. The perquisites of court that he collected were not large, but in 1412-13 they amounted to £14 from five of Romsey's manors.[38]

By the time that records started in the 13th century the court baron was mainly concerned with land tenure on the manor, questions of service, boundary disputes and minor policing. Taking another example from Froyle, the court roll for November 1281 records the business of the court held by the abbess of Winchester's steward, Richard de Holcote, who took a total of £3. 2s. 0d. for the abbey. This comprised 26s. 8d. for entry-fines paid by Henry de Isenhurst on taking over various properties, tallage (tax) from the tenants of 30s. 0d. and 5s. 4d. from 13 small amercements (fines) relating to the grazing of different animals – several of them had strayed onto someone else's land.[39] There is a similar record of just one session of a court at Steeple Ashton in 1262.[40] The sanctions of these court barons were entirely based on the customs of the manor.

By contrast a court leet administered justice on behalf of the king, so the right of jurisdiction that an abbess had in such a court was delegated by the Crown. Its main business was to hear cases involving minor criminal charges, infringements of the assizes of bread and ale (leading to bakers and alewives who overcharged or gave short measure being fined) and occasional pleas of debt. Earlier these courts were known by the name of just one of their rights of jurisdiction, namely the 'view of frankpledge'. This expression was still in use in 1468 when the abbess of Winchester was granted view of frankpledge and assize of bread and ale at Urchfont and All Cannings ' . . . because they are so overburdened with the repairs of their house and church and other possessions and the payment of tenth and other imposts'.[41] One of the rights that went with a view of frankpledge until the 14th century was the right to maintain a gallows and hang any thief caught red-handed within the manor.[42] But in 1263 the abbess of Romsey thought it prudent to apply for a licence before erecting a new gallows on her manor of Romsey; it was said that there had been a gallows there since the tenth-century but as no one had been condemned since the death of the previous abbess the old one had fallen down.[43] (Actually Abbess Matilda had only died two years earlier.)

However, jurisdiction over serious crimes was gradually taken over by the king's courts. In 1400 when the steward of a later abbess of Romsey arrested a barber of the town who had broken into the house of one of the abbey's chaplains and stolen a breviary worth 40s. 0d., he handed him over to the sheriff for trial. But the steward later had to answer for his action in the abbess's court leet.[44]

There was an interesting case at Wherwell in the 1370s that illustrates another way the nunneries could benefit financially from the operation of justice. One of their tenants in Wherwell, Henry Harold, murdered his wife there and then fled to the church for sanctuary. Since he was then a fugitive from justice, the reeve of the abbess seized all his farm stock and crops as well as his household goods on her behalf. From his bull and his ox down to the copper, brass and treen in his house, these goods were worth nearly £35.[45] Perhaps because of their value, the seizure was queried in court afterwards, but in 1384 it was confirmed that the goods all belonged to the abbess and not to the king, and furthermore that she would be entitled to the goods of any other fugitive on her manor during the lifetime of Richard II.[46] (This does of course show the abbey in rather a grasping light, but the business of the court was with property, not social situations.)

Market and fair days were a more normal source of gossip and profit. The nuns of Romsey, Wherwell and Wintney all had charters to hold local markets and fairs which provided their houses with a small income from the owners of booths, from tolls and from the courts of Piepowder that were held at the time of the fairs. St. Mary's Abbey had little benefit from that source, though in 1499 the abbess and convent were granted the right to hold an annual fair at Chalborough Down in the parish of All Cannings, Wiltshire.[47]

Markets were generally held weekly, while a grant to hold a fair was normally made to commemorate the feast day of a patron saint. Thus in the 12th century the abbess and convent of Romsey Abbey had been granted the right to hold a four-day fair in Romsey for the feast of St. Ethelfleda, which fell on 23 October, as well as a market every Sunday. This was confirmed by Henry III in 1268.[48] Four years later he granted them the right to hold an additional fair there for the four days from the feast of SS. Philip and James, which fell on May Day.[49] It seems likely that Romsey Abbey's markets and fairs would have been more profitable than any others owned by the Hampshire nuns on account of the position of the town at the junction of roads from all directions. Indeed the markets probably played their part in helping those roads from Winchester, Salisbury, Stockbridge and Ringwood to develop. Wherwell, by comparison, was off the beaten track and probably too near Andover ever to develop into a major town, but the abbey held a weekly market there on Wednesdays and their annual four-day fair started on 14 September, the feast day of the Exhaltation of the Holy Cross to which their church was dedicated.[50]

In 1228 the prioress of Wintney was similarly granted the right to hold a fair at the time of the feast day of the priory's patron saint, St. Mary Magdalene. This fell on 22 July and the fair was held for the three days from 21 to 23 July.[51] It attracted quite a crowd. By the

1330s it had become so rowdy that Bishop Orleton apparently put a stop to it. His mandate forbidding its being held gives some idea of the robust nature of these annual gatherings:

> Many people have urgently informed us that certain clerics and laymen, whose names are unknown, entering the conventual church of Wintney and its cemetery on the feast of St. Mary Magdalene, have audaciously become accustomed to arouse disputes, cause uproar, attract crowds, and engage in various discussions and disgusting and profane conversations and businesses, and especially the tumult of fairs and much trading, engaging in wrestling and sports, juggling, indecent dancing and the singing of lewd songs.[52]

Valor Ecclesiasticus

The figures for the overall income of the nunneries just before the Dissolution are given in the *Valor Ecclesiasticus* of 1535. This was assessed by commissioners who were appointed under the terms of the Act annexing First Fruits and Tenths to the Crown, which was passed by Parliament in the autumn in 1534. In Hampshire the 15 commissioners appointed in January 1535 were all laymen except the bishop of Winchester, Stephen Gardiner, who was chairman; the others included the mayors of Winchester and Southampton, county landowners and merchants.[53] They were issued with instructions to help them in their enquiries which, at the monasteries, included recording the name of the house, its manorial and other realty, and its rectories and other spiritual income. From that gross figure the commissioners had then to deduct any pensions, rents, alms and fees for which the house was liable before assessing the tenth due to the Crown.

In Hampshire all the enquiries had been completed by 2 May 1535 when Bishop Gardiner wrote to Thomas Cromwell assuring him that 'Neither goodwill nor diligence has been wanting. We delivered the charge into two parts – to know the true value and to grant allowances and deductions'.[54] The survey from the whole country was finished before the end of the year. The returns from most counties gave full details about the different sources of monastic income, but unfortunately the Hampshire returns just gave overall totals of income.

Within their terms of reference the commissioners of 1535 are generally thought to have given a fairly accurate assessment of the income of the monasteries, though they made errors at St. Mary's Abbey, Winchester which will be discussed later. But as a valuation *Valor* figures have two main drawbacks. Firstly the 1530s were a time of inflation but this was not generally reflected in the amount of rent received, so the manors were effectively undervalued, and secondly the value of the monastic buildings and treasury were not included.[55]

In Hampshire the gross incomes of all the monasteries amounted to £6,506 7s. 6d. (net £5,187 11s. 3½d.).[56] The figures for the nunneries were as follows:[57]

	Gross income	Net income	Tenth
St. Mary's, Winchester	£245 17s. 2½d.	£179 7s. 2d.	£17 18s. 8½d.
Romsey Abbey	£528 8s. 10½d.	£393 10s. 10½d.	£39 7s. 1¼d.
Wherwell Abbey	£403 12s. 10d.	£339 8s. 7d.	£33 18s. 10d.
Wintney Priory	£59 0s. 12d. (*sic*)	£43 3s. 0d.	£4 6s. 3¾d.

Chapter Ten

The Economy of the Nunneries:
Expenses and Accounts

EXPENSES

The expenses that the nunneries incurred in the course of a year were numerous. The extension and repair of buildings at home and on their manors; the payment of dues to king, pope and bishop; alms for the poor; legal costs and the upkeep of servants were all a continual drain on their resources, in addition to the everyday costs of food, clothes and hospitality.

Building work and repairs

The actual buildings used by the nuns have had little mention so far. Knowledge about the domestic quarters in particular is very limited, although it is sure to be extended by archaeologists in due course. At Romsey in 1976 Mr. Stubbs made the exciting discovery that part of the refectory was still standing with its late 12th-early 13th century roof, and his other work has enabled him to draw up a plan of the abbey's precinct. The main documentary sources are the records made at the time of the Dissolution which will be discussed later, but there is some earlier evidence of building work, including the Romsey Abbey accounts for 1412-13 which show that nearly 20 per cent of the house's income that year was spent on repairs.[1]

The best recorded period is the 13th century. Work was then in progress at all the nunneries at one time or another and Henry III gave timber to each of them. He was particularly generous to the nuns at Winchester whose abbesses perhaps had more opportunities to mention their community's needs to the king. Over a period of 40 years he made 13 gifts of timber to them, and many of the mandates give the purpose for which it was intended. The first was in 1229 when just one tree was given for repairs to their houses[2] but the following year 50 rafters were sent for their church and six oaks were provided from Alice Holt forest for roofing it in 1252.[3] Another six oaks from the same forest had already been given for making shingles, and a further 10 were provided in 1255.[4] There was then a pause until 1269-71 when a total of 19 oaks were sent,[5] so some project was under way. The timber was not always oak: in 1232 the five trees provided for panelling the nuns' chapter house were beech.[6]

At Romsey there seems to have been fairly continuous activity from the end of the 12th century when work started on the nave of the church. Once the chancel and transepts had been completed and consecrated the nuns worshipped there, so the masons and workmen could move into the area south of the temporary screen that had been erected earlier (see p.31). First of all the late Saxon church was demolished, providing some of the stone for the new work; this was supplemented by other stone from the Isle of Wight. The king had already given the abbey five good oaks in 1231 for the repair of their dormitories.[7] During 1251-2 he provided them with another 22[8] and these were followed up with the gift of 16 more which were specifically for the fabric of their church,[9] though presumably all 38 oaks were used for the nave. Eighteen years later he gave the abbess another six oaks.[10] Once the first four bays of the nave had been completed, a new temporary screen was built across it and building activities were then switched to the domestic range. The screen remained in place for nearly a century before the last three bays and a porch were built on to the west end.[11] The difference in style is immediately apparent.

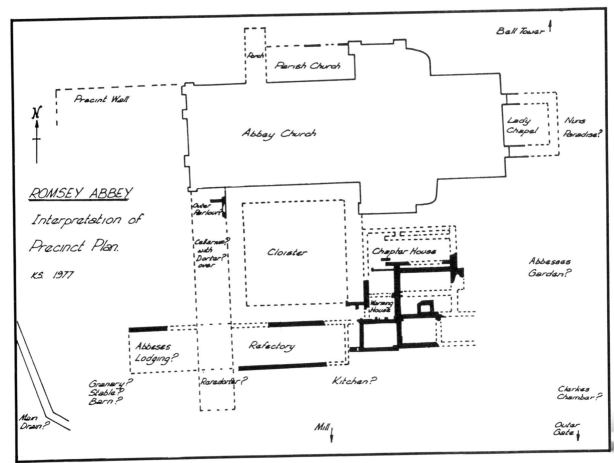

37.   Interpretation of the precinct plan of Romsey Abbey.

Henry III also gave oaks to Wintney Priory. In 1251 he sent a mandate to the custodian of Eversley forest for the prioress to be allowed to carry away 40 oaks to the priory without impediment or paying tolls on them,[12] but unfortunately the mandate does not say how they were to be used. The nuns' new stone church had been dedicated 17 years before[13] but perhaps it was being extended, or the chapter house may date from this time. Earlier in the century Bishop Peter des Roches had given timber to the priory to make their cloister, and he had followed that with a gift of wooden shingles which were presumably used to roof it.[14]

The best recorded building works at that time were at Wherwell Abbey. The Close Rolls show that Henry III gave the abbess 64 oaks altogether between 1234 and 1256,[15] and Edward I presented another 12 in 1277.[16] The 22 that were first given were for repairing their own houses but those given between 1250 and 1256 were for new work; twice this was called 'timbering' but in 1255 it was stated that the 15 oaks were for the fabric of the church.[17] The king also ordered 60 marks to be sent to the abbess in 1251, and chalk from Harewood forest the following year.[18]

All the oaks presented by Henry III were given in the time of Abbess Euphemia, and thanks to the eulogy devoted to her in the Wherwell cartulary the main projects for which they must have been used are known. The whole passage from the cartulary has been printed in translation but the main points will now be summarised, keeping to the sequence of work used by the chronicler since that seems to indicate the order in which it was carried out. She built a new infirmary away from the main convent buildings, with its own dorter and other offices and a watercourse beneath to carry away refuse; behind this she built a Lady Chapel with its own enclosed garden lined with vines and trees to the north. Both this and the quadrangle she designed in the centre of new offices by the river were probably typical of the gardens of the period. Then she turned her attention to the demesne manor. It was evidently in a sordid state. She decided that a clean sweep of the old buildings and squalid out-buildings was needed because of the fire risk from their being too close together; the kitchen was too near the granary and the old hall, and the courtyard

38. The nave of Romsey Abbey as seen from the chancel. The nearest four bays were built in the late 12th century; the other three and the great west window are 13th-century.

was so small that the dirt and dung made it 'a cause of offence to both the feet and nostrils to those who had occasion to pass through'. All the old buildings were demolished, a new hall was built where the manor court could be held, and the courtyard was levelled before the new out-buildings and a wall were erected round it. Gardens, vineyards and shrubberies were planted beyond it. The watermill came next. That too was taken down, though presumably not until the new mill and its sluices had been built at some distance from the new hall. The chronicler added that the mill was constructed with great care so that it would do more work for the abbey than the old one.

Having put Wherwell in better shape, Abbess Euphemia then took a good look at the abbey's manor houses at Middleton and Tufton where she found many of the same defects and the same fire risks that there had been on the demesne manor. At Middleton the original builders had (incredibly in such a well watered area) managed to choose a site without sufficient water and too near the public highway. She demolished it of course, and built a new manor, farmhouse and strong out-buildings on the river bank. Then we are told that she set to work in the same way at Tufton, but as the manor buildings there are still next to the church perhaps no drastic re-siting was needed.

In her last years, in the 1250s, the abbess turned her energy and attention to the nunnery buildings again. The decision to do so was forced on her by the sudden collapse of the bell tower above the dorter one night. Fortunately, 'by an obvious miracle from heaven', none of the nuns was hurt. A new stone spire 'of commanding height and exquisite workmanship' was built and may be glimpsed in the little picture of the church in the corner of Abbess Cowdray's portrait. It may have been the master mason in charge of that work who discovered that the presbytery of the abbey church had been built on poor foundations and was in danger of collapse since, for the first time, 'the advice of skilled builders' is mentioned. With all her previous experience the abbess was probably firm in her guidance to the chapter to take the bold decision. The presbytery was taken down to its foundations and then, finding that the ground underneath was waterlogged, she ordered it to be dug out to a depth of 12 feet until firm, dry ground was found. There she herself laid the first stone of the new foundations. She lived long enough to see the new presbytery completed.

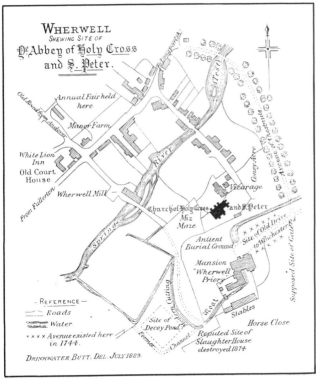

39. Plan of Wherwell, 1889. The abbey was on the site occupied by the house called Wherwell Priory.

The writer of Abbess Euphemia's obituary did not mention the cost of all her building projects. The king's oaks would certainly have helped but even so one can only marvel at her vision and drive, and her evident ability to organise both finance and workforce to achieve her objectives. All abbesses had overall responsibility for the property of their houses and it was not unusual for other women, particularly widows, to run family estates, but Abbess Euphemia's achievements were of another order. As the writer said with admiration, she must indeed have 'seemed to have the spirit of a man rather than a woman'.[19]

There is no other description of building work at the nunneries to compare with that account, but new building and the need for repairs are quite often mentioned in records of the following centuries. How often they were made necessary by fire damage is not known, but it is unlikely that the houses did not have outbreaks at some time or another. The nuns of St. Mary's Abbey, Winchester had 'suffered loss by destruction of its buildings' in 1352,[20] but their petition to the pope does not make it clear whether they were monastic or manorial buildings. Whichever they were, the poor ladies were in trouble and debt and unable to repair their church and house. In 1468 they made a plea to the king about the financial burden of repairing their house, church and other possessions,[21] and 20 years later there were complaints at a visitation that the floors in the dormitory and clothes washing area were in need of repair.[22] But one way or another money must have been found for most necessary work at the abbey for in 1536 the commissioners reported that the house was in a good state of repair.[23]

There were two important building projects at St. Mary's Abbey during its last two centuries. One was the chapel of the Holy Trinity that was built in the nuns' cemetery on the north side of their church early in the 14th century. This is well recorded, and has already been mentioned, but the cost of its construction was entirely borne by the Inkepenne family and not by the nuns themselves.[24] The second was the new Lady Chapel which was built adjoining the choir in 1402-3. Its foundations must lie very close to the south-east corner of the present Abbey House. Nothing is known about its financing or construction except that it was built in one year and 15 weeks.[25] It seems strange that it was still being referred to as the *new* Lady Chapel a century later in the will of John Cornyshe.[26]

It is possible that a drawing of the spire of the abbey church is included in the earliest illustration of Winchester, which was probably made during Edward II's reign. This small sketch at the bottom of a page in a copy of Geoffrey of Monmouth's 'History of the Kings of Britain' has been the subject of an article by Dr. John Harvey.[27] He considers that the drawing may well be based on a sketch made from the western slope of St. Giles's Hill above the East gate and about a quarter of a mile east of the abbey, and that the larger of the two central wooden spires could belong to the cathedral. Concerning the smaller spire, Dr. Harvey has written:

> Allowing for artist's licence in turning the real-life sketch into a picture for the 'chronicle', I do not see any reason why the smaller steeple should not be that of St. Mary's and it seems rather more likely than any other. It could hardly be one of the very small parish churches of the city, and only the Blackfriars has a conceivable possible site, but it would not fit well.[28]

At Romsey the building and repair of the monastic houses 'ruinous by age' were one of the reasons given for the poverty of the abbey in 1351.[29] Later in the century Bishop Wykeham criticised the many repairs that were needed both within the abbey precinct and on its manors, and mentioned particularly the dilapidations in the convent church, the houses of the infirmary and, rather vaguely, 'the rooms needed by the nuns'.[30] Perhaps the Lady Chapel which had been built at the end of the 12th century was one of the areas he had in mind. Certainly plans were in hand by the end of the century to pull it down and rebuild it on a larger scale. Excavations have shown that the floor level was lowered slightly and then tiled, while the roof was supported by a central column.[31] (Unlike the new Lady Chapel at St. Mary's Abbey the work cannot be dated from documentary sources; it is not mentioned in the registers of Wykeham or Beaufort.) A century later the roof of the new Lady Chapel was causing trouble. At the visitation in 1501 several of the nuns said that it was decayed, while one lady complained that if it rained they were unable to remain either in the quire or their beds because of the state of the roofs over the chancel and the dorter.[32]

The buildings at Wintney Priory were on a much smaller scale than at the abbeys, and it seems unlikely that much new work was undertaken after the 13th century since the nuns were so frequently in debt. But repair work on their church was evidently in hand in 1397 when the pope granted indulgences to anyone who visited the priory and gave alms for its repair and conservation.[33] Prioress Alice Fyshide was head of the house then, but early in 1415 she was forced to resign and Johanna Benbury became prioress. Within a few months of her election she was arranging for a new roof to be built on the convent church, and the agreement drawn up between herself and the two carpenters from Basingstoke that September still survives with part of the priory seal attached to it.[34] It has been summarised:

> Agreement with two carpenters to make a flat roof for the church, containing nine beams, with the necessary wallplates, and above it a bell-cote of four posts, with a flat roof; to be finished within about 10 months. The convent shall have the old roof removed and shall provide timber, ropes and lifting machines. The carpenters shall have £22, a pig and a wether, and a gown worth 10s; also

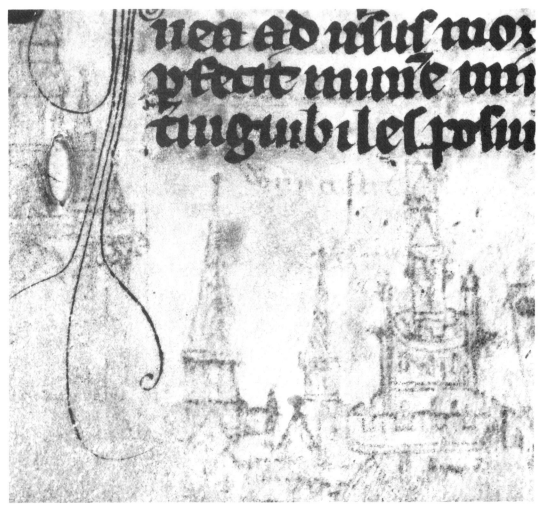

40. A marginal sketch from Geoffrey of Monmouth's 'History of the Kings of Britain' showing the
Winchester spires. The larger central wooden spire may have belonged to the cathedral; the smaller
one may have been the spire of St Mary's Abbey. BL Royal ms. 13 A.iii, f.17v.

lodging and cooking utensils for themselves and their men, and food for six men for a week when
they set up the roof. They produce two sureties for performance of the contract.[35]

Not only does this provide the only known example of part of the cost of a building project
at one of the nunneries, but it also makes clear how such work was organised, with the men
lodging nearby, possibly on the demesne farm, and doing their own cooking. The £22 only
covered the labour costs for the new work. Possibly the prioress arranged for the farmhands
to strip off the old roof, but she still had to meet the expense of the new material – and
however did she organise the hire of lifting machines? It seems likely that all the costs
involved were met by Richard Holt and that it was for this help that he and his wife
Christine were described as benefactors of the foundation in the priory's calendar.[36]

Exactions by King, Pope and Bishop

Taxation is a complex subject that can only be glanced at in this study. The abbeys were liable to pay various taxes on both their spiritual and temporal properties; some were due to the crown, some to the papacy, and some that were imposed by the pope actually benefited the king. Like all taxes they were resented. They were certainly a drain on the resources of the abbeys, as the Winchester nuns pointed out in 1468 when they included 'the payment of tenths and other imposts' among the list of their financial burdens.[37]

The earliest recorded taxes that were paid by the abbeys to the Crown appear in the Pipe Rolls. The first was in 1130-1 when the abbess of St. Mary's, Winchester paid a total of 59s. on the abbey's property in Hampshire, Wiltshire, Lincolnshire and Berkshire.[38] In 1158-9 the abbesses of Winchester and Romsey each paid the 10 marks for which their houses were liable on their Hampshire properties,[39] but eight years later the abbess of Romsey only paid half the 40s. that she owed.[40] Similarly in 1200, when the abbess of Wherwell owed 40 marks for taking 80 acres into cultivation (mainly in Harewood) she paid £20 and remained owing the other 10 marks.[41] On many of the early rolls there are no payments from the Hampshire nunneries, but in 1203 all the abbesses were among the heads of religious houses who made contributions towards the cost of King John's war in France.[42]

Each abbey always had to pay a fine to the king as their patron every time he restored the temporalities of the house to a new abbess after her election, and as tenants-in-chief the three abbesses owed feudal services to the king as well as taxes. Although the abbess of Winchester, a baroness in her own right, was not summoned to Parliament on account of her sex,[43] that factor did not excuse her from knight's service, which was an obligation to provide and maintain fully armed horsemen on demand to serve the king. The abbesses of Winchester, Shaftesbury, Wilton and Barking were all summoned to provide their quota of knights during the troubles in Wales in the early 1260s.[44] The abbess of Romsey was requested to send men-at-arms for service in the north at the beginning of the 14th century,[45] and also for the defence of Southampton in the wake of the French raid of 1338, though she resisted an attempt to make her provide an archer as well.[46] Three years later she and the abbess of Wherwell were each assessed as liable to provide one man-at-arms when requested by the sheriff.[47]

Some taxes of tenths of ecclesiastical income were levied by the pope but granted to the king for a particular cause. Pope Nicholas IV levied a crusading tenth in 1291 but Edward I failed to take the Cross so he should have forfeited the grant; in fact he and the pope shared the spoils between them.[48] In 1294 money intended for the Holy Land included tenths paid by Romsey Abbey, and three years later all three abbeys made contributions for the same cause; the abbess of Winchester paid another 20s. in 1306.[49]

As the number of papal levies increased in the 13th century, new methods of assessment and collection were needed. Three assessments were made between 1254 and 1291, culminating in the *Taxatio* of Pope Nicholas IV.[50] The office of a resident papal collector in England had been established by 1228 to collect the taxes, and the accounts that later collectors rendered to the papal camera between 1317 and 1378 have been studied.[51] In that period there were 12 entries concerning the nunneries at Winchester and Wherwell and five (all between 1363 and 1371) for Romsey Abbey. Most of the items concerned annates that were due for vacant benefices, and several were repeats for money still owing. As an example, £26 13s. 4d. was due from Wherwell Abbey's prebend of Middleton in 1353; between 1363 and 1371 a part payment of £6 13s. 4d. was made, followed by another of £5, but it was not until 1371-9 that a new collector managed to extract the remaining £15. Altogether there were eight entries concerning the one debt.[52] The collectors themselves were entitled to their own procurations from a large number of religious houses. In 1393 the abbesses of

Romsey and Winchester were included in a list of papal debtors for the previous year for their non-payment of procurations, but as it was headed by the archdeacon of Winchester they were in good company![53] (He owed Peter's Pence from the diocese for the previous four years.)

At the start of Cardinal Beaufort's surviving register the lists of taxable ecclesiastical income include the various manors in the diocese held by the nunneries. On these the tenths payable by the abbess of Wherwell were £20 3s. 10d., by the abbess of Winchester £8 4s. 4½d. and by the abbess of Romsey £7 17s. 9d.[54] In 1412-3 the Romsey nuns paid £40 13s. 4d. on all their properties in tenths for the king. By the end of the 15th century the pope had lost his hold on the clerical subsidy which was wholly paid to the king whenever it was ordered by convocation; it was then sometimes in the form of a tenth, but at other times it was a round sum.[55] After Henry VIII's extravagant meeting at the Field of the Cloth of Gold in June 1520 he needed extra finance; in 1522 the abbess of Winchester contributed £200 and the other two abbesses £133 6s. 8d. each towards the 'loan' made to the king for his expenses in France.[56]

Nearer home, the payments that successive bishops of Winchester required from the nunneries were less onerous. The main charge was for procurations which were due whenever the diocesan made a personal visitation, but even then some kindly bishops evidently used their discretion. In the 13th century Bishop Nicholas of Ely did not charge the Wherwell nuns for his visitation to them (it may even have been the occasion when he lent them £30),[57] and Bishop Orleton stayed at Romsey Abbey at his own expense during his visitation in 1334.[58] Early in the 16th century Bishop Fox wrote that he had never taken procurations for a visitation from any of the monastic houses in his diocese.[59] The bishops would have benefited whenever one of the nunneries' benefices in the diocese fell vacant,[60] and more regularly they each received small annual payments for the appropriation of particular churches. Thus 6s. 8d. was due each year from the abbess of Winchester for the appropriation of Froyle, and the same sum from the abbess of Romsey for the appropriation of the prebend of St. Laurence.[61] Later, when Cardinal Beaufort allowed Wherwell Abbey to appropriate the prebendal church of Goodworth Clatford in 1446, the abbess there became liable to pay him and his successors 13s. 4d. a year as well as 6s. 8d. to the archdeacon of Winchester and 10s. to the prior and convent of St. Swithun's.[62] After the Dissolution Bishop Gardiner claimed all these, and other similar payments made by former monasteries each year, from the Court of Augmentations.[63]

Wintney Priory was in a different position from the abbeys. The king was not patron of the house and so the nuns did not have to pay him a fine whenever they elected a new prioress. Cistercian houses were anyway meant to be exempt from taxes, though sometimes they were expected to provide 'gratuities' for the king; but when there was such a collection for Edward I in 1276 the Wintney nuns did not contribute.[64] Other demands were sometimes made to the priory but several bishops of Winchester supported the nuns' pleas to be excused.

In 1285 the papal nuncio evidently tried to obtain procurations from the priory but Bishop Pontissara wrote to him on behalf of the nuns, pleading for him to forbear and pointing out that he himself excused them from all charges on account of their deep poverty.[65] In 1306 Bishop Woodlock 'as instructed' did not press them for the £4 14s. 0d. owing on their rectories of Sparsholt and Hartley Monialium, and in 1297 and 1321 they were granted letters of protection. In 1340 they were excused from the levy on agricultural produce 'as the priory is so slenderly endowed that the goods thereof do not suffice for the maintenance of the prioress and convent'.[67] Further exemptions followed in 1398, 1404 and 1422.[68] Between 1469 and 1484 Bishop Waynflete wrote four times to the Exchequer asking that the poorest religious houses in his diocese might be excused from demands in the king's breves, and the prioress and nuns of Wintney were included each time.[69] (The other houses were the Hospital of St. Cross, Selborne Priory and the Priory of St. Denys, Southampton.) Similar entries appear in the registers of Bishops Courtenay and Langton.[70]

Almsgiving and Pensions

'The poor you have always with you' but under their Rule monks and nuns were expected to be ready with some assistance for people in distress. This help involved simple casual relief for the poor who came to their doors, the distribution of alms and food at particular times of the year, and the provision of sheltered accommodation for the elderly in their own hospitals. By its nature casual relief is rarely recorded, unless it achieves the fame of the Wayfarers' Dole at St. Cross Hospital, but there must have been very many people grudgingly thankful for coarse bread and ale or soup from the kitchens of the nunneries, especially at times of famine or distress. The distribution of foodstuffs and alms on particular festivals was a more organised affair: the traditional times were at Christmas and in Holy Week, especially Maundy Thursday. At St. Mary's Abbey, Winchester, it was customary to distribute bread, ale and cooked food on the eve of the feast of the Purification (1 February) but Bishop Woodlock had to point out to the nuns that the dole was indeed to be given to the poor and not to their own domestic servants.[71]

All three abbeys founded and maintained hospitals for the relief of the elderly and infirm. At Wherwell the site of the hospital is unknown, but was presumably close to the convent buildings as it was at the other two abbeys. Knowledge of such a hospital at Wherwell only rests on the existence of two records: at the end of the 14th century one of Bishop Wykeham's injunctions that were sent to Wherwell ordered that bread intended for the poor women of their hospital each week should not be given to other people;[72] and secondly, in 1504 William Howell of Wherwell bequeathed a shirt or smock to each man and woman in the abbey's hospital.[73] At Winchester the nuns maintained the Sisterne House which, as its name implies, was only for poor women. In 1536 there were 13 'pore systers' living there whose names were all recorded.[74] In the previous century at least one citizen of Winchester, Hugh Craan, had left a small legacy of 6s. 8d. to the sisters there.[75] The Sisterne House lay south of the much larger St. John's Hospital, on a site near the present statue of King Alfred; it continued in use after the Dissolution and the building survived until the end of the 18th century.[76]

At Romsey two separate charities had been founded by King Edgar in the tenth century and were maintained by the nuns until the Dissolution. One was for the benefit of 13 poor and feeble women whose support cost 40s. a year; they lived in the Sisters House near the abbey gate and had their own garden beside pasture land called Rackeclose.[77] The other was the Hospital of St. Mary Magdalene in Spittal Street which took in 'leprous and poor persons'.[78] Originally the hospital had been intended for seven old men,[79] but at the time of the Dissolution there were four men and two women being cared for there.[80]

As well as giving help to the poor, the nunneries were also liable to pay pensions to assist various clergy. Sometimes this was a continuing charge, such as the annual pension of £2 13s. 4d. plus board and lodging that the nuns of St. Mary's Abbey, Winchester gave to their neighbour, the rector of St. Peter's church in Colebrook Street.[81] Sometimes the pension had to be paid to a priest until a benefice in the gift of the nunnery became vacant for him. The nomination of such a recipient was one of the king's prerogatives after the election of a new abbess; invariably the man was a clerk from the royal household having been in offices such as the almonry or chancery,[82] but the priest nominated to Wherwell Abbey in 1518 was chaplain to Queen Catherine.[83] Altogether seven clerks were nominated to receive pensions from St. Mary's, Winchester, nine from Romsey Abbey and eight from Wherwell

Abbey, until they were provided with a benefice. The practice continued until 1527 when Abbess Elizabeth Shelley of Winchester was elected.[84]

At least the clerks waiting for a benefice were only due for a pension, but elderly corrodians nominated by the king had to be provided with board, lodging and suitable clothing at the expense of the nunneries for the rest of their lives. The nuns of Romsey Abbey seem to have been regularly liable to provide such maintenance for an elderly priest: John Belle was sent there in 1391, taking the place of another clerk who had died, and there is a similar record in 1445.[85]

Sometimes the corrodians imposed on the abbeys were lay people to whom the king felt some obligation for their past services. After the election of a new abbess at Winchester in 1313 Edward II exercised his right to nominate a corrodian and sent Juliana de Leygrave, the niece of the foster mother who had suckled him, to the abbey and ordered the community to provide her with financial support and her own chamber within the abbey whenever she wished to stay there.[86] Early in his reign Edward III sent a yeoman who had served his father and grandfather to St. Mary's Abbey;[87] he made similar nominations to Wherwell Abbey, and in Richard II's time one of the yeomen of the king's pantry was sent there.[88] But sometimes a nunnery would manage to escape from the obligation to provide for one of the king's nominees. Thus in June 1310 a mandate was sent to Romsey Abbey for the nuns to make provision for Juliana la Despenser and her maid for the rest of her life, apparently without making preliminary enquiries, but either the abbess or the lady herself raised objections. (Or perhaps it was Bishop Woodlock who disapproved of secular women living permanently in nunneries.) Anyway, seven weeks later the king sent a less preremptory request to the abbess and convent of Shaftesbury asking them to provide a chamber for Juliana and her damsel with all the necessities of life for her in view of her position, since she was the niece of John de London who had served the king well.[89] After that no more is heard of Juliana.

Lesser expenses for the nunneries included occasional donations such as the £10 that the abbess of Romsey paid to Cardinal Beaufort in 1412-3,[90] and the provision of small pensions to other religious bodies. In 1535 the Romsey nuns were paying five annual pensions to Edington Priory amounting to £16 18s. 1d., and they regularly gave their sisters at Wintney a less generous 2s. a year out of their manor of Itchen Stoke.[91] After 1313 the Wintney nuns themselves supported the priest serving the chantry chapel at Sherborne Coudray (the estate that later became The Vyne) out of their property at Herriard and Ellisfield. 'The chantry of ye Vine in Sherborne St. Johns' was still a charge of £4 a year on their former grange in 1548.[92]

Lawsuits

In the previous chapter the dispensing of justice was seen as a source of profit. But there was another side to the law, and being either a plaintiff or defendant in any action was an expensive business. All the nunneries were involved in litigation at one time or another, making them liable to the expense of attorneys, court officials, travelling costs and 'courtesies' (the polite word for bribes). The Romsey Abbey accounts for 1412 show that £5 8s. 0d. was spent on pleas in court that year.[93] Sometimes a case, and its costs, could drag on for years. No wonder that when Archbishop Pecham wrote to Wherwell Abbey he ordered that lawsuits should only be undertaken with the consent of the whole community.[94]

Usually the head of a house would not appear in court herself. At the end of the 13th century one of the clauses in Pope Bonifaces's Bull *Periculoso* warned secular lords against summoning nuns to attend law courts in person; proctors were to represent them instead.[95] At least two of the attorneys who represented the Hampshire nunneries were their tenants. In the 1420s Robert Gyffard, who leased one of the houses owned by Wherwell Abbey in

Jewry Street, Winchester acted as attorney for the abbess of Wherwell in the city court on at least five occasions.[96] And in 1454 the prioress of Wintney was represented by John Lovell, a glover, who lived at the priory's property on the corner of High Street and Colebrook Street (his daughter was a nun at St. Mary's Abbey).[97] Earlier the prioress had been taken to court because of the state of the damaged highway outside this property and had been found liable to repair it.[98]

At least five abbesses of Winchester were involved in actions in the city court between 1361 and 1449,[99] and in October 1454 Abbess Agnes and the abbess of Wherwell were each represented by attorneys at the 'burghmoot' held in the Guildhall. However, although John Lovell was named for Wintney Priory, there are gaps in the record for the names of the two attorneys representing the abbesses.[100] Neither was Abbess Elizabeth Shelley's attorney named in 1528 when she brought an action in the city court against George Baynham, who was also being sued by an innkeeper, William Broker; the case came before the court at weekly intervals between 18 December 1528 and the following 11 February.[101]

Besides litigation in the local courts, the nunneries were sometimes involved in actions heard in the central court which would have cost even more. Among the Curia Regis Rolls for the first half of the 13th century, the abbess of Winchester was directly concerned in seven cases, the abbess of Romsey in five and the prioress of Wintney in four.[102] Most of the actions concerned their manors and lands. The names of four proctors who represented the interests of Romsey Abbey were included in the Close Rolls in the mid-13th century; in the 1250s two were appointed for each action but in 1276 only Robert de Romesy appeared for the abbess when she sued Nicholas de Ichene and others for trespass.[103] The nature of that trespass is not known, but in a later case the abbess recovered 100 shillings from the owner of three greyhounds who killed three of her swans.[104]

Actions involving the abbesses of Wherwell in the 13th century include one that was brought by Abbess Euphemia before the itinerant judges concerning her rights of pasture in Andover.[105] Two later cases were entered in the abbey's cartulary with the names of the judges and the abbey's attorneys.[106] At the end of the century the troubles over the presentation to the prebend of Middleton led to litigation involving the papal court, though the abbess was not one of the parties to the dispute.[107] But in 1308 it was she who took the initiative when she sued the vicar of Middleton for levelling a dike in his parish, felling trees and 'other outrages' which were valued at £20.[108]

ACCOUNTS AND DEBTS

In the aftermath of the Conquest the financial and economic administration of the monasteries had gradually been decentralised, so that each was run without a central treasury or any system of audit. But by the end of the 12th century monastic communities were beginning to follow the example of the state with its royal treasury and exchequer. Monastic revenues were first centralised at Christ Church, Canterbury, but the first audit system in a religious house was initiated by Henry de Blois at St. Swithun's Priory in Winchester about 1163-70. However, there is no evidence that he tried to introduce the same system into the nunneries in his diocese. But by the end of the 13th century the authorities at every level were urging monastic houses to establish a single chest or treasury and to have a regular system of account and audit.[109]

The first bishop of Winchester who is known to have ordered a proper accounting system in the nunneries was Bishop Pontissara. At Romsey Abbey he asked for an account to be rendered twice a year, but that was apparently asking too much. When he next held a visitation there early in 1302 he found that his instructions had been ignored altogether, so he then tried asking for accounts to be presented to the whole convent sitting in chapter just once a year.[110] A week later he repeated this injunction to the nuns at Wherwell Abbey.[111]

No doubt the community at Wintney Priory had had similar orders when he visited them in 1301, though in the letter announcing his intended visitation he confined himself to giving them instructions about the general management of their property.[112] After this time episcopal enquiries about the accounts of a house were an invariable feature of every visitation.

The type of financial administration that the bishops wanted to see in the nunneries is set out in the injunctions that Bishop Stratford sent to St. Mary's Abbey, Winchester in 1326. He ordered that there must be an annual audit of the accounts of their bailiffs, reeves and other ministers during the week after Michaelmas, and that a full statement of the account should then be read in chapter in the presence of the whole convent so that decisions could be made about future expenditure. (The implication being that the abbess was not to make important decisions on her own.) Since there was apparently no central receiver at the abbey at that time, the bishop went on to order the appointment of one. He was to be assisted by two of the older and more discreet ladies, and with their knowledge of the sources of the abbey's revenue he was to receive and record all the income from its manors, rents and other sources of profit and then make the moneys available for the use of the house. He was to make up his accounts annually.[113] This seems to be the first instance of senior nuns being directed to help a male official with the financial management of one of the abbeys. It indicates that the bishop considered that some of the older nuns had a working knowledge of the abbey's sources of income which until then may have been in their own hands.

Earlier, Bishop Pontissara seems to have assumed that at Romsey Abbey the reception and distribution of rents was under the control of the prioress for he ordered that she was to be assisted in the task by 'two of the more influential and discreet ladies' whose advice was to be followed.[114] At Wherwell Abbey Archbishop Pecham had appointed a co-adjutress, whom he made prioress, to assist the abbess with the management of the abbey's property.[115] By the time William of Wykeham sent his injunctions to Romsey and Wherwell in 1387 a receiver would have been part of the normal establishment at each of the abbeys. The bishop did not mention the office, although the abbesses were sent the usual instructions that a full financial statement was to be made each year and that nuns holding office should also render accounts of their administration. No such accounts of an individual office holder have survived, but two charters in the Wherwell cartulary set out the annual income of the sacrist of the house.[116]

Apart from accounts of individual manors, only four account rolls for the nunneries themselves are known to have survived from the period before the Dissolution. The only one that covers a full year is the small roll for Romsey Abbey for the 12 months from Michaelmas 1412; an edited translation of it is printed here, taken from Liveing's *Records of Romsey Abbey*.[117] There is no indication why this one account should have been preserved among the public records. There was no change of abbess that year, though there was a change of sovereign in March 1413 when Henry V succeeded his father.

Two accounts were compiled by John de London of Alton when he had the custody of the abbeys of Wherwell and Romsey during vacancies that occurred during 1279-8. (He has already been mentioned as the uncle of Juliana la Despenser.) The roll for Wherwell Abbey covers the 70-day interregnum that followed the death of Abbess Elena de Percy in December 1297 and lists the income received from the abbey's manors during that period; it amounted to £30 17s. 7½d. of which £13 6s. 8d. was used for the upkeep of the nuns. (This was almost the same figure as the £13 2s. 10½d. which had come in from the rents, farm produce and the mill of the manor of Wherwell itself.) At Romsey the vacancy after the death of Abbess Alice Walerand the following April only lasted 18 days; in that time £11 12s. 1d. came in from the abbey's manors in Hampshire and Wiltshire. Both accounts give

ACCOUNT ROLL OF ROMSEY ABBEY FOR A.D. *1412.

Receipts.

	£	s	d	£	s	d
1.—Aishton.						
Rent	56	2	3¾			
Farm	12	12	0			
Sale of works	6	11	0¼			
Sale of wool (see under Edyndon)						
Sale of corn and stores	20	6	8			
Perquisites of Courts [*i.e.* Manor Courts] ...	6	8	0			
				102	0	0
2.—Edyndon.						
Rent	26	4	8¼			
Sale of works	6	8	4¾			
Sale of wool	30	0	0			
Sale of corn and stores	16	8	0			
Perquisites of Courts	2	0	0			
				81	1	1
3.—Romseye.						
Rent	53	0	11½			
Farm	3	0	0			
Sale of works	2	4	4½			
Sale of wool	30	0	0			
Sale of corn and stores	54	6	8			
Perquisites of Courts	4	0	0			
				146	12	0
4.—More Malewayn.						
Rent	2	0	0			
Sale of corn and stores	10	0	0			
				12	0	0
5.—Sydemanton.						
Rent	3	3	0½			
Sale of works	2	0	3½			
Sale of corn and stores	26	6	8			
Perquisites of Courts	0	12	0			
				32	2	0
6.—Ichenestoke.						
Rent	9	5	7¾			
Sale of works	3	0	11¾			
Sale of corn and stores	17	4	4			
Perquisites of Courts	1	0	0			
				[1] 30	11	0
Total receipts	£404	6	0½	[1] 404	6	1

Totals under Sources of Income extracted from above.

	£	s	d	£	s	d
1.—Rent				149	16	7¾
2.—Farms				15	12	0
3.—Works				20	5	0¾
4.—Wool				60	0	0
5.—Corn and stores				[2] 144	12	8
6.—Courts				14	0	0
Total receipts as above ...	£404	6	0½	[2] 404	6	4¼
Deficit balance				[3] 18	19	2
Total				[3] £423	5	6¼

[1] Error: ½*d.* too much. [2] Error: 4*d.* too much.
[3] £10 too little, by which the account does not balance.

Expenses.

	£	s	d	£	s	d
1.—The Convent.						
(*a*) For clothing	23	7	8			
(*b*) Their kitchen (coquina)	38	4	4			
(*c*) For pittances	18	10	0			
(*d*) The chief kitchen (percoquina)	25	15	10			
				105	17	10
2.—The Abbess.						
(*a*) Provisions for herself and household, and divers expenses, during the year ...	51	4	0			
(*b*) In gifts	8	12	0			
(*c*) In liveries for the household, and spices for the guest-house	18	14	4			
(*d*) In fees of servants	30	6	8			
				[1] 110	6	8
3.—[Extra conventual.]						
(*a*) Repairs of the houses of the Romsey mills	†38	3	10			
(*b*) For pleas (*i.e.*, in courts)	5	8	0			
(*c*) For necessaries	3	6	10			
(*d*) Annuities to the Convent, and to king's clerks	18	13	4			
(*e*) Tenths to the King	40	13	4			
(*f*) Procurations, etc.	1	14	8			
				108	0	0
4.—[Various.]						
(*a*) Alms for the poor	8	19	4			
(*b*) Wine for nobles visiting the Abbess, etc. ...	6	13	4			
(*c*) Broken crockery, and mending pots in divers offices	2	13	8			
(*d*) Shoeing horses of the Lady's household, in horse hire, and expenses of men riding on the Lady's business	3	1	0			
(*e*) In oblations, of the Lady and her household	0	14	0			
(*f*) In a gift to Lord Henry, Bishop of Winchester	10	0	0			
				[2] 32	0	4
5.—Repairs.						
(*a*) Repairing the houses of Aishton Manor, and other expenses there	20	1	6½			
(*b*) Similar expenses at Edyndon	13	3	4			
(*c*) ,, ,, ,, Romesey	22	0	10			
(*d*) ,, ,, ,, Stoke	10	0	0			
(*e*) ,, ,, ,, Sidemanton	8	10	0			
(*f*) ,, ,, ,, Le Mour	3	6	10			
				[3] 77	0	8½
Total expenses	£431	18	8	433	5	6½

	£	s	d
[1]	108	17	0
[2]	32	1	4
[3]	77	2	6½

Errors in addition, by which the total should be less by £1. 6*s.* 10½*d.*, as in the first column.

* 14 Henry IV, ended March 24th, 1413.

† Altered to £46. 4*s.* 6*d.*, but the difference, £8. 0*s.* 8*d.*, is not added to the total.

41. Edited account roll of Romsey Abbey for 1412-13.

the fee that John de London himself received for his custodianship. He was evidently paid at the rate of a shilling a day since he earned 70s. at Wherwell and 18s. at Romsey.[118]

The fourth account is a small roll for Wintney Priory at Christmas 1389 which shows an income of £3 3s. 1½d. having been received from tenants on its lands: 49s. 6½d. was in small rents from 44 tenants and 13s. 7d. had come in from eight *firmae*. On another small roll in the same collection of Herriard Papers there is a memorandum of monies received by Prioress Alice Fyshide (1385-1415) for corrodies sold, for nuns admitted, and from alms, legacies and the sales of stock during her time.[119]

When Dr. Hede made his visitation to the four nunneries in 1501 he was told at St. Mary's Abbey and at Wherwell that the annual balance sheet of each house was presented to the chapter each year; at Wherwell the presentation was made at Michaelmas, and the abbess went on to report that the house was not in debt. Not surprisingly there was some criticism about the accounts of Romsey Abbey and more than one nun reported that the abbess had broken into the convent chest where the seal of the abbey was kept. However, at Wintney the ever-precarious state of the priory's finances had improved a little; Prioress Anne reported that since she had taken office three years earlier the debts of the house had been reduced from 20 marks to 5 marks.[120]

Indebtedness was a state known only too well in all small nunneries throughout the country. Even the abbeys with their more generous endowments often suffered from incomes that were inadequate to meet all their outgoings, particularly after the time of the Black Death. Sometimes this was due to bad management but bad luck in the form of poor harvests or outbreaks of the murain could also be a factor. And, as in all ages, it was impossible to forecast some of the expenses of hospitality and taxes for which the nunneries found themselves liable. At such times money had to be borrowed.

A few records show some of the figures that were involved. The earliest shows that the abbess of Romsey borrowed £11 from a Jewish money-lender at the end of the 12th century; he then became liable to pay the king a shilling in the pound which is why the debt was recorded in the Pipe Rolls.[121] But that way out of a difficulty was closed by the end of the next century when the remaining Jews were expelled from the country.

The nuns at Wherwell borrowed money from at least three bishops of Winchester. It has already been mentioned that Bishop Nicholas of Ely lent them £30 when they were in need, and the debt was later remitted by his executors.[122] A few years afterwards they borrowed £20 from a layman, Robert de la Ber; they repaid £4 in 1304 but Bishop Woodlock helped them to repay money still outstanding at the time of Robert's death.[123] On another occasion they had a loan of £30 from Bishop Adam Orleton.[124] In the 13th century the abbess borrowed money from the apostolic delegate, Cardinal Ottobono, and there is an interesting letter in the abbey's cartulary showing the organisation that was sometimes necessary for making payments in pre-banking days. It was written by the cardinal in 1256 and stated that two named Italians who were companions of Orlando Bonsignori, a merchant of Siena, were authorised to request and receive 100 marks from the abbess and convent of Wherwell who owed that sum to him. The Italians were then to pay the money to the cardinal at the new Temple in London on the following Easter Sunday, nine months ahead.[125] Six years later two other Italian merchants from Florence, Ralph and Matthew Bonfilioli, were responsible for conveying 26 marks out to Italy from the abbess and convent, but that was for the farm of Collingbourne church.[126]

Some of the pleas of poverty and debts that the Winchester nuns made on various occasions in the 14th and 15th centuries have also been mentioned. Usually they were addressed to the king, the pope or the bishop, but another recipient was the archdeacon of Wells, Robert de Wambergh. He was evidently in sympathy with the nuns at St. Mary's Abbey for he endowed a chantry in their church in 1328 and part of the agreement between himself and Abbess Matilda de Pecham was his gift of 100 silver marks, cash down, to help relieve the debts of the house.[127]

Inevitably debts were sometimes owing to the nuns rather than owed by them, but there are few records to prove it. In 1339, following a grant made to the king by Parliament, a promise was enrolled to pay the abbess of Romsey £10 7s. 9d. for wool that had been collected, and two citizens of Romsey had similar promises.[128] More typically there was trouble at the beginning of the 15th century with the bailiff of Romsey who owed £40 18s. 10d. to the abbess, and another £40 to Sir William Asthorp.[129] Arrears of rent must also have been a frequent problem for the stewards, but perhaps the action that the abbess of Winchester took in 1386 to recover arrears of a rent of 20s. a year against John Sethfelde, who held the abbey's prebend of Leckford, was part of a wider clash between them. At any rate he departed for the diocese of Durham the following year.[130]

Chapter Eleven

The Dissolution of the Nunneries

Between 1531 and 1539 Parliament passed a series of acts revoking the authority of the pope in England and bringing the church under the control of the Crown. Above all the Act of Supremacy (1534) confirmed the king as Supreme Head of the Church in England, giving him the power to promulgate doctrine and making the church and all its members subject to the laws of the realm. Shortly afterwards the Act annexing First Fruits and Tenths to the Crown was passed, and led to the compilation of the *Valor Ecclesiasticus* mentioned earlier.[1] In the same year Thomas Cromwell consolidated his personal position by becoming the king's Principal Secretary in succession to Stephen Gardiner, Bishop of Winchester, and in the following January he became Vicar General in matters spiritual. It was the scheming mind and skills of this truly great administrator that lay behind the gradual dissolution of all the monasteries in England between 1536 and 1540.

Bishop Gardiner played no active part in the Dissolution, neither did he attempt to defend the religious houses in his own diocese. He had worked closely with the king at home and abroad from 1527 to 1534 but then his opposition to the policy of the king and Cromwell led to his disgrace and loss of office as Principal Secretary. Later he acquiesced in the measures once they had become law, declaring that an act of Parliament discharged his conscience. In the meantime he had retired to his diocese, but in October 1535 he was sent as ambassador to the French court where he remained for three years, largely because Cromwell feared his opposition at home. It was not until the fall of Cromwell in 1540 that he regained his influence with the king, and by that time the dissolution of the monasteries had been completed.[2]

The Dissolution of the Lesser Monasteries

After Cromwell received the returns of the *Valor* he sent out visitors, who were his agents, to visit many of the monastic houses in the country in order to prepare a case against the monks and nuns that could be presented to Parliament. Two of the visitors sent to Hampshire were Dr. Thomas Legh and John ap Rice, both of them experienced in working for Cromwell. Unfortunately their reports have not survived but from their letters it is known that they both visited at least two of the nunneries in the county at this time. After Dr. Legh had finished his business at Wilton Abbey at the beginning of September, both men were at Wherwell Abbey on 11 September 1535 and then at Wintney Priory a fortnight later on the 24th.[3]

The community at Wherwell must still have been in some disorder on account of the allegations made against the conduct of their abbess, Anne Colte, and the bishop of London, John Stokesley. This has already been mentioned in Chapter 8. The commission to examine the abbess and the questions that she was asked concerning their relationship have survived, together with two letters written at the same time by Sir William Paulet, chief steward of the abbey, to Cromwell, about her examination and return to the nunnery.[4] Between them Sir William and Dr. Legh had the delicate task of persuading the abbess to resign her office and accept a pension, but in their letter to Cromwell they had to admit that 'She has plainly answered she will in no case resign until she has spoken with the king himself'.[5] However, they won their point and on 15 September the *congé d'élire* was issued from Westminster for the prioress and convent to elect a new abbess following the resignation of Anne Colte. Ten

EARL OF ESSEX.

42. Portrait after Holbein of Thomas Cromwell, Earl of Essex, *c.*1485-1540.

days later the king gave his assent to the election of the former prioress, Morpheta Kingsmill, and on the same day Dr. Legh concluded a letter to Sir William on the subject with 'I beg you to remember our fee, and that the late abbess have her pension of £20 that she may be honestly rid from thence'.[6]

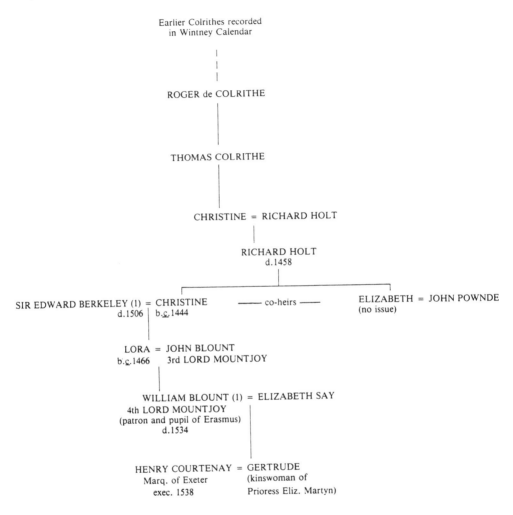

Earlier Colrithes recorded
in Wintney Calendar

ROGER de COLRITHE

THOMAS COLRITHE

CHRISTINE = RICHARD HOLT

RICHARD HOLT
d.1458

SIR EDWARD BERKELEY (1) = CHRISTINE   —— co-heirs ——   ELIZABETH = JOHN POWNDE
d.1506   b.c.1444   (no issue)

LORA = JOHN BLOUNT
b.c.1466   3rd LORD MOUNTJOY

WILLIAM BLOUNT (1) = ELIZABETH SAY
4th LORD MOUNTJOY
(patron and pupil of Erasmus)
d.1534

HENRY COURTENAY = GERTRUDE
Marq. of Exeter   (kinswoman of
exec. 1538   Prioress Eliz. Martyn)

43. Later patrons of Wintney Priory.

At Wintney Priory a new prioress had been in office for a year. When there had been a vacancy in 1534 the election had been in Cromwell's hands as compromissary and he had appointed Elizabeth Martyn, following a letter from Henry Courtenay, Marquess of Exeter, requesting the office for her. She was a kinswoman of his wife Gertrude, (who was herself a direct descendant of Richard and Christine Holt, the 15th-century benefactors of the priory) and in his letter he assured Cromwell

. . . that she is able to execute the same and if she may attain to be prioress of the said place by your good help, wherein I have no doubt, then I trust to see that she shall fully content and satisfy the king of all such duties as shall appertain to his grace.[7]

Unfortunately Dr. Legh and John ap Rice did not comment on either prioress or priory when they wrote jointly to Cromwell from Wintney, but in a second letter written by ap Rice alone he spoke of his concern about the possible results if they carried out their order and dismissed young nuns under 24 years old; he was afraid of the scandal that might ensue, yet Dr. Legh evidently refused to allow him any discretion in such cases.[8] This epitomises the difference in attitude between the two men. Both were career lawyers but Legh was always somewhat harsh and pedantic in carrying out instructions when visiting, whereas ap Rice was rather more sympathetic and sensible in his dealings with the religious. The previous month he had written to Cromwell from the nunnery at Lacock, Wiltshire, pointing out the stupidity of Dr. Legh's attempts to keep monks and nuns perpetually enclosed 'for as many of the houses stand by husbandry they must fall to decay if the heads are not allowed to go out'.[9] But unfortunately that was just the result that Cromwell and Dr. Legh intended.

On the basis of the visitors' reports and the *Valor Ecclesiasticus* the government made a decision some time during the winter of 1535-6 that monasteries with an income of less than £200 a year would be dissolved. Accordingly the Act for the Dissolution of the Lesser Monasteries was passed in March 1536 and another act established the Court of Augmentations to deal with the revenues from the suppressed houses. Commissioners were again appointed from the ranks of the country gentry to carry out surveys of those houses whose incomes brought them within the act, and their reports were later sent to the new court.

According to the *Valor* the nunneries in Hampshire that had incomes of less than £200 were St. Mary's Abbey, Winchester and Wintney Priory; both were therefore visited by the county commissioners: Sir James Worsley, John Paulet, George Paulet, Richard Paulet and William Berners. In addition to being commissioners, Richard Paulet was the Receiver for the court for Hampshire, Wiltshire, Gloucestershire and Bristol, while William Berners was Auditor for the same area from the establishment of the Court of Augmentations in April 1536 until its amalgamation with the Court of Survey in 1547. Both men are considered to have been amongst those many court officials who were both hard working and fair in their dealings with the monasteries and their tenants, unlike the more ruthless Dr. Legh and Dr. Richard Layton.[10]

Two documents survive from the Hampshire visitations of 1536: a detailed survey of St. Mary's Abbey dated 15 May and a schedule summarising the findings of the commissioners at all the lesser houses in the county that was compiled on 30 May.[11] In the schedule each of the questions that the commissioners had to ask was set out at the top of a column and the answers from the six houses were then given underneath. Those from the nunneries are summarised in Appendix 5. The most interesting comment amongst the answers from the abbey is in the column for yearly value; there the income of the house is given as £330 18s. 6¼d. but then comes a note that 'with £150 concealed upon taxation of the Tenths without consent of the abbess and convent as is confessed'. So if only the correct income had been given to the commissioners collecting information for the *Valor* the previous year then St. Mary's Abbey would never have been included with the lesser monasteries under the act of 1536.

Comparing the two surveys St. Mary's Abbey was, of course, in every way the more wealthy house, but Wintney Priory emerges rather more creditably than one might have expected. Certainly the house was in debt but it had stores in hand, its church and the main house were in reasonable condition and the number of nuns had increased from six to ten since the start of the century. Generally the contrast between the houses is one of degree, but in the category for servants and dependants the answers reflect the differences between an urban and a country house. In Winchester there were almswomen, school children and many household officials and domestic servants, while at Wintney the employees included 13 hindes who would have been farm workers. As for the nuns themselves, apart from one lady at the abbey they all wished to continue their profession. The question about their wish to remain was a genuine one since at that time it was not intended that there should be a general suppression of all religious houses and, apart from the head of the house, it was open to those who wished to continue to join one of the larger communities in the same Order.

The detailed survey of St. Mary's Abbey gives the names of all the 102 people living there and fills out the brief answers recorded in the schedule. To take one example the schedule merely gives £182 12s. 6d. for the value of lead and bells, but the survey shows that this was made up of an estimated £154 10s. 0d. for the lead on the church and houses, while the value of the church's five great bells and one little one was put at £28 2s. 6d. When dealing with the reputation of the house the commissioners reported that the nuns 'were of very clean, virtuous, honest and charitable conversation' and went on to say that this was also the opinion of the mayor and citizens who had been pleading with them 'to be suitors unto the King's Highness for toleration of the said monastery'.[12]

But there were some that summer who did not rate the abbey's chances of survival too highly. In June Lord Lisle's agent wrote to him about the prospects for benefiting from the coming suppression of monasteries, saying 'St Mary's in Winchester, as it is showed me, without great friendship to stay it, is like to be of the number'.[13] Great friendship helped no doubt but the abbey also had to pay a large fine of £333 6s. 8d. to obtain exemption from the act.[14] To secure this great sum the evidence points to the abbess and convent surrendering their two Wiltshire manors of Urchfont and All Cannings. They still held them in May 1536 when the farmers there owed the abbey £24 6s. 8d. altogether,[15] but the following month the two manors with the rectory of Urchfont church and the advowson of All Cannings were granted by the Crown to Sir Edward Seymour and his second wife, Anne.[16] (He was brother of the new Queen Jane, and later Duke of Somerset.)

In May 1536 the key to the coffers within the abbey's treasury, which contained their charters and muniments, was apparently put into the custody of Richard Paulet,[17] but in spite of this it does not seem that St. Mary's was ever actually suppressed at that time. Nevertheless, in those changing and troubled times the legal advisers of the abbess evidently thought it was worth spending money on a deed that would put the position of the house beyond all doubt. Accordingly, on 8 August the king made a grant to the abbey 'which should have been suppressed by virtue of the Act 27 Henry VIII' allowing it to continue with its possessions except those at Urchfont and All Cannings, and for Elizabeth Shelley to be its abbess.[18]

The previous month, on 2 July 1536, Prioress Elizabeth Martyn of Wintney was granted an annual pension of £10[19] and on 22 July the priory was formally suppressed and dissolved. Unfortunately only the bare facts of the name of the priory and the date of its dissolution were recorded, along with the same information for the other five houses in Hampshire that were suppressed that summer.[20] The wish of the other nine nuns at Wintney to continue in the religious life was respected. The accounts of Richard Paulet for 1536-7 show that they were given 13s. 4d. for their joint travelling expenses to another monastery as well as 40s. each in alms; Elizabeth Martyn received £4 in alms in addition to her pension, no doubt to meet her travelling costs and the purchase of cloth for secular clothes.[21] The house which the nine nuns joined that summer was not named, but it may well have been the abbey at Tarrant Keynes in Dorset which was the only other Cistercian nunnery in the south of England; it was itself dissolved in March 1539. Earlier in the accounts there is a list of the value of the priory's silver which had been sent to the king; it amounted to £35 2s. 1d. but that figure did not include the 24s. that Richard Paulet himself paid for a silver pyx which had belonged to the nunnery.[22]

The Dissolution of the Abbeys

On the surface 1537 was a comparatively quiet year for monasteries such as the Hampshire houses that were not involved in the opposition movement known as the Pilgrimage of Grace. Yet it must have been a worrying time, full of uncertainty for those remaining monks and nuns who had any imagination. At Romsey the nuns had already seen the nearby Mottisfont Priory dissolved in 1536 and this may have prompted their request to the king for a confirmation of all their charters. He granted that confirmation on 5 November 1537,[23] but it was a waste of their money. In the north, in the wake of the Pilgrimage of Grace, the practice evolved whereby a community surrendered its house voluntarily and it was then forfeited to the Crown. This comparatively simple device was a great help to the government once it had been decided to make an end of all the remaining religious houses in the country – a policy that seems to have been decided some time during the winter of 1537-8. In Hampshire this new and final phase started at the end of December 1537 when Titchfield Abbey was surrendered.

One of the ugly features of 1538 was the organised destruction up and down the country of the shrines of English saints which had been the goal of countless pilgrims throughout the Middle Ages. The shrines of St. Cuthbert of Durham and St. Thomas Becket at Canterbury were just two of the more famous that suffered. That September Thomas Wriothesley, the new owner of Titchfield Abbey, arrived in Winchester with Richard Pollard and John Williams to destroy the ancient shrines there. A letter from them written partly by Wriothesley himself in the cathedral on Saturday, some hours after the 3 a.m. destruction of the shrine of St. Swithun, described their findings and estimated that their work would not be finished until the Monday or Tuesday following,

> which done we intend, both at Hyde and St. Mary's, to sweep away all the rotten bones that be called relics; which we may not omit lest it should be thought we came more for the treasure than for the avoiding of the abomination of idolatry.[24]

44. Thomas Wriothesley, later Earl of Southampton, 1505-50: a chalk drawing by Holbein. He was in charge of the destruction of shrines in Winchester Cathedral, Hyde Abbey and at St Mary's Abbey in September 1538.

Whatever their true motives the effect was the same and one must assume that the shrine of St. Edburga in the church of St. Mary's Abbey was destroyed that week. Its treasures, with those from the other shrines in the city, were then sent to London to swell the funds of the Court of Augmentations.

News of the destruction must soon have travelled to the remaining monastic houses in the county, even if its perpetrators did not. At Romsey the various household officials were evidently as fearful of the future for themselves as for the abbey. Presumably that was why the abbess and convent granted them the several letters patent for their fees, annuities and pensions that were sealed in September. An annuity of £23 6s. 8d. had been granted to John Foster, the abbey's chaplain and steward, in 1536[25] but the long list of other fees to Sir Nicholas Wadham, who was Governor of the Isle of Wight and farmer of Romsey Extra, to John Wintershull, the abbey's principal steward, to Peter Westbroke and Alexander Curtopp, sub-stewards, and to Thomas and John Foster in their capacity as receivers of the manors and lands of the abbey, are all dated 20 September 1538. Annuities were paid to five people out of the same manor of Romsey Extra and to another 10 out of Romsey Infra.[26]

Perhaps these grants, and various leases that either had been or were about to be granted,[27] were matters of common knowledge before the date of their actual sealing since five days earlier Sir Richard Lyster had written to Cromwell from his house at Stanbridge nearby:

> After right humble recommendation pleaseth your good lordship to be advertised that I do perceive very lately that the monastery of Romsey reckon to be in danger of suppression. And by reason of such as hath shown them the danger that they be in, they begin to make grants and leases, and to put goods of their house from them, and so will do daily more and more. Whereof I can do no less than advertise your lordship thereof and if I may know from your lordship if it be the king's pleasure to have them stayed in their doings or how to have them ordered, I doubt not but upon your commands I can stay them from henceforth for doing any great prejudice to the king's highness . . . and to conform them after his grace and pleasure . . .
>
> from Stanbridge, the xv day of September.[28]

It is unlikely that Cromwell would not have responded to this letter fairly soon, but no papers about Romsey affairs have survived from the next two months.

By December Sir Thomas Seymour was making enquiries about Romsey Abbey. He was a brother of the late Queen Jane, who had died in October 1537, and in common with many others in the king's circle at the time he was keen to benefit from some of the monastic spoils that were becoming available. He was personable, vain, ambitious and self-centred. Earlier in 1538 he had obtained Coggeshall Abbey in Essex, but afterwards he had been abroad on the king's business for some months. His particular claim to Romsey Abbey may have been based on a family connection, for the abbesses of Romsey had had a portion in Wolf Hall, his family's seat in Wiltshire, by the early 15th century.[29] Several people would have known of this and may have told him of the likelihood of the abbey's suppression. In his own family there was his brother, Sir Edward, and his sister Elizabeth, who was married to Cromwell's son, may have been well informed; at court he also knew Sir Michael Lyster, son of Sir Richard who had written to Cromwell (the two young men had been knighted on the same day after the christening of Prince Edward). But from the following letter it seems likely that the ladies who were most concerned to help him were his cousins, Katherine and Jane Wadham, who were the sub-prioress and sexton respectively of the abbey. They are likely to have known Sir Thomas since their childhood, and perhaps fallen under the spell of his charm.[30]

By whatever means Sir Thomas actually had Romsey Abbey's situation brought to his notice, he wrote a letter in which he evidently asked questions similar to those that had been put by the commissioners when they visited the lesser monasteries. His letter has been lost, but fortunately the very informative reply to it is still preserved. It was written by John Foster, the chaplain who had been appointed joint receiver of the abbey's manors and lands with his father in 1535. In it he dealt with the value of the abbey's rents and possessions

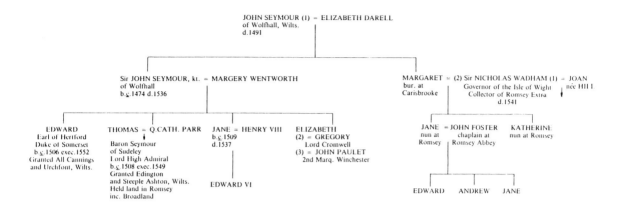

JOHN SEYMOUR (1) = ELIZABETH DARELL
of Wolfhall, Wilts.
d.1491

Sir JOHN SEYMOUR, kt. = MARGERY WENTWORTH
of Wolfhall
b.c.1474 d.1536

MARGARET = (2) Sir NICHOLAS WADHAM (1) = JOAN
bur. at   Governor of the Isle of Wight   née HILL
Carisbrooke   Collector of Romsey Extra
              d.1541

EDWARD
Earl of Hertford
Duke of Somerset
b.c.1506 exec.1552
Granted All Cannings
and Urchfont, Wilts.

THOMAS = Q.CATH. PARR
Baron Seymour
of Sudeley
Lord High Admiral
b.c.1508 exec.1549
Granted Edington
and Steeple Ashton, Wilts.
Held land in Romsey
inc. Broadland

JANE = HENRY VIII
b.c.1509
d.1537

ELIZABETH
(2) = GREGORY
Lord Cromwell
(3) = JOHN PAULET
2nd Marq. Winchester

JANE
nun at
Romsey

= JOHN FOSTER
chaplain at
Romsey Abbey

KATHERINE
nun at Romsey

EDWARD VI

EDWARD   ANDREW   JANE

45. The Seymour and Wadham connection.

46. Sir Thomas Seymour, Baron Seymour
of Sudeley, c.1508-49.

before commenting on the likelihood of the community surrendering voluntarily and their mistrust of the commissioners; as a postscript he wrote out the names of the 26 nuns there. Omitting that list the letter reads:

> In my most hearty wise right worshipful sir I recommend me unto you and according to your request, I do herein signify and subscribe unto you the state of the houses of Romsey, the rents of assize and where they do lie, and the riches of the same, and of Ashton Edington the rents and also the deductions of the same. First you shall understand that the house is out of debt, also the plate and jewels is worth £300 and better, 6 bells be worth £100 at the least. Also the church is a great sumptuous thing all of free stone and covered with lead which as I esteem it is worth £300 or £400 or rather much better.

> The manor and standing rents of the abbey of Romsey.

> Hampshire
> The lordship of Romsey is of the yearly value of £235
> Itm Itchenstoke is worth yearly £28 9s. 0¾d.
> Itm Sidmanton is worth yearly £30 12s.
> Itm Tyleshade [Tinhead, Wilts.] is worth yearly £11 6s. 8d.
> Dorsetshire
> Itm Pewdell [Puddletown] is worth yearly 40s.
> Gloucestershire
> Itm Hownelacy is worth yearly £6 13s. 4d.
> Wiltshire
> Itm the yearly value of the manor of Ashton Edington, deducting the tenths and chief rents is £167 0s. 7¼d.

> And where you wrote unto me by Mr Flemynge that I should ascertain you whether I thought the abbess with the rest of the minys [mincions/nuns] would be content to surrender up the house, the truth is I do perceive throughout the mocyon [?motion] that your kinswomen and other your friends made for you, the[y] will be content at all times to do you any pleasure they may, but I perceive they would be loath to trust to the commissioners gentleness for they hearsay that other houses have been straightly handled. And this fare you heartily well,
>
> at Romsey, the xxviii[th] day of December.
> John Foster[31]

Sir Thomas Seymour lost no time in following up this letter. By the end of January 1539 the abbess had been sent a licence from the king allowing her to grant Sir Thomas the abbey's estates in Wiltshire.[32] When she sealed the deed on 6 February one of the witnesses was William Berners, the local auditor of the Court of Augmentations to which Sir Thomas had to pay dues on the property, so the grant was evidently part of the process of the dissolution of the abbey. The other witness was Robert Flemyng, and in the grant Francis Flemyng was named as the attorney of the abbess and convent.[33]

The exact date of the surrender of Romsey Abbey is not known. It was still in being early in February but the accounts of Richard Paulet show that it had been dissolved by Michaelmas that year.[34] For several reasons it seems likely that the house had been dissolved before the end of April 1539. During the first four months of the year there was a spate of surrenders to commissioners who were acting under the king's privy seal rather than by authority of Parliament. One of these commissioners was Richard Layton who started a letter to Cromwell:

> It may please your lordship to be advertised that this morning, ready to depart towards Romsey in Hampshire according to your commandment, this bill here enclosed . . .[35]

If only he had written after his journey to Romsey instead of before it he might have mentioned affairs at the abbey. Then it was in April that Sir William Paulet bought several former monastic properties in Hampshire, including the abbey's manor and rectory of Itchen Stoke.[36] (Later he became steward of the lands of the former Romsey Abbey.[37]) And a more general reason for thinking that the dissolution of the house took place before the end of April is that there were no surrenders of monastic houses between April and June when Parliament was in session.

Whenever Romsey Abbey was dissolved, no pensions were awarded to the former abbess and nuns by the commissioners of the Court of Augmentations. As the abbey was so well endowed this is most surprising, since the only other nuns who were not awarded pensions were all from small, poor and obscure houses.[38] It has been said that Sir Thomas Seymour paid them pensions and this could be true, before his execution in 1549. The fact that John Foster sent him a list of the names of the nuns could indicate it, but any other written evidence seems to be lacking.[39]

In May 1539 Parliament passed the Act for the Dissolution of the Greater Monasteries which confirmed the process of the surrenders of monastic houses and vested all their property in the king. It then only remained for the surrenders of individual houses to be taken in accordance with the new law. In contrast to Romsey Abbey the surrenders of St. Mary's Abbey, Winchester and Wherwell Abbey are impeccably recorded. The commissioners were in Winchester to receive the surrender of St. Swithun's Priory on 14 November 1539 and they then moved on to St. Mary's Abbey, which surrendered voluntarily on the 17th, and then to Wherwell Abbey whose surrender is dated 21 November. Copies of those three lengthy certificates are bound together amongst the papers of the Court of Augmentations.[40]

The commissioners for taking surrenders in Hampshire, Wiltshire and Gloucestershire were headed by Sir Robert Southwell, who was later Chancellor of the Court of Augmentations and Master of the Rolls.[41] The others were Drs. William Petre, Edward Carne and John London, John ap Rice and John Kingsmill with Richard Paulet and William Berners, the receiver and auditor for the area. Between three and six of them were

47. Portrait of Sir Robert Southwell (d.1560) by a follower of Steven van der Meulen. Southwell headed the Commissioners for the Court of Augmentations who took the surrenders of St Swithun's Priory, St Mary's Abbey and Wherwell Abbey in November 1539.

meant to be present at the time of each surrender, but as their names are only noted at the start of the record one cannot know which of them were actually present on each occasion.

The certificates follow the same order for each house: the annual income, a list of the individual nuns with the amount of pension assigned to each (and 6s. 8d. for the support of each of the almswomen at St. Mary's), the buildings that were to remain and those that were deemed to be superfluous, and then the values of lead, bells and plate. The records of gold and silver were broken down into silver gilt, silver parcel gilt and white silver. Wherwell Abbey with a total of 912 ounces looks much better endowed than St. Mary's Abbey with 117 ounces or even St. Swithun's Priory which had 273 ounces, but the figures for the Winchester houses would presumably have been very different if the assessments had been made before the destruction of their shrines the previous year.

The certificates also recorded the value of goods already sold as well as any debts of the house. At the former St. Mary's Abbey the responsibility for any debts was taken over by Richard Shelley, brother of Abbess Elizabeth Shelley, and in return they were both to receive any sums owing to the house. At Wherwell the commissioners paid debts amounting to £16 18s. 2d. which were owed to various people locally and in Winchester for food and other necessities. No money was owed to the house, though a crossed-out entry shows that it had originally been thought that £11 was owing to the abbess and convent for legal expenses in connection with a case involving the vicar of Middleton.[42]

The size of pensions awarded to the former nuns varied greatly. Basically the amount available was dependent upon the income that the Court of Augmentations could expect to receive from the property of the former house, so the ladies from Wherwell were more generously pensioned than their sisters from Winchester, but the pattern of awards was similar for both. In compensation for their loss of office and income the two former abbesses had much larger pensions than anyone else; Elizabeth Shelley of Winchester was granted £26 13s. 4d. a year, while Morpheta Kingsmill of Wherwell had £40 a year. There was then a sharp drop to £6 for Alice Gilford, the former prioress of Wherwell, and £5 for Agnes Mashame of Winchester; the sub-prioresses each received 20s. less than their superiors and the former sexton of Wherwell had £4. Most of the other former nuns from St. Mary's were awarded 53s. 4d. a year and this was the pension awarded to six of the more junior ladies from Wherwell, but 13 of the more senior were to receive 66s. 8d. In addition a resettlement grant 'of the king's reward' of 40s. was paid to each of the former Winchester nuns except the abbess. Only seven of the Wherwell ladies benefited from a royal reward, three receiving 40s. each and the other four receiving 20s.[43] No reason was given for the neglect of the other former members of the community, but perhaps they had already returned to their families and were not thought to be in need of further assistance.

By the end of 1539 monastic life had come to an end in Hampshire and after the spring of 1540 there was not a monastery left in England. After so many centuries of being an integral and valued part of society, why had it happened? The doctrinal issues of the Reformation are outside the scope of this book and were probably beyond the understanding of most contemporaries too. The main reason for the Dissolution was the king's need for money. Once his matrimonial difficulties had caused the breach with Rome in the 1530s, Thomas Cromwell, who had little respect for old institutions, was quick to seize the opportunity to transfer the wealth of the monasteries to his royal master, as he had seen Cardinal Wolsey do in the previous decade for the benefit of his new foundation at Oxford. Cromwell and his visitors did their best to besmirch the reputations of the monasteries in the eyes of Parliament and the public in order to justify the legislation for their suppression, but by their own admission the commissioners in Hampshire were unable to find any corruption in the nunneries at Winchester, Wherwell and Wintney. However, it is to the credit of the Court of Augmentations, the commissioners and Cromwell himself that the Dissolution proceeded in a legal and orderly manner in the south, and that the officials of the court kept good records which have fortunately survived in considerable numbers.

Chapter Twelve

After the Dissolution

The suppression of the religious houses inevitably brought many social and economic changes. New owners took over the old monastic estates and many of the former monastery buildings were deserted and despoiled, their roofs stripped of lead, their bells melted down and their libraries scattered. In the immediate neighbourhood of well regarded monasteries, especially in the country, there may have been many who felt some lingering sense of loss at the demise of a community that had once seemed so permanent, but the people most affected were of course the former religious themselves. The nuns were in a particularly difficult situation since they did not have the option of becoming parish priests like so many of the monks, but it is clear that some of them remained together.

The people dispossessed

When the Hampshire nunneries were dissolved there were many besides the nuns themselves whose lives were affected. When the whole communities at St. Mary's Abbey and Wintney Priory were counted in 1536 the nuns at both houses only comprised about a quarter of all the people there. It is likely that the ratio of nuns was similar at Romsey Abbey, although at Wherwell there may perhaps have been a slightly higher proportion of nuns since there do not seem to have been any corrodians or other dependants when the house was surrendered. Whatever the actual numbers, there were certainly many former officers and servants of all the nunneries whose lives were changed by the Dissolution.

The schoolchildren at St. Mary's Abbey had presumably been sent back to their families or guardians before the end of 1539. The last reference to one of them is in a letter written by Abbess Shelley to Lady Lisle in September 1538 to inform her that her stepdaughter, Bridget Plantagenet, had gone to stay with friends two weeks earlier 'and since that time she came no more at Winchester'.[1]

The almswomen who lived in the Sisterne House by St. Mary's Abbey remained there, and the place was still being run as a charity at the end of the century.[2] It seems very likely that the former Abbess Shelley continued to visit them there for when she died she left each of the sisters one shilling.[3] In 1536, when the commissioners had noted all their names, there were 13 'poor Sisters' but three years later there were 12 when they were awarded annual pensions of 6s. 8d. each.[4]

Support for the poor also continued at Romsey after the dissolution of the abbey. Two undated lists of names were jotted down at the time: one gave the 10 poor sisters of Romsey who lived near the abbey gate, and the other listed the four almsmen and two almswomen who were cared for at the Hospital of St. Mary Magdalene; in addition the name of Edmund Heliars appears between the two. Some time later the names of those who were still living were re-written and six deaths were noted, including old Edmund Heliars's.[5] There are no records of any almsmen or women still being supported at Wherwell when the abbey was dissolved.

Any wages due to people who had served the nunneries were paid at the time of the surrender of the house. At St. Mary's Abbey 20 officers and servants received a total of £17 11s. 11d. for their wages and liveries, while at Wherwell £25 3s. 0d. was disbursed among them and the former chaplains.[6] Those who had been granted fees or annuities by the abbesses continued to receive them if they were confirmed by the Court of Augmentations.

141

GVIL·MARCHIO·WINTON·THES·ANGL

48. Sir William Paulet, 1st Marquis of Winchester (c.1485-1572). He was Chief Steward of Wherwell Abbey and Wintney Priory before the Dissolution, and of the lands of Romsey Abbey from 1546.

The court could also make grants of its own. In 1546 Sir William Paulet, who was already chief steward of Wherwell Abbey and Wintney Priory, was thus made chief steward of the lands that had belonged to Romsey Abbey.[7] For this he received £6 a year as he did for his stewardship of Wherwell. Both fees were listed among pensions still being paid in 1553 but by then he was not receiving anything out of Wintney.[8] The chief steward for Romsey Abbey when it was dissolved was John Wintershull; his fee of £6 a year and those of the other officers were all recorded.[9] By 1553 only four fees were still being paid out of the income of the three former abbeys: the two already mentioned to the Marquess of Winchester, one of £20 3s. 4d. to John Foster as receiver of Romsey Abbey, and another of £4 to Richard Taylor who had been a chaplain at Wherwell Abbey.[8] No fees were being paid out to officers of St. Mary's Abbey by then; John Shelley had been appointed chief steward in January 1539[10] but after his death the office lapsed.

Annuitants were treated in the same way as fee holders. Provided the annuities were confirmed by the Court of Augmentations they were honoured, however numerous. As Sir Richard Lyster had noted, there had been a flurry of activity at Romsey on the eve of the abbey's dissolution; 15 annuitants were listed in the accounts for 1539-40 and another was added later.[11] By 1553 six of these men were still receiving their annuities, including John Foster who had managed to secure two; in addition Christopher Shorte, the former woodward, and Henry Warner, one of the bailiffs, were being paid the amount of their former fees as annuities. The communities at Winchester and Wherwell had been less profligate over granting annuities and by 1553 the court was only paying two annuitants from each house. John Cooke, registrar to the bishop of Winchester, and Christopher Browne were receiving £1 6s. 8d. and £2 respectively out of the income from Wherwell; and the court's auditor for the area, William Berners, and Walter Dashwood who had been a chaplain at St. Mary's Abbey each had an annuity of £2.[12]

Corrodians could also make claims against the Court of Augmentations since the monastic house to which they had each paid a lump sum in return for board and lodging for life could no longer fulfil its side of the contract. A little is known about the two lady corrodians who were living at Wintney Priory at the time of its suppression, each with her own servant. One of them, Johanne Antile, had bought a corrody in 1528 which entitled her to a chamber in the priory with food and drink provided for lunch and supper, as well as bread and pottage morning and evening for herself and her servant, and firewood and candles for their room. Richard Paulet made her and her fellow corrodian, Margery Trussel, allowances of 20s. each immediately after the suppression to cover the period from 20 July to Michaelmas 1536.[13] Seven years later Mistress Trussel complained to the Court of Augmentations about her situation, taking with her the original agreement that the prioress of Wintney had sealed in June 1523. It appears from this indenture that the widow from Odiham had been assigned a chamber within the inner gate and over the priory vine for the rest of her life, with meat, drink and fuel for herself and her woman servant, and every morning and evening at least one pint of double beer. It had also been agreed that her servant who was there 'to wait and give attendance upon her' should, when she could be spared, be ready to perform similar services for the prioress. All this had cost Margery Trussel one payment of £10 and was only conditional on her remaining a widow. The dissolution of the little priory must indeed have come as an unpleasant shock to her. The court was evidently sympathetic to her loss and awarded her £5 4s. 0d. a year for the rest of her life, plus the arrears, out of receipts from the former priory's properties.[14] Certainly that £10 had been well invested in 1523.

At St. Mary's Abbey three male 'corodiers' were recorded on the certificate of 1536, including Thomas Legh who was the receiver. Thomas Legh himself died the following year leaving a small legacy of 5s. 0d. to his sister Margaret, who was a nun at the abbey, and 30s. 0d. to the community generally. (His daughter Jane was married to William Lambert who was given the charge and custody of the abbey's buildings in 1539.)[15]

However, nunneries were primarily for nuns and it was their lives that were the most affected by the suppression of their houses, but tracing their later lives is not easy. Apart from correspondence concerning Jane Wadham, the main sources of information are the wills that were made by former nuns and the lists that were compiled at intervals showing which former religious were still receiving pensions from the state. Three of the former heads of the nunneries left wills: Elizabeth Shelley who died in 1547, Morpheta Kingsmill of Wherwell who died in 1570 and Elizabeth Martyn who made her will in 1584 but then lived until the summer of 1587, more than 50 years after the suppression of Wintney Priory.[16]

Elizabeth Shelley, who died within a decade of the Dissolution, did not mention in her will that she had been abbess of St. Mary's, merely describing herself as Elizabeth Shelley of Winchester. Perhaps this was modesty, but it may have been expediency in those uncertain times just before the death of Henry VIII. In the more stable days of Elizabeth I Morpheta Kingsmill described herself as 'late abbess of the monastery of Wherwell', and Elizabeth Martyn wrote that she was 'sometime prioress of Wyntney'. It is easy to imagine that all three ladies retained the dignity of their office in the eyes of their contemporaries, even if they had lost the office itself.

The wills of Elizabeth Shelley and Morpheta Kingsmill are particularly interesting because they both indicate that they were each continuing to live with several of the sisters from their former communities. Dame Shelley left bequests to six former nuns from St. Mary's Abbey: Agnes Badgecroft, Jane Wayte, Margaret Shelley, Edburga Stratford, Margaret Sellwood and Maud Aldrich. Apart from her niece Margaret she called each of them 'my sister' when leaving her a legacy, and when she named Walter Dashwood as one of her executors she referred to him as her chaplain. Assuming that she was living in the abbess's lodging at the time of her death, the long inventory of her possessions shows that it was a sizeable house: as well as the hall, kitchen, buttery and domestic rooms called the long house, wood house and fish house, there were seven separate chambers including the great chamber in the gallery.[17] When the king granted the lease of this and other abbey buildings to Thomas Tichborne in May 1540, the deed from the Court of Augmentations mentioned that they were all in the hands and occupation of the former abbess.[18]

Similarly Morpheta Kingsmill left household legacies to six former Wherwell nuns who had presumably been living with her or nearby ever since the surrender of the abbey 30 years earlier. One of them, Elizabeth Hacker, was the wife of Edmund Bathe by 1570, though they may not have been married for very long or else her maiden name would surely not have been used in the will. Master Bathe was probably a local man for Dame Kingsmill chose him as one of her executors and he was one of the three appraisers of her inventory (the others were from Wherwell and Goodworth Clatford). The heading of the inventory seems to confirm that Dame Kingsmill continued to live in Wherwell: after 'The inventory of all such goods as mrs Morveth Kyngesmell Late religious' there is then a gap before 'at Wherwell' so presumably that refers to the whereabouts of the goods. But it is impossible to know whether she continued to live in her former abbess's lodging, although it was among the buildings assigned to remain in 1539.[19] The inventory indicates a much smaller house than Elizabeth Shelley's, though inventories can be deceptive.

In the usual manner all three ladies mentioned their burials in their wills but the most precise directions were given by Elizabeth Martyn. She asked for her body to be buried in the chancel of Hartley Wintney church and above it

> I would that a stone should be laid over my grave with a picture of a woman in a long garment with wide sleeves, her hands joined together holding upon her breast and figured over her head *In te domine speravi non confundar in aeternum. In justicia tua libera me et salva me.* I would that an 'herste' should be standing over my grave by the space of an whole year covered over with black cotton with a cross of white fustian.[20]

She then went on to leave £10 for the payment of burial charges and the transport of her body from Wokingham, where she was living, to Hartley Wintney and another 40s. to the poor of Hartley Wintney. The brass that she describes sounds very similar to one above the grave of an earlier prioress of Amesbury which is in the parish church of Nether Wallop, Hampshire.[21] Unfortunately Elizabeth Martyn's brass has not survived and the gravestones in the chancel of St. Mary's Old Church, Hartley Wintney are all of a later date, but in the centre aisle of the nave there is a large unmarked old tombstone with the remains of metal studs round its edge. It does seem possible that this could be her tombstone.

The two former abbesses were much more vague about their burials. Morpheta Kingsmill asked to be buried 'within the church at what place my friends shall think good'. Elizabeth Shelley only directed that 'my body to be buried in christian burial' but she made John White, the warden of Winchester College, one of the overseers of her will and he evidently arranged for her to be buried in the college chapel. (In 1554 Thomas Basset, who was a priest and fellow of the college, asked to be buried there 'by the grave of Mistress Shelley'.[22]) She had earlier given the college a tapestry carpet, and a small silver gilt chalice on condition that the 'nunnery of St. Mary's in Winchester shall have it again in case it be restored and come up again'.[23]

Three of the Winchester nuns who had benefited under the will of Elizabeth Shelley themselves left wills. Edburga Stratford left 'my sister Baggcroft my kerchief of calico'. Agnes Badgecroft in turn left a small cupboard and other small bequests to Margaret Shelley after asking to be buried within the church of St. Peter, Colebrook Street and leaving her 'professed ring' to be sold to buy a canopy for the sacrament, presumably at that church. Jane Wayte, who described herself as 'late religious woman of St. Maries within the walls of Winchester' also left legacies to four former nuns, referring to each as her sister; they were Agnes Badgecroft, Margaret Shelley, Margaret Sellwood and Maud Aldridge. She also mentioned another sister, Jane Gainsford, who was no longer living,

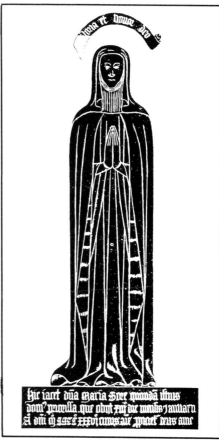

49. (*left*) View of the chancel of St Mary's Old Church, Hartley Wintney, where Elizabeth Martyn asked to be buried (d.1587). The tombstone that may have been hers is by the figure on the left. It was moved into the nave after the red brick floor was laid, possibly *c*.1760, when the Hawley vault was placed under the chancel.

50. (*right*) Brass of Mary Gore, Prioress of Amesbury, 1436, now in the nave of the parish church of Nether Wallop, Hampshire.

from whom she had received four pounds. This will was written when she was sick in 1554 but it was not proved until 1565.[24] No will has survived for Margaret Shelley, but in 1553 it is recorded that she was granted the farm of a tenement and garden in the Soke.[25]

Two other surviving wills were probably made by former nuns. Dame Alice Harwarde whose will was proved in 1553 was surely the Wherwell nun of that name; she was living near the former Netley Abbey and asked to be buried within the churchyard ('the parish Litten') of Hound nearby, leaving the vicar there five marks and some farm produce.[26] The second is rather more doubtful. It was made by Joan Frye who had a shop in Romsey and died in 1548. Was she the Winchester nun of that name who had been awarded a pension of 53s. 4d. in 1539? One only knows for certain that her pension was not among the 11 still being paid to former nuns from St. Mary's Abbey in 1552.[27]

It seems strange that no wills have ever been found that could be attributed to any of the former nuns from Romsey Abbey. The last abbess, Elizabeth Ryprose, and the sisters all disappear from history except for Jane Wadham, one of the two daughters of Sir Nicholas Wadham. According to a disposition that she made in 1541 Jane Wadham had been a reluctant nun at Romsey and

> . . . having both in public and in private always protested against this seclusion, she conceived herself free from regular observance, and in that persuasion joined herself in matrimony with one John Foster *per verba de presenti* intending to have the marriage solemnised as soon as she was free from her religion . . . [28]

This was the John Foster who had been chaplain and receiver at the abbey. His letter to Sir Thomas Seymour was quoted earlier. He also wrote a grovelling letter to Cromwell after the surrender of the abbey and his marriage; his concern was not that his wife might still have been bound by her oath of celibacy, but that he as a priest had married believing that to be possible 'but now by the noise of the people I perceive I have done amiss' and as soon as he realised that clerical marriage was against the king's wishes 'I sent the woman to her friends three score miles from me'.[29] He may have done so, but his new wife showed a fighting rather than a submissive spirit. She petitioned the king and in 1541 he ordered the bishops of Durham, Rochester and Westminster to hold a commission of enquiry into the marriage with the authority to pronounce it valid if they found it to be so.[30] Presumably they did so pronounce because the couple were later living with their children in Baddesley, where John Foster was the incumbent in 1543.[31] Six years later the Court of Augmentations granted him the manor of Baddesley which had belonged to the Hospitallers.[32] As he was also receiving £51 2s. 0d. a year in fees and annuities out of Romsey in 1553[33] the couple had a comfortable income. In a lighter vein this jingle was recorded locally before 1668:

> Mr Foster of Baddesley was a good man
> Before the marriage of priests began,
> For he was the first that married a nun,
> For which he begat a very rude son.[34]

Checks on the people receiving pensions and annuities were held at irregular intervals until 1575. The present writer has seen two of the lists: one relating to Hampshire alone that was compiled in 1552 and Cardinal Pole's list of 1553 for England generally. None of the Romsey nuns was listed at all (though the officers and annuitants are all there) and Elizabeth Martyn was the only pension holder from Wintney Priory. (No doubt the nuns from the priory who had moved when it was dissolved were granted pensions with the other sisters at their new nunnery, but as they were not named in 1536 they cannot be traced.) The returns for the former nuns of Wherwell name 16 ladies in 1552 but three of those names are missing in 1553, including Alice Harwarde whose will has already been mentioned. The returns for the ladies from Winchester are less satisfactory. There are 11 names on each list but the later one includes two names that were not on the earlier one (Agnes Badgecroft and Mary Martyn) and omits one lady, Jane Wayte, who was certainly alive in 1553 (her will was made in 1554) though it is possible that she might have sold her pension rights. Cardinal Pole's list also recorded nuns who had married in spite of their vow of chastity, but none of the ladies from Wherwell or Winchester had done so by 1553.[35] The only Hampshire nuns who are known to have married were Jane Wadham and Elizabeth Hacker.

The pensions were due to be paid in two equal instalments each year, on Lady Day and at Michaelmas. It seems that they were generally paid with fair regularity, but in 1552 there were local difficulties. The record of the inquisition taken at Winchester on 2 November that year before Nicholas Tichborne and Thomas Pace lists many annuity and pension holders who had not been paid. In the commissioners' often repeated phrase they had 'been yet living and unpaid for one year to our knowledge, and have not sold or assigned over their annuities'.[36] Elizabeth Martyn from Wintney was one of them; there was a group of four ladies from St. Mary's Abbey, and another group of 10 from Wherwell, headed by Morpheta Kingsmill. After both those entries there is a list of former nuns from the two abbeys who were not accounted for that day (five from Winchester and six from Wherwell); as the commissioners wrote ' . . . we be not certain whether [they] been yet living or no'.

When payments were actually made the recipients had 4d. in the pound deducted by the court or commissioners, and they were also liable to be taxed on their pensions whenever an ecclesiastical tenth was levied.[37] However, the assessors of Morpheta Kingsmill's inventory ignored deductions when they noted that £20 was due to her at Lady Day 1570 for a pension.[38]

The real value of the pensions and the extent that they helped to keep the former nuns in the manner to which they had become accustomed is another matter, especially as there was a bad period of inflation during the 20 years that followed the Dissolution. The two abbesses of Wherwell and Winchester on £40 and £26 a year respectively had adequate provision, but the ladies who received less than £5 a year would certainly have needed further help from their families. There is an interesting item about the cost of living in the inventory for Edburga Stratford (d.1551) who lived near the abbey in the parish of St. Peter, Colebrook Street: among her debts was six months' rent for her board at 14d. per week.[39] If this sum is multiplied by 52 the annual cost comes to £3 0s. 8d. yet her pension was only £2 13s. 4d.

Looking further ahead to the last record of one of the nuns, there is no indication that Elizabeth Martyn was in difficult circumstances in her old age and her inventory of 1587 shows that she was still in possession of her silver salt, her six silver spoons and her silver bowl when she died.[40]

The sites of the nunneries

Once a monastery was dissolved its site passed into the hands of the Court of Augmentations until such time as it was given or granted to one of the king's subjects. In the meantime it was administered by the court's receiver and auditor for the area. The responsibilities of Richard Paulet as receiver included paying off any outstanding debts incurred by the community, collecting in any sums that were due to it and arranging for the auction of any moveables that remained on the site after the valuable goods had been sent to London for the use of the king. During this period a custodian was usually appointed who was responsible for the day-to-day management of the site and its demesne. The manors and other properties that had belonged to the former house were dealt with in the same way.

In the following pages the new owners of the sites of the Hampshire nunneries are mentioned and those of their manors and other properties can be found in Appendix 3. All the grants that were made to them carried financial obligations. Several of the new leasehold owners of manors and farm land already occupied them as tenants of the nuns, and nearly all the men who obtained the sites of the nunneries themselves had some prior knowledge of or connection with the house. The only exception was Lord de la Warr who was successful in supplanting the brother of the last abbess as the grantee of Wherwell Abbey. It is remarkable the extent to which these men were inter-related and known to one another – and can be encountered in the correspondence of Lord Lisle and his family.

Wintney Priory was one of the lesser monasteries dissolved in Hampshire in 1536 that were given by the king as rewards to those who had served him well.[41] In his receiver's accounts for Michaelmas 1537 Richard Paulet assessed the value of the former priory's assets at £224 11s. 1d. altogether; this came from the income of its properties, the value of its jewels and silver sent to the king and 24s. for the silver pyx that he bought himself, the value of the lead on the buildings and the one church bell, its church ornaments sold, and the value of its grain and livestock (with details). The outgoings incurred had been £35 19s. 4½d.

51. Interpretation of the 17th-century portrait of Sir John
Mason (1503-66), painted in 1966 by G. McIvor.

for payments to the departing nuns, to the two corrodians and to the guardian, William Martyn.[42] In those accounts Richard Hill, sergeant of the king's cellar, was described as the farmer and collector of rents for Wintney manor.[43] He lived in Odiham nearby and through his wife Elizabeth he had connections with several people in influential positions. (They included John Dudley, Duke of Northumberland, who was related to Henry, Marquess of Exeter, whose wife was related to the last prioress of Wintney.) It was presumably some time during the two-year period when Richard Hill had just the farm of the manor that Richard Paulet wrote to him, criticising his conduct at the priory and pointing out to him that he had only been granted

... the keys as to the farm thereof. I therefore with the assent of other the said commissioners do command you and ... also straightly charge you that upon the site hereof ye cease to raze or deface any further of the housing and buildings there (being as yet the king's possessions) than that my lord's letter will testify you that the king's grace hath given you, the which is only the cloister and dorter until such time the king's commissioners come thither again.[44]

In June 1538 Richard Hill and his wife became masters of the whole site. The king granted them the property in tail male in consideration of Master Hill's good and faithful services. It comprised the house and site of the priory with its church, bell tower and cemetery, all other buildings and houses, barns, stables, dovecot, orchards, gardens and the land for seven paces all round the site; also the manor and advowson of Hartley Wintney and the rents in Winchester that had belonged to the priory. The total annual value of the properties was £26 14s. 9d. a year but on this the normal tenth of £2 13s. 6d. had to be paid annually to the Crown.[45]

Within a year Richard Hill was dead. He may have died in London as John Husee wrote from there to both Lord and Lady Lisle on 28 April 1539 with news of his death the previous day:

The xxvii[th] day of this month deceased the Sergeant of the Cellar, suddenly, God pardon his soul.[46]

That year it was the widowed Elizabeth who paid the £2 13s. 6d. to the receiver.[47] In 1540 the interests of Elizabeth Hill and her son Henry in the Wintney Priory property were

52. The site of Wintney Priory in 1965. The large Tudor barn is on the left and the smaller Tudor building on the right, adjacent to a shed.

53. The site of Wintney Priory, 31 January 1984. The large Tudor barn faces the motorway. Little remains of the smaller Tudor building on the left but the position of the pond just beyond it can be seen. Evidence of former buildings can be seen in the turf to the right.

confirmed, but Mistress Hill lost her former home at Odiham which passed to the king in return for his settling £500 of debts left by her husband, as Richard Hill had requested on his deathbed.[48] She soon remarried and had one more child, Thomas Mason, whose tomb is still in Winchester Cathedral. Her second husband was Sir John Mason whose varied career included being clerk of the Privy Council, Member of Parliament for Southampton and the only lay dean of Winchester Cathedral. However, he was not too busy to complain to the Court of Augmentations that the rector of Dogmersfield had failed to pay him, as husband of Elizabeth, the 20s. pension that he and his predecessors had formerly paid to the priory. In fact, the poor man had been paying it to the receiver.[49] Sir John and Lady Mason were evidently in residence sometimes at Hartley Wintney because when Sir John died in 1566 his will mentioned household stuff there.[50]

The site of the priory has suffered severely during the past quarter century. Photographs taken in 1964/5 show an early 16th-century barn and a smaller building of the same date still in reasonable condition, apart from the loss of tiles from the latter, but since then the M3 motorway has been constructed right alongside the farm buildings, destroying much potential evidence of the priory. While the work was in progress a local historian managed to get on the site for a couple of days and noted several 14th-15th century wall foundations and many animal bones (some possibly human) which had been unearthed by the bull-dozers, but there has never been a proper archaeological investigation of the site.

Through neglect the smaller of the two Tudor buildings collapsed in 1976; it had been a two-storey structure of four bays (12.0m. long, 5.2m. in breadth). The barn with its seven equal sized bays (25.0m. long, 6.5m. breadth, 5.0m. wallplate height) is still standing in 1987, minus most of its tiles, but a question mark hangs over its future. Originally both buildings had been wholly framed but certain lower sections were later replaced with brick. The employment of close studding for the main facade framing of both structures is particularly interesting as it is a type more usually found in better quality domestic buildings around the turn of the 15th and in the early 16th century. The surviving barn features large panel framing with bold arch braces on the east and both gable walls, while the main west frontage is formed of close studding with ogee profiled braces and diagonally set brick nogging.[51]

Although both buildings can be ascribed to the first half of the 16th century, in the absence of any documentary evidence it is impossible to know whether they were built before or after the Dissolution. However, on the basis of the known poverty of the nuns it does seems more likely that they would have been built just afterwards by one of the husbands of Elizabeth Hill/Mason, and since Sir John Mason had both more time and more money than his predecessor he would seem the more likely builder.

At Romsey no one individual was granted the site and lands of the abbey within the parish. The accounts that the bailiff, Henry Warner, submitted to the Court of Augmentations for the period after the surrender of the abbey show how fragmented the nuns' former estate had become. They give descriptions and some measurements of the site which, with two exceptions, was rented at that time by Francis Fleming who had been the community's attorney. (He also rented their 23 acres of meadowland in Romsey.) The site of the abbey included gardens, orchards, the cemetery, ponds and waters, while the abbess's lodging in the outer court had its own chapel, kitchen, granary, stable and a new barn.[52] In December 1546 he purchased that area from agents who had been granted it the previous month by the Court of Augmentations.[53] The following year he acquired both a knighthood and the parcel of land in the parish that included Broadland, which the abbess had leased to Thomas Foster in 1538 and had then been held by Sir Thomas Seymour.[54] The two parts of the site that were not included in Francis Fleming's holding were the clerk's chamber with its adjacent buildings and the land called Paradise which were let to one of the under-stewards, Peter Westbrook; the other was the gatehouse with its room above and the adjacent receiver's lodging which were held by John Richards.[55] The bailiff also noted the abbey's various mills and their leaseholders in his accounts, and among the records of the Court of Augmentations are a valuation of the Town Mills and a complaint by one of the millers, Robert Burnham, that he was being double charged.[56]

In 1544 John Foster and Richard Marden paid £900 for various monastic properties in Hampshire. Those in Romsey included the profits of the two annual fairs, the former Sisters' house at the gate of the abbey, various lands and also a house and its closes that had belonged to the Braishefield chantry within the abbey which had been in John Foster's occupation.[57]

The farm of the rectory of Romsey with all its tithes had been leased by the abbess and convent to John Taylor in 1538 for 80 years at £26 13s. 4d.[58] From 1541 John Taylor paid this sum to the new owners of the rectory and advowson, the newly founded Dean and Chapter of Winchester Cathedral.[59]

The abbey church itself was surely in danger after the abbey surrendered, but thanks to the parish church of St. Laurence having always been part of its building on the north side, the churchwardens and parishioners were allowed to buy the whole magnificent church in February 1544 for £100. Included in the sale were some adjoining land, extra land for the cemetery and a processional way all round the church. The deed can still be read in the church today. The sale did not include the six bells as they had already been removed and sold by Richard Paulet on behalf of the Court of Augmentations to John White, a citizen of London, together with 25 other bells from former monastic houses within his area. Together the 31 bells had fetched £363 10s. 0d.[60]

54. The site of the Lady Chapel of Romsey Abbey.

It is not known when the Lady Chapel was pulled down, but it seems likely that it may have occurred between the surrender of the abbey and the sale of the church. Perhaps it may have been the sight of it being torn down that spurred the churchwardens to negotiate for the sale of the rest of the church – but that is pure conjecture.

At Winchester the ownership of the site of St. Mary's abbey is easier to understand, but how long it took for every trace of its former buildings above ground to disappear is another matter. In the certificate of November 1539 Sir Robert Southwell and his fellow commissioners divided the abbey buildings into two groups. Those that were assigned to remain were put into the custody of William Lambert 'to the use of the king's majesty'; they were:

The late Abbess lodging stretching from the Church to the Frater north and south, with houses of offices to the same as Buttery, Pantry, Kitchen and Larder. The Gatehouse, the Barn, the Baking and Brewing houses, the Garner next to them, the Stable and the Mill.[61]

These were let to Thomas Tichborne the following May for a term of 21 years; as already mentioned, the lease noted that the former abbess still occupied them[62] and she probably continued to reside in the abbess's lodging with a few of the former nuns until her death in 1547. It is open to doubt whether the other ladies continued to live there after that but one of them, as we have seen, was still living in the parish of St. Peter, Colebrook Street in 1551. The commissioners' list is repeated in an undated valuation made by the court's auditor, William Berners, and he also mentions gardens, orchards, courts and grounds in the 5 acres $1\frac{1}{2}$ rods which were let for 53s. 4d. a year.[63]

The buildings that the commissioners deemed to be superfluous were also put in the custody of Master Lambert. They were:

> The Church, the cloister, the chapter house, the Dormitory, the Frater, the Infirmary, the convent kitchen, the two Garners on the south side of the court, the Lodging called Mistress Lane's Lodging, the priests Lodging and the plumber's house.[64]

55. Abbey Gardens, Winchester, part of the site of St Mary's Abbey.

The certificate then continues with the weights of the five bells in the steeple and the lead on the church, its aisles and steeple, on the cloister and other houses.

In November 1546 the Court of Augmentations granted the site to two agents who were much involved with the disposal of monastic lands, John Bellowe and John Broxholme. Their grant lists the buildings still standing, starting with the abbess's lodging and including all the others that were to remain, as well as the church and frater which had not yet been pulled down. After mentioning the fruit trees in the orchards and the gardens, a note at the end of the grant says that no other buildings remained on the site of the late monastery,[65] so all the other 'superfluous' parts of the abbey had presumably been pulled down within the lifetime of Elizabeth Shelley. Two months later the agents were given a licence to convey the abbess's lodging and certain gardens to Thomas White and his wife Agnes.[66] Finally, in 1554, all the property that the abbey had owned in Winchester was granted to the Corporation of the city in recompense for the expenses it had incurred at the time of Queen Mary's marriage to Philip of Spain in the cathedral.[67] The city still owns part of the site today.

The dereliction of parts of Winchester following the Dissolution is apparent in one of Bishop Gardiner's letters written in 1546. When pleading on behalf of the two remaining hospitals in the city he wrote:

> ... for the country is poor and very poor, and these two houses somewhat garnish the town, which by reason of friars, monks and nuns, whose houses stand all to torn, with the decay of the inhabitants, is now much defaced.[68]

During the last half of the century stones from the demolished buildings of St. Mary's Abbey were used for local work. Some were incorporated in the walls of Winchester College and others were used for repairs at St. Peter Chesil whose parish accounts for 1582-3 include the sum of 6d. which had been spent 'For the carriage of a load of stones from Saint Mary's'.[69] However, it was still possible for William Camden to sense something of the grandeur that had been when he visited the site for he wrote later,

> I cannot but take notice of the nunnery ... it having been so noble a pile (as the ruins of it still show).[70]

It had originally been intended that John Kingsmill, who was a brother of the last abbess, should be granted the site of Wherwell Abbey. He had already tried to obtain the prebend of Wherwell when it came vacant in 1538. No doubt Morpheta Kingsmill did her best to further his interests, and two of Cromwell's undated memoranda concerning the monasteries include a note, 'Mr Kingsmill for Wherwell'.[71] However, in the end he had to be content with lesser spoils that included two manors in the parish of Kingsclere where his family had become established; one was Sydmonton which had belonged to Romsey Abbey. (Among the Kingsmill papers is a memorandum that was signed by Morpheta Kingsmill in 1569, discharging the executors of Sir John Kingsmill 'my dear and well beloved brother' of all debts due to her.[72])

Instead Wherwell Abbey and its adjacent lands were granted to Sir Thomas West, Lord de la Warr. According to his own account he had been born within 20 miles of Wherwell, but his country seat was at Halnaker in Sussex where he had entertained the king in 1526, six years after attending him at the Field of the Cloth of Gold. He was an occasional correspondent of Lord Lisle for whom he and Cromwell were appointed proxies in 1533 when Lisle went to Calais. He was a staunch catholic and a friend of the Marquess of Exeter. A contemporary described him as

> ... the whole stay of our corner of Sussex, for if we lacked him we might well say to have lost the greatest part of our wealth and catholics, for he is surely a good lord and a just.[73]

But naturally this had not deterred him from benefiting from the Dissolution. In 1536 he was granted Boxgrove Priory which had been founded by his family and lay close to his home, but by 1539 he was having to face the loss of his Sussex estate. It is difficult to be certain quite why. The previous December he had been committed to the Tower for three weeks, apparently because he refused to sit on the jury of peers trying his friends Exeter and Montague. This surely made him more vulnerable to any intended take-over by the king or his servants, but it has also been suggested that the authorities feared he might restore monks to Boxgrove.[74]

By the end of the year Lord de la Warr was resigned to having to exchange his Sussex

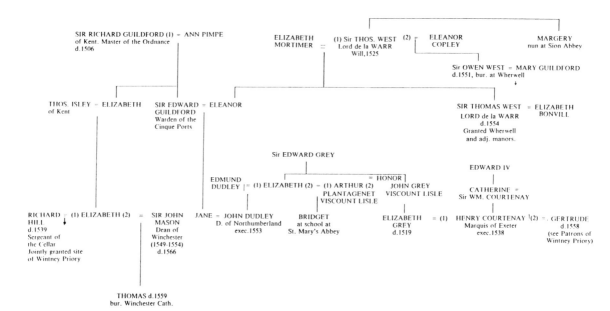

56.   Grantees of Wherwell Abbey and Wintney Priory.

property for another monastic site. Wherwell had evidently been suggested, so on 18 November he wrote to Cromwell:

> I would gladly have the said nunnery because it stands wholesomely in the country where I was born, and my wife has no house to dwell in if I should die before her: and this is but a reasonable house as I hear say. I beg your favour that I might obtain the said abbey before the surveyors of the same come to the king, for fear he should grant it to another.[75]

He followed this up with another letter next day after the surveyors had been to Halnaker (which he always called 'Halfnakyd'). He continued:

> . . . I do hearsay that the abbeys of Horwell [sic] is like to be dissolved within this two or three days and I do hearsay that it standeth in Hampshire in a wholesome country and within xx miles there as I was born . . . [76]

He then went on to compare the values of his own and the Wherwell lands. Incidentally, his sources of information were most accurate; the abbey was indeed surrendered within two or three days – two to be precise.

The indenture for the exchange of de la Warr's Sussex property for the Wherwell estate was dated 3 March 1540. On 24 March the Court of Augmentations enrolled the grant to Sir Thomas West, Lord de la Warr and his wife Elizabeth of the site and circuit of the former monastery with all its buildings including the water mill, the waters and 30 acres of land there, as well as the contiguous manors of Wherwell, Westover, Middleton, Tufton Bullington, Goodworth Clatford and Little Anne, with the advowson of the church of Wherwell and the prebend of Goodworth. Their rent was £137 3s. 8d. a year.[77] (Five years later the priest who held the prebend of Wherwell resigned and was granted an annuity of £30 by the Court of Augmentations.)

It is possible that his widow may have used the house but it seems unlikely that Lord de la Warr ever lived at Wherwell. He had other manors and lands in Wiltshire and Sussex, as well as part of the manor of Oakhanger in Selborne which had been in his family since the 14th century. However, it is clear from the will of the younger half-brother, Sir Owen West, that he himself lived in Wherwell where he was buried in 1551; his tomb may now be seen in the new parish church. Before the Dissolution Lord de la Warr had built a beautiful chantry chapel in the chancel of Boxgrove Priory church, where it still stands. It was never used for burials, so when he died in 1554 de la Warr was interred near his father in the parish church of Broadwater nearby. He had no children but was eventually succeeded by his nephew, Sir William West.[78] The Wherwell property continued in the family until the end of the 17th century.

The commissioners' certificate shows that all the abbey buildings were put into the custody of Lord de la Warr from the day of the surrender. As at St. Mary's Abbey they were divided into two groups by the commissioners. The buildings assigned to remain were:

> The late Abbess' lodging with the houses within the Quadrant as the water leadeth from the East side of the cloister to the Gate; the [In]firmary, the Mill and Millhouse with the Slaughter house adjoining. The brewing and Baking houses with the Granaries to the same. The Barn and Stables in the outer court.

57.   Fifteenth-century effigy of an abbess of Wherwell, now in the parish church of Wherwell.

58. An 1830 watercolour of the former Wherwell parish church showing the 15th-century south aisle (*see also* plate 17).

59. Gateway into the churchyard from the present Wherwell Priory. Medieval coffin lids lie on either side and the 17th-century inscription concerning the fate of the abbey is set into the wall.

Those that were deemed to be superfluous were:

> The Church 'Quyer' and steeple covered with lead, the Cloister covered with tiles and certain gutters of lead. The Chapter house, Frater, Dormitory, Convent Kitchen, and all the old lodgings between the Granary and the hall door covered with tiles.[79]

The commissioners then recorded their estimations of the weight of lead on the buildings and the five bells in the steeple; these were later bought by Lord de la Warr for £100.[80]

Nothing now remains of the abbey buildings above ground, although some early fragments of sculpture remain which were taken into the parish church in 1939.[81] Two coffin lids can also be seen by the gate that leads from the present Wherwell Priory into the churchyard. The most interesting survival in the church is the 15th-century effigy of a nun; her wimple and much of her face are still clear and her dog squats at her feet, but her hands which were once joined in prayer are now missing. The surprising feature is that she does not hold a crosier which would have indicated that she was an abbess, but the lack of one is perhaps the clue to her identity. Juliana Overey was abbess for over 40 years at the end of the 15th century (1452-94) but at the end of that period she was not dead, only resigned. At the election that followed, her kinsman, Thomas Overey, was present so she was still in touch with her family. It is surely a not unreasonable hypothesis that they may have commissioned the effigy when she eventually died.

Although the abbey church was destroyed after the dissolution of the abbey, the parish church just to the north of it remained until it was pulled down and replaced in 1858. Fortunately two water-colours were painted in the 1830s which show that the north aisle (with the bell turret over the west gable) seems to have been of 13th-century origin, and probably had a narrow south aisle lit by the two-light west window of lancets divided by a slender shaft; the cusped outer arch above the three-light west window is characteristically 13th century. The second painting shows the later south aisle (with porch) which apparently swallowed up the earlier narrow one. Its width, buttresses and windows with square heads under label moulds all show it to be 15th-century work, probably mid-late in the century but before 1485.[82] The unusual row of panels that can be seen on this south side are mentioned in the description made by Baigent, Hampshire's great antiquarian. He visited the old parish church and wrote this note on 4 July 1851:

> Wherwell – The building used as a church might have been some building connected with the abbey, but not the abbey church. A large perpendicular building with no exterior division of a chancel, and has neither tower nor bells. On the north side of [the] nave is a large parlour pew with a carpet and fireplace. On the floor remain a number of encaustic tiles, several stones forming the pavement have matrices from which the brass plates have been taken, among them is the matrix of the figure of an abbess with pastoral staff, and another stone gives the upper portion of a good canopy. A large number of coffin shaped stones form a portion of the pavement and some of these are probably reversed. In the north aisle is a very shallow stone coffin [illustrated]. An altar tomb is built into the east wall of the north aisle. The side or front of it is divided into three compartments, the centre one has a shield of arms, and upon the other compartments is an inscription. The first words are nearly erased being cut away intentionally . . . [re. Sir Owen West, 1551] There are two pieces of stone panelling built into the south wall of the nave, externally, which once formed the front or sides of a tomb. Each is divided into five compartments, in each of these is a shield hanging from a band or guige. None of these shields exhibits any trace of bearings upon them. About the middle of this wall there is built into it a shield charged with two bars and a label of five points.[83]

In the 17th century, in the year of King Charles's execution, a memorial stone was erected near the ruins of the abbey which was noted in *The Gentleman's Magazine* in the following century. It is still in place in a wall near the church today and its words may fittingly conclude this account.

Anno Dom 1649
Here was the Monastery of Wherwell. Erected by Queene Ethelred. Demolished by the overacted zeale or avarice of King Henry, and of its last ruines here buried there yet remains this monument.

Abbreviations used in the Appendices and References

(For episcopal registers, see bibliography)

Ancient Deeds	Calendars of Judicial Records: *Ancient Deeds*
BL (BM)	British Library (British Museum)
Book of Fees	Calendars of Exchequer Records: *Book of Fees*
Biddle, *W.S.1*	Biddle, M., *Winchester Studies*, vol.1 (see bibiliography)
Cant. and York. Soc.	Canterbury and York Society
Cal. Ch. Rolls.	Calendar of Charter Rolls
Cal. Cl. Rolls.	Calendar of Close Rolls
Cal. Fine Rolls.	Calendar of Fine Rolls
Cal. Inq. Misc.	Calendar of Inquisitions Miscellaneous
Cal. Inq. P.M.	Calendar of Inquisitions Post Mortem
Cal. Lib. Rolls.	Calendar of Liberate Rolls
Cal. Pat. Rolls.	Calendar of Patent Rolls
Cal. Pap. Reg.	Entries in the Papal Registers relating to Great Britain and Ireland
Curia Regis Rolls	Calendars of Judicial Records: *Curia Regis Rolls*
E.H.D.	*English Historical Documents* (see bibliography)
Feudal Aids	Calendars of Exchequer Records: *Feudal Aids*
H.F.C. Proc.	Proceedings of the Hampshire Field Club
HRO	Hampshire Record Office
HMC	Historical Manuscripts Commission
Keene, *W.S.2*	Keene, D., *Winchester Studies*, vol.2 (see bibliography)
Leningrad Cal.	Calendar of Wherwell Abbey now in Leningrad
L. and P.	Letters and Papers, Foreign and Domestic, Henry VIII
Liveing	H.G.D. Liveing, *Records of Romsey Abbey (1906)*
Power	Eileen Power, *Medieval English Nunneries*, (1922)
PRO	Public Record Office
R.S.	Rolls Series
v.; r.	*verso; recto* (where specified)
Valor Eccl.	*Valor Ecclesiasticus*
VCH	*Victoria County History of Hampshire and the Isle of Wight* (1900-14)
VCH, (county)	*Victoria County History* for county specified
Wher.Cart.	Cartulary of Wherwell Abbey. BL MS. Egerton 2104a
Wint.Cal.	Calendar etc. of Wintney Priory. BL MS. Cotton Claud D.iii.

Appendix 1

The Heads of the Nunneries

Nunnaminster - St. Mary's Abbey, Winchester

Etheldritha	by 924	Osbert of Clare
(St. Edburga?)	d. c.951	*ibid.*; Biddle, *W.S.1*, p.555 on her death
Ethelthryth	963 x 984	Knowles, Brooke, London, *Heads of Relig. Houses*, p.223
Eadgifu	c.975	*ibid.*
Alfghena (Alvena?)	963 x 984	Osbert of Clare; Clapham, 'Three Bede-Rolls', p.42
Alfleda	after Alfghena	Osbert of Clare
Beatrice	d. 1084	*Winchester Annals*, p.34; Clapham, *Three Bede Rolls*, pp.42, 51
Alice (Athelitz)	from 1084	Knowles et al., p.223
	occ. 1102	*Winchester Annals*, p.34
(Adela?)		obit. of Adela, abba., on 15 Jan. (Romsey Psalter)
Lucy	occ. 1142 & after	Knowles et al., p.223
Emma	occ. 1159 x 1181, prob. d.-1173	*ibid.*
Claricia	apptd. 1174	*ibid.*
	occ. 1207	BL Add. MS. 39977, fol.251
Isabella	occ. 1219, 1223	Berks. Fines, CP 25/1/7/6, 8
	d. 1236	*Cal. Pat. R., 1232-47*, p.137
(Natalia	invalid election	*Cal. Cl. R., 1234-7*, p.251)
Agnes	election process May-June 1236	*Cal. Pat. R., 1232-47*, pp.147-9;
	d. 30 Aug. 1265	*Winchester Annals*, p.102; *Cal. Pat. R., 1258-66*, p.447
Euphemia	elec. Sept. 1265	*Cal. Pat. R., 1258-66*, p.449; *Winchester Annals*, p.102
	d. 20 Nov. 1270	*ibid.*, p.109
Lucy	elec. Dec. 1270	*ibid.*; *Ann. Wigornia*, p.460 *Cal. Pat. R., 1266-72*, p.496
	d. (unknown)	
Matilda	occ. 1281, her 5th year in office d. 14 Dec.	BL Add. Ch. 17519 obit in Romsey Psalter
(abbess)	May 1284, very aged	*HMC. Var. Coll.*, vol.4, p.153
(abbess)	1282 x 1288	Bp. Pontissara writes re. death of abbess, n.d., no name. Reg. Pontissara, fol.48
Mary	occ. 1285	PRO Ancient Deeds, E42/481

Christina de Wintonia	elec. Feb. 1288	*Cal. Pat. R., 1281-92*, pp.290-1
	d. Jan. 1299	*ibid., 1292-1301*, p.393
Agnes de Ashley	elec. Feb. 1299	*ibid.*, pp.394-5
	d. by 1 April 1313	*ibid., 1307-13*, p.559
Matilda de Pecham	elec. April-May 1313	*Reg. Woodlock*, pp.610-1; *Cal. Pat. R., 1307-13*, pp.561, 567
	d. Nov. 1337	*ibid., 1334-8*, p.546
Matilda de Spyne	elec. Nov.-Dec. 1337	Reg. Orleton, fols.66v-7; *Cal. Pat. R., 1334-8*, pp.555, 557
	d. May 1349	*ibid., 1348-50*, p.297
Margaret de Molyns (Molyneux)	elec. June 1349	*Reg. Edington*, vol. 1, items 577, 588-93; *Cal. Pat. R., 1348-50*, pp.302, 304
	d. Oct. 1361	*ibid., 1361-4*, p.83
Christina la Wayte	elec. Oct.-Nov. 1361	*Reg. Edington*, vol.1, items 1471-4; *Cal. Pat. R., 1361-4*, pp.100, 106.
	d. July 1365	*ibid., 1364-7*, p.160
Alice de la Mare	elec. July-Aug. 1365	*ibid.*; *Reg. Edington*, vol.1, items 1694-1701
	d. Feb. 1385	*Cal. Inq.P.M.*, vol.16, p.118; *Cal. Pat. R., 1381-5*, p.525; *Reg. Wykeham*, vol.1, p.153
Johanna Denemede	elec. March 1385	*ibid.*; *Cal. Pat. R., 1381-5*, pp.534, 544
	d. April 1410	*ibid., 1408-13*, p.184
Matilda Holme	elec. April 1410	Reg. Beaufort, vol.1, fols.26-31[+]; *Cal. Pat. R., 1408-13*, pp.170, 188
	d. April 1415	*ibid., 1413-16*, p.296
Christina Hardy	elec. April 1415	*Cal. Pat. R., 1413-16*, pp.299, 303
	d. April 1419	*ibid., 1416-22*, p.216
Agnes Denham	elec. April 1419	*ibid.*, pp.216-7
	d. April 1449	*ibid., 1446-52*, p.234
Agnes Buriton	elec. April-May 1449	Reg. Waynflete, vol.1, fols. 10v-14; *Cal. Pat. R., 1446-52*, pp.240, 243
	d. April 1488	*ibid., 1485-94*, p.221
Johanna Legh	elec. April 1488	Reg. Courtenay, fols.4-6; *Cal. Pat. R., 1485-94*, pp.221, 229.
	d. 11 May 1527	*L. and P.*, vol.4 (2), item 3117
Elizabeth Shelley	elec. May-June 1527	Reg. Fox, vol.5, fols.130-8; *L. and P.*, vol.4 (2), items 3133, 3182, 3224.
	(Abbey dissolved Nov. 1539) d. by 16 April 1547	Date of inventory, HRO D2/A/1/134

Note: The obits of all the abbesses from 1100 to 1419 are recorded in the so-called Romsey Psalter, except Mary (occ. 1285) and Agnes de Ashley (d. 1313) and there is only one Lucy (Liveing, pp.299-300)

Romsey Abbey

(Elfleda?) (dau. of Edward the Elder)	10th century	(ed.) Zettl, *Anon. Short English Metrical Chronicle*, p.21
	d.959 (?)	*VCH*, vol.2, p.132
St. Merewenna	occ. 967 x 975	(ed.) Birch, *Liber Vitae*, pp.58, 94; Knowles et al., p.218
Elwina	? 990s	Knowles et al., p.218
St. Ethelfleda (Elfleda)	? 990s	Knowles et al., p.218; Birch, *Liber Vitae*, p.58
Wulf(w)ynn	prob. 11th century	*ibid.*, p.62
Elfgyfu (Christina?)	prob. 11th century	*ibid.*
Athelitz	c.1086+	Knowles et al., p.219
Hadewidis	occ. prob.-1102	*ibid.*
	1130 x 1133	(ed.) Blake, *Cartulary of St. Denys, Southampton*, p.215
Matilda	1133 x 1155	*ibid.*, p.216
	d. 1155	*Winchester Annals*, p.55
Mary de Blois	resigns 1160 (d.1182)	Knowles et al., p.219
Juliana	1174 x 1199	(ed.) Goodman, *Winchester Cathedral Chartulary*, pp.213-4.
	d. 1199	*Winchester Annals*, p.71
Matilda Patriz. (sister of Walter Walerand)	elec. 3 June 1199	*ibid.*, p.72; Knowles et al., p.219
	d. 14 Dec. 1230	*Cal. Pat. R., 1225-32*, p.418
Matilda de Barbeflé	elec. process Dec. 1230-Jan.1231	*ibid.*, pp.418, 420
	d. April 1237	*ibid., 1232-47*, p.180
Isabella de Neville	elec. April-May 1237	*ibid.*, pp.180, 182; *Cal. Cl. R., 1234-37*, p.443
	d. (unrecorded)	
Cecilia	elec. prob. 1238 occ. 1244	Liveing, pp.64-5 *ibid.*; Hants. Fines, CP25/1/203/8 n.38
	d. (unrecorded)	
Constance de la Rochele	elec. Sept. 1247	*Cal. Pat. R., 1232-47*, p.509; *Cal. Cl. R.,1242-7*, p.537
	d. prob. 1260 (6 months vacancy)	*Cal. Pat. R., 1258-66*, p.153; Liveing, p.64
Amicia de Sulhere (Sullye)	elec. May-June 1261	*Cal. Pat. R., 1258-66*, pp.153, 156-7
	d. July 1268	*ibid., 1266-72*, p.244
Alice Walerand	elec. July 1268	*ibid.*, pp.244, 249
	d. April 1298	PRO SC6-983-34; *Cal. Pat. R., 1292-1301*, p.342
Philippa de Stokes	elec. April 1298	*ibid.*, pp.342, 345, 347
	d. Sept. 1307	*ibid., 1307-13*, p.5
Clementia de Gildeford	elec. Sept.-Oct. 1307	*ibid.*, pp.5, 8, 12; *Reg. Woodlock*, pp.216-7, 224
	d. Dec. 1314	*Cal. Pat. R., 1313-17*, p.206

Alice de Wyntershull	elec. Jan.-Feb. 1315	*ibid.*, pp.210, 216
	d. May 1315	*ibid.*, pp.281, 327, 403
Sybil Carbonel	elec. July-Aug. 1315	*ibid.*, pp.333, 340
	d. June 1333	*ibid.*, *1330-4*, p.452
Joan Icthe	elec. June-July 1333	*ibid.*, pp.453, 460; Reg.
		Stratford, fols. 81v-83
	d. April 1349	*Cal. Pat. R.*, *1348-50*, p.278
Joan Gerveys	elec. May 1349	*ibid.*, pp.285, 296; *Reg.*
		Edington, vol.1, items 514, 544.
	d. Oct. 1352	*Cal. Pat. R.*, *1350-4*, p.348
Isabella Cammoys	elec. Nov. 1352	*ibid.*, pp.360-1; *Reg.*
		Edington, vol.1, items 916-921.
	d. April 1396	*Cal. Pat. R.*, *1391-6*, p.686
Lucy Everard	elec. April-May 1396	*ibid.*, pp.686, 698, 714;
		Reg. Wykeham, vol.1, pp.202-3.
	d. July 1405	*Cal. Pat. R.*, *1405-8*, p.54
Felicia Aas	elec. July-Aug. 1405	*ibid.*, pp.39, 42, 54
	d. Oct. 1417	*ibid.*, *1416-22*, p.124
Matilda Lovell	elec. Nov. 1417	*ibid.*, pp.125-7
	d. April 1462	*ibid*, *1461-7*, p.182
Johanna Brygges	elec. April-May 1462	*ibid.*, pp.182, 185, 187-8;
		Reg. Waynflete, vol.1,
		fols.119v-121.
	d. May 1472	*Cal. Pat. R.*, *1467-77*, p.337
Elizabeth Brooke	elec. June 1472	*ibid.*, pp.339, 344; Reg.
		Waynflete, vol.2, fols.12-13
	resigns Aug. 1478	Reg. Waynflete, vol.2,
		fol.64
	re-elec. Aug.-Oct. 1478	*ibid.*, fols.64-80; Liveing,
		pp.211-6
	d. by 6 June 1502	Reg. Fox, vol.1, fol.21
Joyce Rowse	elec. June 1502	*Cal. Pat. R.*, *1494-1509*,
		pp.254, 310; Reg. Fox,
		vol.1, fols.21-4.
	resigns Sept. 1515	*L. and P.*, vol.2 (1), item 914
Anne Westbroke	elec. Sept. 1515	*ibid.*, items 935, 942, 1008
	d. by 1 Dec. 1523	*ibid.*, vol.3 (2), item 3589
Elizabeth Ryprose	elec. Dec. 1523-Jan. 1524	*ibid.*, vol.4 (1), item 66;
	(Abbey dissolved 1539)	Reg. Fox, vol.5, fols.54-62
	d. (unknown)	

Wherwell Abbey

(Wenfleda?)	occ. c.960s	Knowles et al., p.222
Heanfled	occ. 1002	Finberg, *Early Charters of Wessex*, item 149
sister of Edward the Confessor (name unknown)	occ. 1051	Anglo-Saxon Chronicle, *EHD*, vol.2, p.125
Aelstrita	before 1113	Clapham, 'Three Bede-Rolls', p.43
Matilda	before 1113	*ibid.*
Alberada	before 1113	*ibid.*
(Agnes?)	dates unknown	obit 29 August, in St. John's Coll., 68
Matilda de Bailleul	c.1170s (abbess for 40 years)	Wherwell Cart., ch.60, fol.44v
	occ. 1194	*Papsturkunden in England*, vol.1 no.318
	d. 1207 x 1219	obits: 13 Dec. in St. John's Coll., 68; 14 Dec. in Leningrad Cal.; Thomson, *MSS from St. Alban's Abbey*, pp.8, 58, 123
Euphemia (niece of Matilda de Bailleul whom she succeeded; dau. of Margaret de Walliers)	occ. May 1219	Berks. Fines, CP25/1/7/7 n.46; Wherwell Cart, ch.59, fol.43v
	d. 26 April 1257	*ibid.*; obit in Leningrad Cal.
Mary	elec. April-May 1257	*Cal. Pat. R., 1247-58*, pp.552, 555; *Cal. Cl. R., 1256-58*, p.59.
	d. Feb. 1259	*Cal. Pat. R., 1258-66*, p.13
Constance	elec. March 1259	*ibid.*, pp.14-15
	d. Oct. 1262	*ibid., 1266-72*, appendix, p.738; *Cal. Cl. R., 1261-4*, p.162
Mabel de Tichburne	elec. Nov.-Dec. 1262	*Cal. Pat. R., 1258-66*, p.237
	d. Dec. 1281	*ibid., 1281-92*, p.6; obit 12 Dec. in St. John's Coll., 68
Elena de Percy	elec. Jan.-Feb. 1282	*Cal. Pat. R., 1281-92*, p.9
	d. 2 Dec. 1297	PRO SC6-983-34;
	news to king 17 Jan. 1298	*Cal. Pat. R., 1292-1301*, p.326
Isabella de Wyntreshulle	elec. Jan.-Feb. 1298	*ibid.*, pp.326, 329; Wherwell Cart., ch.436, fols.184v-185v
	resigns by Oct. 1333	*Cal. Pat. R., 1330-4*, p.478
Matilda de Littleton	elec. Oct.-Dec.1333	*ibid.*, pp.478, 483, 488; Reg. Stratford, fol.139
	d. March 1340	*Cal. Pat. R., 1338-40*, p.442; obit, Fitzwilliam Mus. McClean 45
Amicia Ladde	elec. March-April 1340	*Cal. Pat. R., 1338-40*, pp.442, 449, 461; Reg. Orleton, vol.1, fol.87; Wherwell Cart., ch.111, fol.69
	d. Sept. 1361	*Cal. Pat. R., 1361-4*, p.74

Constancia de Wyntreshulle	elec. Sept.-Oct. 1361	*ibid.*, pp.74, 87, 91; *Reg. Edington*, vol.1, items 1464-70; Wherwell Cart., ch.282, fols.129v-130 and ch.351, fol.151v
Joan Cokerell (Cotterell)	d. November 1361 elec. Nov.-Dec. 1361	*Cal. Pat. R., 1361-4*, p.125 *ibid.*, pp.125, 134, 136; *Reg. Edington*, vol.1, items 1480-3; Wherwell Cart, chs. 349, 350; fol.151v
Cecily Lavyngtone	d. Sept. 1375 elec. Sept.-Oct. 1375	*Cal. Pat. R., 1374-7*, p.168 *ibid.*, pp.168, 172, 183; *Reg. Wykeham*, vol.1, pp.69-74
Alice Parys	d. May 1412 elec. May-July 1412	*Cal. Pat. R., 1408-13*, p.400 *ibid.*, pp.398, 400, 408; Reg. Beaufort, vol.1, fols.48v+-49+.
Sibyl Bolde	d. Nov. 1437 elec. Nov.-Dec. 1437	*Cal. Pat. R., 1436-41*, p.119 *ibid.*, pp.119-20
Anna Quarley	d. Nov. 1451 elec. Nov. 1451	*ibid., 1446-52*, pp.496, 504 *ibid.*, pp.496, 504, 514; Reg. Waynflete, vol.1, fols.40v-41
Alice Serle	d. Oct. 1452 elec. Oct. 1452	*Cal. Pat. R., 1452-61*, p.21 *ibid.*, pp.21, 33; Reg. Waynflete, vol.1, fol.50
Juliana Overey	d. 9 Dec. 1452 elec. Dec.-Jan. 1452-3	*ibid.*, fol.50v; *Cal. Pat. R., 1452-61*, p.29 *ibid.*, pp.29. 36; Reg. Waynflete, vol.1, fols.50v-56
Matilda Rowse	resigns June 1494 elec. June-July 1494 d. 24 Jan. 1518	*Cal. Pat. R., 1485-94*, p.468 *ibid.*, pp.468, 470; Reg. Langton, fols.46v-50 *L. and P.*, vol.2 (2), item 3920
Avelina Cowdrey	elec. Feb.-Mar. 1518	*ibid.*, items 3920, 3970, 4006; Reg. Fox, vol.4, fols.20-4
Anne Colte	d. July 1529 elec. July-Aug. 1529 resigns Sept. 1535	*L. and P.*, vol.4 (3), item 5799 *ibid.*, items 5799, 5838; *Reg. Wolsey*, pp.17-48 *L. and P.*, vol.9, items 344, 439, 504 (4)
Morpheta Kingsmill	elec. Sept.-Oct. 1535 (Abbey dissolved Nov. 1539) d. 8 April 1570	*ibid.*, items 504 (4, 15), 729 (5, 21) Will and inventory, HRO Bp. 1570

Wintney Priory

The Wintney Calendar and Martyrologium (BL MS. Cotton Claud D.iii) contain the names of the earliest known prioresses but only give the dates of their obits, marked with a * in the chronological list. The following nine names are all original entries in the calendar:

Sabina	15 March	fol.147
Isilia	31 March	fol.148
Claricia	5 May	fol.148v
Lucia (I)	21 May	fol.151v
Juliana	15 July	fol.155
Alicia	21 July	fol.155v
Hawiisa (sic)	2 September	fol.156v
Cecilia	10 September	fol.157
Roisa	29 September	fol.158

The obits of the following three prioresses were added later:

Emma	7 January	fol.140v
Lucia (II)	23 July	fol.155v
Edmunda	6 September	fol.37 (in martyrologium)

***

Chronological order of prioresses

Roisa	occ. April 1219	Hants. Fines, CP25/1/203/4 no.55
	obit 29 Sept.*	
Lucy (I)	occ. 1223 x 1224	*London and Middlesex Fines*, p.215
	obit 21 May*	
Sabina	occ. April 1228	Hants. Fines, CP25/1/203/5 no.42
	obit 15 March*	
Hawisia	occ. Jan. 1236, June 1248, Feb. 1249	Hants. Fines, CP25/1/203/6 no.32; 203/8 no.14; 203/8 no.65
	obit 2 Sept.*	
Lucy (II)	occ. April 1256, July 1258	Hants. Fines, CP25/1/204/9 no.88; 204/10 no.9
	occ. April 1263	*HMC Var. Coll.*, vol.4, p.148
	obit 23 July*	
Cecilia Banastre	occ. c.1270 x 1280	*ibid.*, p.150
	occ. Feb. 1280	Hants. Fines, CP25/1/204/12 no.56
	cession accepted October 1294	*Reg. Pontissara*, pp.xxxv, 67
	obit 10 Sept.*	
Claricia de Meleburne	d. as prioress pre- 13 May 1301	Memoranda Roll, 28-9 Edward I, m.44
	obit 5 May*	
Alicia de Dummere	elec. May 1301 resigns 1309	*Reg. Pontissara*, pp.xxxv, 98 *Reg. Woodlock*, p.343
	? obit 21 July*	
Christiana	d. by June 1329 (no obit but memorandum on fol.18 of Martyrologium)	Reg. Stratford, fol.115

Alicia de Westcote	elec. June 1329 resigns Nov. 1336	Reg. Stratford, fol.115 Reg. Orleton, vol.1, fol.46v
Covina/Camina de Marys	elec. Nov. 1336 occ. May 1337 d. by 17 July 1349	*ibid.* *HMC Var. Coll.*, vol.4, p.154 *Reg. Edington*, vol.1, item 632. (re. incorrect surname see chap. 8, n.21)
Emma de Wynterburn	elec. July 1349 d. (unknown) obit 7 Jan.*	*Reg. Edington*, vol.1, item 632
Alice Fyshide	elec. c.1385 resigns by March 1415	Had been prioress 'about 20 years' in 1405; *Cal. Pap.* *Reg. (Letters)*, vol.6, p.55 Reg. Beaufort, vol.1, fol.50[+]
Johanna Benbury	el. March 1415 d. (unknown)	*ibid.*

It is possible that there could have been other prioresses between 1415 and 1447, the period of the missing Reg. Beaufort, vol.2.

Eleanor Squerell	d. by March 1453	Reg. Waynflete, vol.1, fol.58v
Alice Somerset	elec. March 1453 d. 2 April 1460	*ibid.* *ibid.*, fol.102v
Petronilla Pygeon	elec. April 1460 resigns by Feb. 1498	*ibid.*, fols. 102v-103 Reg. Langton, fol.51
Anne Thomas	elec. Feb. 1498 d. by April 1534	*ibid.*, fols.51-2 BL MS. Cotton Vespasian, F.xiii, fol.178
Elizabeth Martyn	elec. post 7 April 1534 (Priory dissolved July 1536) d. by 6 July 1587	*ibid.* date of inventory; will proved 1587, Wilts. R.O.

Appendix 2

Churches from which the Nunneries
Derived Income

St. Mary's Abbey, Winchester

Hampshire

Leckford

> Prebendal to the abbey
> Advowson: probably in the patronage of the abbey by the Conquest. After becoming prebendal, the prebend presented vicars. Vicarage by 1305. (*Reg. Woodlock*, p.889)
> 1291 valuation of church: £6 13s. 4d.[1]
> 1333-45 valuation of prebend: 10 marks[2]
> 1535 valuation of prebend: £9
>> of vicarage: £8 16s[3]
>
> 1539 valuation of prebend: £10 (PRO E315-494, fol.15)
> 1539-40. Pension of £1 a year paid by prebend to abbess (PRO SC6-Henry VIII-3342)
> 1544. Grant of advowson and pension (See Appendix 3)

Itchen Abbas

> Prebendal to the abbey
> Advowson: probably in the patronage of the abbey by the Conquest. The abbess and convent presented rectors.
> 1291 valuation of church: £10
>> of prebend: £3 6s. 8d.
>
> 1333-45 valuation of church: 15 marks
> 1535 valuation of rectory: £14 1s. 4d.
>> of prebend: £4 6s. 8d.
>
> 1539 valuation of rectory: £13 6s. 8d.
>> of prebend: £4 (PRO E315-494, fol.15)
>
> 1544. Grant of advowson (*L. and P.* vol.19 (1), item 610 (4, 116)

Froyle

> Advowson: probably in the patronage of the abbey by the Conquest. The abbess and convent appropriated the rectory by 1354 (*Cal. Cl. Rolls, 1354-60*, p.107[4]; *Reg. Edington*, vol.1 item 1008) and then presented vicars.
> 1291 valuation of church: £26 13s. 4d
> 1333-45 valuation of church: 40 marks
>> of pension paid to the prebend of Itchen (Abbas): 2 marks
>
> 1535 valuation of vicarage: £11 12s. 1½d
> 1539 valuation of vicarage: £10 (PRO E315-494, fol.15)
>> of the farm of the rectory: £17 (PRO SC6-Henry VIII-3342)

St. Peter's Church, Colebrook Street, Winchester

> Advowson: abbess and convent were patrons; they presented rectors to whom they gave a pension. (*Reg. Gardiner*, pp.69-70)
> 1333-45 valuation of church: 40s.
> 1535 valuation of church: £3 13s. 4d.
> 1539 valuation: £3 6s. 8d. (PRO E315-494, fol.15)

All Saints in the Vines Church, Winchester
>Advowson: abbess and convent were patrons. In c.1370 the church was closed and may have been absorbed into the parish of St. Michael outside King's Gate and St. Faith (Keene, *W.S.2*, p.134).

Priory of St. Denys, Southampton
>Two pensions of 7s. and 1s. 3½d. a year paid to the abbey. (*Cartulary of the Priory of St. Denys, Southampton*, pp.277-8, 280)

Wiltshire
All Cannings, with the chapel of Etchilhampton
>Partly prebendal to the abbey by the late 13th century.
>Advowson: always held by the abbess and convent until 1536; they presented rectors. (*VCH Wilts.*, vol.10, pp.25. 30)
>Pensions paid to the abbess: from church £2 5s.
>from prebend £1
>(*Valor Eccl.*, vol.2, p.129)
>1291 valuation of prebend: £13 6s. 8d.
>of church: £13 6s. 8d. (undervalued)
>1535 valuation of prebend: £14
>of church: £31 16s. 10d

Urchfont
>Partly prebendal to the abbey by the 13th century. Prebends continued after the rectory was appropriated in 1382. (*Reg. Thomas Langton of Salisbury, 1485-93*, item 58; *VCH Wilts.*, vol.10, pp.186-7).
>Advowson: the abbess and convent presented rectors before 1382 and vicars thereafter until 1536.
>1291 valuation of church: £13 6s. 8d.
>1535 valuation of prebend: £14
>of church: £15 15s. 4d.

Lincolnshire
Greatford
>Advowson: probably granted to the abbess and convent with the manor by 1212. (*Book of Fees*, vol.1, p.182.)
>Until the Dissolution they presented rectors who paid the abbess a pension of 13s. 4d. a year by the end of the 13th century. (*Rolls and Register of Oliver Sutton*, Cant. and York Soc., 1948), vol.1, p.33.
>1291 valuation of church: £26 13s. 4d.
>1352. Appropriation of church granted by Pope Clement VI (*Cal. Pap. Reg. (Petitions)*, vol.1, p.230) but not recorded in the Lincoln Episcopal Registers. (Apparently not carried out.) valuation of church: 40 marks
>1535 pension of 13s. 4d. payable by rector to prioress [sic] (*Valor Eccl.*, vol.4, p.110)
>1539 valuation of parsonage: £20 (PRO E315-494, fol.15)

Berkshire
Coleshill
>Abbess and convent were patrons until 1351 when the church was alienated to John de Edyngdon. (BL Add.MS. 71758; *Cal. Pat. R., 1350-4*, p.63; *Cal. Cl. R., 1354-60*, pp.107-8).
>1291 valuation of church: £16

Hagbourne
>Abbess and convent received a pension out of Hagbourne, probably following a dispute in 1298. (*Registrum Simonis de Gandavo*, pp.552-4)
>It is listed in 1539-40 but nothing had been received. (Dugdale, *Monasticon Anglicanum*, vol.2, p.458 records £1 in error.)

Sparsholt
>   1291: a portion of 13s. 4d. a year was paid to the nuns of Winchester; also recorded in *Reg. Simonis de Gandavo*, p.373.
>   Unrecorded in 1535 and later.

Woolley
>   Abbess and convent were patrons of a portion of the church and presented a keeper or co-portioner. 'This portion is situated next to Poughley Priory in Chaddleworth parish'. *Reg. of Thomas Langton of Salisbury, 1485-93*, item 168.

Wherwell Abbey

Hampshire

Wherwell with the chapels of Tufton and Bullington
>   Prebendal to the abbey.[5]
>   Advowson: probably in the patronage of the abbey by the Conquest. Vicars were presented by the prebend by 1318 (*Reg. Sandale*, p.149)
>   1228. (Parish) church of the Holy Trinity with its chapels of the B.V.M. and St. Michael, the 'churches' of 'Tokyntone' and 'Bolyndone', and the tithes of the assarts of Tufton for which a pension of 2s. a year was paid out of its church, all included among the possessions of the abbey confirmed in a Bull of Pope Gregory IX.[6]
>   1291 valuation of church of Wherwell with chapel: £40
>   1333-45 valuation of church with chapel: 60 marks
>   1535 valuation of prebend: £44 11s.
>   of vicarage: £14
>   1539. Prebend listed in the dissolution valuation of the abbey, but no values given for any of the seven churches of which the nuns were patrons. (PRO E315-494, fol.21).

Middleton
>   Prebendal to the abbey.
>   Advowson: probably in the patronage of the abbey by the Conquest. Right of presentation disputed in 1295 (*Reg. Pontissara*, pp.804-21, 830-5).
>   By 1304 vicars were presented by the prebend (*ibid.*, p.172)
>   1291 valuation of church: £26 13s. 4d.
>   1333-45 valuation of prebend: 40 marks
>   1535 valuation of prebend: £18 9s. 4d.   ⎰ no pension to
>   of church: £8   ⎱ abbess
>   1539. Prebend listed but no valuation (PRO E315-494, fol.21)
>   1539-40. Pension of £1 6s. 8d. paid out of church to Lord de la Warr (PRO SC6-Henry VIII-3342)

Goodworth (Clatford)
>   Prebendal to the abbey until appropriation in 1444. (Greatrex, *Register of the Common Seal*, p.108)
>   Advowson: abbess and convent would have been patrons before the Conquest. By 1321 the prebend presented vicars (*Reg. Asserio*, p.444) and continued to do so until appropriation; thereafter they were presented by the abbess and convent.
>   1228. Church of St. Peter of Godewirda included in papal confirmation of abbey's possessions.[7]
>   1291 valuation of church: £12
>   1333-45 valuation of prebend: 18 marks
>   1535 valuation of vicarage: £10
>   1539. Vicarage listed but no valuation (PRO E315-494, fol.21)
>   1539-40 'prebend of Good alias Goodworth' listed in error. (PRO SC6-Henry VIII-3342)

Over Wallop
>   1197, 1201, 1231: episcopal confirmations to the abbey included certain tithes in Wallop.[8] These were not included in the 1228 papal confirmation, and were later disputed.

1270. Composition between the rector of Wallop and Abbess Mabel; rector agreed to pay abbess 30s. a year.[9]

1333-45 valuation of certain tithes of abbess: 30s.

1539-40. Pension of £1 10s. a year from the rector of Over Wallop recorded. (PRO SC6-Henry VIII-3342)

Drayton, in Barton Stacey

1197, 1201, 1231: episcopal confirmations to the abbey included certain tithes in Drayton.[10]

1228. All the tithes of Drayton included in papal confirmation to the abbey.[11] They were payable out of two crofts.[12]

1229/30. Dispute and composition between rector of Barton and abbess.[13]

1267-70. Litigation between the same.[14]

1302. Abbess deemed not entitled to the tithes. (*Cal. Inq. Misc. (Chancery)*, vol.1, p.519)

1333-45 valuation of abbess's sheaves of corn: 2 marks

1539-40. Pension of 10s. a year out of Drayton in Barton Stacey recorded. (PRO SC6-Henry VIII-3342)

Cholderton

1197, 1201, 1231: episcopal confirmations to the abbey included tithes from three virgates of land in Chelewarton.[15]

1228. Included in papal confirmation.[16]

Church of St. Martin in Parchment Street, Winchester

Advowson: abbess and convent were patrons and presented rectors. (Biddle, *W.S.1*, fig.12 for location.)

1228. Included in papal confirmation to abbey.[17]

Between 1438 and 1446 the church was absorbed into the parish of St. Mary Kalendar. (Keene, *W.S.2*, p.134)

Isle of Wight

Langbridge and Newchurch

1228. For tithes from the church of Langbridge, an annual pension of half a mark from the parish church of Newchurch included in papal confirmation,[18]

1250. Dispute between the rector of Newchurch and the abbess about tithes due to the abbey from a mill and a turbary in Langbridge. The abbess granted him the turbary tithes for the sake of peace but kept the tithes from the mill.[19]

Wiltshire

Collingbourne Ducis

Advowson: abbess and convent were patrons and presented rectors.

1201. Bishop Herbert Poore of Salisbury confirmed the churches of Collingbourne and Everleigh to the convent; this repeated an earlier confirmation by Bishop Jocelin de Bohun (1142-84).[20]

1220. Confirmation of 12 marks to be paid out of the church of Collingbourne to the abbess and convent.[21]

1291 valuation of church: £6 13s. 4d.
     of pension to abbess: £8

1535 valuation of rectory: £16 6s. 8d.
     of pension to abbess: £8

1539. Parsonage listed but no valuation. (PRO E315-494, fol.21)

1539-40. Pension recorded: £8 (PRO SC6-Henry VIII 3342)

1544. Grant of advowson to Edward, Earl of Hertford. (*L. and P.*, vol.19 (2), item 527 (14))

Everleigh

1201. Confirmation as for Collingbourne church.[22]

Advowson: abbess and convent were patrons. There was apparently a vicarage by 1291, but from the 14th century they presented rectors. (*VCH Wilts.*, vol.11, p.140)

1291 valuation of church: £8
             of vicarage: £5 6s. 8d.
             of pension to abbess: £2
1535 valuation of rectory: £16 4s. 2½d.
             of pension to abbess: £2
1539. Parsonage listed but no valuation. (PRO E315-494. fol.21)
1539-40. Pension recorded: £2. (PRO SC6-Henry VIII 3342)
1544. Grant of advowson (*L. and P.*, vol.19 (1), item 610 (4, 116)

Milston

12th century. All the tithes of Milston ('Mildestona') inter alia confirmed to the abbess and convent by Jocelin de Bohun, bishop of Salisbury.[23]
1201, 1232-3. further episcopal confirmations.[24]
1291. Portion of Prior' [sic] of Wherwell in the tithes, £1 a year
1325. Abbess Isabella makes a grant of the tithes for a term of 5 years.[25]
1539-40. Payment from a portion of the tithes: £2 (PRO SC6-Henry VIII-3342)

Hannington

12th century. Two parts of the tithes of Hannington ('Hannedona') i.a. confirmed by Jocelin, bishop of Salisbury, and by later bishops in 1201, 1232-3 as for Milston (above).
1291 valuation of church of 'Havindon': £13 6s. 8d.
   portion of abbess of Wherwell: £1 8s.
1304. Dispute between the rector and the abbess and convent about the two parts of the tithes.[26]
1533. Abbess and convent grant a 31-year lease of a messuage and its portion of the tithes 'called Wherewelles portion' to William Prowte of Hawkesbury, Glos. (PRO E315-238-32).
1539-40. Payment made for messuage and tithes: £1 13s. 4d. (PRO SC6-Henry VIII-3342)

(*Note*. Neither Milston nor Hannington were included in the papal confirmation of 1228.)

Somerset

Bathwick, with the chapel of Woolley

Prebendal to the abbey. It came into possession after the death in 1093 of Bishop Geoffrey of Coutance who held in 1086.
1228. Both included in confirmation of abbey's possessions by Pope Gregory IX.[27]
Advowson: After a vicarage was ordained in 1321 the prebend presented vicars. (*HMC, Wells Cathedral*, vol.1, pp.389-90)
1291 valuation of church (Wyk Abbisse): £8
             of pension to abbess: £1 6s. 8d.
1535 valuation of rectory: £3 6s. 2¾d.
             of vicarage: £8 3s. 4d.
             of pension to abbess: £1 6s. 8d. (*Valor Eccl.*, vol.1)
1539. Prebend listed but not valued. (PRO E315-494-21)
1539-40. Pension listed: £1 6s. 8d. (PRO SC6-Henry VIII-3342)

Berkshire

Compton

Prebendal to the abbey, annexed to the prebend of Goodworth, Hants., probably by 1304 (*Reg. Simon de Gandavo*, pp.635-7) and certainly by 1309 (*Reg. Woodlock*, p.405).
1228. Included in papal confirmation.[28]
Advowson: vicars presented by the prebend before the appropriation of Goodworth prebend in 1444, and by the abbess and convent thereafter.
1234. Composition between abbess and vicar about tithes.[29]
1291 valuation of church: £13 6s. 8d.

1535 valuation of vicarage: £11 13s. 3½d.

1539. Vicarage of Compton listed but not valued. (PRO E315-494-21)

1539-40. Farm of the rectory or prebend of Compton and a portion of the tithes of 'Fowleston' (unidentified). (PRO SC6-Henry VIII-3342).

Inkpen

12th century: two parts of the tithes of Inkpen were confirmed to the abbess and convent by Jocelin de Bohun, bp. of Salisbury.[30]

1201-33: further episcopal confirmations.[31]

1228: included in papal confirmation.[32]

13th century: Abbess Euphemia assigned 4 marks from the tithes of Inkpen and 1 mark from those of 'Fughelescote' to the infirmarian.[33]

1291 valuation of church: £6 13s. 4d.
            of portion of abbess: £5

1320-5: litigation between rectory of Inkpen and abbess.[34]

1535 valuation of rectory: £11 14s. 5½d.

1540-1. 6s. 8d. received from Inkpen (PRO SC6-Henry VIII-3342).

Bradfield

12th century as for Inkpen; two parts of the tithes of Bradfield were confirmed to the abbey by Bishop Jocelin de Bohun.[35] They were confirmed again in 1201 but not in 1232-3.

1228. Included in papal confirmation.[36]

Romsey Abbey

Hampshire

Romsey

1. A portion in the parish church of St. Laurence (within the abbey church) with Timsbury and the chapel of Imber, Wilts.

   Prebendal to the abbey.

   1291 valuation of prebend: £28 13s. 4d.; portion of £5 6s. 8d. a year paid to abbess out of Imber.

   1333-45 valuation of prebend: 43 marks

   1535 valuation of 'Imber' prebend: £17 9s. 8d.

   1546: surrender of prebend by John Mason, prebendary, and grant of it to (the same) John Mason, French secretary, for £100. (*L. and P.*, vol.21, items 562, 716 (11)).

2. Co-portion of St. Laurence within the abbey church.

   Prebendal to the abbey until the appropriation by abbess and convent in 1351.[37]

   1291 valuation of prebend: £20
               of abbess's portion: £10 13s. 4d.

   1333-45 valuation of prebend: 30 marks
               of abbess's portion: 16 marks

Advowson: a perpetual vicarage was appointed in the prebendal church in 1321. (*Reg. Asserio*, pp.451-2, 506-8). From 1321-1381 vicars of Romsey were presented by the prebendaries;[38] from 1400 by the abbess and convent, except in 1482.

1333-45 valuation of vicarage: 18 marks

1535 valuation of rectory: £26 13s. 4d.
            of vicarage: £20 17s. 11½d.

1538-9. Payment for the farm of the rectory: £26 13s. 4d. and pension of £1 out of the tithes of Comptons held by the former Mottisfont Priory. (PRO SC6-Henry VIII-3341).

Itchen Stoke

The abbess and convent were probably patrons by the Conquest. They appropriated the rectory in 1317.[39] They presented rectors before 1317 and vicars thereafter.

1291 valuation of church: £10

1333-45 valuation of church: 15 marks
1535 valuation of rectory: £6 13s. 4d.
1538-9 valuation of rectory: £8 10s.

Wiltshire

Edington, with the chapel of Bradley
Abbess and convent were probably patrons before the Conquest.
Prebendal to the abbey until surrendered in 1351. (*VCH, Wilts.*, vol.8, pp.247. 320)
Advowson, with messuage and 2 acres in Edington granted to William de Edyngdon in 1351.
(*Cal. Pat. R., 1350-4*, p.64).
1291 valuation of church: £33 6s. 8d.

Steeple Ashton, with the chapel of Semington.
Abbess and convent were probably patrons before the Conquest. They appropriated the rectory
between 1247 and 1252. (*VCH, Wilts.*, vol.8, p.211).
Advowson: after appropriation the abbess and convent presented vicars.
1291 valuation of church: £26 13s. 4d.
              of vicarage: £13 6s. 8d.
1535 valuation of vicarage: £17 2s. 6d.
              for chaplain of Semington: £10 12s. 6d.

Imber
The abbess and convent held the chapel and presented to it from an unknown date until c.1316.
It remained part of the prebend of St. Laurence. (Liveing, p.155)
1291 valuation of 'church': £10
              of the abbess's portion: £5 6s. 8d.[40]
(The Le Rous family succeeded them as patrons. In the 15th century the church building was
still a free chapel. *Reg. Robert Hallum*, Cant. and York. Soc. (1982), items 518, 674)

In Wolf Hall in Grafton
By 1405 the abbess had a portion in Wolf Hall (the seat of the Seymour family) but no details
are known. Timmins, *Reg. John Chandler, Dean of Salisbury*, items 62, 279, 354.

Gloucestershire

Chapel of the manor of Hullasey with Tarleton in the parish of Coates.
The abbess and convent received the tithes of the chapel (**PRO** SC6-Henry VIII-3341) and owned
the 'advowson'. (*Cal. Cl. R., 1454-61*, pp.266-7).

Worcestershire

Weston
1291 valuation of pension of abbess out of church of Weston: £9 3s. 4d. (*VCH*, vol.2, p.127)

Wintney Priory

Hampshire

Hartley Wintney, als. Hartley Monialium
The church of Hurtlege was granted to the church and nuns of Wintney by Geoffrey fitz Peter at
or soon after the foundation of the priory.
(*Cal. Ch. R.*, vol.4, pp.391-2). It was appropriated to the priory.
Advowson: As patrons, the prioress and convent were presenting vicars by 1302. (*Reg. Pontissara*,
p.145)
1291 valuation of church: £10
              of pension: 5s.

1333-45 valuation of rectory: 15 marks
              of pension: 5s.
1535 valuation of vicarage: £4 0s. 7½d.
1535-7 farm of the rectory: £4 (£2 a year) (PRO SC6-Henry VIII-3327)

Sparsholt

By grant of Bishop Godfrey de Lucy (1189-1204) the rectory of Westspersolte was to be appropriated to the nuns of Wintney after the death of the existing incumbent, provided a perpetual vicarage was then instituted in the church. (*Cal. Ch. R.*, vol.4, p.394).
1238: church appropriated by the prioress and convent and perpetual vicarage instituted, following the death of the parson, William de Londoniis (*ibid.*).
Advowson: In 1204 a dispute about the advowson between John de Caritate and Alan de Spersholte was taken to court (Knowles, C., *Sparsholt and Lainston*, pp.19-20, 36). Later, Bishop Peter des Roches (1205-38) witnessed a grant of the advowson of the church that was being given to the prioress and convent by Philip, son of Alan de Spersholte (*Cal. Ch. R.*, vol.4, p.393). The first recorded presentation of a vicar by the prioress and convent as patrons was in 1307 (*Reg. Woodlock*, p.723).
1291 valuation of vicarage: £10 13s. 4d.
          of pension (to St. Swithun's Priory): 2s.
1333-45 valuation of rectory: 25 marks
          of vicarage: 16 marks
          of pension: 2s.
1535 valuation of vicarage: £16 10s. 1d.
1535-7 farm of the rectory: £20 (£10 a year) (PRO SC6-Henry VIII-3327).

Herriard

The rectory was appropriated by the prioress and convent between 1335 and 1337, following the grant of the advowson to them by Thomas de Coudray in 1334 (*Cal. Pat. R., 1330-4*, p.527; Reg. Orleton, fols. 54v-55)
1333-45 valuation of rectory: 25 marks
          of vicarage: 100s.
1535 valuation of vicarage: £7 6s. 4d.

Dogmersfield

Pension of 20s. a year paid to the prioress and convent by the rector of Dogmersfield. The original gift to the church and nuns of Wintney out of the church of Dogmersfield was apparently made by Prior Walter (d.1198) and the monks of Bath Abbey (*Cal. Ch. R.*, vol.4, p.395)[41]; but this may have been at the request of Reginald FitzJocelin (Bishop of Bath 1174-91) who held the manor of Dogmersfield where he died on 26 December 1191, one month after he had been elected archbishop of Canterbury.[42]
1333-45 valuation including pension of 20s.
1535-7 pension recorded as £2 (£1 a year) (PRO SC6-Henry VIII-3327)
1538-9 accounts of receiver record 20s.[43] (PRO E315-442, fol.2v)

Romsey Abbey

1535-7 Pension of 4s. from Romsey Abbey recorded, payable out of their manor of Itchen Stoke (2s. a year) (PRO SC6-Henry VIII-3327)

Southwick Priory

Gave two quarters of salt each year to the nuns of Wintney, according to a deposition made by the last prioress in 1572.[44]

Berkshire

Reading Abbey

1535-7 Pension of £1 6s. 8d. from the abbey (13s. 4d. a year). (PRO SC6-Henry VIII-3327) (Wintney is not mentioned in the abbey's cartulary.)[45]

Surrey

Newark Priory (de Novo Loco)

John, prior of Newark (d.1226) bound the canons of Newark to pay the Wintney nuns 30s. a year.[46]

1337 confirmation of the bond (*Cal. Ch. R.*, vol.4, p.397).

1535-7 pension of £4 from the priory (£2 a year) (**PRO** SC6-Henry VIII-3327).

Appendix 3

Manors and Realty held by the Nunneries

St. Mary's Abbey, Winchester

MANORS

The chief manor of Froyle, Hampshire
>1086. Always held by the abbey.[1]
>1291. Rents etc. from Froyle: £34.[2]
>1539-40. Payments from the manor: £47 3s. 8½d.[3]
>1541. Granted to William Jefson and wife Mary of London (together with the rectory and advowson). (*L. and P.*, vol.16, p.463 (54))
>A fine collection of compotus rolls (1236-1537) and court rolls (1281-1514) are in the BL MSS. department.

The manor of Itchen Abbas, Hampshire
>Held by the abbey before 1066 but temporarily lost after the Conquest and therefore not amongst its possessions in 1086. Later restored to it by William I. (*VCH*, vol.1, p.419; vol.4, p.191)
>1291. Rents etc. from 'Ichene': £17 15s.
>1296. Action re. common pasture. (*Reg. Asserio*, p.485, n2)
>1539. Granted to Sir William Paulet (together with the advowson). (*L. and P.*, vol.14 (1) item 906 (1))

The manor of Leckford Abbas, within the parish of Leckford, Hants.
>1086. Held by the abbey.
>1291. Rents etc. from Leckford: £10
>   Payments from the manor: £17 6s. 4d.
>1544. Granted to Sir Richard Lyster, chief baron of the Exchequer, and William Thorpe (together with the advowson of the prebend and 20s. pension out of the rectory. (*L. and P.*, vol.19 (1), item 278 (43))

The chief manor of Timsbury, Hants.
>1086. Always held by the abbey
>1291. Rents etc. from 'Timberbury': £8
>   Payments from the manor: £14 13s. 7½d.
>1543. Granted to Thomas Knight, the king's servant, with certain meadows (named) in Timsbury. He sold to Thomas Wriothesley in 1546. (*L. and P.*, vol.18 (2), p.57 (44); vol.21 (2), item 648 (62)).

The manor of Liss Abbas/Abbess, in the parish of Liss, Hants.
>1086. Always held by the abbey
>1291. Rents etc. from Liss: £6 8s.
>   Payments from the manor: £7 8s. 9d.
>After the Dissolution the manor apparently remained crown property until 1610. (*VCH*, vol.4, p.84)
>(The start of a 13th-century compotus for Liss is on the verso of BL Add. Ch. 17477)

The manor of Ovington, Hants.
>1086. Domesday Book recorded that 'Yavington' was held by both the bishop of Winchester and the abbey, its income supplying the needs of the nuns.
>Before 1284 the nuns appear to have sold their interest. (*VCH*, vol.3, p.331)

The manor of All Cannings, Wilts.
>   1086. Held by the abbey.
>   1291. Rents etc. from 'Albecaning', Swindon and 'Hakeburne': £41 16s. 8d. a year.
>   1523. Rent of demesne farm: £26 6s. 8d. a year (*VCH, Wilts.*, vol.10, p.26)
>   1535-6. Six months rents from farm: £13 3s. 4d. + 33s. 4d.
>   from customary tenants: £15 2s. 8⅞d.
>   (Blatcher, *Bath, Longleat, vol.4: Seymour Papers*, pp.320-1)
>   1536. Granted to Sir Edward Seymour (later Earl of Hertford, Duke of Somerset) and wife Anne
>   (together with advowson of parish church). (*L. and P.*, vol.10, item 1256 (6))

The manor of Urchfont, Wilts.
>   1086. Held by the abbey
>   1291. Rents etc. from 'Orchesfunte': £47 a year
>   1535-6. Six months rent from farm: £13 4s. 6d.
>   from customary tenants: £18 0s. 11d.
>   (Blatcher, *Bath, Longleat, vol.4*, p.320)
>   1536. Granted to Sir Edward Seymour and wife Anne (together with rectory and advowson of
>   parish church of Urchfont). (ref. as above)
>   Several compotus and court rolls (1450-1531) are in the BL MSS department; others at HRO.

The manor of Greatford, Lincs.
>   Given to the abbess by Berengarus de Toni by 1207. (*Pipe Roll 9 John*, N.S., vol.22, p.28; *Book of
>   Fees*, vol.1, p.182)
>   1234. King grants abbess and her successors and all her men of the manor of Greatford exemption
>   from various dues. Inspeximus in 1268. (*Cal. Cl. R., 1231-4*, p.391; *Cal. Ch. R.*, vol.2, p.115)
>   1539-40. Payments from the manor: £22 9s. 4¼d.
>   1541. Grant of the site and chief messuage of the manor to Edmund Hall who had a farm there,
>   following letter (4 March 1540) from Charles, Duke of Suffolk, to Cromwell requesting it for
>   him. (*L. and P.*, vol.15, item 296, p.121; vol.16, item 503 (5), p.238)
>   1541. Grant of stewardship of the manor to Richard Snell. (PRO E315-240, fols.21-2)
>   (N.B. note re. Braceborough, Lincs. below)

The manor of Coleshill, Berkshire
>   1086. Held by the abbess.
>   1291. Rents etc. from Coleshill: £10 + £3 2s. 6d.
>   1351-4. Rents (and advowson) granted to John de Edyngdon. (*Cal. Pat. R., 1350-4*, p.63; *Cal. Cl.
>   R., 1354-60*, pp.107-8.)
>   (16th-century memo on demesne lands: E315-81, fol.11)
>   The Edington Cartulary (BL MS. Lansdowne 442) includes several charters of the abbess of
>   Winchester concerning the manor (fols.150v-160). It is now published: Stevenson, Janet H., (ed.),
>   *The Edington Cartulary*, Wilts. Record Soc., (1987)

OTHER PROPERTY HELD IN HAMPSHIRE

In Winchester
>   1148. The abbess received £6 1s. 9½d. from rents in the city. (Biddle, *W.S.1*, p.356, figs.14, 19,
>   table 11)
>   By 14th century abbey had custody of the East Gate, with right to collect tolls. (Keene, *W.S.2*,
>   vol.1, p.44)
>   1539-40. Payments from city interests, incl. mill: £17 19s. 4d.
>   1553-4. When the city acquired the former abbey's estate in the city from the Crown the rents
>   due from 37 properties were £12 12s. 8d. (Keene, *W.S.2*, vol.1, p.199-200; vol. 2 for individual
>   properties)

In Longstock

    1086. The abbey held 'Stoches' which they had always held; it included a mill.
    1233-7. Tenement with two mills confirmed to the use of Mottisfont Priory. (Loyd, L.C. and
    Stenton, D.M., *Sir Christopher Hatton's Book of Seals*, (1950), p.325)
    1539-40. Rents including a mill: £4 15s. 6d.

In Liss

    The abbey held a property called Whetham with its lands.
    1539-40. Payments from Whetham: £3 16s. 8d.
    1542. Granted to Nicholas Deryng of Liss. (*L. and P.*, vol.17, pp.32 (37), 211 (5ii))

In Godsfield

    1539-40. Payment of rent: 12s. a year

In Shamblehurst, in the parish of South Stoneham

    1539-40. Payment of rent of assize: 2s.

PROPERTY HELD IN OTHER COUNTIES

In Swindon, Wilts.

    The abbess held land in the manor of Even Swindon by 1210-12, when it was worth £4 a year.
    (*VCH, Wilts.*, vol.9, p.120)
    1539-40. Payment of rent of assize: £4

In Shipton Moyne, Glos.

    The abbey held a tenement in Shipton Moyne by 1216; it was later called Oaksey's Place. By
    1260 the rent was 40s. a year. (*VCH, Glos.*, vol.11, p.252)
    1539-40. Payment of rent of assize: £2

In Blandford St. Mary, Dorset

    The abbey held a messuage and land in the parish.
    1291. Rents from 'Bloneford Mar': £1
    1539-40. Payments from property: £1
    1543, 1544: two grants to Sir John Rogers, the king's servant, of lands and a messuage with rights
    of common in St. Mary Blandford. (*L. and P.*, vol.18 (2), p.143 (31); vol.19 (1), item 278 (40))

In Braceborough, Lincs.

    The abbey owned property in 'Bressingburgh' by the mid-13th century.
    1539-40. Payments from it: £7 5s. 9½d.
    The Herriard papers at the HRO include 11 grants and quitclaims concerning Greatford and
    Braceborough. They are undated but those involving the abbey cover the period of Abbesses
    Lucy, Christina and Agnes (1270-1313). (HRO 44 M 69-409, 411-6)
    Also in the parish of Braceborough, the abbey held property in Barnthorpe (a hamlet, now
    extinct) and Fletelond Mill.
    1539-40. Payments from Barnthorpe: £11 18s. 10½d.
    1540. Land in Barnthorpe and Braceborough was included with the grant of the manor of
    Greatford to Edmund Hall of Greatford. (Linc. Archive Off., TB 4/5/1).

In Pitton, Wilts., in the forest of Clarendon

    1327. 82 acres held of abbess for 10s. a year and 1 lb. of pepper by William de Putton. (*Cal.
    Inq.P.M.*, vol.7, item 58).
    1382. Rent paid to abbess for a moiety of the manor: 100s. a year. (*Cal. Inq.P.M.*, vol.15, item
    774)
    1500. 120 acres held of abbess by Joan Warre, widow. (*Cal. Inq.P.M.*, vol.2, item 368)

***

Wherwell Abbey
MANORS
The manors in the Hundred of Wherwell

The abbey held the manors of Wherwell (with Westover), Middleton (now Longparish), Tufton, Bullington and Goodworth (Clatford). Together with the manor of Little Ann nearby, it held them all before the Conquest and until the Dissolution. (Only the tithing of Fullerton near Wherwell was not part of the abbey's estates, being always in the possession of Hyde Abbey.) The abbess held the jurisdiction of the hundred.

1086. The abbey held Wherwell village, Tufton, Goodworth, Ann, Middleton and Bullington.

1291. These were assessed at:

Wherwell: £59 13s. 6d.
Middleton: £39 6s.
Tufton: £15 16s.
Bullington: £18 12s. 8½d.
Goodworth: £10 0s. 9d.
Ann: £9 3s. 4d. Total: £152 12s. 3½d

1228. Bull of Pope Gregory IX confirmed to the abbey the manors of Wherwell, Goodworth, Tufton, Bullington, Ann ('Buna'). The manor of Middleton was not mentioned, only the church; but the vills of Forton and Aston within the parish were both included. (Dugdale, *Monasticon*, vol.2, p.638)

1540. Sir Thomas West, Lord de la Warr, and wife Elizabeth were granted the site of the abbey with the mill, 30 acres of land and the manors of Wherwell (with advowson), Westover, Middleton, Tufton, Bullington, Goodworth Clatford and Little Ann. In 1539-40 the rents from this property, with other small rents in Hampshire were £137 3s. 8d. (*L. and P.*, vol.15, item 436 (72); PRO C66-689-m.4)

The Wherwell Cartulary (BL MS. Egerton 2104a) includes numerous charters concerning these manors. As the cartulary has never been published the number of charters concerning land and tenements in each place is given below, while the actual charter numbers in the MS. are in the references.

Wherwell: 53 charters. Mid-13th century-1360
  field names in charters 359, 361
  all charter numbers[4]; Harewood forest[5]
Middleton: 34 charters. Late 13th century-1364
  fulling mill in charters 163, 170, 301-3, 305, 307, 324-6, 328-9
  field names in charters 309, 311, 319
  all charter numbers[6]
Forton, in the parish of Middleton: 11 charters. 1234-1321
  all charter numbers[7]
Aston (East), in parish of Middleton: 10 charters. 1254-1329
  all charter numbers[8]
  for mill called Knightbridge see below, p.181
Gavelacre, in parish of Middleton: 1 charter, no.50 (1258)
Tufton, including 'Toppemulle': 10 charters. 1299-1323
  all charter numbers[9]
Bullington: 110 charters. 1241-1364
  mill, unspecified, mentioned in charters 213, 218, 377
  mill in East Bullington, charter 88
  mill in West Bullington and St. Elizabeth College, Winchester, charters 300, 463
  charters with three or more field names: 375, 379, 381, 386, 389, 393
  all charter numbers[10]
Goodworth: 10 charters. 1285-1343
  fulling mill next to the bridge between Goodworth and (Upper) Clatford, charter 167
  all charter numbers[11]

(Little) Ann: 3 charters. Mid-13th cent.
   mill mentioned in charter 14
   all charter numbers[12]
N.B. The tenants in 1496 in East Aston, West Aston, Bullington, Ann and Clatford are listed in the cartulary, fol.222.

The manor of Ashey, with Langbridge, Isle of Wight
   1228. Both confirmed to the abbey by Pope Gregory IX.
   1291. Assessed at £41 6s. 2d.
   1539-40. Payments from the manor: £40 19s. 9d.
   1544. Granted to Giles Worsley with other property in the parish of Newchurch. He and his wife, Elizabeth, had been the tenants there since 1539. (*L. and P.*, vol.19 (1), item 278 (56))
   Wherwell Cart. charter numbers[13]
   (N.B. There is a collection of records from 13th-19th centuries relating to the manor of Ashey in the BL MSS. department. Refs.: BL Add. MSS. 46520-46524; Add. Charters 74487-74759)

The manor of (East) Compton, Berks.
   Held by the abbey by 1220. (*Book of Fees*, pp.296, 863)
   1228. Confirmed to the abbey by Pope Gregory IX.
   1291. Valuation of £13 15s.
   1539-40. Payments from the manor: £27 15s. 7d. (PRO E315-446, fols.34ff)
   1542. Granted to Richard Andrews and Leonard Chamberleyne of Woodstock, with leave to alienate it. (*L. and P.*, vol.17, p.259 (39-11)).
   Although charter 12 in the Wherwell Cartulary concerns the tithes of Compton, there are apparently no charters concerning the manor.

The manors of Bathwick and Woolley, Somerset
   1228. Both confirmed to the abbey by Pope Gregory IX. ('Wyca' and 'Wlleghe')
   1291. Assessed together at £12 5s.
   1311, 1314. Estate extended. (*Cal. Pat. R., 1307-13*, p.382; *1313-17*, p.200)
   1539-40. Payments from Bathwick manor with Tetbury and Wringmershe: £31 14s. 6½d. (and details of lease of Thomas Stele of Bath, clothier, m.86v)
   1543-7. Robert Stele farmer and collector of rents. (PRO E315-446, fols. 38ff)
   1539-40. Payments from Woolley manor: £11 1s. 8d.
   1543-7. As in 1540, Juliane Benstye/Bonstie was the farmer and collector of rents. (*ibid.*, fol.42)
   Wherwell Cartulary: Bathwick charters[14]; Woolley charters[15]

OTHER PROPERTY HELD IN HAMPSHIRE

In Winchester
   By the 11th century the abbess of Wherwell held one of the seven great fiefs in the city. It comprised 21 properties and her own house within the city walls, and the mill (City Mill) outside East Gate,[16] Both the extent and value of this estate declined greatly in the later Middle Ages; even the mill had ceased to operate by the mid-16th century.[17] In 1554 the city acquired all the remaining property of the former abbey there.
   1148. Value of 27 rents: £2 2s. 2d. (Keene, *W.S.2*, p.200)
   1228. Property in the city confirmed to the abbey by Pope Gregory IX.
   1291. Valuation of rents: £8
   1539-40. Payments from properties: £1 16s. 4d.
   1553-4. Rents received from 4 tenements and 2 gardens of the former abbey: £1 7s. (Keene, *W.S.2*, p.200)
   Wherwell Cartulary: mill, charter numbers[18]; all charter numbers[19]

In Southampton
   1228. Pope Gregory IX confirmed to the abbey its rent and possessions in the town.
   The property was in a small block along English Street in the parish of St. Lawrence. In 1304 it comprised four houses with upper storeys[20] and by 1454, two cottages and a tenement.[21]

1539-40. Rents from property: £2 2s. 8d.
Wherwell cartulary charter numbers[22]

Other properties
     In 1539-40 total rents of £6 11s. were received from various small properties in Hampshire:
Upton rents of assize: 5s.
     The hamlet of Upton lay partly in Hurstbourne Tarrant and partly in Vernham Dean. Two rents
     in it were given to the abbey in the 13th century.[23] Other Wherwell Cartulary numbers[24]
Heckfield and Bramley ('Hethefylde et Bromeley') rents of assize from the two together: £1. The two parishes are
     in N.E. Hampshire, within five miles of each other.
     Separate payments:
     Heckfield, rent for land: 6s. 8d.
     Wherwell Cartulary charter 11 includes a gift of 10s. a year rent from 'Hecfeld'.
     Bramley, rent of 8s. for land near Lyle Mill.
     (No charters in Cartulary.)
Appleshaw rent 13s. 4d.
     This rent of assize of one mark was given to the abbey in the 13th century. (Wherwell Cartulary
     charter 96.) The village is near Andover.
Week ('Wyke') rent for land: 6s. 8d.
     The tithing of Week was in the parish of St. Mary Bourne. The abbey held the mill there in the 13th
     century[25] and 4 crofts at the Dissolution.[26] Other Wherwell Cartulary numbers[27]
Hursley rent for one tenement: 10s.
     This property may have been given to the abbey after the 14th century since there are no Hursley
     charters in the Cartulary.
Mattocksford in the parish of Botley payment for the farm of the manor: £2 8s.
     1436. the reversion of this property granted to the abbey; it comprised 7 houses and 564 acres. (*Cal.
     Pat. R., 1429-36*, p.501) It is unrecorded in the Cartulary.
     At the Dissolution it was included in the grant to Lord de la Warr (*VCH*, vol.3, p.467)
East Aston in the parish of Middleton rent for the mill called Knightbridge: 13s. 4d.
     1544. Grant of the fulling mill and its garden. (*L. and P. Henry VIII*, vol.19 (2) item 690 (14))

(No rents from Sutton Scotney or Newton Stacey were recorded in 1539-40 but the Wherwell Cartulary
includes charters concerning them.[28])

PROPERTY HELD IN OTHER COUNTIES
In Newbury, Berks.
     1228. Pope Gregory IX confirmed a mill and other property at Newbury to the abbey.
     1539-40. Rent for property: £3 16s.
     1545. Grant of the former abbey's messuage near the parish church. (*L. and P.*, vol.20 (1)
     item 465 (70)).
     (No charters in Wherwell Cartulary.)

In Inkpen, Berks.
     1539-40. Rent of assize for land: 6s. 8d.
     (This comprised 2 meadows and 13 acres of land. PRO E315 448, fol.42)
     Wherwell Cartulary charter numbers[29]

'Ertingdon', Surrey
     The abbey was given 20s. rent out of the manor of Hertingdon near Guildford in the 13th century.[30]
     1539-40. Payment of rent: £1 1s. 2d.

Guildford, Surrey
     1253. Abbess recompensed for damage done to her mills. (*Cal. Lib. R., 1251-60*, p.125)
     1278. Mill belonging to the abbess and others was on the west side of the water near the church of
     St. Nicholas. (*Cal. Inq. Misc.*, vol.1, p.345)

1539-40. Rent paid for a field called Milmede: 1s. 4d. and for land of St. Nicholas church: 7½d. (No charters in Wherwell Cartulary.)

Penwith and Cornagh, Cornwall

Early 13th century. Grants to abbey by Matilda and Isabella de Lucy. (Wherwell Cartulary, charters 142-3)

1262 x 1281. Granted by abbess. (*ibid.*, ch.281)

1329. Ralph de Beaupre held of the abbess. (*Cal. Inq.P.M.*, vol.7, item 232)

(No record in 1539-40)

In Bristol

By 1257. Grant of land and buildings to abbey by Matilda, widow of Henry, marshal of Bristol. (Wherwell Cartulary charter numbers[31])

(No record in 1539-40.)

***

Romsey Abbey

MANORS

Romsey Manors

1086. The abbey always held the whole vill of Romsey.

1263. Right of Abbess to raise a gallows in Romsey confirmed. (*Cal. Pat. R.*, *1258-66*, p.276)

1316. In addition to the town of Romsey, the abbess was assessed for the vills of 'Cupernam, Haltreworth, Whytenharpe, Asshefelde, Wopbury, Lee and Welles' in the Hundred of Somborne. (*Feudal Aids*, vol.2, pp.309-10.) (N.B. all these vills are within the boundaries of the Anglo-Saxon charter of King Edgar)

1412-13. Total manorial income from Romsey: £146 12s.[32]

1538-9. The Ministers' Accounts cited below were given for each manor separately. (see n.3)

1539-40. Accounts of the receiver, Sir Richard Paulet (not cited). (PRO E315-446, fols. 2-28)

i. *Romsey Extra*

1538-9. Rents of assize: £15 12s. 10½d.

Rents of customary tenants: £60 3s. 2d.

Farm of the site of the former abbey: £42 1s. 8d.

Pannage of pigs: £1 10s.

Perquisites of court: £1 16s. 10d.

Total manorial income: £121 4s. 6½d.

(Account of Henry Warner, bailiff for Romsey Extra and Infra, see n.3)

1538-9. Balance account of the bailiff: £31 1s. 8d.[33]

The manorial properties were divided up after the dissolution of the abbey. They are listed in PRO E315-446, fols.2-6. Court rolls from some of the Halmotes (Courts Baron) for Romsey Extra with Wools, Woodbury, Lee, Cupernham and Romsey from 1395 to 1597 are at the PRO. Those from the period before the Dissolution are SC2-201-38, 39, 39a, 40 and see Liveing, pp.198ff.

ii. *Romsey Infra*

1538-9. Rents of assize: £5 0s. 2d.

Rents of tenants: £41 4s. 5½d.

Market fees: 12s. 4d.

Perquisites of court: 11s. 3d.

Total manorial income: £48 4s. 2½d. (see n.3)

1538-9. Balance account of the bailiff: £7 0s. 6d.[34]

1544. Granted to John Foster and Richard Marden (*L. and P. Henry VIII*, vol.19 (2), p.473) but R.M. surrendered his interest to J.F. the following year.

iii. *More Abbess and More Malwyn*

    More Abbess belonged to the abbey from an early date but More Malwyn only from the 14th century. (*VCH*, vol.4, p.455)

    1412-13. Manorial income from More Malwyn: £12[35]

    1538-9. Farm of the site of the manor and lands: £22 12s.

    (Account of Richard Dowce, farmer there, see n.3)

    1542. Both granted to Edward Seymour, Earl of Hertford at 46s. rent. (*L. and P.*, vols.17, p.322 and 21 (2), item 648 (11)).

The manor of Itchen Stoke, Hants.

    1086. The abbey always held (Itchen) Stoke.

    1291. See Romsey manors.

    1316. Held by the abbess. (*Feudal Aids*, vol.2, p.306)

    1412-13. Total manorial income: £30 11s.[36]

    1538-9. Rents of assize £2 8s. 5d.

    Rents of customary tenants: £11 7s. 8d.

    Farm of the manor, incl. rectory: £16 9s. 6d.

    Pannage of pigs: 5s.

    Perquisites of court: 1s. 8d.

    Total income: £30 12s. 3d.

    (Account of Leonard Palmes, see n.3)

    1539. Granted with the rectory and advowson to Sir William Paulet. (*L. and P.*, vol.14 (1), item 906 (1))

The manor of Sydmonton in the parish of Kingsclere, Hants.

    1086. Always held by the abbey.

    1291. See Romsey manors.

    1297/8. Lease and extracts from accounts (PRO E315-446, fols.20-1)

    1316, 1346, 1428. Held by abbess. (*Feudal Aids*, vol.2, pp.308, 330-1, 345)

    1412. Total manorial income: £32 2s.[37]

    1538-9. Rents of assize: £3 2s. 1d.

    Rents of customary tenants: £16 4s. 8½d.

    Rent for moveable goods: 2s.

    Farm of the site of the manor and lands: £14 13s. 8d.

    Pannage of pigs: 5s.

    Perquisites of court: 6s. 6d.

    Total income: £34 13s. 11½d.

    (Account of Thomas Wethers, farmer there, see n.3)

    1540. Granted to John Kingsmill and wife Constance, of Whitchurch, Hants. (*L. and P.*, vol.15, item 611 (43))

Sway, in the parish of Boldre, Hants.

    The abbey's property in Sway is not referred to as a manor in the Ministers' Accounts of 1538-9, although a court was evidently held there. It was sometimes known as Sway Romsey or South Sway. (*VCH*, vol.4, p.620)

    1086. The abbey always held one hide in Sway.

    1316. Abbess included in assessment with the abbot of Quarr and the prior of Christchurch. (*Feudal Aids*, vol.2, p.316).

    1538-9. Rents of assize: 12s.

    Perquisites of court: 12s.

    (Account of John Foster, see n.3)

    1543. Lands and mill granted to Sir John Williams and Anthony Stringer. (*L. and P.*, vol.18 (1), p.131)

The Hundred of Whorwellsdown, Wilts.

    The abbess of Romsey held the jurisdiction of the hundred; it may have been included in the original

10th-century grant of Steeple Ashton to the abbey. Within the hundred the abbey held the manors of Steeple Ashton and Edington. On 6 February 1539 these manors were granted by the abbess, with the king's licence, to Sir Thomas Seymour, together with the abbey's property in the hundred in Keevil, North Bradley, Tinhead, West Ashton, Southwick, Hinton, Semington and Littleton. (*L. and P.*, vol.14 (1), p.75; PRO E328-329) Sir Thomas Seymour rendered an account without details for the two manors for 1538-9 of £20 1s. 7d. (PRO SC6-Henry VIII-3341, fol.66 which also repeats the grant.)

i. *The manor of (Steeple) Ashton*
   1086. Held by the abbey. (The manor then included North Bradley and Southwick (*VCH, Wilts.*, vol.8, p.194)
   1291. Valued at £63
   1412-13. Total manorial income: £102[38]
   1537/8. Indenture between Abbess Ryprose and William Bailly about Gayford Mill. (PRO E326-B12295)

ii. *The manor of Edington*
   1086. Held by the abbey.
   1291. Valued at £37
   1351. On the foundation of William of Edington's chantry the manor remained with the abbey, but it became divided into their capital manor known as Edington Romsey and a mesne manor called Edington Rector which the new foundation held of the abbey (*V.C.H., Wilts.*, vol.8, p.241)
   1412-13. Total manorial income: £81 1s. 1d.[39]
   (In 1539 the grant to Sir Thomas Seymour did not include the premises of the manor of Edington.)

The manor of Tinhead, Wilts. ('Titleshide')
   1291. Valued at £5.
   1356. Release to abbess and convent of messuages and lands formerly held by Reginald de Morheye. (*Cal. Ancient Deeds in PRO*, vol.1, p.223, B.71).
   1538-9. Farm of the manor: £11 6s. 8d.
   (Account of Richard George, see n.3)
   By 1540 the manor was apparently held by the college of Edington. (*L. and P.*, vol.15, item 1029 (61)

The manor of Hullasey with Tarleton, Glos. ('Hunlacy with Torleton iuxta Cotes')
   By 1268, abbey held 1½ hides in Hullasey. (*Cal. Ch. R.*, vol.2, p.103)
   1316. Abbess included in assessment for Cotes. (*Feudal Aids*, vol.2, p.270)
   1457. Agreement, following dispute about lands and chapel. (*Cal. Cl. R., 1454-61*, pp.266-7)
   1538-9. Farm of the manor, incl. tithes of the chapel of the manor: £6 13s. 4d.
   (Account of Anne Pole, widow of Henry Pole, farmer there, see n.3)
   1542. Grant to Giles Pole of Sapperton, Glos., the king's servant, of the reversion of the lease of the manor with tithes granted in 1528 by abbess and convent to Henry Pole and his wife, Anne (details). (*L. and P.*, vol.17, p.567 (49))

Bardolfeston manor in the parish of Puddletown, Dorset
   1285. Abbess included in assessment. (*Feudal Aids*, vol.2, p.16)
   1339. Abbey had 2 marks a year rent out of Puddle Bardolfeston. (*Cal. Cl. R., 1339-41*, p.217)
   1538-9. Farm of the manor: £2
   (Account of Sir Thomas Trenchar', farmer there, see n.3)
   1544. Sept: Lands in Bardolfeston in the tenure of Sir Thomas Trencharde granted to agents. Nov: Agents given licence to alienate property to Robert Martyn of Athelhampton and wife, Elizabeth. (*L. and P.*, vol.19 (2), items 340 (10), 690 (67)).

OTHER PROPERTY HELD BY ROMSEY ABBEY
None of these properties appear to have been recorded at the Dissolution except Testwood.
In Winchester
   1148. Abbess held one of the great fiefs; the 12 properties were all within the walls and produced total rents of £1 a year. (Biddle, *W.S.1*, p.356, table 11, figs.14, 19)

By the early 13th century only one rent of 20d. was due to the abbess for a property in Gold Street; this later became a waste, then a garden by 1417. (Keene, *W.S.2*, vol.1, pp.184-5; vol.2, item 638)

In the parish of Eling, Hants.

The abbey's interests are difficult to ascertain but included:

i. *In Totton*

1086. Abbess held one hide, including mill and salt-house.
1268. Confirmation of charters included ¼ part of the mill of 'Todintona'. (*Cal Ch. R.*, vol.2, p.102 (5))

ii. *In Testwood*

1174 x 1199. Abbess Juliana granted 1½ hides in Terstwode and ly Wada to William of Terstewode in fee farm for £4 10s. and a pint of honey a year. She also granted Totyngtone mill to Richard of Terstewode for 40s. a year, 12 dishes of eels at the feast of St. Martin and 2s. to the lord of Welewede on behalf of the convent. (Goodman, *Winchester Cathedral Chartulary*, items 502-3; see also 505-6)
1376 Reversion of property granted to abbess. (*Cal. Cl. R., 1374-7*, p.449)
By 1386. Property, apparently manorial, held in fee farm by Sir Thomas West for £6 10s., 6½ lbs. of honey, one salmon and 300 eels a year. (*Cal. Inq.P.M.*, vol.16, item 495)
Held by abbey until Dissolution. (*VCH*, vol.4, p.549)

iii. *Marchwood Romsey*

Manor held of the abbey by fealty. (*VCH*, vol.4, p.553)

iv. *In La Hangre*

1362. 6 acres held of the abbess by Walter de Russyngton for 2s. 6d. a year. (*Cal. Inq.P.M.*, vol.11, item 418)

In Trowbridge, Wilts.

1341-2. Eight tenants of the abbess held between them 9 messuages, a grove, a croft, 17 acres of arable and 2 meadows in Lovemead. (*VCH, Wilts.*, vol.7, p.133)

In Whaddon

1286. A wood in the manor of W. was held of the abbess by Humphrey de Waddone for 8d. a year. (*Cal. Inq.P.M.*, vol.4, item 467)

In Imber, Wilts.

Manor of Imber South held by abbey and the family of Le Rous. (Liveing, p.155)
1183. Abbess Juliana granted Richard Ruffo all the abbey's land in 'Hynbemere' in fee farm for £10 a year. (Charter in Edington Cartulary quoted in BL Add. MS. 39974, fol.145)
1301/2. Deed between Abbess Philippa and Matthew Owayn of Imber. (PRO E326-B9842)

In Wingfield, Wilts.

1350. 36 acres in La Frithe in the parish of Wingfield held by Philip de Welislegh from abbess for 5s. a year. (*Cal. Inq. P.M.*, vol.9, item 564)

In Enborne, Berks.

By 1220. Abbess held 6 carucates of land in East Enborne. (*Book of Fees*, vol.1, p.296; *VCH, Berks.*, vol.4, p.171)
1307. Thomas de Abbresbury als. Apperbury held a capital messuage, 56 acres and rents in Enborne from abbess for 55s. a year. (*Cal. Inq.P.M.*, vol.4, item 432)

In Littlemore, (?Oxon.)

1411, Oct. 15 acres of meadow in Littlemore quitclaimed to Abbess Felicia Aas and convent by Sir John Berkley and wife Elizabeth. (Agreement in court transcribed in BL Add. MS. 39974, fol.158)

Wintney Priory

The manor of Hartley Wintney

> The priory owned part of the manor from its foundation in the 12th century, and all of it by 1258. (*VCH*, vol.4, p.79)
>
> 1316. Prioress assessed for the vill of Hartley Monialium. (*Feudal Aids*, vol.2, p.314)
>
> 1535-7. Rents of assize: £31 18s. 6d.
>
> Farm of the site of the manor of former priory and demesne lands: £20[40]

In the city of Winchester

> In the 12th century the priory was granted property in Colebrook Street and the mill at Newbridge by its founder, Geoffrey fitz Peter. (*Cal. Ch. R.*, vol.4, pp.392-3) At least by the mid-14th century two holdings by the High Street end of Colebrook Street were known as tenements of the prioress and convent of Wintney. The two were adjacent but divided by the stream that powered Newbridge mill. In Keene, *W.S.2.*, they are numbered 118 and 571 (pp.532-4, 852; figs. 60, 95). The mill at Newbridge was still functioning in the 14th century. The nuns also owned the Postern mill (no.556) at the angle of Colebrook Street by the cathedral. Both mills were run by the same stream and were managed by the same miller. The mill at Newbridge had ceased to exist by 1417; by then the site, on the corner of Colebrook Street and High Street, had been incorporated into the nuns' tenement no.571 and four cottages had been built on it. The Postern mill lasted longer; it was still there in 1489 but it was not mentioned in the account of rent for 1535-7. (Keene, (*W.S.2.*, pp.846-7, 852-3)
>
> 1535-7. Rent from two tenements and four gardens: £2 5s.[41]

In Well, in the parish of Long Sutton, Hants.

> In the 12th century the priory was granted a messuage, a virgate of land and grazing rights in Well ('La Welle') by Hugh de Wyngeham (fl. c.1170). In 1337 it was confirmed that the nuns held enclosed land and rights of common for 45 sheep in Well.[42] (*Cal. Ch. R.*, vol.4, pp.395-7; Keene, *W.S. 2*, p.1395)
>
> 1538. Property (unspecified) in Sutton was included in the grant to Richard Hill.

4 June 1538. Richard Hill, sergeant of the king's cellar, and Elizabeth his wife were granted in tail male the house and site of the former priory with its church, steeple and churchyard, the rectory and advowson of Hartley Wintney, and all the above property (i.e. the manor and all the land and rights that the nuns had held in Hartley Wintney, Sutton, Wyntney and the city of Winchester) which produced: £26 14s. 9d. a year. (*L. and P.*, vol.13 (1), p.485; PRO C66-678-m.16)

Wintney Herriard Grange, in the parishes of Herriard and Ellisfield, Hants.

> Before 1221, Richard de Hereard, son of Richard de Hereard and wife Ella, had granted the nuns 1½ virgates in Southrope[43] and 'Eslande' with the wood of 'Petsete' for the maintenance of a chaplain. This charter was confirmed by Edward I in 1290/1.[44] (Dugdale, *Monasticon*, vol.5, p.722)
>
> 1221. Matilda de Heriard, sister and heir of the above, and her husband Richard de Sifrewast entered upon all the land that had belonged to her deceased brother. (*VCH*, vol.3, p.368)
>
> 1230. Dispute concerning their interest in the 1½ virgates which they had warranted to the prioress and convent. (*Curia Regis Rolls*, vol.14, p.25)
>
> The prioresses of Wintney continued to hold these 1½ virgates which became known as Wintney Herriard Grange.
>
> 1230 x 1240. Agnes, daughter of Edith Pechy[45] granted the priory church of St. Mary Magdalene at Wintney 6 acres of land in Southrope, lying in a croft called Hamcroft. (HRO 44 M 69/226)
>
> c.1240. Matilda de Heriard, widow of Richard de Sifrewast, granted the priory church of St. Mary Magdalene 20s. a year rent from four of her named tenants in Southrope. (HRO 44 M 69/225).[46]
>
> 1230/46. Matilda de Heriard, widow of R. de S., granted the prioress and convent all her land in Ellisfield; part of it lay along the road to Basingstoke and part of it between Ellisfield and Herriard.[47] (*Cal. Ch. R.*, vol.4, pp.393, 397)

By 1246. 3½ marks were payable to the priory out of Southrope. (*Cal. Inq.P.M.*, vol.1, pp.15-16)

1281. Edward I granted the nuns a virgate of land and 5 marks rent in Southrope which he had lately demanded against them. (*Cal. Pat. R., 1272-81*, p.463; *VCH*, vol.3, p.368)

1428. Prioress assessed for half a knight's service in Herriard. (*Feudal Aids*, vol.2, p.344)

1536. (1 August) Grant to Sir William Paulet of all the lands, rents and services in Wintney Herriard that had belonged to the former priory (together with the advowson of Herriard church). (*L. and P.*, vol.11, item 385 (3); PRO C66-670-m.21)

(*Polling, in the parish of Odiham, Hants.*)

The history of the manor of Polling in the *VCH* (vol.4, pp.92-3) does not mention any connection with Wintney Priory; it is only included here on account of Sir John Seymour's Inq.P.M. The name is now preserved in Poland Farm.

1305. Henry Sturmy held the manor of Polling at the time of his death. (*VCH*, vol.4, p.92) (He had been one of the priory's benefactors.[48])

1492. Sir John Seymour of Wolfhall held the manor, worth £10 a year, from the prioress of Wintney for services unknown. (*Cal. Inq.P.M. Henry VII*, vol.1, p.328)

1541. The lands exchanged by Edward Seymour, Earl of Hertford, for the former Amesbury Abbey included Polling. (Blatcher, *Bath, Longleat, vol.4: Seymour Papers*, p.376.[49])

(*Mabley mill, in the parish of Greywell, Hants.*)

In a deposition made in 1572, the former prioress, Elizabeth Martyn, said that the priory had had a yearly rent from Mabley mill in Greywell. (PRO E178-2018).

Appendix 4

Surviving Books formerly owned by a Hampshire Nunnery or Nun

All the following except two marked * are listed in Ker, N.R., *Medieval Libraries of Great Britain: A list of surviving books*, RHS Handbook no.3 (1964).
The bibliographies given below are selective.

St. Mary's Abbey, Winchester

Liber Precum	BL MS. Harley 2965. (Foundation collection, 1753), 9th century

Bibliography:
Cat. of the Harleian Manuscripts in the BM, vol.2, p.722
Birch, W. de Gray, *An Ancient Manuscript*, Hants. Record Society (1889)
Ker, N.R., *Cat. of Manuscripts containing Anglo-Saxon* (1957), item 237

Liber Precum   BL MS. Cotton Galba A.xiv. (Foundation collection), ?11th century

Bibliography:
Cat. of Manuscripts in the Cottonian Library deposited in the BM, vol.1, p.242
Ker, N.R., *Cat. of Manuscripts containing Anglo-Saxon*, item 157

Kalendarium   BL MS. Cotton Nero A.ii, fols.3-13 (Foundation collection), ?11th century. Originally probably part of Cotton Galba A.xiv. (see above)

Bibliography:
Cat. of Manuscripts in the Cottonian Library deposited in the British Museum, vol.1, p.202
Ker, N.R., *Cat. of Manuscripts containing Anglo-Saxon*, item 157

Smaragdus etc.   Oxford MS. Bodley 451. Given to the Bodleian in 1605 by Sir William Billesby.
12th century, with 15th-century English binding.
Includes: Smaragdus, a moral treatise and 14 sermons, perhaps by St. Augustine.

Bibliography:
Summary cat. of Western Manuscripts in the Bodleian Library, vol.2 (1), item 2401

Psalterium*
with
kalendarium   Trinity College Library, Cambridge, MS. B.11.4
Provenance uncertain, but probably donated by a benefactor. James suggests that it might be the 'Psalterium cum picturis' mentioned on fol.115 of the library's 17th-century *Memoriale*.
13th century, before 1220 (Rickert).

Bibliography:
James, M.R., *The Western Manuscripts in the Library of Trinity College, Cambridge*, (1900), vol.1, item 243
Rickert, M., *Painting in Britain: The Middle Ages*, pp.122, 132 n.30
See chapter 6 for St. Mary's Abbey connection.

Psalterium   Romsey Abbey parish church. Bought from Quaritch in 1900. Ownership signature T.H. Lloyd.
15th century, first half.

Bibliography:
Davy, F.W. Hyne, 'The Romsey Psalter', in Liveing, *Records of Romsey Abbey*, pp.285-302
Ker, N.R., *Medieval Libraries*, p.164 re. rejection as a Romsey Abbey book.

Ordo
consecrationis
sanctimonialium

Cambridge University Library, MS. Mm.3.13
Presented to the Library by George I in 1715, together with the rest of the library of John Moore, Bishop of Ely (d.1714). Previously owned by Richard Smyth of London whose books were sold in 1682.
Early 16th century. Given to the abbey by Richard Fox, Bishop of Winchester.

Bibliography:
Cat. of Manuscripts Preserved in the Library of the University of Cambridge, item 2329
Maskell, W., *Monumenta Ritualia Ecclesiae Anglicanae* (1846 edn.), vol.2, pp.307-31; (2nd edn.), vol.3, pp.333-59.
(Ellis, H., *The Obituary of Richard Smyth*, Camden Soc., Old ser., vol.44 (1849).)

Romsey Abbey
Chronicon etc.

BL MS. Lansdowne 436. The Lansdowne collection was purchased by the BM in 1807 having been collected by William Petty, 1st Marq. of Lansdowne (d.1805). Possible earlier ownership marks on fol.1: 'Heb. Dhun, E.B.' and 'No 54 JP'.
14th century, first half.
On fol.1: 'Iste liber est de librario ecclie sce' Marie et sce' Ethelflede virginis, de Romesey'.
Includes: Breve chronicon Regum Saxonicorum, Vitae Sanctorum Angliae.

Bibliography:
Cat. of the Lansdowne Manuscripts in the BM, vol.2, p.121.

Psalterium

Royal College of Physicians Library, London, MS.409, 'Wilton Psalter'. The psalter was part of a bequest of the Marquess of Dorchester in 1680. Earlier it had belonged to Sir Nicholas Saunder (b. c.1563, M.P.1588-1626) and to his grandfather. (MS. fol.1; Millar, pp.57-8)
Mid-13th century, possibly written in the scriptorium of Salisbury Cathedral. Given to a Romsey nun in 1523. See chapter 6.

Bibliography:
Ker, N.R., *Medieval Manuscripts in British Libraries*, vol.1: *London* (1969), p.226
Millar, E.G., 'Les MSS. à peintures des bibliothèques de Londres', in *Bulletin de la Société française de réproductions de manuscrits à peintures*, vol.4 (1914-20), pp.48-69
Rickert, M., *Painting in Britain: The Middle Ages*, pp.117, 133 n.53

Wherwell Abbey
Kalendarium

Saltykov-Shchedrin State Public Library, Leningrad, USSR, MS. Lat.Q.v.I.62
12th century
At the end of the 18th century this was acquired by a Russian collector, P.P. Dubrovskii, who was secretary of the Russian embassy in Paris at the time of the Revolution. In 1805 his collection was bought by Alexander I

and became the basis of the Russian Imperial manuscripts collection which is now owned by the state. Dubrovskii ownership signature. Earlier ownership signature: John Sawyer on fol.1

Bibliography:
Thomson, R.M., *Manuscripts from St. Alban's Abbey*, pp.30, 37-8, 123
(Voronova, T.P., 'P.P. Dubrovskii, 1744-1816' in *The Book Collector*, Winter 1978, pp.469-78)

Psalterium

St. John's College Library, Cambridge, MS. C.18
Given to the library in 1634 by Thomas, 4th Earl of Southampton; presumably part of the large collection of MSS. which his father, Henry, had purchased from William Crashaw. Earlier ownership mark: R. Benet on fol.1.
12th century, with calendar.

Bibliography:
James, M.R., *A descriptive catalogue of the manuscripts in the Library of St. John's College, Cambridge* (1913), item 68
Thomson, R.M., *Manuscripts from St. Alban's Abbey*, pp.56-60, 120-1

Psalterium

Fitzwilliam Museum, Cambridge, MS. McClean 45
Purchased from Quaritch after its sale at Sotheby's in May 1897 (lot 622). Earlier it was in the collection of Sir Thomas Phillipps (MS.2635). A much earlier owner was Symon Choppares of Odiham (flyleaf inscription).
Two vols., 13th-14th century, with calendar.

Bibliography:
James, M.R., *Cat. of McClean Manuscripts*, item 45

Psalterium

BL Add. MS.27866. Purchased by the BM from Boone's on 13 June 1868. Bookplates of Cecil D. Wray, F.C.C., Manchester. Given by Rev. P. Knapp, rector of Shenley, Bucks. to William Cole in 1764 (fols. 4v, 5). Cole bookplate.
14th century, with calendar. Ownership inscription of Johanna Stretford, nun at Wherwell (fol.131v).

Bibliography:
Cat. of Additions to the Manuscripts in the BM, 1854-75

Cartularium*

BL MS. Egerton 2104a. Purchased by the BM from W. Cutter, 29 Oct. 1869. Until the 19th century the cartulary had apparently passed with the ownership of Wherwell manor from 1540, for Dugdale saw it in the hands of Charles, 5th Baron de la Warr in 1669, and it was produced in court by the Iremonger family on 5 November 1762 (fol.1)
14th century, with later additions.

Bibliography:
Cat. of Additions to the Manuscripts, 1854-75
Davies, G.R.C., *Medieval Cartularies of Great Britain*, item 1031
Dugdale, *Monasticon Anglicanum*, vol.2, p.635

Wintney Priory

Martyrologium etc.

BL MS. Cotton Claud. D.iii. Foundation collection. Ownership signature of Robert Cotton, fol.3.

Late 13th century. Includes martyrologium, Rule of St. Benedict and calendar.

Bibliography:

Cat. of Manuscripts in the Cottonian Library deposited in the BM, vol.1, p.196

Schroer, A., *Die Winteney Version der Regula S. Benedicti* (1888)

The connections of the following are no longer accepted

St. Mary's Abbey

BL MSS. Royal 2 B.v; 4 A.xiv

Bodleian MS. Laud misc.664

Romsey Abbey

BL MSS. Add.28188; Cotton Vit. A.vii;

Romsey parish church Psalterium.

(ref. Ker, N.R., *Medieval Libraries*, pp.164, 202).

ARTICLES OF INQUISITION 30 MAY 1536 PRO SC12 - 33/27 f.l.

	Value in Valor Ecc.	Clear value of possessions & demesnes	Numbers of religious & how many wish to remain in religion	Numbers of servants & dependants	State of house. Value of lead and bells	Value of goods & ready money	Debts	Acres & sale value of woods owned
Wintney Priory	£43.0.3 (n)	£50.5.8	10 All wished to continue. Good reputations.	29 (2 priests 1 waiting servant 13 hindes 9 women servants 2 corrodians 2 servants to corrodians)	Church and mansion good (except tiling) kitchen & brewing house in great decay. £28.1.4	£188.17.0 (plate & jewels £35.0.10 ornaments £6.11.6 household stuff £16.0.6 grain £16.19.8 stocks & stores £114.4.6)	owed by house £72.17.0	Great woods: 34 acres Coppice woods: 55 acres £42.14.10
St. Mary's Abbey, Winchester	£179.7.2	£330.18.6½ (with £150 concealed upon taxation of tenths without consent of Abbess & convent)	26, of whom 25 wished to continue and one wished for a capacity. All living virtuous lives	76 (2 priests 13 lay sisters 9 women servants 20 household officers & waiting servants 3 corrodians 26 children)	Church and mansion & other houses all in very good estate & well repaired. £182.12.6	£880.10.11 (plate & jewels £371.18.4 ornaments £89.10.0 ready money £15.13.8 household stuff £27.3.8 grain £51.9.8 stocks & stores £324.15.7)	owed to house £30.9.4 but £24.6.8 in the hands of servants	Great woods: 146 acres Coppice woods: 78 acres £231.7.4

Note: (n) sic Valor Ecclesiasticus II p.13 gives the correct £43.3.0

SOME POINTS FROM THE COMMISSIONERS' CERTIFICATES FOR SURRENDER OF NUNNERIES. NOVEMBER 1539

	Yearly value of possessions, less annuities granted	Number and annual value of nuns' pensions	Buildings to remain	Buildings deemed superfluous	Lead and bells / Silver	Value of goods sold
St. Mary's Abbey, Winchester	£160.6.3	23 = £91.13.4 p.a	Abbess's lodging and offices Gatehouse Barn Baking and brewing houses Garner adjacent Stable Mill	Church cloister Chapter house Dormitory Frater Infirmary Convent kitchen 2 garners, s. of court Mistress Lane's lodging Priest's lodging Plumer's house	5 bells Lead on church choir, aisles and steeple, on cloister and other houses = 120 foders ————— weight of silver: 117 ozs	£69.15.4
Wherwell Abbey	£352.7.8½	25 = £123.6.8 p.a.	Abbess's lodging Infirmary Mill and mill-house Slaughterhouse Brewing and baking houses with granary Barn Stables to the outer court	Church, choir and steeple Cloister Chapter house Frater Dormitory Convent kitchen Lodgings between granary and hall door	5 bells Lead on houses = 60 foders ————— weight of silver: 912 ozs	£95.1.11

Ref. E315-494 - ff. 11-15, 17-21

References to Chapters

Chapter One

1. Asser, *Life of King Alfred*, in *E.H.D.*, vol.1, p.300
2. Biddle, M., 'Felix Urbs Wintonia' in (ed.) D. Parsons, *Tenth Century Studies*, pp.125-32
3. Translation by Dr. A.R. Rumble for the forthcoming *Winchester Studies* (*W.S.*), vol. 4, pt. 3 from BL MS. Harley 2965; also Biddle, *W.S.1*, p.322, n.8
4. The traditional view that Alfred was one of the founders of Nunnaminster is no longer accepted because it was based on a corrupt passage from William of Malmesbury. Biddle, *W.S.1*, p.321, n.9
5. Asser, *Life of King Alfred*, ed. W.H. Stevenson, pp.lx-lxii
6. *Liber Monasteria de Hyda*, p.83
7. Florence of Worcester, *Chronicle*, ed. T. Forester, p.88
8. Smith, L.T., *The Itinerary of John Leland*, vol. 1, p.272; Edwards (ed.), *Liber Monas. de Hyda*, pp.lxxv-lxxvii
9. Campbell, A., (ed.), *The Chronicle of Aethelweard*, p.52
10. Biddle, *W.S.1*, pp.321-2
11. '... abbatissa Edeldrida nomine, femina generosa ex regali progenie orta'. Braswell, L., 'St. Edburga of Winchester', *Medieval Studies*, vol. 33, p.330, which quotes from BL MS. Lansdowne 436
12. For her dreams: Wulfstan, *Life of St. Ethelwold*, in *E.H.D.*, vol. 1, p.904, n.1; for her installation: Osbert of Clare quoted in Braswell, p.300
13. Braswell, p.301, n.43
14. Biddle, *W.S.1*, 1, pp.555-6
15. Osbert of Clare quoted in Braswell, p.302, n.47
16. Braswell, pp.294-8. In 1150 a note concerning King Alfred, St. Neot and St. Edburga was written into the Smaragdus which belonged to St. Mary's Abbey (Bodley MS. 451, f.ii)
17. *Liber Monas. de Hyda*, p.112
18. Florence of Worcester, *Chronicle*, p.103
19. There were digs in 1973-5, 1977 and 1979, led by Mr. Kevin Stubbs, then Field Director of the Test Valley Archaeological Committee
20. Hinton, D.A., *Alfred's Kingdom*, p.99
21. All archaeological information kindly supplied by Mr. Stubbs
22. Hill, D., 'The Burghal Hidage', *Journal of Medieval Archaeology*, vol.13, p.87
23. Stenton, F.M., *Anglo-Saxon England*, pp.432-3; Loyn, H.R., *Anglo-Saxon England and the Norman Conquest*, p.240
24. Stenton, F.M., p.439
25. Richard of Cirencester, *Speculum*, Rolls Series, 30, vol.2, p.51
26. William of Malmesbury, *The History of the Kings of England*, in (ed.) J. Stevenson, *The Church Historians of England*, vol.3, pt.1, p.110
27. Zettl, E., *An Anonymous Short English Metrical Chronicle*, pp.21-2; *Liber Monas. de Hyda*, pp.112-13
28. *V.C.H.*, vol. 2, p.126; The two are compared in Liveing, *Records of Romsey Abbey*, app.A, pp.325-6
29. see n.26 above
30. *Liber Monas. de Hyda*, p.112
31. Athelstan's laws were issued at Grateley, Hants., c.926-30. *E.H.D.*, vol. 1, p.240
32. *ibid.*, pp.303-4
33. Sawyer, P.H., *Anglo-Saxon Charters*, no. 446; Finberg, H.P.R., *The Early Charters of Wessex*, no. 57
34. Meyer, M.A., 'Women and the Tenth Century English Monastic Reform', *Révue Bénédictine* (1977), pp.38-44
35. Whitelock, D., *Anglo-Saxon Wills*, pp.34-7, 137-41

36. Birch, W. de Gray, *Cartularium Saxonicum*, vol. 2, no.787. The first two witnesses to this charter are the king and his mother. For another possibility re. Sydmonton see Liveing, pp.17-18 and Meyer, M.A., 'Patronage of the West Saxon Royal Nunneries in late Anglo-Saxon England', *Révue Bénédictine*, vol.91, pp.340-1. Both these are based on the 'Vita Ethelfledae' in Horstman, C., *Nova Legenda Angliae*, vol. 1, pp.379-81

37. Braswell, L., 'St. Edburga of Winchester', *Medieval Studies*, no.33, p.309

38. Eadred's grant to Eadwulf in 947: Sawyer, *Anglo-Saxon Charters*, no.526; Finberg, *The Early Charters of Wessex*, no.66. Eadwulf's grant to New Minster and Nunnaminster between 947 and 955: Sawyer, no.1419; Finberg, no.74; Robertson, A.J., *Anglo-Saxon Charters*, no.29, pp.54-5, 311

39. *E.H.D.*, vol.1, pp.554-6; Finberg, no.75, pp.45, 90-1; Gelling, M., *Early Charters of the Thames Valley*, p.43

40. Knowles, D., *The Monastic Order in England*, pp.31-42

41. John, Eric, *Orbis Britanniae*, pp.162-3, 249ff.

42. *E.H.D.*, vol.1, p.909, chs. 18-19

43. *Anglo-Saxon Chronicle*, Rolls Series, 23, vol.2, p.93

44. *Monastic Breviary of Hyde Abbey*, vol.5, which transcribes Bodleian Gough MS. Liturg.8. July is on fol.G7. St. Edburga's feast day was 15 June (fol.G6v)

45. Sawyer, no.807; Finberg, no.101

46. Sawyer, no.1449; Finberg, no.121. Translations: Birch, W. de Gray, *An Ancient Manuscript*, pp.129-32 and Robertson, no.49, pp.102-5. Since the publication of Birch's translation it has been accepted that Nunnaminster received two mills in exchange for the watercourse, but the more recent translation by Miss Robertson seems to imply that the first mill became part of the Old Minster's property as it lay within its new bounds, while the second mill was exchanged with the nunnery in return for the watercourse.

47. Biddle, *W.S.1*, p.119 and fig.8

48. William of Malmesbury, *De Gestis Pontificum*, Rolls Series, 52, p.174

49. Information from Winchester Archaeology Office

50. Symons, T., *Regularis Concordia*, pp.xxiv, 10; Biddle, 'Felix Urbs Wintonia', p.139 and Symons, '*Regularis Concordia*: History and Derivation', pp.41-2 in Parsons (ed.), *Tenth Century Studies*

51. Symons, *Regularis Concordia*, p.2; Bullough, 'The continental background of the reform', in Parsons, (ed.), *Tenth Century Studies*, pp.34-6

52. Symons, *Regularis Concordia*, pp.4-5

53. *Historians of the Church of York and its Archbishops*, Rolls Series 71, 'Vita Sancti Oswaldi', p.438

54. *E.H.D.*, vol.1, p.908 (ch.17, n.3)

55. Robinson, J. Armitage, *The Times of St. Dunstan*, p.168; see n.48 above

56. Braswell, 'St. Edburga of Winchester', *Medieval Studies*, p.302

57. Robertson, pp.136, 348n.; Knowles, Brooke, London (eds.) *The Heads of Religious Houses*, p.223

58. Symons, in *Tenth Century Studies*, pp.40-2

59. *Florence of Worcester*, p.103; *Worcester Annals*, Rolls Series 36, vol. 4, p.368

60. Horstman, C., *Nova Legenda Angliae*, p.379; *Liber Monas. de Hyda*, p.191

61. William of Malmesbury, *De Gestis Pontificum*, p.175. Both are recorded in a list of ladies in the *Liber Vitae* of Hyde Abbey, p.58

62. Liveing, p.20, translation from BL MS. Lansdowne 436

63. All three years are given in different versions of the Anglo-Saxon Chronicle, *E.H.D.*, vol.1, p.227

64. *Florence of Worcester*, p.104

65. Birch, *Cartularium Saxonicum*, vol.3, no.1187; Finberg, no.123 gives translation of gifts.

66. Sawyer, no.812 lists those who regard it as suspicious; Finberg, no.123 and John, Eric, *Orbis Britanniae*, pp.198-9 accept its authenticity

67. Berrow, P., *When the Nuns ruled Romsey*, pp.22-38; Grundy, G.B., 'The Saxon land charters of Hampshire', *Archaeological Journal*, vol.84, pp.199-206

68. Sawyer, no.765; Finberg, no.304; for boundaries: Grundy, in *Archaeological Journal* vol.77, pp.80-4

69. Whitelock, D., *Anglo-Saxon Wills*, no.X, pp.24-7, 125-8; *Liber Monas. de Hyda*, pp.133ff., 343; Finberg, no.125

70. Whitelock, no.VIII, pp.20-3, 118-21; Gelling, *Early Charters of the Thames Valley*, p.75; Sawyer, *op.cit*, no.1484. Elfgifu may have been the wife of Edgar's brother, Eadwig. (Liveing, p.35, is mistaken)

71. *Leechdoms, Wortcunning and Starcraft in Early England*, R.S., 35, vol.3, pp.416, 441; Robinson, J. Armitage, *The Times of St. Dunstan*, pp.121-2; Clemoes (ed.), *Anglo-Saxon England*, vol.3, p.138, n.2

72. *E.H.D.*, vol.1, p.922; *Leechdoms*, . . . (see above), p.443

73. Stenton, F.M., *Anglo-Saxon England*, p.367; *E.H.D.*, vol. 1, p.914; Keynes, S., *The Diplomas of King Aethelred 'the Unready'*, p.166

74. *Florence of Worcester*, p.106

75. *E.H.D.*, vol.1, pp.230-1; Stenton, F.M., pp.367-8; Keynes, pp.169-70. Folklore example: *The South English Legendary*, vol.1, pp.110-8

76. Stenton, F.M., p.368; Keynes, pp.166-9; Whitelock, *Anglo-Saxon Wills*, p.123n.

77. *E.H.D.*, vol.1, p.596; Whitelock, no.XX; Keynes, p.187, n.117. In his will Athelstan granted land at Rotherfield to Nunnaminster (BL MS. Stowe Charter 37)

78. Symons, *Regularis Concordia*, p.2; *E.H.D.*, vol.1, p.922

79. Keynes, p.269

80. Wherwell Cartulary (BL MS. Egerton 2104a), ch.58, fol.43 and ch.353, fols.152v-153

81. *Cal. Pat. Rolls*, 1343-5, pp.386-7. Petition dated 25 June 1344

82. *E.H.D.*, vol.1, p.227. Alfred is not otherwise known to be the brother of Elfthryth though in 964, when the king granted land in Berkshire to her, the diploma was attested both by her father Ordgar (still a thegn then) and by Alfred, another thegn. Sawyer, no.725. Elfthryth's known brother was called Ordulf.

83. William of Malmesbury, *History of the Kings of England*, pp.139-41; *Winchester Annals*, R.S., 36, vol.2, p.12

84. Farmer, D., 'The progress of the monastic revival', in (ed.) Parsons, *Tenth Century Studies*, pp.14, 209 n.6; Barlow, F., *The English Church 1000-1066*, p.32 n.1; Clutterbuck, R.H., *Notes on the parishes of Fyfield, . . . and Wherwell*, pp.153-4

85. Wherwell Cartulary, ch.62, fol.45

86. Hase, unpublished Ph.D. thesis, p.85

87. Keynes, pp.176-7

88. Meyer, 'Women and the Tenth Century English Monastic Reform', *Révue Bénédictine*, no.87, pp.58-61

89. Keynes, p.210 n.203

90. This was probably in East Dean, in the rape of Hastings where Countess Goda was the landholder in 1086. Wherwell Abbey is not mentioned in the Sussex entries in Domesday Book

91. Keynes, p.258

92. Finberg, pp.103-4

N.B. After the gravestone of Frithburga was found in the parish church at Whitchurch in 1868, it was suggested that the lady might have been a nun at Wherwell. This inaccuracy is still quoted locally although it was known by the end of the 19th century that the stone pre-dated the abbey. A mid-ninth century date is now assigned to it.

Minns, Rev. G.W., 'On a Saxon Sepulchral Monument at Whitchurch', *HFC Proc.*, vol.4, pp.171-4

Green, A.R. and P.M., *Saxon Architecture and Sculpture in Hampshire* (1951), pp.53-4.

Chapter Two

1. Stenton, F.M., *Anglo-Saxon England*, pp.369-87; *E.H.D.*, vol.1, pp.232-251

2. *E.H.D.*, vol.1, p.240. Raid on Cannings: *ibid.*, p.244

3. Horstman, *Nova Legenda Angliae*, vol.1, p.379; Liveing, p.26

4. *Winchester Annals*, p.16

5. Horstman, p.379

6. Birch, W. de Gray (ed.), *Liber Vitae*, pp.58, 62-3; from: BL MS. Stowe 944 (not as in Birch, p.i)

7. Birch, *Liber Vitae*, p.49n.

8. Carpenter Turner, B., 'Emma: A 900th Anniversary', *Winchester Cathedral Record*, no.21, pp.8-12

9. Backhouse, J., Turner, D.H., and Webster, L., *The Golden Age of Anglo-Saxon Art 966-1066*, pp.144-5; *E.H.D.*, vol.1, pp.138-9, 350-3
10. *E.H.D.*, vol.2, pp.111-12; *Florence of Worcester*, pp.145, 152; *Winchester Annals*, pp.20-4; Barlow, F., *Edward the Confessor*, pp.76-8
11. *Cal. Lib. Rolls, 1240-5*, p.292
12. Barlow, *Edward the Confessor*, pp.xlix, 80-5, 89-90, 115-6; Stenton, F.M., pp.553-60
13. *E.H.D.*, vol.2, pp.124-5
14. *Florence of Worcester*, p.152; Stubbs, W. (ed.), *Chronica Magistri Rogeri de Hovedene*, vol.1, p.98
15. Barlow, F. (ed.), *Vita Edwardi Regis*, p.23
16. Barlow, F., *The English Church 1000-1066*, pp.312-15
17. Barlow, *Vita Edwardi Regis*, pp.46-8, 95-7
18. Carpenter Turner, B., *A History of Hampshire*, map p.28
19. Carpenter Turner, B., *Winchester*, pp.21-2
20. Clover, H. and Gibson, M. (eds.), *The Letters of Lanfranc, Archbishop of Canterbury*, pp.166-7
21. Knowles, D., *The Monastic Order in England*, pp.92-4; Barlow, F., *The English Church 1066-1154*, pp.178-9
22. Meyer, M.A., 'Patronage of the West Saxon Royal Nunneries . . .', *Révue Bénédictine*, no.91, p.357
23. *Winchester Annals*, p.34; Schmitt, F.S. (ed.), *S. Anselmi, Cantuariensis archiepiscopi*, vol.4, pp.190-1
24. Schmitt, pp.144-5; Knowles, Brooke, London, *Heads of Religious Houses*, p.219
25. see Appendix 1
26. Strickland, Agnes, *Lives of the Queens of England* (1857 edn), vol.1, p.92
27. *E.H.D.*, vol.2, p.162
28. Knowles, Brooke, London, p.219
29. Chibnall, M. (ed.), *Orderic Vitalis*, vol.4, p.273
30. Southern, R.W., *Saint Anselm and his Biographer*, pp.182-5
31. Eadmer, *History of Recent Events in England*, trans. G. Bosanquet, pp.127-8
32. Southern, pp.188-93; Chibnall, M., *Anglo-Norman England*, p.68
33. Hallam, E.M., *Domesday Book through nine centuries*, p.18, quoting from the Anglo-Saxon Chronicle.
34. Finn, R.W., *Domeday Book. A Guide*, pp.8-9, 25-7
35. *Domesday Book: Wiltshire* (Phillimore), items 14-15
36. *Domesday Book: Hampshire* (Phillimore), items 14-16
37. *Salina* was translated as saltpan in *VCH* vol.1, p.475 but as salt-house in the Phillimore edn. (15-4). A pan or group of pans must have at least one boiling house. In Lymington a saltern was made up of eight pans which were probably worked from one boiling house. (Information from Mr. A.T. Lloyd, author of 'The Salterns of the Lymington area' *HFC Proc.*, vol.24 (1967), pp.86-102)
38. *Domesday Book: Hampshire* (Phillimore), items 14-6; *ibid.: Berkshire*, item 14
39. BL MS. Egerton 2104a, fol.153
40. BL MS. Lansdowne 442.

Chapter Three

1. *VCH*, vol.2, pp.10-11; Chibnall, M., *Anglo-Norman England*, pp.68-70
2. Schmitt, F.S., *S. Anselmi, Cantuariensis Archiepiscopi*, vol.4, no.276 (trans.)
3. *ibid.*, no.236, apparently written before the Council of London, 1102; Brett, M., *The English Church under Henry I*, p.83; for Earl Waltheof: Knowles, D., *Monastic Order in England*, p.242. He was executed outside Winchester
4. Schmitt, vol.4, no.237 (trans.)
5. Knowles, *Monastic Order in England*, pp.173, 190
6. Schmitt, vol.4, no.242, vol.5, nos.317, 384, 400. Her seal is illustrated in *English Romanesque Art 1066-1200*, p.305
7. Clapham, Sir A., 'Three Bede-Rolls', *Archaeological Journal*, vol.106, (1949 supp.), pp.42-3; Barlow, F., *English Church 1066-1154*, p.219, n.15
8. Clapham, pp.47-51
9. Blake, E.O. (ed.), *Cartulary of the Priory of St. Denys*, pp.xxxvii, 215-6
10. Biddle, *W.S.1*, p.322, n.10

11. *ibid.*, and p.556
12. *Regesta Regum Anglo-Normanorum*, vol.2, no.687, p.41. The editors suggest that 'Storunella in the New Forest' may be Wherwell. The charter sealed concerned Andover church.
13. Peers, Sir C., 'Recent Discoveries in Romsey Church', *Archaeologia*, vol.57 (1901), pp.317-20; *VCH*, vol.4, pp.460-7; Hearn, M.F. 'A note on the chronology of Romsey Abbey', *Journal of the British Archaeological Association*, vol.32 (1969), pp.30-7; Information from Mr. K. Stubbs
14. Schmitt, vol.4, no.237
15. Liveing, p.49
16. *Abingdon Annals*, Rolls Series, 2, vol.2, p.126; *Regesta Regum Anglo-Normanorum*, vol.2, pp.40-1
17. *Regesta Regum Anglo-Normanorum*, vol.2, pp.54, 95
18. *ibid.*, p.237; *Cal. Ch. Rolls*, vol.5, pp.318-9; Liveing, pp.44-5
19. Poole, A.L., *From Domesday Book to Magna Carta*, pp.125-31
20. William of Malmesbury, *Historia Novella*, ed. Potter, p.51
21. Poole, pp.142-3; *E.H.D.*, vol.2, pp.301-3
22. *Winchester Annals*, pp.52-3; William of Malmesbury, *Historia Novella*, p.59; Biddle, *W.S.1*, pp.297ff, 318-9
23. Potter, K.R. and Davis, R.H.C., *Gesta Stephani*, pp.131-3; *Florence of Worcester*, p.285; Wm. of Malmesbury, *Historia Novella*, p.60
24. Potter and Davis, *Gesta Stephani*, p.133. In 1883 eight skeletons were found at Wherwell and it was thought that they dated from this battle. Clutterbuck, R.H., *Notes on the parishes of Fyfield, . . . and Wherwell*, p.163
25. Potter and Davis, *Gesta Stephani*, pp.133-7; Poole, pp.144-5
26. Luce, Sir R., *Pages from the History of Romsey and its Abbey*. pp.19-20
27. *Regesta Regum Anglo-Normanorum*, vol.3, pp.265-6
28. Saltman, A., *Theobald, Archbishop of Canterbury*, pp.379-80
29. *ibid.*, pp.52-4; *Waverley Annals*, Rolls Series, 36, vol.2, p.238
30. Liveing, pp.56-7
31. Knowles, *Monastic Order in England*, p. 289
32. Tewkesbury Register, BL Add. MS. 36985, fol.14v. This reference is given by Knowles (*Monastic Order in England*, pp.137 n.6, 727) but he was mistaken in saying it referred to one of the sisters being abbess of Romsey. For the possibility that ROBERTUS may be Earl Robert, see Luce, Sir R., *Pages from the History of Romsey and its Abbey*, pp.19-20
33. Knowles, *Monastic Order in England*, pp.721-6
34. *ibid.*, pp.230, 248-9
35. Thompson, S., 'The problem of the Cistercian nuns in the 12th and early 13th centuries', in Baker (ed.), *Medieval Women*, p.230
36. Knowles, D. and Hadcock, R.N., *Medieval Religious Houses*, pp.271-7
37. Thompson, S., pp.227-40
38. This Geoffrey fitz Peter should not be confused with the later justiciar of that name who became Earl of Essex in 1199, died 1213 and whose wives were Beatrice and then Aveline.
39. Biddle, *W.S.1*, p.106, no.509
40. *Regesta Regum Anglo-Normanorum*, vol.3, p.303, no.823. Pipe Roll Society, *7 Henry II*, p.57, *13 Henry II*, p.179
41. Knowles, Cecilia, *Sparsholt and Lainston*, p.20
42. *Cal. Ch. Rolls*, vol.4, pp.392-7. The prior was William de Basingstoke; the inspection was probably c.1294-5 (*Reg. Pontissara*, pp.xxxv, 509)
43. *Cal. Ch. Rolls*, vol.4, p.392. Her husband is not known, but in 1112 a Roger fitz Peter witnessed Henry I's subscription to a charter. (Farrer, Wm., *An Outline Itinerary of Henry I*, p.63)
44. Biddle, *W.S.1*, p.284 and fig.8
45. Pipe Roll Society, *28 Henry II*, p.146; also *31 Henry II*, p.214 and *32 Henry II*, p.177
46. Wintney Cal., fol.147v
47. Knowles, Brooke, London, *Heads of Religious Houses*, p.147
48. *Cal. Ch. Rolls*, vol.4, p.394
49. *ibid.*, p.392
50. Wintney Cal, fol.3v
51. *Waverley Annals*, p.292

52. *VCH*, vol.4, pp.79, 110
53. Wintney Cal., fols.146v (stone church), 157
54. *ibid.*, fol.148
55. HRO, Herriard Papers, 44 M 69-225. In her widowhood Matilda dropped the name Sifrewast
56. Wintney Cal.: Agnes domina de Colrythe, fol.34; Alesia domina de Colrythe, fol.40v; Dionisia domina de Colrythe, fol.149
57. *ibid.*, fol.157v. The connection, if any, between Matilda de Quincy and Seyer de Quincy, Earl of Winchester is not known.

Chapter Four

1. Talbot, C.H., *The Life of Christina of Markyate* (1959)
2. *Cal. Pat. Rolls, 1225-32*, p.418
3. *ibid., 1232-47*, p.180
4. *ibid.*, p.137
5. *ibid., 1247-58*, p.552
6. *ibid., 1292-1301*, p.326; Reg. Stratford, fol.66
7. *Cal. Pat. Rolls, 1330-34*, p.452
8. *ibid, 1334-38*, p.546; *ibid., 1348-50*, p.297
9. *Cal. Lib. Rolls, 1260-67*, p.120
10. *Cal. Pat. Rolls, 1377-81*, pp.64, 86
11. *ibid., 1381-85*, p.399; *Cal. Cl. Rolls, 1377-81*, pp.166, 263
12. *Reg. Edington*, vol.2, item 427
13. *Reg. Wykeham*, vol.2, pp.501, 519
14. *Register of Henry Chichele, Archbishop of Canterbury*, (ed.) E.F. Jacob, vol.4, pp.96, 382
15. Reg. Stratford, fols.37v, 41
16. *Cal. Pap. Reg. (Petitions)*, vol.1, p.98; *ibid. (Letters)*, vol.3, pp.193, 287, 578; vol.4, pp.483, 495
17. Power, Eileen, *Medieval English Nunneries*, p.455
18. *Cal. Pat. Rolls, 1232-47*, p.397
19. Parsons, J.C., *Court and Household of Eleanor of Castile in 1290*, pp.19, 86
20. Reg. Stratford, fol.86v; Reg. Orleton, vol.1, fol.96v
21. *Reg. Pontissara*, p.252
22. *Reg. Wykeham*, vol.2, p.501
23. Power, pp.25-38
24. Martin, C.T. (ed.), *Reg. Epistolarum Johannis Peckham, Arch. Cantuar.*, vol.2, letter DIV, p.653
25. *Reg. Woodlock*, p.761
26. Reg. Fox, vol.5, fols.69v, 130; *Reg. Gardiner*, p.39. Their ages were 14 (2), 15, 17 (2), 20 (2), 23 and 31
27. *Reg. Wykeham*, vol.2, pp.60-1, 461-2
28. Maskell, Wm., *Monumenta Ritualia Ecclesiae Anglicanae*, vol.2, pp.308-9. Original MS.: C.U.L. Mm.III.13
29. BL MS. Lansdowne 451, fol.63v
30. Wherwell Cart., ch.59, fol.43v; *VCH*, vol.2, p.133
31. *Reg. Pontissara*, p.252
32. *ibid.*, p.321
33. *ibid.*, pp.xxxiii, 546
34. *Reg. Woodlock*, p.517
35. *ibid.*, pp.528, 532. Liveing, pp.103-4 numbers this as item 8. In the register it is item 9 in the Latin version while the French one is unnumbered
36. *VCH*, vol.2, p.130
37. *Reg. Woodlock*, pp.551-2
38. *ibid.*, pp.322-3
39. *ibid.*, p.761
40. Reg. Stratford, fol.8v
41. *ibid.*, fol.10v
42. *ibid.*, fol.16

43. *ibid.*, fol.176r, v
44. *ibid.*, fol.23
45. *ibid.*, fol.23r, v
46. *ibid.*, fol.33v
47. *ibid.*
48. *ibid.*, fol.82
49. *ibid.*, fol.86v
50. *Reg. Edington*, vol.2, item 34
51. *Reg. Edington*, vol.1, items 117, 125, 148
52. *ibid.*, item 289
53. *Cal. Pap. Reg. (Petitions)*, vol.1, p.122
54. Luce, *HFC Proc.*, vol.17 (1), p.36
55. Reg. Beaufort, vol.1, fol.50$^+$; Reg. Langton, fols. 51-2; An edition of the Register of John Moreton, Archbishop of Canterbury (thesis by C. Harper-Bill), p.55
56. Reg. Beaufort, vol.1, fol.50$^+$
57. Reg. Langton, fol.51
58. *Reg. Pontissara*, p.182
59. Wherwell Cart., fols.184v-185v. This letter was not included in the bishop's register
60. *Reg. Woodlock*, pp.343-4
61. *ibid.*, pp.606-7, 610-1
62. Reg. Stratford, fols.81v-82
63. Reg. Waynflete, vol.1, fols.50v-53
64. Reg. Courtenay, fols.4-6
65. Reg. Waynflete, vol.2, fols.64-8
66. *Cal. Pap. Reg. (Letters)*, vol.13 (2), pp.803-4
67. Liveing, pp.217-223
68. Reg. Stratford, fol.115
69. Reg. Fox, vol.5, fols.130-8; *Reg. Wolsey*, pp.xix-xx
70. *Reg. Edington*, vol.1, items 916 (Romsey), 1480 (Wherwell); *Reg. Wykeham*, vol.1, p.153 (St. Mary's, Winchester)
71. Reg. Orleton, vol.1, fol.87; Haines, R.M., *The Church and Politics in Fourteenth Century England*, pp.64, 253; *Reg. Wykeham*, vol.1, pp.69-74
72. Reg. Wykeham, vol.1, fol.260. (Not included in the edited register.)
73. Reg. Orleton, vol.1, fol.46v
74. Reg. Beaufort, vol.1, fols.26-31
75. Reg. Waynflete, vol.2, fol.80
76. Reg. Langton, fol.49
77. e.g., BL MS. Lansdowne 451, fols.59v ff
78. Reg. Langton, fols.46v-47.
79. Reg. Beaufort, vol.1, fol.50$^+$
80. PRO E318-4-126 (14)
81. Clutterbuck, *Notes on the parishes of Fyfield, . . . and Wherwell*, p.165; VCH, vol.4, p.453
82. *Reg. Epistolarum Peckham*, p.662; Liveing, pp.82-4; Power, p.62
83. Liveing, p.221
84. *ibid.*, p.229
85. Power, p.63
86. see Appendix 1
87. Reg. Stratford, fols.66, 139
88. Except Eleanor Warblington whose obit is in the Wintney Calendar, fol.148v
89. Reg. Fox, vol.4, fol.20v (Wherwell); vol.5, fol.130 (Winchester)
90. Wherwell Cart., fols.200-211
91. Reg. Langton, fol.51
92. Reg. Fox, vol.4, fol.20v
93. *ibid.*, vol.1, fol.21
94. Leningrad Cal., fol.2v

 95. Wintney Cal., fol.49v
 96. *ibid.*, fol.158v
 97. *Reg. Woodlock*, pp.760-1
 98. Wherwell Cart., fol.14v
 99. *Reg. of John Pecham*, vol.2, pp.218-9. He was dismissed in order to restore peace in the convent.
100. Visitations of 1492 and 1501. Liveing, pp.217-226
101. *Reg. Woodlock*, p.760
102. Luce, *HFC Proc.*, vol.17 (1), p.40.

Chapter Five

 1. Green, A.R., 'The Romsey Painted Wooden Reredos', *Archaeological Journal*, vol.90 (1933), pp.306ff.; Croft-Murray, E., *Decorative Painting in England 1537-1837*, vol.1, pp.173-4
 2. Duggan, C., 'From the Conquest to the death of John' in (ed.) C.H. Lawrence, *The English Church and the Papacy in the Middle Ages*, pp.105-7
 3. Sayers, J.E., *Original Papal Documents in the Lambeth Palace Library*, p.17
 4. Wherwell Cart., fols.17v-24 (Popes Innocent III, Gregory IX, Celestine IV, Alexander IV)
 5. *ibid.*, sacrist ch.4, fols.200v-201; Cheney (ed.), *The Letters of Pope Innocent III concerning England and Wales*, pp.32, 209
 6. *Cal. Pap. Reg. (Letters)*, vol.1, p.540; Wherwell Cart., ch.35, fols.33v-35, sacrist ch.8, fols.202v-3
 7. St. Mary's: *Cal. Pap. Reg. (Petitions)*, vol.1, pp.122, 230; Wintney: *Cal Pap. Reg. (Letters)*, vol.5, p.71
 8. *ibid.*, vol.2, p.160; vol.8, pp.342-3; Goodman, A.W., *Chartulary of Winchester Cathedral*, pp.56-7; Keene, *W.S.2*, vol.1, p.195
 9. *Cal. Pap. Reg. (Letters)*, vol.11, p.626
10. Lawrence, C.H., 'The Thirteenth Century', pp.147-51; Pantin, W.A., 'The Fourteenth Century', pp.183-93, both in Lawrence, C.H. (ed.), *The English Church and the Papacy in the Middle Ages*. The only later provision was made at Wherwell in 1402: *Cal. Pap. Reg. (Letters)*, vol.5, p.492
11. Wherwell Cart., ch.32, f.32v (n.d. but the authority of the Council of Oxford (1222) quoted). Generally, Cheney, C.R., *Episcopal Visitation of Monasteries in the Thirteenth Century*, pp.22-3
12. *ibid.*, pp.33, 40
13. *Reg. Woodlock*, pp.546, 551-2
14. *ibid.*, pp.322-3
15. Haines, R.M., 'Adam Orleton and the diocese of Winchester', *Journal of Ecclesiastical History*, vol.23 (1972), p.22
16. Thompson, A. Hamilton, *The English Clergy and their organisation in the later Middle Ages*, pp.178-9
17. Harper-Bill, C. 'An edition of the register of John Morton, Archbishop of Canterbury' (Ph.D. thesis), pp.433-6
18. Cheney, *Episcopal Visitation of Monasteries . . .* , p.108
19. *Annales Monastici*, vol.2, Rolls Series, 36, pp.110, 118
20. Wherwell Cart., ch.61, fol.45
21. Wintney Cal., fol.143
22. *Reg. Epistolarum Peckham*, vol.2, Rolls Series, 77, pp.650-4, 658-65
23. *ibid.*, vol.1, pp.40-1, 265-6
24. *Reg. Edington*, vol.1, item 1702; Wintney Cal., fol.41v
25. *Reg. Wykeham*, vol.2, pp.360-2
26. Luce, *HFC Proc.*, vol.17 (1), p.44
27. Wherwell Cart., fol.14v
28. *VCH*, vol.2, pp.124, 129-31 (incorrect date p.129), 135, 151
29. Wintney Cal., fols.157, 151, 141, 142, 162 respectively
30. *ibid.*, fols.18, 146v
31. Liveing, pp.163-4
32. *VCH*, vol.2, p.124; Spence, C., *The Abbey Church of Romsey*, pp.106-7

33. Chandler, R., *The Life of William Waynflete*, pp.219, 380
34. Will of Thomas Langton, 1501, quoted in Baigent MS: BL Add. MS. 39977, fol.266
35. Bishop Fox's translation, *The Rule of Seynt Benet*. Introduction, spelling modernised. The whole intro. is in (ed.) Allen, *Letters of Richard Fox*, pp.86-8. The two surviving copies are in the BL and the Bodleian. (*The Benedictines and the Book*, item 6)
36. Wherwell cart., ch.54, fols.39-40; auditing: *ibid.*, ch.56, fol.41; annual audit: *Reg. Woodlock*, p.518; Reg. Stratford, fol.176v
37. *VCH*, vol.2, p.127
38. Wherwell Cart., ch.57, fol.42v
39. *ibid.*, ch.55, fol.40; exchange: *Cal. Pap. Reg. (Petitions)*, vol.1, pp.211, 219; *Cal. Pat. Rolls, 1348-50*, p.564
40. Wherwell Cart., ch.40, fols.35v-36
41. *Reg. Pontissara*, pp.xli-ii, 804-821, 830-5
42. 1328: *Cal. Pap. Reg. (Letters)*, vol.2, pp.276-7; 1331: *ibid.*, p.325. Liveing, p.131
43. *Cal. Pap. Reg. (Petitions)*, vol.1, p.14; *Cal. Pap. Reg. (Letters)*, vol.3, p.78
44. *Cal. Cl. Rolls, 1339-41*, p.263; *Cal. Pap. Reg. (Petitions)*, vol.1, p.216; *Cal. Pap. Reg. (Letters)*, vol.3, p.166
45. *Cal. Pat. Rolls, 1343-5*, pp.28, 35; *Cal. Pap. Reg. (Petitions)*, vol.1, p.98
46. Wherwell Cart., ch.4, fols.18v-20 (privileges); Greatrex, J., *The Register of the Common Seal*, p.108 (Goodworth)
47. Wherwell Cart., ch.54, fol.39r
48. *Cal. Pat. Rolls* for 1323, 1349, 1361, 1392
49. *VCH (Wilts)*, vol.10, pp.25, 30; appendix 2
50. *ibid.*, pp.181, 186; appendix 2
51. *ibid.*, vol.8, pp.246-7; Liveing, p.146ff; appendix 2
52. Reg. Beaufort, fols.11 (income), 14 (pension); appendix 2
53. Liveing, pp.135-9; Goodman, *Chartulary of Winchester Cathedral*, pp.24-6
54. Haines, R.M., 'Adam Orleton and the diocese of Winchester', *J. Eccles. Hist.*, p.26
55. *Reg. Asserio*, pp.451-3; Liveing, pp.127-8. In 1400 the vicar was presented by the abbess and convent (*Reg. Wykeham*, vol.1, p.226)
56. Wherwell cart., ch.57, fol.42v
57. *Reg. Sandale*, p.149
58. *Reg. Pontissara*, pp.xxxv, 509
59. *ibid.*, p.145
60. Will of Henry Sewghel, 1508. HRO, WR1, fol.374
61. *Reg. Edington*, vol.2, item 114
62. *Reg. Wykeham*, vol.2, pp.158, 185-6
63. *ibid.*, pp.548-9; Liveing, pp.180-2
64. Wherwell Cart., ch.57, fol.42v
65. *ibid.*, fol.42r
66. *ibid.*, fols. 213v-214
67. Keene, *W.S.2*, p.109
68. *Reg. Wykeham*, vol.2, p.315
69. Smith, L.T., *The Itinerary of John Leland in or·about the years 1535-43*, vol.1, p.270
70. Reg. Stratford, fols.110v-111; *Cal. Pat. Rolls, 1327-30*, p.259
71. *Cal. Pat. Rolls, 1330-4*, pp.181, 258, 318; Liveing, pp.115-7; Reg. Orleton, vol.1, fol.117v
72. *Cal. Pat. Rolls, 1467-77*, p.569. The chapel of St. Peter was also a chantry (*Cal. Pat. Rolls, 1396-99*, p.257)
73. Wherwell Cart., chs.73; 83, fols.53v-54, 58
74. *Reg. Sandale*, p.90; *VCH*, vol.2, p.28
75. *Reg. Pontissara*, pp.xxxii, 251
76. Reg. Stratford, fols.19, 177
77. *Reg. Edington*, vol.2, item 488; *Reg. Wykeham*, vol.2, p.315
78. *Reg. Wykeham*, vol.2, pp.268, 440
79. *ibid.*, pp.469, 118; Luce, *HFC Proc.*, vol.17 (1), p.39
80. Reg. Langton, fols. 78, 80v.

Chapter Six

 1. Luce, *HFC Proc.*, vol.17 (1), p.43
 2. *Reg. Epist. Peckham*, vol.2, pp.651-2
 3. *Reg. Pontissara*, p.126; Liveing, p.100
 4. *Reg. Woodlock*, pp.516-7, 520-1
 5. *ibid.*, pp.526-7; Liveing, p.102
 6. *Reg. Woodlock*, p.758
 7. Reg. Stratford, fol.176
 8. Luce, *HFC Proc.*, vol.17 (1), p.33
 9. Harper-Bill, C., 'Edition of the Register of John Morton . . .' (Ph.D. thesis), p.435; Liveing, p.221
10. *VCH*, vol.2, p.124
11. Luce, *HFC Proc.*, vol.17 (1), p.43
12. Deanesly, M., *The Lollard Bible*, pp.110-13
13. Power, *Medieval English Nunneries*, p.240
14. Liveing, pp.30-1
15. Thomson, R.M., *Manuscripts from St. Alban's Abbey*, pp.56-60
16. *VCH*, vol.2, p.133
17. James, M.R., *The Western Manuscripts in the Library of Trinity College, Cambridge*, p.333 (trans.)
18. Wherwell Cart., sacrist, ch.26, fol.209; *VCH*, vol.2, p.134
19. Royal College of Physicians MS.409, fol.144; A post-Dissolution note on fol.1 reads 'This was my great-grandmother's father's book and therefore for the antiquities sake I keep it. Nich. Saunder'.
20. Liveing, p.285
21. Leningrad Cal., fol.12v; Thomson, R.M., *op.cit.*, pp.37-8, 123
22. Maskell, Wm., *Monumenta Ritualia Ecclesiae Anglicanae*, vol.2, p.308. The whole MS. is transcribed pp.307-31
23. PRO E315-400, fol. 27. An 'almere' was an aumbry, a cupboard sometimes used for books.
24. *VCH*, vol.2, p.124
25. Luce, *HFC Proc.*, vol.17 (1), p.43
26. Power, *Medieval English Nunneries*, p.253
27. Reg. Stratford, fol.176v
28. Fox, Bishop Richard, *The Rule of Seynt Benet*, intro. p.Aii
29. see Legge, Mary Dominica, 'The French Language and the English Cloister' in Ruffer and Taylor (eds.), *Medieval Studies presented to Rose Graham*, pp.146-62; French oath: *Reg. Wykeham*, vol.1, p.153
30. Clapham, Sir A., 'Three Bede-Rolls', *Archaeological Journal*, vol.106 (1949 supp.), p.51; Reg. Fox, vol.1, fol.21
31. Leningrad Cal., fols.11-12
32. Wherwell Cart., fol.2; and see Knowles, *The Religious Orders in England*, vol.1, pp.305-7
33. *HFC Proc.*, vol.17 (1), p.44; Davis, G.R.C., *Medieval Cartularies of Great Britain*, pp.41, 118
34. Ellis, R.H., *Catalogue of Seals in the PRO, vol.1: Monastic Seals*, pp.77, 99. Abbess 'Lucy' is incorrect on p.99: the deed of 1285 refers to Mary, abbess of Winchester.
35. Himsworth, S., *Winchester College Muniments*, vols. 1-3. Romsey Abbey's seals: nos. 16348, 16378; Romsey merchant: no.16031; St. Mary's Abbey: nos. 808a, 1266, 1271, 1281. I am grateful to Mr. T.A. Heslop for commenting on these seals.
36. HRO, Herriard Papers, 44 M 69 – C351 (13th century); Herriard Papers, 44 M 69 – C80, C83 (1337); Kingsmill Papers, 19 M 61 – 149 (1415)
37. *Reg. Epist. Peckham*, vol.2, pp.651, 662-3; Liveing, p.83
38. Salt: *VCH*, vol.5, p.469; pepper: *Cal. Inq, P.M.*, vol.7, p.32. General information about food from Mrs. Maggie Black, author of *Food and Cooking in Medieval England*, (1985)
39. Power, appendix 1, note A, pp.563-8
40. BL Add. Charters, 17.471 (c.1256), 17.482 (1367-8)
41. Information from Winchester Archaeology Office
42. *Cal. Cl. Rolls, 1234-7*, p.445; *ibid., 1256-8*, p.376
43. *ibid., 1264-8*, p.194; *ibid., 1268-72*, p.77
44. *ibid., 1256-8*, p.17; *ibid., 1264-8*, p.421

45. *Cal. Pat. Rolls, 1381-5*, p.399
46. *Reg. Woodlock*, pp.518, 762
47. Coleman, O., *The Brokage Book of Southampton, 1443-4*, vol.1, pp.62, 273
48. *ibid.*, pp.95, 102, 177-8. On 10 Feb. the red herrings were listed as 'v cades' and the white as 'ii barellis'; a cade held 600 herrings and a barrel 1000 herrings. Easter Day was on 12 April 1444.
49. Stevens, K.F. and Olding, T.E., *The Brokage Book of Southampton, 1477-8 and 1527-8*, p.135
50. Luce, *HFC Proc.*, vol.17 (1), p.43
51. Coleman, pp.299-300
52. Stevens and Olding, p.44
53. Keene, *W.S.2*, pp.259-60, fig.32
54. Information from Winchester Archaeology Office
55. 'Piscarys' were included in a lease of the site in 1540. PRO E315-212, fol.133
56. Liveing, p.202
57. Goodman, A.W., *Chartulary of Winchester Cathedral*, pp.213-4; *Cal. Inq.P.M., XVI, 1384-92*, p.187 (Sir Thomas West)
58. *ibid., III, 1291-1300*, p.155 (Nich de Barflet, als. Barbeflet)
59. BL MS. Add. Ch. 17471
60. Information from Winchester Archaeology Office
61. Greatrex, J., *The Register of the Common Seal*, p.108; Power, p.568 n.1 has a 15th-century recipe for 'cripcis'.
62. Wherwell Cart., ch.56, fol.41v
63. *Reg. Woodlock*, p.517, inj.9 (trans.)
64. *ibid.*, p.528, inj.8
65. *ibid.*, p.762
66. Reg. Stratford, fol.176v (trans.)
67. Luce, *HFC Proc.*, vol.17 (1), p.38
68. *ibid.*, p.43
69. Liveing, p.195
70. *L. and P.*, vol.21 (2), p.240. Before 1385 a fit man from Urchfont manor would be chosen to make beer for the abbess of Winchester. *VCH, Wilts.*, vol.4, p.39; vol.10, p.182
71. PRO SC12-33/27
72. Harper-Bill, C., 'The Labourer is Worthy of his Hire? – Complaints About diet in Late Medieval English Monasteries', in Barron, C.M. and Harper-Bill, C., *The Church in Pre-Reformation Society*, pp.99-102
73. Harper-Bill, 'Edition of Reg. of John Morton' (Ph.D. thesis), pp.433-6
74. *VCH*, vol.2, p.130
75. Coleman, *Brokage Book of Southampton*, p.127
76. Stevens and Olding, *Brokage Book of Southampton*, pp.77, 99
77. *ibid.*, pp.133, 142, 169, 179 (Wherwell); pp.135, 154 (Romsey)
78. *Cal. Lib. Rolls, 1245-51*, p.78; *ibid., 1260-7*, p.120
79. Romsey: *Cal. Cl. Rolls, 1268-72*, p.481; Wherwell: *Cal. Lib. Rolls, 1226-40*, p.431; *Cal. Cl. Rolls, 1237-42*, p.18; *ibid., 1251-3*, p.398; *ibid., 1264-8*, p.420
80. *Cal. Lib. Rolls* for 1237, 1246 (2), 1247, 1248 (2), 1249 (4), 1251 (2), 1252 (2), 1255 (2), 1256 (2), 1257, 1269
81. Turner, H.T., *Manners and Household Expenses of England in the Thirteenth and Fifteenth Centuries*, pp.6, 11, 16, 19, 23, 29, 41
82. PRO E315-103, fol.112v (Wintney); *VCH*, vol.2, p.133 (Wherwell)
83. Liveing, p.83
84. *Reg. Woodlock*, p.762 (trans.)
85. Power, pp.316-7; Knowles, *Religious Orders in England*, vol.1, pp.280-3
86. Luce, *HFC Proc.*, vol.17 (1), p.39
87. Wintney Cal., fol.3v
88. *VCH*, vol.2, p.124
89. Knowles, vol.2, p.360
90. Reg. Langton, fol.65

91. Liveing, p.83; *Reg. Epist. Peckham*, vol.2, p.lxxii
92. *Reg. Epist. Peckham*, p.651 (trans.)
93. *VCH*, vol.2, p.150; *Register of John Morton*, vol.1, item 232 (ii).

Chapter Seven

  1. Thompson, A. Hamilton, *The English Clergy*, p.172
  2. Battiscombe, C.F., *The Relics of St. Cuthbert*, pp.375-432; Kendrick, T.D., *Anglo-Saxon Art*, pp.217-9
  3. Turner, H.T., *Manners and Household Expenses of England in the Thirteenth and Fifteenth Centuries*, p.18; MacGregor, P., *Odiham Castle, 1200-1500*, p.57
  4. *VCH*, vol.2, p.133
  5. Will of John de Inkepenne, 1361, in Himsworth, S., *Winchester College Muniments*, vol.3, p.1050
  6. Spence, C., *The Abbey Church of Romsey*, pp.64-5; also Walcott, Mackenzie, *The Minsters and Abbey Ruins of the United Kingdom*, p.75; Liveing, p.197. It was exhibited in Winchester in 1845
  7. BL Add.MS. 26.777, fols.132v-133
  8. *ibid.*, shield at fol. 134; Liveing, opp. pp.198, 202 illustrates both fireplace and embroidery. Other information about pall and powdered panel from Textiles and Dress Department at Victoria and Albert Museum. Vestments such as the copes were generally preserved by recusant families.
  9. Morton, J., *The Nun's Rule, being the Ancren Riwle Modernised*, p.318
 10. Power, p.255
 11. *ibid.*, pp.315, 322-3
 12. *Cal. Lib. Rolls, 1240-5*, p.278
 13. *VCH*, vol.2, p.133
 14. Liveing, p.195
 15. *Cal. Ch. Rolls, 1257-1300*, p.257
 16. *Reg. Woodlock*, p.762
 17. *Cal. Pap. Reg. (Letters)*, vol.6, p.55
 18. Thompson, S., 'The Problem of the Cistercian Nuns', *Medieval Women*, pp.246-7
 19. Morton, J., p.318
 20. Douie, D.L., *Archbishop Pecham*, p.156
 21. *Reg. Woodlock*, p.517 (trans.)
 22. Luce, *HFC Proc.*, vol.17 (1), p.37
 23. Will of William Thornton, 1504, HRO WR1, fol.145
 24. Will of Sir William Bonevyle, 1409: Hingeston-Randolph, *Register of Bishop Stafford of Exeter* (1886), p.392; Will of Thomas Naile, 1505: HRO WR1, fols.323-4
 25. Chaucer, Geoffrey, *Canterbury Tales*, Prologue
 26. Liveing, p.244
 27. Morton, J., p.316
 28. Chaucer, *Canterbury Tales*, Prologue
 29. *Reg. Epistolarum Peckham*, p.660; Power, pp.306-7
 30. Luce, *HFC Proc.*, vol.17 (1), p.42
 31. *Cal. Cl. Rolls, 1247-51*, p.417; *ibid., 1264-68*, p.88 (Winchester); *ibid., 1288-96*, p.178 (Romsey)
 32. Marginal illustration in Bodleian MS. 264, fol.22
 33. Warton, Thos., *History of English Poetry*, (ed.) W.C. Hazlitt, vol.2, p.231. This cites the payment made to the boys in a mutilated fragment of a compotus of St. Swithun's for 1441. (Wharton (1728-90) was a brother of Joseph Wharton, headmaster of Winchester College.)
 34. Reg. Stratford, fol.177 (trans.)
 35. *Reg. Asserio*, pp.xxv, 418-9, 576. For Winchester processions see Keene, *W.S.2*, pp.128-9
 36. Luce, *HFC Proc.*, vol.17 (1), p.35
 37. Reg. Wykeham, vol.2, fols.65v ff (orig. MS.); *Reg. Wykeham*, vol.2, p.158
 38. Hardy, T.D., *A Description of the Patent Rolls, with an Itinerary of King John*
 39. Gough, Henry, *Itinerary of King Edward I*, vol.1, p.43. Liveing, p.71 suggests that his visit may have been for the consecration of the Lady Chapel

40. *Cal. Cl. Rolls, 1330-3*, p.403; *Cal. of Signet Letters of Henry IV and Henry V*, p.153; Byrne, M. St. Clare,(ed.), *Lisle Letters*, vol.2, p.589
41. *Cal. Pat. Rolls, 1232-47*, p.442
42. *Reg. Wykeham*, vol.2, pp.162-3
43. *Cal. Cl. Rolls, 1339-41*, p.236 (order dated 16 July 1339)
44. Liveing, p.195
45. *Cal. Pat. Rolls, 1467-77*, p.138; *VCH*, vol.2, pp.123-4
46. *Reg. Epist. Peckham*, vol.2, p.653
47. *Reg. Wykeham*, vol.2, pp.73-4; Power, p.401
48. *Reg. Epist. Peckham*, vol.2, p.663
49. *Reg. Pontissara*, pp.xxxiii, 546; Reg. Stratford, fol.176; *HFC, Proc.*, vol.17 (1), p.41
50. *Reg. Epist. Peckham*, vol.2, pp.652, 664; Power, pp.407-8
51. Liveing, pp.84, 165; *Reg. Epist. Peckham*, vol.2, p.653
52. *Reg. Wykeham*, vol.2, p.7
53. *Reg. Woodlock*, pp.325, 527
54. Reg. Stratford, fol.177
55. *Reg. Edington*, vol.2, items 449, 450
56. *Cal. Pat. Rolls, 1374-7*, pp.222, 295; *1377-81*, p.314; *1381-5*, p.122
57. *Reg. Woodlock*, pp.529, 759
58. *Reg. Epist. Peckham*, vol.2, p.653
59. *VCH*, vol.2, p.130
60. *ibid.*, p.124
61. Byrne, *Lisle Letters*, vol.3, letters 537, 539; vol.5, letter 1226. For schoolgirls in nunneries see Power, chap. 6
62. Luce, *HFC Proc.*, vol.17 (1), p.39
63. *Reg. Epist. Peckham*, vol.1, pp.265-6; vol.2, p.664
64. Power, p.373
65. Turner, H.T., *Manners and Household Expenses of England . . .* , p.6
66. *Reg. Pontissara*, p.127; *Reg. Woodlock*, p.528
67. Liveing, p.218
68. Reg. Stratford, fol.176
69. *ibid.*, fol.177 (trans.).

Chapter Eight

1. Liveing, pp.236-7. Voting lists for 1478 and 1523
2. Keene, *W.S.2*, pp.394-5
3. *Reg. Epist. Peckham*, vol.2, pp.652, 663
4. Labarge, M.W., *Women in Medieval Life*, pp.169-171; Jones, P.M., *Medieval Medical Miniatures*, pp.33-4, 124 (illumin. showing a lady 'cupping').
5. Liveing, pp.100, 103
6. *Reg. Woodlock*, pp.518, 522/11
7. *ibid.*, pp.529/11 (Romsey), 762 (Wintney)
8. *VCH*, vol.2, p.133; Wherwell Cart., fol.43v
9. Wherwell Cart., fols.121v-122, ch. 259. Four marks were from Inkpen and one from Fullerton
10. PRO E315-494, fols.13 (Winchester), 19 (Wherwell)
11. Knowles, *Religious Orders in England*, vol.2, p.360
12. Power, pp.361 n.2, 344. There was a lepers' hospital at Romsey, *Reg. Sandale*, p.268
13. *Reg. Edington*, vol.2, item 166; vol.1, pp.xii-xiii; Gasquet, F.A., *The Great Pestilence*, pp.107-9; Liveing, pp.119-21; Ziegler, P., *The Black Death*, pp.144-5
14. Gasquet, pp.108-9
15. *ibid.*
16. Ziegler, p.145. See also Shrewsbury, J.F.D., *A History of Bubonic Plague in the British Isles*, pp.90-1
17. It is now in the south aisle. Dr. Latham's drawing of it is in Liveing, opp. p.120

18. *Cal. Pat. Rolls, 1348-50*, pp.278, 285, 296; *Reg. Edington*, vol.1, items 514, 554; vol.2, item 214
19. *ibid.*, vol.1, items 611, 619, 663
20. *Cal. Pat. Rolls, 1348-50*, p.297
21. *Reg. Edington*, vol.1, item 632. The more likely reason for the scribe writing Gervaise is that he may have had before him the previous episcopal record for the priory which was the bishop's presentation to it of Isabella, daughter of Roger Gervais (item 289). It was also the name of the new abbess of Romsey.
22. Liveing, pp.112-13
23. Shrewsbury, p.145
24. *Reg. Woodlock*, p.528/8
25. Reg. Fox, vol.4, fol.20v
26. Information from Winchester Archaeology Office
27. *Reg. Woodlock*, pp.517, 521
28. *ibid.*, p.529
29. Luce, *HFC Proc.*, vol.17 (1), p.35
30. *Reg. Woodlock*, pp.758-9 (trans.)
31. Power, chap.11
32. *Reg. Wykeham*, vol.2, p.395; *VCH*, vol.4, pp.289-90
33. *Reg. Wykeham*, vol.2, p.437
34. *ibid.*, p.498, dated from Wolvesey 12 April 1400
35. *VCH*, vol.2, p.150
36. *Reg. Wykeham*, vol.2, p.556
37. *Cal. Pap. Reg. (Letters)*, vol.6, p.55
38. *ibid.*, p.485. The prioress was called Joan and the diocese Lincoln
39. Reg. Beaufort, vol.1, f.50+ (trans.)
40. Reg. Waynflete, vol.1, fols.58v-59
41. *ibid.*, fol.33* (trans.)
42. *ibid.*, fols.102v-103. The other three were Johanna Fabyan (sub-prioress), Johanna Taylard and Agnes Lymbroke
43. Reg. Langton, fols.51-2
44. *Reg. Woodlock*, pp.437-8
45. *ibid.*, pp.606-7, 610-11. Her election had been disputed because it was uncanonical but she was later appointed by Bishop Woodlock.
46. Reg. Stratford, fol.56
47. *ibid.*, fol.57v (trans.)
48. *ibid.*, fol.79 (trans.)
49. Reg. Orleton, vol.1, fol.10v. His visitation was held on 9 November 1334 (not 9 April as in *VCH*, vol.2, p.124)
50. *ibid.*, fol.29v. The commission was not dated but January 1336 has been suggested by R.M. Haines in *The Church and Politics in Fourteenth Century England*, p.75, n.105, and in 'Adam Orleton and the Diocese of Winchester', *Journal of Ecclesiastical History*, vol.23 (1972), p.12 n.4; p.11 for M. John de Usk.
51. *ibid.*, fol.41
52. *ibid.*, fol.54v – on 15 May 1337
53. *Cal. Pat. Rolls, 1334-8*, p.546
54. *Cat. Pat. Rolls, 1367-70*, p.353. Commission of oyer and terminer on the complaint of the abbess dated 20 Jan. 1369
55. *Reg. Wykeham*, vol.2, pp.100-2
56. *ibid.*, pp.114-5; Power, p.451
57. *Reg. Wykeham*, vol.2, pp.360-2
58. *ibid.*, p.469
59. *Cal. Pat. Rolls, 1313-17*, p.281
60. *ibid.*, p.327
61. *ibid.*, p.403. 'intoxicated' should read 'poisoned'.
62. *Reg. Woodlock*, p.629. Translated summary in Liveing, p.92
63. *Reg. Edington*, vol.2, item 114

64. *Reg. Wykeham*, vol.2, pp.77-9
65. Liveing, pp.211-26
66. *Cal. Pap. Reg. (Letters)*, vol.13, pp.803-4
67. Power, p.361 n.1
68. Liveing, p.219
69. *ibid.*, pp.225, 236
70. Reg. Fox, vol.2, fol.42v; Liveing, pp.228-9
71. Reg. Fox, vol.2, fol.41v; Liveing, p.228
72. Reg. Fox, vol.5, fol.55v lists her among those tacitly professed, but the list in Liveing, p.237, incorrectly puts her among the fully professed.
73. Reg. Fox, vol.4, fol.80; Liveing, pp.245-7.

Chapter Nine

1. Wherwell: *Cal. Pat. Rolls, 1327-30*, p.468; *1330-4*, p.72; Cartulary: chs. 78-9, 295; also fols.215, 216v Romsey: *Cal. Pat. Rolls, 1301-7*, p.527; *1334-8*, p.223 (fines: £20 for each month of interregnum) Winchester: *Cal. Pat. Rolls, 1401-5*, p.491 (fine: 10 marks); *ibid., 1461-7*, p.383, confirmed 1527 (fine: £5 for first month, 50s. for each succeeding month)
2. Froyle and Urchfont by St. Mary's Abbey; Itchen Stoke and the co-portion of St. Laurence by Romsey Abbey; Herriard by Wintney Priory
3. Wherwell Cart., chs. 54-7, fols.39-43 (n.d. but Nicholas de Talemarche was prebendary at the time and he occurs in 1350 (*Cal. Pat. Rolls, 1348-50*, p.564)
4. Deposition by the late prioress of Wintney. PRO E178-2018
5. Himsworth, *Winchester College Muniments*, vol.3, p.1050
6. Keene, *W.S.2*, p.129
7. Will of John Burgess, 1521, HRO Bp; Thomas Faukes: Himsworth, *Winchester College Muniments*, vol.2, pp.556-7 (will proved 8 May 1490)
8. Wherwell Cart., ch.452, fol.193v (n.d. but in the time of Abbess Euphemia)
9. Liveing, pp.163-4
10. Will of John Cornyshe, 1503, HRO WR1, fol.149. Translated literally the bequest was 'a pair of beads with 60 *Aves* bound in gold'; this means a rosary consisting of six decades of *Ave Marias*
11. Will of William Howell, 1504, HRO WR1, fol.138; Will of John Burgess, 1521, HRO Bp
12. Will of Henry Sewghell, 1508, HRO WR1, fol.374
13. Will of Ralph Hall, 1518, HRO Bp. The five communities were St. Swithun's Priory, the Holy Ghost chapel at Basingstoke, the brotherhood of Alresford, Netley Abbey and the Observants of Southampton.
14. Will of Gilbert Stanton, 1522, HRO Bp
15. Farrer, William, *An Outline Itinerary of King Henry I*, pp.41, 47
16. Reg. Stratford, fol.176v (trans.)
17. Luce, *HFC Proc.*, vol.17 (1), p.40. Injunction only to Romsey
18. Royal College of Physicians MS. 409, fol.144.
19. Keene, *W.S.2*, p.195
20. *ibid.*, p.199
21. Inquisition certificate: PRO SC12-33/27
22. Dyer, C., *Lords and Peasants in a Changing Society*, pp.51-2
23. The status of this office increased in time; c.1525 abbess Aveline Cowdrey of Wherwell granted it to her brother John who lived at Wherwell. Wherwell Cart., fol.199
24. Dyer, pp.64-6; Harvey, P.D.A., *Manorial Records*, pp.5-6
25. Harvey, P.D.A., *Manorial Records of Cuxham*, pp.21-2
26. Listed with others for Urchfont and one for Timsbury in *Index to Charters and Rolls in the British Museum*, vol.2, p.800
27. BL Add.Ch., 17457
28. BL Add.Ch., 13339
29. *Serviens* has been variously translated. J.S. Drew found *ballivus* and *serviens* used indiscriminately to describe a bailiff: 'Manorial Accounts of St. Swithun's Priory, Winchester', *English Historical Review*,

vol.62 (1947), p.22 n.3. Prof. Harvey has suggested 'servant' or 'official' rather than 'sergeant' which has also been used. Harvey, *Manorial Records*, p.6

30. BL Add.Ch., 17477, dated 26-7 Abbess A(gnes). Prof. Harvey suggests Michaelmas 1235-6 as the first accounting year of Abbess Agnes: *Manorial Records of Cuxham*, p.22 n.28. This has been followed. Agnes became abbess in June 1236, *Cal Pat. Rolls, 1232-47*, pp.147-9

31. HRO 19 M 61 – 550

32. Hare, J.N., 'The Monks as Landlords, The Leasing of the Monastic Demesnes in Southern England', in Barron and Harper-Bill (eds.), *The Church in Pre-Reformation Society*, pp.85-6, 89

33. Blatcher, M., *Bath, Longleat, vol.4: Seymour Papers*, HMC, 58, pp. 320-1

34. BL Add.Ch., 17514 rot.1 (1425); rot.2 (1430); rots. 2-5. By 1453 Thomas atte Mere was lessee.

35. Hockey, S.F., *Insula Vecta*, p.66

36. In 1208 the abbess of Wherwell paid 40s. to secure her discharge from having to attend court: *Pipe Roll 10 John*, N.S., vol.23, p.117

37. Inq.P.M. of Richard de Wyndesore who owed suit at Froyle, *Cal. Inq. P.M.*, vol.12, pp.153-4

38. Liveing, p.194

39. BL Add.Ch., 17519

40. Maitland, F.W., *Select Pleas in Manorial and other Seignorial Courts*, Selden Society (1889), p.183. The abbess of Romsey also held the franchise of the Hundred Court of Whorwelsdown, Wilts.; a commentary and the pleas for the court held in June 1262 are on pp.176-82. Liveing, pp.151-3

41. *Cal. Pat. Rolls, 1467-77*, p.138; *1441-6*, pp.153, 180

42. Harvey, *Manorial Records*, p.47; pp.44-8 for manorial courts generally

43. *Cal. Pat. Rolls, 1258-66*, p.276; *Cal. Inq. Misc.*, vol.1, item 275

44. *Cal. Inq. Misc.*, vol.7, item 189

45. *ibid.*, vol.3, item 1033

46. *Cal. Pat. Rolls, 1381-5*, pp.488-9

47. *Cal. Ch. Rolls*, vol.6, p.273

48. *Cal. Ch. Rolls*, vol.2, pp.102, 104. The fair was to be 15 days from the feast of St. Denis (9 October)

49. *ibid.*, p.179. They also had a grant for a market and fair at Steeple Ashton, *ibid.*, vol.3, p.128

50. Fair granted 12 April 1215. *Rott. Litt. Claus, 1204-24*, (Close rolls) p.194; Wherwell Cart., chs. 182, 238; Market granted 3 May 1267, *Cal. Ch. Rolls*, vol.2, p.75

51. *Cal. Cl. Rolls, 1227-31*, p.55

52. Reg. Orleton, vol.1, fol.62v (trans.), (n.d. but previous entry 1338)

53. *Valor Ecclesiasticus*, vol.2, p.1 lists them all: Bishop of Winchester, Sir Richard Lyster, Sir Thomas Lysle, Sir William Berkeley, Richard Andrews, George Poulet, Robert Bager – mayor of Winchester, Harry Huttoft – mayor of Southampton, Thomas Haydok, John Ringwood, John Milles, Thomas Wellis, Thomas Pace, Nicholas Ticheborne and William Hawles.

54. *L. and P.*, vol.8 (1535), item 654

55. Knowles, *Religious Orders in England*, vol.3, pp.244-7

56. Savine, A., 'English Monasteries on the Eve of the Dissolution', in P. Vinogradoff (ed.), *Oxford Studies in Social and Legal History*, p.98

57. *Valor Ecclesiasticus*, pp.4, 16, 7, 13 respectively.

Chapter Ten

1. PRO SC6-981-21; Liveing, p.195

 2. *Cal. Cl. Rolls, 1227-31*, p.169

 3. *ibid.*, p.344; *1251-3*, p.299

 4. *ibid.*, *1247-51*, p.481; *1254-6*, p.256

 5. *ibid.*, *1268-72*, pp.79-80, 451

 6. *ibid.*, *1231-4*, p.47

 7. *ibid.*, *1227-31*, p.483

 8. *ibid.*, *1247-51*, p.464; *1251-3*, p.295

 9. *ibid.*, *1251-3*, p.375

10. *ibid.*, *1268-72*, p.448

11. Information from Mr. K. Stubbs
12. *Cal. Cl. Rolls, 1247-51*, p.434
13. On 4 October 1234. Wintney Cal., fol.158v
14. Holt, N.R., *The Pipe Roll of the Bishopric of Winchester, 1210-11*, pp.41-2
15. *Cal. Cl. Rolls, 1231-4*, p.372; *1247-51*, pp.168, 392; *1254-6*, p.252; *1256-8*, p.15
16. *ibid., 1272-9*, p.391
17. *ibid., 1254-6*, p.252
18. *ibid., 1251-3*, p.69; *Cal. Lib. Rolls, 1245-51*, p.366
19. *VCH*, vol.2, pp.132-3, from which all quotations are taken. Wherwell Cart., ch.59, fols.43v-44v
20. *Cal. Pap. Reg. (Petitions)*, vol.1, p.230
21. *Cal. Pat. Rolls, 1467-77*, p.138
22. Harper-Bill, 'Register of John Morton' (Ph.D. thesis), p.432
23. PRO E315-400, fol.26
24. Keene, *W.S.2*, pp.129, 195-6, 231
25. *Reg. Wykeham*, vol.2, p.549
26. Will of John Cornyshe, 1503, HRO WR1, fol.149
27. Harvey, J.H., 'Had Winchester Cathedral a Central Spire?',*Winchester Cathedral Record*, no.27 (1958), pp.9-13. Sketch: BL MS. Royal 13 A iii, fol.17v
28. In a letter to the author, 3 April 1984
29. *Cal. Cl. Rolls, 1354-60*, p.102
30. Luce, *HFC Proc.*, vol.17 (1), pp.40-1
31. *Medieval Archaeology*, vol.18 (1974), p.189
32. *VCH*, vol.2, p.130
33. *Cal. Pap. Reg. (Letters)*, vol.5, p.71
34. HRO 19 M 61 /149
35. Salzman, L.F., *Building in England down to 1540*, p.492. (p.52 is misleading in referring to 'Hartley Wintney church'; the work was at the priory church, not the parish church.)
36. Wintney Cal., fol.157v
37. *Cal. Pat. Rolls, 1467-77*, p.138
38. *Magnus Rotulus Scaccarii [exchequer] de anno 31 Henry I* (1833), pp.23, 41, 121, 125
39. *Pipe Roll, 5 Henry II*, (Pipe Roll Soc.), vol.1, p.46
40. *Pipe Roll, 13 Henry II*, vol.11, p.179
41. *Pipe Roll, 2 John*, N.S., vol.12, p.201. 40 marks = £26 13s. 4d., 10 marks = £6 13s. 4d.
42. *Pipe Roll, 5 John*, N.S., vol.16, p.148
43. Power, *Medieval English Nunneries*, p.185
44. *Cal. Cl. Rolls, 1259-61*, p.194; *1261-4*, pp.305, 379
45. Liveing, p.97
46. *Cal. Cl. Rolls, 1339-41*, pp.215, 217
47. *Cal. Inq. Misc.*, vol.2, p.444
48. Lawrence, C.H., 'The Thirteenth Century' in (ed.) C.H. Lawrence, *The English Church and the Papacy in the Middle Ages*, p.134
49. *Cal. Pat. Rolls, 1292-1301*, pp.97, 262; *1301-7*, p.453
50. Lawrence, pp.134-5
51. Lunt, W.E. and Graves, E.B., *Accounts rendered by Papal Collectors in England, 1317-78*
52. *ibid.*, pp.144, 189, 216, 229, 259, 270, 326, 366
53. *Reg. Wykeham*, vol.2, pp.437-8
54. Reg. Beaufort, vol.1, fols.10-11
55. Scarisbrick, J.J., 'Clerical Taxation in England, 1485-1547', *Journal of Ecclesiastical History*, vol.11 (1960), p.45
56. *L. and P.*, vol.3 (2), item 2483
57. Wherwell Cart., ch.61, fol.45
58. Haines, R.M., 'Adam Orleton and the Diocese of Winchester', *J. Eccles. Hist.*, vol.23 (1972), p.22 n.9
59. Allen, P.S. and H.M., *Letters of Richard Fox, 1486-1527*, p.151
60. Haines, p.21
61. Reg. Beaufort, vol.1, fol.14

62. Greatrex, J., *The Register of the Common Seal*, p.108
63. *Reg. Gardiner*, pp.63-4; PRO E315-101, fol.40
64. Hockey, S.F., *The Beaulieu Cartulary*, pp.254-5
65. *Reg. Pontissara*, p.299
66. *Reg. Woodlock*, p.916; *Cal. Pat. Rolls, 1292-1301*, p.267; *Reg. Asserio*, p.598. Abbess of Romsey given protection in 1297. *Cal. Cl. Rolls, 1296-1302*, p.88
67. *Cal. Cl. Rolls, 1339-41*, p.510
68. *Reg. Wykeham*, vol.2, pp.479, 553; *Cal. Pat. Rolls, 1422-9*, p.6
69. Reg. Waynflete, vol.2, fols. 1, 3, 9v-10, 21v
70. Reg. Courtenay, fol.34; Reg. Langton, fol.61
71. *Reg. Woodlock,*, pp.518, 522
72. Luce, *HFC Proc.*, vol.17 (1), p.36
73. Will of William Howell, 1504, HRO WR1, fols.138-9. The garments were called *camisea* for the men and *interula* for the women
74. PRO E315-400, fol.31
75. In 1401. Himsworth, *Winchester College Muniments*, vol.3, item 1346
76. Carpenter Turner, B., *Winchester*, pp.50, 92
77. PRO E315-446, fol.7a; *L. and P.*, vol.19 (2), item 800 (24)
78. Liveing, p.204
79. PRO E315-446, fol.8
80. *ibid.*, fol.1; Liveing, p.272
81. In 1542 the rector was granted the pension and another £6 2s. 0d. in compensation for the value of the board etc. *Reg. Gardiner*, pp.69-70. This supports the suggestion that St. Peter's originated as an oratory within the precincts of the abbey. Keene, *W.S.2*, p.112
82. *Cal. Cl. Rolls, 1409-13*, p.113; *1447-54*, p.112
83. *L. and P.*, vol.2 (2), item 4031
84. *ibid.*, vol.4 (2), item 3213 (3)
85. *Cal. Cl. Rolls, 1389-92*, p.494; *1441-7*, pp.345, 409
86. *ibid., 1307-13*, pp.581-2
87. *ibid., 1327-30*, p.393
88. *ibid., 1385-9*, pp.158, 254
89. *ibid., 1307-13*, pp. 267, 328
90. Liveing, p.195 gives 'on his return from the Holy Land', but the original does not state that: PRO SC6-981-21.
91. *Valor Ecclesiasticus*, vol.2, p.142; PRO SC6-Henry VIII-3327m.3
92. *VCH*, vol.3, p.368. Chantry certificate: PRO E301-52-6
93. Liveing, p.195
94. *Reg. Epist. Peckham*, vol.2, p.652
95. Power, p.201 n.2
96. Keene, *W.S.2*, vol.2, pp.660-1, 1249
97. *ibid.*, pp.533, 1287
98. *ibid.*, vol.1, p.52 n.7. Date: 1396
99. Noted without details by Baigent: BL Add.MS. 39977, fol.317
100. Winchester City Archives, HRO W/D1-61
101. *ibid.*, W/D1-71. For Baynham and Broker: Keene, *W.S.2*, vol.2, pp.1157, 1175
102. *Curia Regis Rolls*, vols. 1-16
103. *Cal. Cl. Rolls, 1247-51*, pp.359-60; *1251-3*, p.480; *1272-9*, p.353
104. *Cal. Inq. P.M.*, vol.14, item 64
105. *Cal. Cl. Rolls, 1227-31*, p.40
106. Wherwell Cart., chs.405 (1242), 407 (1279)
107. *Reg. Pontissara*, pp.xli-xlii, 804-21, 830-5. There was another dispute about the prebend in 1400, *Cal. Pap. Reg. (Letters)*, vol.5
108. *Reg. Woodlock*, p.940
109. Knowles, *Religious Orders in England*, vol.1, pp.55-7; vol.2, pp.309-10
110. *Reg. Pontissara*, p.126

111. *ibid.*, p.125
112. *ibid.*, pp.xxxv, 112
113. Reg. Stratford, fol.176v
114. *Reg. Pontissara*, pp.xxxiv, 126
115. *Reg. Epist. Peckham*, vol.2, pp.654-5
116. Wherwell Cart., fols.208v-9; sacrist ch.24 is an inspeximus of the sacrist's income of £3 12s. 10d.
117. Liveing, pp.194-5. The totals of each section have been checked and are correct, as in PRO SC6-981-21
118. Account rolls for Wherwell and Romsey: both PRO SC6-983-34. John de London, fl. 1316, is recorded in Keene *W.S.2*, vol.2, p.1286
119. *HMC, Various Collections*, vol.4, p.155
120. *VCH*, vol.2, pp.124, 130, 135, 151
121. *Pipe Rolls*, vols.37-8, N.S. vols.1-2 (1186-92)
122. Wherwell Cart., ch.61, fol.45
123. *ibid.*, chs. 165, fol.89; 248, fol.118v-119
124. *ibid.*, ch.179, fol.93
125. *ibid.*, ch.415, fols.175v-176. The Italians were Aldebrand Aldebrandini and Rayner Bonacurpi
126. *ibid.*, ch.416, fol.176
127. Reg. Stratford, fol.111
128. *Cal. Pat. Rolls, 1338-40*, p.296
129. *Cal. Pat. Rolls, 1401-5*, p.76
130. *Reg. Wykeham*, vol.1, p.164; vol.2, p.593. It has been assumed that John Segefeld and John Sethfelde are the same man.

Chapter Eleven

1. Dickens, A.G. and Carr, D. (eds.), *The Reformation in England*, pp.46-68 for a summary of the legislation. As women the nuns did not have to take any oaths.
2. Muller, J.A. (ed.), *The Letters of Stephen Gardiner*, pp.xxv-xxviii
3. *L. and P.*, vol.9 (1535), item 344 (from Wherwell); *ibid.*, item 424 (from Wintney)
4. *L. and P.*, vol.7 (1534), items 528-9, 907; and see *ibid.*, vol.9, p.142 dating letters to 1535
5. *L. and P.*, vol.7, item 527. The letter is not dated but as it was from Wherwell it was presumably written at the time of Dr. Legh's visit in September 1535
6. *L. and P.*, vol.9 (1535), item 439. Congé: item 504 (4). Assent: *ibid.*, items 504 (15), 729 (5)
7. BL MS. Cotton Vespasian, F.xiii, fol.178. The Marquess of Exeter was himself a grandson of Edward IV through his mother Catherine. He later fell foul of Cromwell and was executed in 1538
8. PRO SP1-96-230; *L. and P.*, vol.9, item 423. Cromwell later decided that none over the age of 20 were to be compelled to go, Knowles, *Religious Orders in England*, vol.3, p.282
9. *L. and P.*, vol.9, item 139
10. Richardson, W.C., *History of the Court of Augmentations*, pp.49, 55, 81-2
11. Survey of St. Mary's: PRO E315-400, fols.26-35, 42; Schedule: PRO SC12-33/27
12. PRO E315-400, fol.26
13. Byrne, M. St. Clare, *The Lisle Letters*, vol.3, item 714
14. Youings, J., *The Dissolution of the Monasteries*, p.220
15. PRO E315-400, fol.42
16. *L. and P.*, vol.10 (1536), item 1256 (6)
17. PRO E315-400, fol.27
18. *L. and P.*, vol.11 (1536), item 385 (20)
19. PRO E315-232, fol.35
20. PRO E315-400, fol.23a
21. PRO SC6-Henry VIII-7415-m.9v
22. *ibid.*, m.1
23. PRO E313-11-66; *L. and P.*, vol.12 (2) (1537), item 1150 (5)
24. Cook, G.H. (ed.), *Letters to Cromwell and others on the Suppression of the Monasteries*, pp.197-9. This letter was written on a Saturday but is otherwise undated. Mr. Cook attributes it to early September since

Pollard was in Reading by the 15th, in which case it was probably written on 7 September. Cheney, C.R., *A Handbook of Dates*, Table 15. This is a fortnight earlier than the date suggested in *L. and P.*, vol.13 (2), item 401

25. PRO E315-446, fol.7
26. *ibid.*, fols.6a-7a, 11-11a. One annuity was shared between three men.
27. *ibid.*, fol.3-6
28. PRO SP1-136, fol.126; *L. and P.*, vol.13 (2), item 352. Sir Richard Lyster was Chief Baron of the Exchequer. Besides the Stanbridge estate, his property in Hampshire lay in Southampton and included the great house that is now the Tudor House Museum. Platt, C., *Medieval Southampton*, p.249
29. Timmins, T.C.B., *The Register of John Chandler, Dean of Salisbury*, items 62, 279, 354. For Wolf Hall: Jackson, J.E., 'Wulfhall and the Seymours', *Wilts. Arch. and Nat. Hist. Magazine*, vol.15 (1875), pp.140-207
30. Their mother was Margaret Seymour, the second wife of Sir Nicholas Wadham; she was buried in the Priory church of St. Mary, Carisbrooke, I. o. W. She was the eldest daughter of John Seymour of Wolf Hall (1450-91) and his first wife, Elizabeth. St. Maur, H., *Annals of the Seymours*, pp.16-17. Pedigree of 1576 at Longleat House. Liveing, p.259 is incorrect. It is possible that another nun at Romsey, Elizabeth Hill, may have been related to the Wadham sisters since their father's first wife, Joan, had been the daughter of Robert Hill of Wiltshire.
31. BL MS. Royal 7.C.xvi, fols.147-8. Liveing , p.253 transcribed the names of the 26 nuns; those listed 7th-9th should read: Jane Rensall, Agnes Pottenall, Alys Gorphyn; 12th, Elysabeth Hyll; 17th, Bone Pownde.
32. *L. and P.*, vol.14 (1) (1539), p.75, no.38, dated 27 Jan.
33. PRO E328-389 (in poor condition); recited in SC6-Henry VIII-3341-mm.66-7
34. PRO E315-442, fols.8v-9
35. PRO SP1-140, fol.218; *L. and P.*, vol.13 (2) item 1175. Dr. Layton did not date his letter, but Cromwell's office marked it 'Anno xxx' (i.e. 22 April 1538-21 April 1539). Thus, either it was written early in 1539, in which case Dr. Layton may well have been the commissioner who took the surrender of the abbey, or it was written the previous year. In 1538 he had been in Hampshire to take the surrenders of Beaulieu Abbey (2 April) and Southwick Priory (7 April) but after that there is no reason to suppose he was in the county for the rest of the year.
36. *L. and P.*, vol.14 (1), item 906 (1)
37. PRO E315-236, fol.143, dated 18 Jan. 1546
38. Jacka, H.T., 'The Dissolution of the English Nunneries' (M.A. thesis), p.118
39. Baskerville, G., *English Monks and the Suppression of the Monasteries*, p.222. The original HMC calendar of Seymour Papers was made by Baskerville but there is no mention of any Romsey pensions in Blatcher, *Bath, Longleat vol.4: Seymour Papers 1532-1686*, HMC. Earlier Baskerville included Sir Thomas Seymour in his list of private payers of monastic pensions in 'The Dispossessed Religious after the Suppression of the Monasteries' in (ed.) H.W.C. Davis, *Essays in History*, p.444 n.2. The only Romsey reference he cites has been searched without result.
40. PRO E315-494, fols.1-21. St. Mary's, fols.11-15; Wherwell fols.17-21. See Appendix 5
41. *DNB*. Although Southwell was knighted in 1537 he is called 'esquier' in PRO E315-494, fol.1
42. PRO E315-494, fols.15, 20-1
43. *ibid.*, fols.11-12, 14, 17-18, 20. Also E315-234, fols.213b-220

Chapter Twelve

1. Byrne, *Lisle Letters*, vol.5, pp.221-2
2. Atkinson, T., *Elizabethan Winchester*, p.107; Carpenter Turner, B., *Winchester*, p.92
3. Will of Elizabeth Shelley, 1547, HRO Bp. no.98
4. 1536: PRO E315-400, fol.31; 1539: E315-494, fol.12
5. PRO E315-446, fol.1; Liveing, p.272
6. PRO E315-494, fols. 14, 20

7. PRO E315-236, fol.143. His title by then was Lord St. John; he became Marquess of Winchester in 1551. The Court of Augmentations' decree (4 March 1540) awarding him an annuity for his stewardship of Wherwell Abbey survives with the seal, HRO 19 M 61 – 553
8. PRO E164-31, fol.11
9. PRO E315-446, fols.6a, 10-11
10. Confirmation of office, 21 April 1540, which recites the grant under seal of 18 Jan. 1539, PRO E315-95, fol.62
11. PRO E315-446, fols.7, 11
12. PRO E164-31, fol.11r, v
13. PRO SC6-Henry VIII-7415-m.8v
14. PRO E315-103, fols.112v-113
15. 1536: PRO E315-400, fol.32 (corrodians), fol.26 records Thomas Lee, auditor, and Thomas Legh, receiver. Custody in 1539: E315-494, fol. 13. Paul, J., 'Dame Elizabeth Shelley', *HFC Proc.*, vol.23 (1965), p.66
16. Will of Elizabeth Shelley, see above n.3; will and inv. of Morpheta Kingsmill, 1570, HRO Bp. no.251; will of Elizabeth Martyn, 1587, Wilts. R.O. Reg. fol.147, and inventory
17. Inventory: HRO D2/A/1/134
18. PRO E315-212, fol.133
19. PRO E315-494, fol.19
20. see above n.16. This will, but not the inventory, was printed in *Notes and Queries for Somerset and Dorset*, vol.3 (1892-3), pp.55-6
21. It is of Mary Gore, d.1436, and is in the centre aisle of St. Andrew's church.
22. Paul, J., 'Dame Elizabeth Shelley', *HFC Proc.*, vol.23, p.70, quotes his will
23. *ibid.*, quoted from a college inventory of 1 Dec. 1556
24. Will of 'Edboro' Stratford, HRO. An unproved copy of the will and inventory is dated 1551 (Unclassified, 1551, no.185-6); the proved copies of both are filed for 1552 (Unclassified, no.61-2). She died at Winchester on 23 March 1551, and Jane Gainsford on 2 November 1551. PRO E101-76-15, fol.11v. Will of Agnes Badgecroft, 1556, HRO Bp. with inventory; will of Jane Wayte, 1565, HRO Bp. no.119
25. Keene, *W.S.2*, item 824
26. Will of Dame Alice Harwarde, 1553, HRO Unclassified, no.100
27. Will of Joan Frye, 1548, HRO Bp. no.28 with inventory which lists a few haberdashery items in the shop
28. *L. and P.*, vol.16 (1541), item 947 (25); Liveing, p.255
29. Letter from Foster to Cromwell, 18 June [1539?]: BL MS. Cotton Cleop. E.4, fol.140; Wright, T., *Three Chapters of Letters relating to the Suppression of the Monasteries*, pp.160-1
30. see above n.28
31. Ecclesiastical Visitation of Hampshire, 1543, BL Add. MS.12483
32. PRO E315-220, fol.183
33. PRO E164-31, fol.11. The sum comprised his fee as receiver of £20 3s. 4d. and annuities of £23 6s. 8d. and £7 12s. 0d.
34. Liveing, p.257. There is an entry for Foster in *Alumni Oxon.*
35. 1552: PRO E101-76-15; 1553: E164-31, fols.11-12. For some reason the pensions of Agnes Badgecroft, Mary Martyn and Cecily Gaynesford were administered separately in the 1540s. *L. and P.*, vol. 17, pp.131-3 for 1541; later entries for 1542-7
36. PRO E101-76-15, fol.11r, v
37. Knowles, *The Religious Orders*, vol.3, p.407
38. see above n.16. There is also a note in the inventory of Agnes Badgecroft (1556) that 31s. had been received for her pension; and one would like to know some details about her 'certain old books and other older trupery' that were assessed at 3s. 6d.
39. see above n.24; the debt appears in both her inventories
40. see above n.16
41. Kennedy, J., 'Laymen and Monasteries in Hampshire, 1530-58', *HFC Proc.*, vol.27, pp.78ff for others
42. PRO SC6-Henry VIII-7415-mm.1, 8v-9v

43. Richard Hill also had the collectorship of the subsidy of the port of London, *L. and P.*, vol.10 (1536), item 870

44. Letter from Richard Paulet written from Herriard, n.d., PRO SP1-133-249; *L. and P.*, vol.13 (1) (1538), item 1292

45. Grant to Richard Hill and wife, dated 4 June 1538. PRO C66-678-16

46. Byrne, *Lisle Letters*, vol.5, p.452

47. PRO E315-442, f.2v

48. *L. and P.*, vol.15 (1540), item 498 (c.68).

49. Bill of complaint and answer of Thomas Ryggeby, clerk: PRO E321-1/85-82-3. For payment, see above n.47

50. Hurd, D.G.E., *Sir John Mason, 1503-66*, p.41

51. Information on barn and smaller building from Mr. Richard Warmington who surveyed them in 1973 and 1985. Mr. David Gorsky was the local historian who was briefly on the site during the construction of the M3.

52. 30-31 Henry VIII: PRO SC6-Henry VIII-3341-mm.60-6; 31-33 Henry VIII: PRO E315-446, fols.2-12; site: fols.4a-5

53. *L. and P.*, vol.21 (2), items 476 (85), 648 (62)

54. Foster: PRO E315-96, fols.113v-114; Seymour: E315-242. fol.88v; Fleming: *VCH*, vol.4, p.454

55. PRO E315-446, fols.5-5a. Both men paid 6s. 8d. p.a. Westbrook was granted a lease in Nov. 1545, *L. and P.*, vol.20 (1), item 1336

56. Valuation: PRO E315-204, fol.138; complaint: E321-19/82

57. *L. and P.*, vol.19 (2) (1544), item 800 (24)

58. PRO E315-446, fol.5a

59. Kitchin and Madge (eds.), *Documents relating to the Foundation of the Chapter of Winchester, 1541-1547*, H.R.S. (1889), p.98

60. PRO E315-442, fol.14v. Other bells were hung in the church later, Liveing, p.271

61. PRO E315-494, fol.13

62. PRO E315-212, fol.133

63. PRO E315-204, fol.137

64. PRO E315-494, fol.13

65. Particulars for grants: PRO E318-4-126 (14)

66. *L. and P.*, vol.21 (2) (1546), item 771 (37)

67. Carpenter Turner, *Winchester*, p.92

68. Muller, *The Letters of Stephen Gardiner*, p.219, (spelling modernised)

69. Williams, J.F., *The Early Churchwardens Accounts of Hampshire*, p.223. College: Carpenter Turner, *Winchester*, p.91

70. Camden, W., *Britannia*, ed. E. Gibson, vol.1, p.216

71. BL MS. Titus B.1, fol.471; *L. and P. Henry VIII*, vol.14 (2), items 425, 427

72. Kingsmill Papers, HRO 19 M 61-1301. Amongst the papers is a letter from Lord de la Warr to John Kingsmill addressing him as cousin (*ibid*.1298). Morpheta and Sir John Kingsmill were children of John Kingsmill, d.1509, one of the justices of the Court of Common Pleas

73. Letter from Antony Wayte to Lady Lisle, 9 Oct. 1534, Byrne, *Lisle Letters*, vol.2, 270. See also vol.1, pp.189, 469, 575

74. Cook, *Letters to Cromwell and others on the Suppression of the Monasteries*, pp.89-92. For Dec. 1538: Byrne, *Lisle Letters*, vol.5, pp.320-2

75. *L. and P.*, vol.14 (2) (1539), item 544

76. PRO SP1-155, fols.3-4; *L. and P.*, vol.14 (2), item 547

77. PRO C66-689-m.4; *L. and P.*, vol.15 (1540), item 436 (72). Accounts for 1543-7: PRO E315-446, fol.29. Prebend: *L. and P.*, vol.20 (1), p.677

78. Clutterbuck, *Notes on the Parishes of Fyfield, . . . and Wherwell*, pp.178-85, for genealogy and wills. *The Story of Boxgrove Priory* (on sale in the church) describes and illustrates the chantry

79. PRO E315-494, fol.19

80. *L. and P.*, vol.19 (2) (1544), item 328, p.171

81. Atkinson, T.D., 'Fragments of Architecture and Sculpture at Wherwell Church', *HFC Proc.*, vol.14 (3), (1940), pp.369-71. Early graves were found south of the garden gate when the Priory gardens were

altered this century, and in 1986 a small archaeological excavation in its grounds uncovered a 13th-14th century boundary ditch filled with building material fragments, including thick medieval slate. Report of Test Valley Archaeological Trust.
82. Based on information from Dr. John Harvey
83. BL Add. MS. 39977, fol.529.

References to Appendix 2

1. All 1291 valuations from *Taxatio Ecclesiastica of Pope Nicholas IV*, (1802)
2. All 1333-45 valuations from *Reg. Wykeham*, vol.1, p.xi and Appendix 1
3. All 1535 valuations from *Valor Ecclesiasticus*, vol.2, unless otherwise stated
4. For appropriation see also: *Cal. Pat. R., 1327-30*, p.499; *Cal. Pap. Reg. (Petitions)*,vol.1 p.122; Reg. Orleton, vol.1, fols.122v-3. From 1354 the abbess and convent paid the bishop of Winchester 6s. 8d. a year for their appropriation of Froyle (Reg. Beaufort, fol.14)
5. Wherwell Cartulary – BL MS. Egerton 2104a: ch.54, fols.39-40 for chaplains serving the two chapels; ch.446, fols.190v-1 for tithes
6. *ibid.*, ch.3, fols.17v-18; Dugdale, *Monasticon*, pp.638-9
7. as above n.6
8. Wherwell Cart., chs.190-1, 212, fols.98-9, 108v
9. *ibid.*, sacrist ch.7, fols.210v-2; sacrist chs.24-5. Also for Wallop: chs.194-5, sacrist ch.4
10. as above n.8
11. as above n.6
12. Wherwell Cart., sacrist ch.13, fols.204-5
13. *ibid.*, sacrist ch.5, fol.201
14. *ibid.*, chs.266-280, fols.124-8
15. as above n.8
16. as above n.6
17. as above n.6
18. as above n.6
19. Wherwell Cart., ch.231, fol.114v; Hockey, S.F., *Insula Vecta*, p.67
20. Wherwell Cart., ch.188, fol.97v
21. *ibid.*, ch.264, fols.123v-4; also for Collingbourne church: chs. 255, 258, 260-1, 265, 414-6
22. as above n.20
23. Wherwell Cart., ch.184, fol.96
24. *ibid.*, chs.185-7, fols.96-7
25. *ibid.*, ch.457, fol.196
26. *ibid.*, ch.352, fol.152
27. as above n.6
28. as above n.6
29. Wherwell Cart., ch.12, fols.24v-5; ch.189
30. as above n.23
31. as above n.24
32. as above n.6
33. Wherwell Cart., ch.259, fols.121v-2
34. *ibid.*, chs.66-7, 104, 107-9, 183
35. as above n.23
36. as above n.6
37. *Cal. Pat. Rolls, 1350-4*, p.59; *Cal. Cl. Rolls, 1354-60*, p.102
38. Presentation was made by both prebends in 1321; by the first with the consent of the second in 1334; by the first in 1349 (twice) and 1381. *Reg. Asserio*, p.452; Reg. Orleton, vol.2, fol.45v; Reg. Edington, vol.1, fols.54, 56v; *Reg. Wykeham*, vol.1, p.113
39. *Cal. Pat. Rolls, 1313-17*, p.642; *Reg. Sandale*, p.269
40. as above n.1
41. Prior Walter had previously been sub-prior of Hyde Abbey. He died at Wherwell Abbey and is commemorated in the Winchester Annals, *Annales Monastici*, vol.2, p.68; Knowles, Brooke and London, *Heads of Religious Houses*, p.29.

42. For Reginald Fitz Jocelin see Cheney, C., 'Two Mortuary Rolls from Canterbury' in (ed.), D. Greenway, C. Holdsworth and J. Sayers, *Tradition and Change* (1985), pp.108ff

43. After the Dissolution (n.d., post-1539) John Mason and his wife complained that this pension was no longer being paid. PRO E321-1/85-82, 83

44. PRO E178-2018. Two obits of priors of Southwick were entered in the Wintney Calendar, BL MS. Cotton Claud D iii, fols.157, 160v: Guy, who was prior by 1185 (Knowles, Brooke, London, *Heads of Religious Houses*, p.184) and Wakelin (d.1234)

45. The obit of Elias, abbot of Reading (1200-12) was in the Calendar (fol.153v) as one of the benefactors of the house.

46. The obit of John, prior of Newark, was entered in the Calendar (fol.162) as one of the benefactors of the house.

References to Appendix 3

1. All 1086 references from Domesday Book, Phillimore editions
2. All 1291 valuations from *Taxatio Ecclesiastica of Pope Nicholas IV*
3. Ministers' Accounts (temporal income only):

St. Mary's Abbey:	PRO SC6-Henry VIII-	3342-mm.65-75
Wherwell Abbey:	,, ,, ,, ,,	mm.81-90
Romsey Abbey:	,, ,, ,, ,,	3341-mm.60-66
Wintney Priory:	,, ,, ,, ,,	3327-mm. 2-3;
		also 3328-3336

Basic headings to these accounts, which include spiritualities, are given in *List of Ministers' Accounts*, vol.2: *Lands of Dissolved Religious Houses* (PRO).

Summary figures from the MSS. are printed in Dugdale, *Monasticon Anglicanum*. The figures for St. Mary's Abbey (vol.2, pp.457-8) and Wintney Priory (vol.5, p.722) are correct. Those for Wherwell Abbey (vol.2, pp.642-3) are correct except for the following corrections:

perquisites of court for Ashey, 73s.; East Compton, 3s. 10d.; Bathwick, 2s. 8d.; Woolley, 2s. pannage of pigs for East Compton, 3s. 2d.

However, the Romsey Abbey figures must have been abstracted on one of Dugdale's off days. His list (vol.2, p.510) had many omissions and nine of the 18 figures given are incorrect. They have therefore been quoted in greater detail than for the other nunneries.

4. Wherwell, charter nos. 16-17, 19-21, 43, 74, 83, 98, 106, 110, 123-4, 131, 135-6, 138, 140-1, 173, 177, 257, 263, 284-6, 289-91, 296-8, 328, 341, 357-61, 368, 370, 390, 411, 432-3, 449-50, 456, 459. Sacrist charter nos. 14-17
5. Harewood forest, charter nos. 39, 68-71, 353, 417; office of woodward, nos. 228-9, 331 and fol.199
6. Middleton, charter nos. 198, 200, 304, 306, 308-23
7. Forton, charter nos. 24-8, 31, 34, 38 (mill), 45, 65, 288. Sacrist charter no.30
8. East Aston, charter nos. 41-2, 44, 64, 83, 201-2, 204, 404, 413
9. Tufton, charter nos. 92-3, 133, 150-6
10. Bullington (West and East Bolyndon) charter nos. 73-4, 76-7, 86-90, 106, 115-7, 119-21, 126-9, 134-5, 141, 171, 175, 205, 213-16, 218, 220-7, 239, 252-3, 256, 284-5, 300, 332-4, 335, 337-48, 362, 366, 369-403, 412, 418-9, 434, 444, 448, 450, 458, 463. Sacrist charter nos.17-18
11. Goodworth, charter nos. 83-5, 159, 167, 196-8, 262, 460
12. Little Ann, charter nos. 13-14, 209
13. Ashey, charter nos. 80, 192-3, 231-2, 234-5, 237, 241, 439-40; See Hockey, *Insula Vecta*, pp.66-70, 247 nn.4-6
14. Bathwick, charter nos. 81-2, 110-11, 114, 210-1, 240, 364
15. Woolley, charter nos. 230, 236, 240
16. Biddle, *W.S.1.*, pp.356-7
17. Keene, *W.S.2.*, pp.61, 1046
18. City mill, charter nos. 299, 423, 425, 437, 453
19. Winchester charter nos. 164, 169, 180, 292-3, 299, 368, 408-9, 420-31, 435, 437, 445, 447, 452-5, 461-2
20. Wherwell Cartulary, nos. 75, 95, 172
21. Burgess, *The Southampton Terrier of 1454*, p.46
22. Southampton, charter nos. 33, 75, 95, 157-8, 172
23. Wherwell Cartulary, nos. 11, 148
24. Upton, charter nos. 145-7, 149
25. Wherwell Cartulary nos. 118, 438
26. *L. and P.*, vol.19 (2) item 800 (24)
27. Week, charter nos. 102, 122, 125, 174, 202, 204. Sacrist charter no.29

28. Sutton Scotney, charter nos. 91, 106, 131, 135-6, 141, 217, 285, 341, 344, 368-70, 450; Newton Stacey, charter nos. 137, 341, 433, 459
29. Inkpen, charter nos. 36-7, 97, 99, 105, 183, 287. Sacrist charter no. 20
30. Wherwell Cartulary no.254
31. Bristol, charter nos. 46-8, 53, 178
32. PRO SC6-981-21; Liveing, pp.194-5
33. PRO E315-442, fol.8v
34. *ibid.*
35. PRO SC6-981-21; Liveing, pp.194-5
36. *ibid.*
37. *ibid.*
38. *ibid.*
39. *ibid.*
40. The Ministers' Accounts (see n.3) cover two years from Mich. 1535 (ten months before the dissolution of the priory) until Mich. 1537. The figures quoted are as recorded but need to be divided by two for the annual income. The account was rendered by the king's bailiff there, Richard Hill.
41. *ibid.*
42. The obit of Hugh de Wyngeham is in the Wintney Calendar: BL MS. Cotton Claud. D.iii, fol.142.
43. Southrope lay to the south of the Herriard to Ellisfield road. See Milne's map of Hampshire, 1791.
44. It is probably his obit in the Wintney Calendar on fol.157. It seems likely that it was Richard de Hereard senior who rebuilt the nuns' church in stone; that is recorded with his obit on fol.146v. The obit of Ella is on the same folio.
45. Her brother, John Peche, had been involved in the action of 1230.
46. This charter still carries her large seal. Her obit is in the Wintney Calendar, fol.148 as 'Matild' Cifrewast, domina de Herierd'.
47. Re. date: as Maud was a widow it was after 1230; she herself died in 1246. *Cal. Inq.P.M.*, vol.1, pp.15-16.
48. Confirmation of his grant of meadow and moor between his wood and the meadow of the nuns as the dikes enclosed it, with the fishery and mill. (*Cal. Ch. R.*, vol.4, p.397) No location was given but it was presumably near the priory because a later Henry Sturmy was allowed to impark 600 acres in Elvetham and 'Wyntneyhertle' in 1359. (*Cal. Ch. R.*, vol.5, p.164)
49. *L. and P.*, vol.16, item 779 (7).

Bibliography

1. WINCHESTER EPISCOPAL REGISTERS, with abbreviations.

Published

Reg. Pontissara	*Registrum Johannis de Pontissara, episcopi Wintoniensis 1282-1304*, ed. Cecil Deedes, Cant. and York Soc., vols. 19, 30 (1915-24)
Reg. Woodlock	*Registrum Henrici Woodlock, diocesis Wintoniensis 1305-16*, ed. A.W. Goodman, Cant. and York Soc., vols. 43, 44 (1940-1)
Reg. Sandale	*The Registers of John de Sandale and Rigaud de Asserio, Bishops of Winchester 1316-23*, ed. F.J. Baigent, Hants. Record Soc. (1897), pp.3-384
Reg. Asserio	*supra.*, pp.387-619
Reg. Edington	*The Register of William Edington, Bishop of Winchester 1346-66*, ed. Dom S.F. Hockey, Hants. Record Series, vol.7 (2 vols. 1986-7)
Reg. Wykeham	*Wykeham's Register*, ed. T.F. Kirby, Hants. Record Soc. (2 vols. 1896-99)
Reg. Wolsey	*Registrum Thome Wolsey, cardinalis ecclesie Wintoniensis administratoris*, ed. F.T. Madge and Herbert Chitty, Cant. and York Soc., vol.32 (1926)
Reg. Gardiner	*Registra Stephani Gardiner et Johannis Poynet, episcoporum Wintoniensium*, ed. Herbert Chitty, Cant. and York Soc., vol.32 (1930)

Unpublished registers at the Hants. Record Office

Reg. Stratford	Register of Bishop John Stratford 1323-33 (HRO A1/5)
Reg. Orleton	Register of Bishop Adam Orleton 1333-45 (HRO A1/6)
Reg. Beaufort	Register of Cardinal Henry Beaufort 1405-47 vol. I, (1405-1418), (HRO A1/12)
Reg. Waynflete	Register of Bishop William Waynflete 1447-86 2 vols., (HRO A1/13-14)
Reg. Courtenay	Register of Bishop Peter Courtenay 1487-92 (HRO A1/15)
Reg. Langton	Register of Bishop Thomas Langton 1493-1501 (HRO A1/16)
Reg. Fox	Register of Bishop Richard Fox 1501-28, 5 vols. (HRO A1/17-21)

2. MANUSCRIPT SOURCES

British Library, London, and see appendix 4
Add. charters and rolls:
  compotus rolls of Froyle, Hants.: 13338-9, 17457, 17460, 17465, 17470-82, 17497, 17509-12, 17514, 17516-8
  court rolls of Froyle: 17519-22, 17533
  compotus rolls of Urchfont, Wilts., 19717, 19719, 19726, 19728, 19731
  court rolls of Urchfont: 19724-5
Add. manuscripts:
  12483. Ecclesiastical visitation of Hants., 1543
  26774-26780. Dr. John Latham's collections for a history of Romsey, Hants., 7 vols.
  39974. F.J. Baigent's collection re. Hants. religious houses, incl. Romsey Abbey
  39977. *ibid.*, incl. the abbeys of Wherwell and St. Mary's Winchester, and Wintney Priory
MS. Cotton Claud D.iii. Martyrologium and Calendarium of Wintney Priory
MS. Cotton Cleop. E.4.fol.140. Letter of John Foster to Cromwell
MS. Cotton Vespasian F.xiii.fol.178. Letter of Marquis of Exeter to Cromwell, 7 April [1534]
MS. Egerton 2031-4. Alchin's Index to the Registers of the Bishops of Winchester
MS. Egerton 2104a. Wherwell Cartulary
        b. Index to charters 1-64 (numbered) and 65-263 (unnumbered)

MS. Harley Roll I. 13, 14. Compotus rolls of receiver for Hampshire, 28, 32-3 Henry VIII
MS. Lansdowne 388. Pontifiçal
MS. Lansdowne 442. Edington Cartulary
MS. Lansdowne 451. Pontifical
MS. Royal 7. C.xvi. fols.147-8. Letter from John Foster to Sir Thomas Seymour, 28 December [1538]

Hampshire Record Office

Episcopal registers, *supra*.
Probate records
44 M 69. Herriard Archive collection
19 M 61. Kingsmill Archive collection
W/D 1. Winchester City court rolls

Public Record Office, London

Chancery	C66. Chancery grants, Henry VIII
Exchequer	E164-31. Pension list, 1553
	E178. Special commissions of inquiry
	E301. Augmentations Office. Chantry certificates
	E310. *ibid.* Particulars for leases
	E313. *ibid.* Letters patent (original)
	E315. *ibid.* Miscellaneous Books
	E318. *ibid.* Particulars for grants
	E321. *ibid.* Proceedings of the court
	E328. *ibid.* Ancient deeds. Series BB

Special collections	
	SC2-201-38/9. Romsey court rolls
	SC6. Ministers and receivers accounts
	SC12. Rentals and surveys

State Papers Office	
	SP1, 5. State Papers, domestic. Henry VIII

Saltykov-Shchedrin State Public Library, Leningrad, U.S.S.R
Lat. Q.V.I. no.62. Wherwell Abbey calendar

Wiltshire Record Office, Trowbridge
Will and inventory of Elizabeth Martyn, 1587

3. PRINTED SOURCES

Abingdon Annals, Rolls Series, 2, vol.2
Allen, P.S. and H.M., *Letters of Richard Fox 1486-1527* (1929)
Annales Monastici, (ed.) H.R. Luard, R.S. 36 (1864-8): vol.2, 'de Wintonia et de Waverleia' (*Winchester Annals* and *Waverley Annals*); vol.4, 'de Oseneia et de Wigornia' (for *Worcester Annals*)
Anglo-Saxon Chronicle, Rolls Series, 23, vol.2
Asser, *Life of King Alfred*, ed. W.H. Stevenson, with article on recent work on Asser's *Life* by Dorothy Whitelock (1959)
Atkinson, T., *Elizabethan Winchester* (1963)
Atkinson, T., 'Fragments of Architecture and Sculpture at Wherwell Church', *HFC Proc.*, vol.14 (3), (1940)
Backhouse, J., Turner, D.H., and Webster, L. (eds.), *The Golden Age of Anglo-Saxon Art 966-1066* (1984)

Barlow, Frank, *The English Church 1000-1066* (1979 edn.) *The English Church 1066-1154* (1979) *Edward the Confessor* (1970) (ed.), *Vita Edwardi Regis*: The Life of King Edward who rests at Westminster (1962)

Baskerville, Geoffrey, *English Monks and the Suppression of the Monasteries* (1940 edn.) 'The Dispossessed Religious after the Suppression of the Monasteries' in (ed.) H.W.C. Davis, *Essays in History* (1927)

Battiscombe, C.F. (ed.), *The Relics of St. Cuthbert* (1956)

Beckingsale, B.W., *Thomas Cromwell* (1978)

Benedictines and the Book, The, Bodleian Library catalogue (1980)

Benedictines in Britain, The, BL catalogue (1980)

Bennett, H.S., *Life on the English Manor* (1937)

Berrow, Phoebe, *Drawing the map of Romsey*, LTVA Study Group Paper I (1977) *When the nuns ruled Romsey*, LTVA Study Group Paper II (1978)

Berrow, Phoebe, Burbidge, B., and Genge, P., *The Story of Romsey* (1984)

Berry, William, *County Genealogies: Pedigrees of the families of the county of Hampshire* (1833)

Biddle, Martin (ed.), *Winchester in the Early Middle Ages: Winchester Studies*, vol. I (1976) [*W.S.1*] 'Felix Urbs Wintonia: Winchester in the Age of Monastic Reform' in (ed.) D. Parsons, *Tenth-Century Studies* (1975)

Birch, W. de Gray, *An Ancient Manuscript*, Winchester Record Society (1889) *Cartularium Saxonicum*, 3 vols., (1885-93) *Liber Vitae: Register and Martyrology of New Minster and Hyde Abbey*, Winchester Record Society (1892)

Blake, E.O. (ed.), *Cartulary of the Priory of St. Denys, near Southampton*, Southampton Record Series, vols. XXIV and XXV (1981)

Blatcher, Marjorie, *Report on the Manuscripts of the Marquess of Bath, preserved at Longleat*, vol. IV: Seymour Papers, 1532-1686, HMC, 58 (1968)

Braswell, Laurel, 'St. Edburga of Winchester, a study of her cult, 950-1500', *Medieval Studies*, No.33, (1971)

Brett, M., *The English Church under Henry I* (1975)

Brooke, Christopher, 'St. Bernard, the patrons and monastic planning', in (eds.) C. Norton and D. Park, *Cistercian Art and Architecture in the British Isles* (1986)

Burgess, L.A., *The Southampton Terrier of 1454*, HMSO and Southampton Record Series, vol.15 (1976)

Byrne, M. St. Clare (ed.), *The Lisle Letters*, 6 vols., (Chicago, 1981)

Calendar of Charter Rolls

Calendar of Close Rolls

Calendar of Fine Rolls

Calendar of Inquisitions: Miscellaneous

Calendar of Inquisitions Post Mortem, 1st and 2nd series

Calendar of Liberate Rolls

Calendar of entries in the Papal Registers, Letters and Petitions

Calendar of Patent Rolls

Calendar of Signet Letters of Henry IV and Henry V

Calendars of Judicial records: *Curia Regis Rolls*

Ancient Deeds, series B

Calendars of Exchequer records: *The book of Fees*

Feudal Aids, vols. 2 and 3

Camden, William, *Britannia*, ed. Edmund Gibson, vol. 1 (1772)

Campbell, A. (ed.), *The Chronicle of Aethelweard* (1962)

Carpenter Turner, B., *A History of Hampshire* (1978) *Winchester* (1980) 'Emma: a 900th Anniversary', *Winchester Cathedral Record*, no. 21 (1952)

Chandler, Richard, *The Life of William Waynflete* (1811)

Chaucer, Geoffrey, *The Canterbury Tales*, trans. Nevill Coghill (Folio Soc. 1956-7)

Cheney, C.R., *Episcopal Visitation of Monasteries in the Thirteenth Century* (1931) *Medieval Texts and Studies* (1973)

Cheney, C.R. and M.G., *The Letters of Pope Innocent III (1198-1216)* concerning England and Wales (1967)

Chew, H.M., *The English Ecclesiastical Tenants-in-Chief and Knight Service* (1932)

Chibnall, Marjorie (ed.) *The Ecclesiastical History of Orderic Vitalis*, vols. 1, 4, 5. *Anglo-Norman England 1066-1166* (1986)

Clapham, Sir Alfred, 'Three Bede-Rolls', *The Archaeological Journal*, vol. 106 (1949 supp.)

Clover, H. and Gibson, M. (eds.), *The Letters of Lanfranc, Archbishop of Canterbury* (1979)

Clutterbuck, R.H., *Notes on the parishes of Fyfield, Kimpton, Penton Mewsey, Weyhill and Wherwell* (1898)

Coleman, Olive, *The Brokage Book of Southampton 1443-4*, 2 vols., Southampton Record Series (1960-1)

Cook, G.H. (ed.), *Letters to Cromwell and others on the Suppression of the Monasteries* (1965)

Croft-Murray, E., *Decorative Painting in England 1537-1837*, vol.1

Davis, G.R.C., *Medieval Cartularies of Great Britain*: a short catalogue (1958)

Davis, H.W.C. (ed.), *Essays in History*, (1927)

Deanesly, Margaret, *The Lollard Bible* (1920)

Dickens, A.G., *Reformation Studies* (1982)

Dickens, A.G. and Carr, D. (eds.), *The Reformation in England to the Accession of Elizabeth I*, Documents of Modern History (1967)

Dickinson, J.C., *The Later Middle Ages. An ecclesiastical History of England, from the Norman Conquest to the Eve of the Reformation* (1979)

Dictionary of National Biography

Domesday Book: Hampshire, Wiltshire and Berkshire vols., Phillimore edn.

Douie, D.L., *Archbishop Pecham* (1952)

Dugdale, Sir William, *Monasticon Anglicanum*, (ed.) Caley, Ellis and Bandinel, vols. 2, 5 (1817-30)

Dyer, Christopher, *Lords and Peasants in a Changing Society: The Estates of The Bishopric of Worcester 680-1540* (1980)

Eadmer, *History of Recent Events in England*, trans. G. Bosanquet (1964)

Eckenstein, Lina, *Women under monasticism* (1896), esp. chapters on saint lore and convent life between 500 and 1500

Ellis, Sir Henry (ed.), *The Pylgrymage of Sir Richard Guyldforde to the Holy Land, 1506*, Camden Society (1851)

Ellis, R.H., *Catalogue of Seals in the P.R.O.: Monastic Seals*, vol. 1 (1986)

English Historical Documents, vol. 1, c.500-1042, (ed.) D. Whitelock (1979 edn.)

English Historical Documents, vol. 2, 1042-1189, (ed.) D.C. Douglas and G.W. Greenaway (1953)

English Romanesque Art 1066-1200, Exhibition catalogue (1984)

Farrer, William, *An Outline Itinerary of King Henry I* (1920)

Fell, Christine, *Women in Anglo-Saxon England* (1984)

Finberg, H.P.R., *The Early Charters of Wessex* (1964)

Finn, R. Welldon, *Domesday Book: A Guide* (1973)

Florence of Worcester, *The Chronicle of Florence of Worcester*, (ed.) Thomas Forester (1854)

Fox, Bishop Richard, *The Rule of Seynt Benet* (1517)

Gasquet, F.A., *The Great Pestilence* (1893)

Gelling, Margaret, *The Early Charters of the Thames Valley* (1979)

Gibson, Margaret, *Lanfranc of Bec* (1978)

Goodman, A.W., *Chartulary of Winchester Cathedral* (1927)

Gough, Henry, *Itinerary of King Edward I. 1272-1307*, 2 vols. (1900)

Greatrex, J., *The Register of the Common Seal*, Hants. Record Series, vol.2 (1978)

Green, A.R., 'The Romsey Painted Wooden Reredos', *Archaeological Journal*, vol. 90 (1933)

Green, A.R. and P.M., *Saxon Architecture and Sculpture in Hampshire* (1951)

Greenway, D.E., 'Two Bishops of Winchester: Henry of Blois and Peter des Roches', *History Today*, vol. 27, no. 7 (1977)

Grundy, G.B., in *Archaeological Journal*, vol.77

Habakkuk, H.J., 'The Market for Monastic Property, 1539-1603', *Economic History Review*, 2nd series, vol.10 (1957-8)

Haines, R.M., *The Church and Politics in Fourteenth Century England: the career of Adam Orleton c.1275-1345* (1978) 'Adam Orleton and the Diocese of Winchester', *Journal of Ecclesiastical History*, vol. 23 (1972)

Hallam, E.M., *Domesday Book through nine centuries* (1986)

Hamel, Christopher de, *A History of Illuminated Manuscripts* (1986)

Hardy, T.D., *A description of the Patent Rolls, with an Itinerary of King John* (1835)

Hare, J.N., 'The Monks as Landlords: The Leasing of the Monastic Demesnes in Southern England', in (eds.) C.M. Barron and C. Harper-Bill, *The Church in Pre-Reformation Society* (1985)

Harper-Bill, C., 'The Labourer is Worthy of his Hire? – Complaints about Diet in Late Medieval English Monasteries', in *The Church in Pre-Reformation Society*, see above

Harvey, J.H., 'Had Winchester Cathedral a central spire?', *Winchester Cathedral Record*, no. 27 (1958)

Harvey, P.D.A., *Manorial Records of Cuxham, Oxfordshire c.1200-1359*, HMC (1976) *Manorial Records*, British
   Records Association, Archives and the User, no.5 (1984)
Hatcher, John, *Plague, Population and the English Economy 1348-1530* (1977)
Hearn, M.F., 'A Note on the Chronology of Romsey Abbey', *Journal of the British Archaeological Association*,
   3rd series, vol.32 (1969)
Heslop, T.A., 'Cistercian seals in England and Wales', in *Cistercian Art and Architecture in the British Isles*
   (1986) 'Seals', in *English Romanesque Art 1066-1200* (1984)
Hill, David, 'The Burghal Hidage: The establishment of a text', *Journal of Medieval Archaeology*, vol. 13
   (1969)
Himsworth, Sheila (ed.), *Winchester College Muniments*, 3 vols. (1976-84)
Hinton, D.A., *Alfred's Kingdom: Wessex and the South 800-1500* (1977)
Historians of the Church of York and its Archbishops, Rolls Series 71
Historical Manuscripts Commission: Reports on Manuscripts in various collections, vol. 4 (1907), for the Manuscripts
   of F.H.T. Jervoise, Esq. preserved at Herriard Park, Hampshire
Hockey, Dom. S.F., *The Beaulieu Cartulary*, Southampton Record Series, vol. 17 (1974) *Insula Vecta: The Isle
   of Wight in the Middle Ages* (1982)
Hodgett, G.A.J., 'The Unpensioned ex-Religious in Tudor England', *Journal of Ecclesiastical History*, vol.
   13 (1962)
Holt, N.R. (ed.), *The Pipe Roll of the Bishopric of Winchester 1210-1211* (1964)
Horstman, Carl, *Nova Legenda Angliae*, vol.1 (1901)
Hovedene, Roger de, *Chronica Magistri Rogeri de Hovedene*, (ed.) William Stubbs, vols. 1-2, Rolls Series, 51
   (1868)
Hunt, Noreen, 'Notes on the History of Benedictine and Cistercian Nuns in Britain', *Cistercian Studies*, no.8
   (1973)
Hurd, D.G.E., *Sir John Mason 1503-66* (1975)
Jackson, J.E., 'Wulfhall and the Seymours', *Wiltshire Archaeological and Natural History Magazine*, vol. 15
   (1875)
Jewell, H.M., *English Local Administration in the Middle Ages* (1972)
John, Eric, *Orbis Britanniae and other studies* (1966)
Jones, P. Murray, *Medieval Medical Miniatures* (1984)
Keene, Derek, *Survey of Medieval Winchester: Winchester Studies 2*, 2 vols. (1985) [*W.S.2*]
Kendrick, T.D., *Anglo-Saxon Art to A.D. 900* (1938)
Kennedy, Joseph, 'Laymen and Monasteries in Hampshire 1530-58', *Proceedings of the Hampshire Field Club*,
   vol. 27 (1970)
Ker, N.R., *Catalogue of Manuscripts containing Anglo-Saxon* (1957) *Medieval Libraries of Great Britain: a list of
   surviving books*, 2nd edn., Royal Historical Society (1964) *Medieval Manuscripts in British Libraries*, vol.1
   London (1969)
Keynes, Simon, *The Diplomas of King Aethelred 'the Unready', 978-1016* (1980)
Kitchin and Madge (eds.), *Documents relating to the Foundation of the Chapter of Winchester, 1541-1547*, H.R.S.
   (1889)
Knowles, Cecilia, *Sparsholt and Lainston* (1981)
Knowles, David, *The Monastic Order in England 940-1216*, 2nd edn. (1966) *The Religious Orders in England*,
   vols. 1-3 (1948-59)
Knowles, D. and Hadcock R.N., *Medieval Religious Houses in England and Wales* (1971 edn.)
Knowles, D., Brooke, C.N.L., and London, V. (eds.), *The Heads of Religious Houses: England and Wales 940-
   1216* (1972)
Labarge, M. Wade, *Women in Medieval Life* (1986)
Lawrence, C.H. (ed.), *The English Church and the Papacy in the Middle Ages* (New York 1965) 'The Thirteenth
   Century' in above
Le Neve, John, *Fasti Ecclesiae Anglicanae, 1066-1300 Monastic Cathedrals*, vol.2, ed. D.E. Greenway (1971),
   and *1300-1541* vol.4, (ed.) B. Jones (1963)
Leechdoms, Wortcunning and Starcraft in Early England, (ed.) O. Cockayne, vol. 3, Rolls Series, 35 (1866)
Legge, Mary Dominica, 'The French Language and the English Cloister' in Ruffer and Taylor (eds.),
   Medieval Studies presented to Rose Graham (1950)
Liber Monasteria de Hyda, (ed.) Edward Edwards, Rolls Series, 45 (1866)

Liveing, H.G.D., *Records of Romsey Abbey 907-1558* (1906)

Luce, Sir Richard, 'Injunctions made and issued to the abbess and convent of the monastery of Romsey after his visitation by William of Wykeham, A.D.1387' in *Proceedings of the Hampshire Field Club*, vol.17 (1) (1949) *Pages from the History of Romsey and its Abbey* (1948)

Lunt, W.E. and Graves, E.B., *Accounts rendered by Papal Collectors in England, 1317-78* (Philadelphia 1968)

MacGregor, P., (ed.) B. Stapleton, *Odiham Castle, 1200-1500* (1983)

Maitland, F.W., *Select Pleas in Manorial and other Seignorial Courts*, Selden Society (1889)

Maskell, William, *Monumenta Ritualia Ecclesiae Anglicanae*, vol.2 (1846)

Meyer, M.A., 'Patronage of the West Saxon Royal Nunneries in late Anglo-Saxon England', *Révue Bénédictine*, vol.91 (1981)

Meyer, M.A., 'Women and the Tenth Century English Monastic Reform', *Révue Bénédictine*, vol.87 (1977)

Monastic Breviary of Hyde Abbey, (ed.) J.B.L. Tolhurst, Henry Bradshaw Society, vol.5 (1934)

Morton, James, *The Nun's Rule, being the Ancren Riwle Modernised* (1905)

Muller, J.A. (ed.), *The Letters of Stephen Gardiner* (1933)

Pantin, W.A., 'The Fourteenth Century', in (ed.) C.H. Lawrence, *The English Church and the Papacy in the Middle Ages* (New York 1965)

Parsons, David (ed.), *Tenth Century Studies*: Essays in Commemoration of the Millenium of the Council of Winchester and 'Regularis Concordia', (1975)

Parsons, J.C., *Court and Household of Eleanor of Castile in 1290* (Toronto 1977)

Paul, John, 'Dame Elizabeth Shelley, Last Abbess of St. Mary's Abbey, Winchester', *Proceedings of the Hampshire Field Club*, vol. 23, pt.2 (1965)

Peers, Sir C., 'Recent Discoveries in Romsey Church', *Archaeologia*, no. 57 (1901)

Pipe Roll Society publications

Platt, Colin, *Medieval Southampton: The port and trading community 1000-1600* (1973)

Poole, A.L., *From Domesday Book to Magna Carta* (1951)

Potter, K.R. and Davis, R.H.C. (eds.), *Gesta Stephani* (1976)

Power, Eileen, *Medieval English Nunneries c.1275-1535* (1922) *Medieval Women*, ed. M.M. Postan (1975)

Regesta Regum Anglo-Normannorum, 1066-1154
    vol.2, ed. C. Johnson and H.A. Cronne (1956)
    vol.3, ed. H.A. Cronne, R.H.C. Davis and H.W.C. Davis (1968)

Register of Henry Chichele, Archbishop of Canterbury 1414-43, (ed.) E.F. Jacob, vol. 4, Cant. and York Society, vol.47 (1947)

Registrum Simon de Gandavo, diocesis Saresberiensis, 1297-1315, (ed.) C.T. Flower and M.C.B. Dawes, Cant. and York Soc., vols.40-41 (1934)

Register of Robert Hallum, Bishop of Salisbury 1407-17, (ed.) Joyce M. Horn, Cant. and York Soc., vol.72 (1982)

Register of Thomas Langton, Bishop of Salisbury 1485-93, (ed.) D.P. Wright, Cant. and York Soc., vol.74 (1985)

Register of John Morton, (ed.) C. Harper-Bill, vol.1, Cant. and York Soc., vol.75 (1987)

Register of John Pecham, Archbishop of Canterbury 1279-92, (ed.) F.N. Davis, Cant. and York Society, vols. 64-5 (1969)

Reg. Epistolarum Johannis Peckham, Arch. Cantuar., (ed.) C.T. Martin, vol.2, Rolls Series, 77

Richard of Cirencester, *Speculum*, Rolls Series, 30, vol.2

Richardson, W.C., *History of the Court of Augmentations 1536-54* (Baton Rouge, Louisiana 1961)

Rickert, Margaret, *Painting in Britain: The Middle Ages* (1954)

Robertson, A.J. (ed.), *Anglo-Saxon Charters* (1956)

Robinson, J. Armitage, *The Times of St. Dunstan* (1923)

Rollason, D.W., 'Lists of saints' resting places in Anglo-Saxon England', in (ed.) Peter Clemoes, *Anglo-Saxon England*, no.7 (1978) 'The cults of murdered royal saints in Anglo-Saxon England', in (ed.) Peter Clemoes, *Anglo-Saxon England*, no.11 (1983)

Ruffer, V. and Taylor, A.J. (eds.), *Medieval Studies presented to Rose Graham* (1950)

St. Maur, H., *Annals of the Seymours* (1902)

Saltman, Avrom, *Theobald, Archbishop of Canterbury* (1956)

Salzman, L.F., *Building in England down to 1540: a documentary history* (1952)

Savine, A., 'English Monasteries on the eve of the Dissolution', in (ed.) Paul Vinogradoff, *Oxford Studies in Social and Legal History* (1909)

Sawyer, P.H., *Anglo-Saxon Charters: an annotated list and bibliography*, Royal Historical Society (1968)

Sayers, J.E., *Papal Judges Delegate in the Province of Canterbury 1198-1254* (1971) *Original Papal Documents in the Lambeth Palace Library: a catalogue*, B.I.H.R. Special Supplement no. 6 (1967)

Scarisbrick, J.J., 'Clerical Taxation in England 1485-1547', *Journal of Ecclesiastical History*, vol.11 (1960)

Schmitt, F. Salesius, *S. Anselmi, Cantuariensis Archiepiscopi: Opera Omnia*, vol. 4 (1949)

Shrewsbury, J.F.D., *A History of Bubonic Plague in the British Isles* (1970)

Smith, L. Toulmin, *The Itinerary of John Leland in or about the years 1535-43*, 5 vols. (1907-10)

South English Legendary, The, I, (eds.) C. d'Evelyn and A.J. Mill, Early English Text Society (1956)

Southern, R.W., *Saint Anselm and his biographer: a study of monastic life and thought 1059-c.1130* (1963)

Spence, Charles, *An Essay descriptive of the Abbey Church of Romsey in Hampshire*, 4th edn. (1st edn. 1862)

Stafford, Pauline, *Queens, Concubines and Dowagers: The King's wife in the early Middle Ages* (1983)

Stenton, D.M., *The English Woman in History* (1957)

Stenton, F.M., *Anglo-Saxon England*, 2nd edn. (1947)

Stevens, K.F., and Olding, T.E., *The Brokage Books of Southampton 1477-8 and 1527-8*, Southampton Record Series, no.28 (1985)

Symons, Thomas, *Regularis Concordia: The monastic agreement of the monks and nuns of the English nation* (1953) '*Regularis Concordia*: History and Derivation', in (ed.) D. Parsons, *Tenth Century Studies* (1975)

Tanner, Thos., *Notitia Monastica* (1787)

Taxatio Ecclesiastica Angliae et Walliae, auctoritate Papae Nicholai IV, c.1291 (1802)

Thompson, A. Hamilton, *The English Clergy and their organisation in the later Middle Ages* (1947)

Thompson, Sally, 'The problem of the Cistercian nuns in the 12th and early 13th centuries' in (ed.) Derek Baker, *Medieval Women* (1978)

Thomson, R.M., *Manuscripts from St. Alban's Abbey 1066-1235* (University of Tasmania 1982)

Timmins, T.C.B. (ed.), *The Register of John Chandler, Dean of Salisbury 1404-17*, Wiltshire Record Society (1984)

Turner, H.T. (ed.), *Manners and Household Expenses of England in the Thirteenth and Fifteenth Centuries* (1841)

Valor Ecclesiasticus, temp. Henrici VIII, vols. 1, 2, 4 (1810-34)

Victoria County History: Hampshire, 6 vols., (1900-1914)

　　ibid.: Berkshire

　　ibid.: Wiltshire

Walcott, Mackenzie, *The Minsters and Abbey Ruins of the United Kingdom* (1860)

Waverley Annals, see *Annales Monastici*

Whitelock, Dorothy, *Anglo-Saxon Wills* (1930)

William of Malmesbury, *De Gestis Pontificum*, Rolls Series, 52 *Historia Novella*, (ed.) K.R. Potter (1955) *The History of the Kings of England*, in (ed.), J. Stevenson, *The Church Historians of England*, vol.3, pt.1 (1854)

Williams, J.F., *The Early Churchwardens Accounts of Hampshire* (1913)

Winchester Annals, see *Annales Monastici*

Wood, Susan, *English Monasteries and their Patrons in the thirteenth century* (1955)

Woodward, G.W.O., *The Dissolution of the Monasteries* (1966)

Wright, Thos., *Three Chapters of Letters relating to the Suppression of the Monasteries*, Camden Society, (1843)

Youings, Joyce, *The Dissolution of the Monasteries* (1971) 'The Terms of the Disposal of the Devon Monastic Lands, 1536-58', *English Historical Review*, vol. 69 (1954)

Zettl, Ewald, *An Anonymous Short English Metrical Chronicle*, Early English Text Society (1935)

Ziegler, Philip, *The Black Death* (1969)

4. UNPUBLISHED THESES etc.

Harper-Bill, C., 'An edition of the register of John Morton, Archbishop of Canterbury, 1486-1500' (Ph.D. thesis, London, 1977)

Hase, P.H., 'The Development of the Parish in Hampshire, particularly in the 11th and 12th centuries' (Ph.D. thesis, Trinity Coll., Cambridge, 1975)

Jacka, H.T., 'The Dissolution of the English Nunneries' (thesis submitted for M.A., London, 1917)

Kennedy, Joseph, 'The Dissolution of the Monasteries in Hampshire and the Isle of Wight' (thesis submitted for M.A. London, 1953)

Yorke, Barbara, 'The written evidence for the Nunnaminster/St. Mary's Abbey' (King Alfred's College, 1981) 'Nunnaminster/St. Mary's Abbey in the early Middle Ages' (King Alfred's College, 1984).

Index

(Bishops: of Winchester, unless otherwise specified; Places: Hampshire, unless otherwise specified)